Understanding Business

Accounting and Financial Decisions

New edition

D.R. Myddelton

Understanding Business
Series editor: Richard Barker

Titles in the series:
Accounting and financial decisions
Marketing and production decisions
Organizational decision making
Quantitative decision making
Case studies for decision making

Longman

Understanding Business

Accounting and Financial Decisions

New edition
D.R. Myddelton

Understanding Business

Accounting and Financial Decisions

Revs edition

D.R. Myddelton

Acknowledgements

We are grateful to the following for permission to reproduce copyright material. They bear no responsibility for any interpretation.

The Controller of Her Majesty's Stationery Office: for the Retail Prices Index statistics, used in Appendix 1 on Inflation, also used in Figure 8.1, 8.5, 16.1 and 17.3; and for the data on compulsory liquidations in Figure 19.3.

Express Newspapers for material from *The Standard* on which problem B10 in Chapter 14 is based. The *Financial Times*, for statistics used in Figure 17.3. Richard D. Irwin Inc. for material from which the following cases have been adapted: Newman Machines (Chapter 13, B13) and Bexhill Manufacturing (Chapter 18, B13); Park Products Ltd and Langley Engineering Ltd (Chapter 18, B12); and for the discount tables in Appendix 3.

International Baccalaureate for questions from past 'Organisation and Management Studies' examination papers and University of Cambridge Local Examinations Syndicate for questions from past International Examination GCE 'A' Level papers.

The author acknowledges a general debt to co-authors of other accounting text-books: Michael W. Allen, co-author of *Essential Management Accounting* (Prentice Hall, 1987), and Professor Walter Reid, co-author of *The Meaning of Company Accounts* (Gower Press, 4th edition, 1988).

Longman Group UK Limited
Longman House
Burnt Mill, Harlow, Essex CM20 2JE, England
and Associated Companies throughout the world

© Cambridge Business Project Trust 1976, 1977, 1978, 1983, 1984, 1991

First published 1991
Second impression 1991
ISBN 0582 04091 4

Set in 10/12 Plantin, Linotronic 202

Produced by Longman Singapore Publishers Pte Ltd
Printed in Singapore

Contents

Contents

Introduction to the series

This series produces a new approach to the teaching of business decision making. It has been developed over the last two decades to give an understanding of the nature and purpose of business activity, whilst also stimulating the mind. It is suitable for young managers, students and academic sixth-formers.

The material provides an analytical understanding of people's problems and behaviour within organizations. The texts discuss the nature of problems, and explore concepts and principles which may be employed to aid their solution. Test materials have been selected from industrial and commercial organizations; from the private and public sector and from non-profit-making institutions. The material is as much to provide general understanding of industrial society and the workings of organizations, as it is to help those who are already engaged in their business or professional career.

Decision-making, as an approach, draws together ideas, and produces significant elements of reality; it gives purpose and challenge to the reader. Any organization is striving towards more or less closely defined objectives by deciding how to carry out, and control, its activities within constantly changing conditions. The programme looks carefully at these processes of decision-making; it provides the student with an understanding of their overall nature. The scene is set in *Organizational Decision Making* with an examination of the nature of organizations, the economic and legal environment in which they operate and the way people are involved in decision-making. Two books look at the key aspects of management information. Numerate information is considered in *Quantitative Decision Making*. The principles and practice of management control through accounting and finance are examined in *Financial and Accounting Decisions*. Aspects of these three books are then applied, along with relevant additional concepts, to the areas of marketing and production in *Marketing and Production Decisions*. A collection of decision-making case studies (*Case studies for Decision Making*) draws ideas together and tests students' ability to apply their skills.

This revised series of five books has been designed to meet the needs of students (and their lecturers/teachers) studying the business world. The up-to-date materials provide many ideas and activities from which the teacher can choose. Lecturers on management courses may use the books to introduce analytical concepts to practitioners; tertiary management courses may use them as a first text and as a source of well-tried and up-to-date cases; 'AS' and 'A' Level students may use individual books in the series or the complete course. To meet these different needs, each book has been designed to stand either as a part of the whole, or complete in its own right.

The four central books have the same chapter format:
> a chapter objective and synopsis so that the purpose and pattern are clear;
> a factual/explanatory text with case examples where applicable;
> a participative work section to provide materials for learning, application and discussion.

The participative sections are an integral part of the text and allow students to gain understanding by doing. They are usually divided into three parts. Firstly, some simple revision questions. Secondly, a series of exercises and case problems to test their application and to increase their knowledge of the area. Thirdly, a set of essay questions.

There is a teachers' book accompanying each student text which introduces the topic area, clarifies possible objectives, suggests approaches to the selected materials and provides additional themes. The teachers' books also provide solutions, where appropriate, to the participative sections, including the case studies.

The philosophy, approach and materials have been forged in discussion with businessmen, lecturers and teachers, and experience has refined the texts and most of the participative work. The Cambridge Business Studies Project Trust has co-ordinated the work. My particular thanks go to Professor John Dancy (who was the founding father), Sir Michael Clapham, David Dyer, Sir Nicholas Goodison, Professor David Myddelton, Professor Sir Austin Robinson and Peter Tinniswood; also, for generous financial assistance from, amongst others, the Wolfson Foundation, the Esmé Fairbairn Trust, Shell International, B.P. and the Department of Trade and Industry. I am also grateful to the individual authors who have been willing to draw their own considerable expertise into the format and approach required by the series.

Richard Barker
Series Editor

Preface

Accounting and Financial Decisions is for people who are studying business decisions. It aims to introduce the concepts, language and methods of accounting and financial management in the context of business decision-making. The book deals with many of the basic problems in modern accounting and finance and contains plenty of participative material to interest students. It should be useful for people in business as well as for students in business schools, polytechnics and colleges of further education, and for sixth-formers on business studies courses.

The book is intended for readers working on their own as well as for students enrolled on formal courses. For teachers an extensive Teachers' guide is available. The Teachers' guide contains detailed summaries of key points in each chapter, suggestions for alternative ways of using the text, worked answers to all the B exercises and problems, and an analysis of the B questions by chapter section and by 'difficulty' grading.

Accounting and Financial Decisions combines two previous books in the Understanding Business series: *Accounting and Decision Making* (3rd edition) and *Financial Decisions* (2nd edition). It also includes material from chapters 3 to 7 of *Production Decisions* by John Powell. Compared with the previous editions, chapter 8 on Inflation Accounting has been reduced, but it is not yet possible to omit it completely. Chapter 11 now includes new material on break-even analysis; and chapters 16 and 17 have been substantially rewritten. The entire text has been revised and updated.

At the start of each chapter there is a list of contents, together with a statement of objectives and a brief synopsis. As with the other books in this series, the end of each chapter (except the first) contains many revision questions, exercises, case studies and essay questions.

The A section contains about 25 revision questions. These relate to the text and are set out in the same order. They are meant to be helpful as "instant revision".

Most of the chapters contain 10 to 15 B exercises and case studies. I have retained nearly all the B questions from the earlier editions. It is essential for students to have the opportunity to work on a number of detailed problems to give both practice and confidence.

The C section contains essay questions. These may sometimes form a suitable topic for class discussion, rather than a written essay. Clearly there are many more B and C questions than any one person is likely to want, so there is a need to be highly selective in using them.

A feature of this book is the Glossary at the end. It contains definitions and descriptions of about 300 common words and expressions used in accounting and finance. These are shown in **bold letters** the first time they appear in the text.

I have tried to write as simply and clearly as possible and to avoid unnecessary jargon. However, students need to be familiar with the language of accounting and finance. Whenever you come across a word or phrase you don't understand, it is good practice to look it up *at once* in the Glossary. Otherwise you may think you understand the text when you don't. Appendix 2 lists common abbreviations and acronyms. Other Appendices deal with Inflation and with Discount Tables.

Finally there is an extensive Index. The letter G as the first item after an index entry indicates that the word or phrase appears in the Glossary.

I would like to acknowledge the significant extent to which this book is based on the earlier editions. In particular, chapters 1 to 12 draw heavily on Peter Corbett's editions of *Accounting and Decision Making;* chapters 13 to 19 use many of the questions developed by Roger Davies in his edition of *Financial Decisions;* and chapters 10 to 12 use some of the text and many of the questions from chapters 3 to 7 of John Powell's book, *Production Decisions.*

I would also like to acknowledge with thanks many helpful comments from Marek Kwiatkowski, John Powell, Ron Stevens and Peter Tinniswood at Marlborough College, and especially from Richard Barker, Headmaster of Sevenoaks School, the series editor. I would also like to thank Professor Peter Forrester, then Director of Cranfield School of Management, for providing time, as well as financial support, to enable me to write previous editions of this book. Finally my thanks to Doris Rogers for doing such a good job in preparing the text for the publishers, and to my secretary Sheila Hart for being so helpful over so many years.

D.R. Myddelton,
Cranfield School of Management,
January 1991.

1

Background

Plan of the chapter:

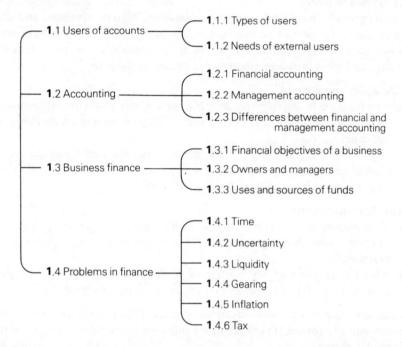

Fig.1.0

Objective: *To explain who uses accounts; the differences between financial and management accounting; the financial objectives of a business; and to identify six key problem areas in finance.*

Synopsis: *'Outsiders' (mainly shareholders and lenders) use financial accounts, while 'insiders' use management accounts. Financial accounting, originally based on 'stewardship', reports regularly on a business's financial performance and position. Management accounting deals more with the future: it helps managers to plan and control, and often concerns only part of a business.*

The main financial objective of a business enterprise is to maximize the wealth of the owners. Large businesses are now run by professional managers, not owners, and their interests may not always coincide. A business gets funds from selling its products, from owners who provide share capital, and from lenders who provide long-term or short-term loans. A business uses funds on operating costs and other expenses, on acquiring fixed assets, and on short-term assets such as stocks. Six problem areas in finance are: time, uncertainty, liquidity, gearing, inflation and tax.

1.1 Users of accounts

1.1.1 Types of users

Accounts provide financial facts about a business. Who needs them, and why? We can show the role of accounting in business decisions by asking some typical questions. They are of two kinds: from 'outsiders' (people external to the firm), and from 'insiders' (managers working in the firm).

'Outsider' questions

- *As a trade union official on behalf of the workers, you are pressing the managers for a wage increase. How can you find out if they are right to say the firm can't afford it?*
- *A golfing friend who runs a local furniture business walks into the branch bank of which you are manager. He asks for a bank loan to tide his firm over a sticky patch. How will you decide what to do?*

'Insider' questions

- *As managing director of a large firm with branches all over the country, how can you control their performance? How can you measure your firm's success or failure?*
- *After several years of making a good profit, your company suddenly finds itself making a loss. How will you discover the reasons for this?*

To answer any of the above questions, you need financial facts. This is what accounts aim to provide. There are many different potential users of accounts, as figure 1.1 shows.

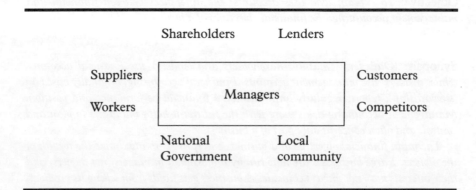

Figure 1.1 Potential users of accounts

1.1.2 Needs of external users

Not all external users have the same needs. Moreover their desire for financial information must be set against the cost of producing it, as well as the possible need to maintain commercial secrecy. In publishing accounts, company directors must comply with legal requirements to give a 'true and fair view' and with **statements of standard accounting practice** (see 3.1.3). But they still have some discretion over how much to disclose, and in what form.

Shareholders are legal owners of shares in a company. They are entitled to know how well the managers are running their business.

Bankers and other lenders will need to satisfy themselves that a borrower can pay regular interest and repay the loan in due course.

Customers may wish to ensure regular supply, including spares for products with a long life. They may also want to be confident that a supplier is financially sound if they make payments in advance.

Competitors may wish to compare themselves with other companies in the same industry, perhaps by means of schemes of inter-firm comparison (see 11.3.2).

The local community will care about prospects for local employment, and any plans to increase or reduce output. Companies' annual reports represent one potential source of such news.

The national government needs to know how a company is doing, for purposes of taxation. It may also wish to compile and publish certain economic statistics.

Workers may want to know about profits to indicate both the chance of wage increases and the long-term prospects for secure employment.

Suppliers providing goods and services on credit will want to be sure that buying firms are able to pay.

1.2 Accounting

1.2.1 Financial accounting

Financial accounting provides information for external users, while business managers use **management accounting** to help run their firms. This section discusses some differences between the two.

Before the Industrial Revolution, the accounting needs of business firms were not complex. The village cobbler was clearly doing all right if, after buying his leather, he earned enough surplus cash to feed, clothe and house his family properly.

But the last two hundred and fifty years have brought a vast expansion in the need for accounting information. From about 1750 the numbers of English people living in towns grew rapidly. As a result, the amount of trading by means of market exchanges greatly increased. People specialized and were no longer self-sufficient. This caused an expansion of the number of different business firms .

As the size of firms increased, from about 1850 the emergence of **limited companies** began to separate a firm's ownership from its day-to-day management. This required regular reports on their **stewardship** from the managers to the owners.

Finally the increasingly world-wide nature of business since about 1950 has led to growth in the size of many **multinational companies**. It has also led to complex problems of translating foreign currencies.

Early accounting was often simply 'venture accounting'. A ship set sail from Plymouth for the Indies, laden with supplies. When it returned months or years later, the value of the treasure on board, less the value of the initial supplies, represented **profit.** Ships which never came back were a total loss.

Modern business firms, in contrast, aim to last for decades, not just for a specific venture. Moreover the use of long-lasting assets, such as buildings and capital equipment, makes it difficult to prepare accurate reports every year.

The need for regular accounting statements requires the flow of a modern enterprise's existence to be 'chopped up' into somewhat artificial short periods. Figure 1.2 portrays this. We shall see later how this gives rise to important problems of valuing assets and measuring profit or loss.

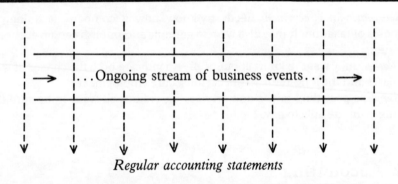

Figure 1.2 'Chopping up' the life of a business into short time periods

1.2.2 Management accounting

Management accountants aim to help managers to make good decisions. A great deal of accounting information is essential to run a modern business of any size. Of course, accounting alone is not nearly enough. Managers also need production data about technology and raw materials, market research about customers' wants and competitors, and much else.

Management accounting relies on many of the same principles as financial accounting. It makes full use of internal balance sheets, profit and loss accounts, funds flow statements, and ratio analysis. These may apply only to certain parts of the firm, or for periods shorter than twelve months. Two key standards for comparison in management accounts are trends over time and internal budgets (see 9.1.2).

Two different disciplines underlie management accounting: economics, dealing with the use of scarce resources, and behavioural science, dealing with how people behave in firms. Management accounting has four main purposes, covering different time periods:

1 Score-keeping   past
2 Problem-solving   present
3 Controlling   present
4 Planning   future

The score-keeping function is much the same as for financial accounting.

The sorts of problems that management accounting may be able to help solve are:

(a) Should the firm accept low prices for bulk orders if a factory is below capacity?
(b) Is it worth installing a new machine which will reduce costs?
(c) Why is the Newcastle office so much more expensive than the larger Birmingham one?
(d) Should we base salesmen's pay at least partly on the profitability of the products they sell?

Controlling involves monitoring actual outcomes against agreed budgets, and taking corrective action if needed.

Planning involves co-ordinating different parts of a business, and gaining the agreement of various responsible managers to their part in the plan.

Managers need information which is up-to-date, in enough detail, and available to the right people. Monthly management accounts allow frequent regular control of the firm's business

Management accountants must produce as much useful data as they can within certain cost limits. This requires not only the skill to keep the costs down, but also the imagination to see what extra information other managers might find useful. The general notion of **cost/benefit analysis** is that something's cost should not exceed its value. Measuring the cost of providing management information is often not easy; still less so is valuing the benefits.

Modern computers are so powerful that management accountants can easily supply too much data. Managers may not use the information provided, either because it is not relevant, or because they don't know how to. To some extent, therefore, management accountants may act as teachers. They should take care to present reports in a way which people can understand, without too much detail.

1.2.3 Differences between financial and management accounting
Figure 1.3 outlines several differences between financial accounting and management accounting.

		Financial accounting	*Management accounting*
1	Use	External	Internal
2	Time focus	Past and present	Present and future
3	Coverage	Whole company	Divisions and sub-groups
4	Accounting unit	Money *	Money * or physical units
5	Nature of data	Somewhat technical	For use by non-accountants
6	Governed by	Company law, SSAPs	Managers' needs
7	Ideal criteria	Objective, verifiable, consistent	Relevant, useful, understandable
8	Emphasis	Accuracy	Speed
9	Period	Usually one year	Various as appropriate

* Or unit of constant purchasing power (see Chapter 8).

Figure 1.3   Differences between financial and management accounting

Financial accountants supervise the **book-keeping** records, and once a year they summarize them in the company's published **accounts.** (Larger companies also publish **interim accounts** during the year.) Acting as independent external **auditors,** financial accountants check that a company's accounts give a **true and fair view** of its affairs.

Financial accountant
1 Knowledge of: (a) accounting techniques for all likely situations;
                     (b) company law and auditing requirements;
                     (c) taxation law, especially as it affects companies.
2 Ability to: (a) work to schedule under severe time pressure;
                     (b) control office staff of all ages;
                     (c) deal with people at all levels in a firm, from store-keepers to top management and auditors.
3 Numeracy and a liking for precision.

Management accountant
1 Knowledge of: (a) financial accounting concepts and methods;
                     (b) data processing methods and equipment;
                     (c) economics and modern management methods.
2 Ability to: (a) present relevant information clearly;
                     (b) grasp the inter-relationships of different parts of a business;
                     (c) work with employees at all levels.
3 Imagination and a persistent nature.

Figure 1.4 Qualities needed by financial and management accountants

Management accountants obtain and present information to help managers plan and control business. They provide data for specific decisions, as well as preparing routine monthly financial reports. Larger firms employ management accountants as **internal auditors** to review their management information systems.

Many new accountants now are university graduates, but their degree may be in almost any subject. Practical training is also essential to qualify as a professional accountant. The professional examinations cover both financial and management accounting. Other subjects include: company law, taxation, economics.

Figure 1.4 lists some of the main qualities which financial and management accountants in industry require. Clearly there is much common ground, as well as a number of differences.

1.3 Business finance

1.3.1 Financial objectives of business

The main **financial objective** of a business enterprise is to maximize the wealth of its owners. This means nearly the same as 'maximizing profits', except that wealth takes into account the *timing* of profits.

Why are profits desirable? From an owner's point of view, because larger profits will help make him 'better off', by enlarging his purchasing power. From society's point of view, because – in normal competitive markets – both buyer and seller can expect to benefit from a voluntary market exchange. In general, therefore, the higher total profits, the more individuals will have become better off as a result of market transactions. It is basic fallacy to suppose that if the seller makes a profit, the buyer must *lose* to the same extent! (We must also bear in mind that much business activity is between one enterprise and another. Companies selling to individuals, or vice versa, represent only a small part of the total.)

Why are profits ever possible, above a 'normal' rate of interest on capital invested? Essentially because of ignorance. If people dealing on markets *knew* everything there was to be known, the prices of products would already fully reflect consumers' valuations. This **arbitrage** view of profit emphasizes the *information* content of price signals in the market.

1.3.2 Owners and managers

Few large businesses are managed by their owners. The directors of the largest 100 UK companies between them own less than one-tenth of one per cent of the ordinary shares in the firms. They are professional managers, not owners. The possibility of profits acts as an incentive for owners of businesses (and for their agents, the managers); and profit or loss reflects success or failure.

Owners of small businesses may not always aim to maximize their business profits. For example, the owner of a small shop may prefer to close early, and not open on Saturdays, in order to enjoy more leisure. As a sole owner, he is perfectly entitled to do this. But it would hardly please the owners of a large business if its managers deliberately failed to maximize profits in order to enjoy more leisure! A competitive market would soon replace such managers with others who *would* try to serve the owners by maximizing profits.

Business firms aim to make a profit by *satisfying customers*. Thus it is a mistake to regard managers and workers as two 'sides' of industry. The real distinction is between *consumers* on the one hand, and *producers* – owners, managers, and workers – on the other.

1.3.3 Uses and sources of funds

As a rule there is no shortage of finance for good projects: the main problem in business is finding profitable things to do.

How firms spend money depends on the nature of the business. A major film may cost tens of millions of pounds. This goes on acquiring the story, writing the screenplay, buying equipment and building the sets, hiring actors and others, shooting the film, and promoting it – all *before* the first customer pays any cash. A gold mine will take many years to develop: surveying the land, buying it, digging the mine, equipping it, hiring miners and others, extracting and refining the ore – all *before* any metal is sold for cash.

Such long-term projects have to be financed. Indeed most businesses need financing 'in advance of sales' to some extent. This applies to a firm which is expanding, as well as to a new business. Firms may also need short-term finance to tide them over the ups and downs which occur in most businesses from time to time.

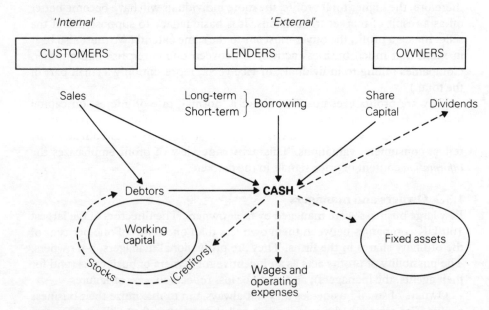

Figure 1.5 Main flows of funds

Thus a business *spends* money on:

1 long-term ('fixed') assets, such as buildings and equipment,
2 short-term ('current') assets, such as stocks of materials,
3 wages and other operating expenses.

And a firm *gets* money from:

1 owners, who starts the business with equity ('share') capital,
2 lenders (banks and others), who provide long-term or short-term funds,
3 customers, in respect of goods or services sold.

Funds deriving from sales to customers (whether on credit or for cash) are sometimes referred to as **internal finance,** funds from owners or lenders as **external finance**. Figure 1.5 shows the major uses and sources of funds (including the payment of cash dividends to shareholders, out of profits).

1.4 Problems in finance

1.4.1 Time

The difference between the near and distant future is important in finance, as in other areas of business. Long-term investments may involve expenditures promising 'returns' only after many years; while long-term borrowing can provide funds which need not be repaid for a long time.

In business one may often choose to 'sacrifice' a smaller profit soon in the hope of a larger profit later: for example, pricing low with a new product in order to build up market share. Maximizing the wealth of a firm's owners therefore requires some way to compare profits in different future periods. This is done by using the rate of interest, in effect, as an 'exchange rate through time'. In trying to forecast cash receipts and payments in the uncertain future, we must worry not only about the *amount* of cash flows, but also about their *timing*.

In general, firms often try to 'match the maturities' of their liabilities (sources of finance) with those of their assets (uses of funds). So do financial institutions. 'Borrowing short and lending long' can clearly be dangerous: a firm might have to repay the borrowings at short notice without being able to demand repayment of its own long-term investments.

1.4.2 Uncertainty

The future is uncertain. Hence financial plans, like any others, may go wrong. Financial managers try to allow sufficient margin of error to cover most risks, without playing it so safe that little *profit* remains. Chapter 15 discusses some ways of trying to cope with uncertainty.

There are many different aspects to business uncertainty. It is likely to be high, for example, where:

1 a firm is heavily dependent on a single product line;
2 market conditions make accurate sales forecasts difficult;
3 technological changes are altering the industry's cost structure;

4 senior managers change;
5 an interfering government changes its policies.

1.4.3 Liquidity

Liquidity means the ease with which an asset can be turned into cash. In a perfect capital market this would not matter, since the owner of assets would always be able to borrow against them. But in the real world, it is often true that 'it's easier to turn cash into assets than assets into cash'.

As with other aspects of business, financial managers need to seek a *balance*. Holding too little liquidity might create immediate problems in paying bills, while holding too much might lead to a relatively low rate of return.

1.4.4 Gearing

The two main forms of finance are borrowing ('debt') and ordinary shareholders' funds ('equity'). They are discussed in Chapters 16 and 17. A company is 'highly geared' when borrowing forms a large proportion of its total capital structure. In Chapter 18 we note some rules of thumb about how much financial gearing a firm can take on without undue alarm.

Financial gearing (or **'financial risk'**) refers to how a company finances its investment of funds, while operational gearing (or **'business risk'**) refers to the nature of a firm's business and how it has invested its funds. How a firm invests funds is probably far more important than how it finances the business. This is because most financial markets are more competitive, with better information, than most factor markets dealing in 'real' goods and services. So, in general, financing decisions provide fewer opportunities for significant profit or loss.

'Operational gearing' sometimes refers to the level of fixed expenses as a proportion of total expenses. Thus most of a school's expenses are fixed, whereas most of a street trader's would be variable. Where most expenses are fixed, the amount of profit is very sensitive to the level of sales revenue.

1.4.5 Inflation

The problems caused by inflation are both important and complicated; and any rate of inflation above three or four per cent a year is serious. Inflation affects: (a) the required rates of return on new investments; (b) the basis of valuing assets; (c) the management of working capital; (d) the appropriate extent and type of borrowing; and (e) the accuracy of accounts using money as the unit of measurement (Chapter 8 discusses 'inflation accounting'). So clearly inflation, where it exists, is crucial in finance.

In discussing financial numbers, we must be careful to distinguish between 'money' amounts and 'real' amounts. Another critical question is whether a particular rate of inflation was *anticipated* or not. We must also concern ourselves with *fluctuations* in the inflation rate.

1.4.6 Tax

Businesses are subject to many taxes – on wages, on property, on capital. But business finance is mainly concerned with three: (a) corporation tax on a firm's 'taxable profits' (both **mainstream** and **advance corporation tax**); (b) personal income tax on dividends to shareholders; (c) capital gains tax.

A business which aims to maximize the owners' wealth has to take account of the tax effects on individuals. But it is trying to maximize the after-tax profits, not to 'minimize taxes'. Unfortunately, inflation complicates the impact of tax, since the tax system doesn't always properly allow for it. Hence there are some distortions which affect the best way to finance a firm.

Work section

A Revision questions

A1   What two kinds of user may require accounting information?

A2   Name three different external users of accounts.

A3   For whom are internal accounts prepared?

A4   Name two modern developments which have affected accounting.

A5   Name aspects of management accounting dealing with:
(a) the past, (b) the present, (c) the future.

A6   What do you understand by (a) planning, (b) control?

A7   How is cost/benefit analysis relevant to management accounting?

A8   Why do management accountants need imagination?

A9   Name four differences between financial accounting and management accounting.

A10 What is the role of the financial accountant in industry?

A11 What is the role of the management accountant in industry?

A12 Identify as many personal qualities as you can which are needed by *both* financial accountants and management accountants.

A13 What is the main financial objective of a business?

A14 Why is it not true that if the seller makes a profit, the buyer must lose to the same extent?

A15 What are three main kinds of business uses of funds?

A16 What are three main kinds of business sources of funds?

A17 How can profits in different future periods be compared?

A18 Name three instances where business uncertainty is likely to be high.

A19 Define 'liquidity'.

A20 Why is how a firm *invests* funds likely to be more important than how it *finances* the business?

C Essay questions

C1   'A company with no accounts would be like a ship without a rudder.' Discuss.

C2   Write a memo to the managing director of your company explaining why you think she should create a department of management accounting.

C3   As personnel officer, design a questionnaire to be filled in by an applicant for the post of:
(a) financial accountant, (b) management accountant.

C4 In what ways would accounting information, when prepared for internal management, differ from that compiled for the use of other interested parties?

C5 What kind of information would a supplier require of a new customer ordering £1 million worth of raw materials on a regular basis?

C6 Might you be suited to a career in accounting? Why or why not?

C7 Explain why management accounting depends both on economics and on behavioural science.

C8 Why is the so-called 'separation' between owners and managers likely to be more significant in large than in small businesses?

C9 Why can inflation have important effects on business?

C10 What are the implications of trying to maximize after-tax profits, rather than to minimize taxes on profits?

2

The financial statements

Plan of the chapter:

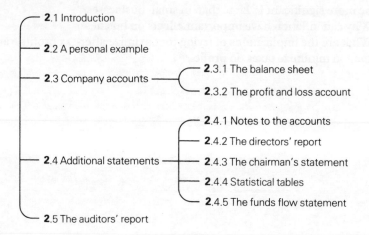

Fig.2.0

Objective: *To outline the purpose of the two main accounting statements, the balance sheet and the profit and loss account; and to describe the other statements comprising a company's 'accounts', together with the auditors' report.*

Synopsis: *The balance sheet shows the financial position of a business at a point in time, while the profit and loss account shows how much profit or loss it has made in a period (usually one year).*

The balance sheet lists assets (what a business owns or controls) and liabilities (what it owes to others). The difference represents the owners' equity in the business ('shareholders' funds' for a limited company). The profit and loss account for a period deducts expenses from sales revenues to determine profit or loss.

The other component parts of a company's 'accounts' are: notes to the accounts, the directors' report, and (for larger companies) a funds flow statement. Other statements, not formally part of the accounts, may be useful; such as the chairman's statement and tables of statistics covering a number of past years. Finally the auditors write a report saying whether they think each company's accounts 'give a true and fair view' of its affairs.

2.1 Introduction

Business accounts try to answer two different kinds of question:

1 What profit or loss has the business made during a given period?
2 What is its financial position at the end of that period?

A simple analogy can illustrate the difference between them.

Imagine that you set out to record on video tape a day in the life of a local market trader. During the day many people visit his stall: some buy fruit, while others just look and then move on. Those who buy hand money to the trader, who puts it in a cash drawer behind the stall.

When you get home that evening, you want to find out what the position was at 12 noon. So you run the tape through, and freeze it when you get to that moment. You can see how many apples, bananas, and so on the trader had left on his stall, and the amount of cash in the drawer. A complete list of these things would be a 'stock' of his possessions: it would describe the state of affairs of the business at the instant at which the film was frozen.

You may then want to know what the trader sold between 12 noon and 4.00 p.m. You re-start the film; and, as it runs through, you note down what fruit is handed to customers, and how much money they pay the trader. If you summarized all these transactions, you would have a measure of the 'flow' of events for the four-hour period.

When the film is again frozen, you can make a second list of the trader's stock of possessions at 4.00 p.m.

A company regularly buys and sells goods and services during its life. It needs to summarize its position from time to time, and its transactions in between. In this way, accounts can provide both 'stock' and 'flow' information.

Of course purely physical descriptions cannot summarize the transactions and position of a business. The various kinds of activities and possessions are too different for that. Instead *money* is the 'common denominator' allowing accounts to add or compare different events and objects. So a company translates all physical amounts into terms of money, in order to express the measures of 'stocks' and 'flows' in a single unit of account.

2.2 A personal example

To illustrate these principles, we can look at a year in a person's life, before going on to consider the more complex affairs of a company in business.

Example: On 1 January, Alison Robbins sits at her desk and lists her possessions. Next to each she writes an estimate of its money value. Then she calculates a total from the individual values, as shown in figure 2.1.

	£
One semi-detached house	40,000
Furniture and household goods	8,000
One three-year-old car	3,600
Current account at the bank	200
Total	**51,800**

Figure 2.1 Alison's possessions at the start of the year

It might seem that Alison's 'wealth' amounts to £51,800; but she almost forgot that she owes the building society £24,000, which she borrowed four years ago to buy her house. So her net wealth is not £51,800 but only £27,800.

Exactly one year later, Alison sits down again, and summarizes her financial transactions during the past year (figure 2.2). She gets this information from the records she has kept. Her pay slips tell her how much she has earned in her job, and her cheque book counterfoils show how much she has spent, and on what. She lists separately her receipts and her payments; and then subtracts the total of the payments from the total receipts.

	£
Receipts	
Monthly wages (less PAYE tax deductions)	10,000
Payments	
To building society (of which £1,400 interest)	3,000
Light, heat, etc.	1,800
Housekeeping	2,400
Car running expenses	1,000
Clothing, holiday, etc.	1,200
	9,400
Surplus of receipts over payments	600

Figure 2.2   Alison's receipts and payments during the year

During the year Alison has received £600 more than she paid out. But does this mean her 'wealth' is now exactly £600 more than it was at the start of the year? When she lists her possessions again (figure 2.3), she finds, of course, that she has

£600 more cash in her current account with the bank than she had a year earlier. But she owes less to the building society, since £1,600 of the £3,000 paid during the year was to reduce the loan outstanding (the rest being interest). She also recognizes that not all the values shown a year ago still apply. The car and the household furniture have partly worn out during the year, and are now worth somewhat less than before (Chapter 6 discuss such 'depreciation'). On the other hand, she believes the house has risen in value. Alison identifies all these changes in figure 2.3, and compares her list of possessions at the beginning of the year (shown in Column A) with those at the end of the year (Column B).

	A	B
	Start of year	*End of year*
	£	£
One semi-detached house	40,000	46,000
Furniture and household goods	8,000	7,200
One four-year-old car	3,600	2,800
Current account at bank	200	800
	51,800	56,800
Less: Owing to building society	24,000	22,400
Net 'wealth':	27,800	34,400

Figure 2.3 Alison's 'wealth' at the start and end of the year

Alison's net 'wealth' appears to have increased by £6,600 during the year, which is much more than the £600 increase in her bank balance. In the light of the adjustments she made to the valuations of her various possessions, Alison is able to prepare a statement (figure 2.4) showing the sources of her increase in wealth during the year.

		£
Increase in value of house	+	6,000
Fall in value of car, furniture, etc.	−	1,600
Surplus of net income (£10,000) over living expenses (£7,800*)	+	2,200
Net increase in wealth during the year	+	6,600

* = £9,400 less £1,600 mortgage repaid.

Figure 2.4 Alison's increase in wealth during the year

2.3 Company accounts

In the last section we saw how someone might work out how much her possessions and liabilities amount to in money terms at a particular date. (Don't worry if you found it hard to see exactly where all the numbers came from: at this stage it's the general idea that matters.)

A company produces each year a statement called a **balance sheet** which is broadly similar to Alison's statement of 'wealth' in figure 2.3. A company also produces a **profit and loss account,** which describes the result of a year's trading, rather like figure 2.4.

The accounting ideas involved in a domestic example also mostly apply to limited companies. The main changes are in terminology and degree of complexity. A company's 'accounts' consist of a balance sheet and a profit and loss account, together with certain other statements described later in this chapter. Here we merely outline the two main statements: we discuss them in more detail in Chapters 4 and 5.

2.3.1 The balance sheet

The balance sheet of a company at a particular date shows the equivalent of the 'wealth' of a person - with one important exception. Companies usually value their possessions (called **assets)** at the original cost **(historical cost)**, not - as Alison did - at their current market values. Chapter 4 discusses the balance sheet in more detail.

Companies must produce balance sheets at yearly intervals, but they can choose when to end their **financial years.** Many companies choose the calendar year, ending on 31 December; others choose 31 March. Other companies choose year ends which suit the nature of their business; for example, department stores often end their year on 31 January, after the end of the post-Christmas sales; and universities on 31 July, at the end of the academic year.

2.3.2 The profit and loss account

The profit and loss account summarizes changes in shareholders' funds (owners' equity) due to trading and other operations during a period (normally one year). Chapter 5 discusses in detail how firms determine **sales revenues** (turnover) for a period, and how they estimate the amount of expenses. The surplus is the profit for the period (or any deficit is called a **loss,** if total expenses exceed sales revenue).

Figure 2.5 outlines the link between the profit and loss account for a year and the start-of-year and end-of-year balance sheets. We already know that the amount of profit may not be reflected in an identical increase in the asset *cash;* so the profit for the year is simply added to *total* assets, as well as to owners' equity.

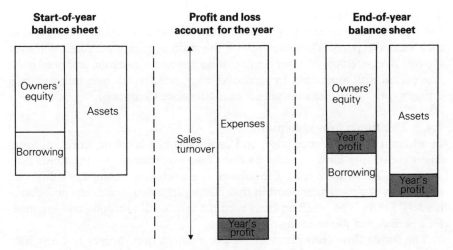

Figure 2.5 Link between profit and loss account for a year, and start-of-year and end-of-year balance sheets

2.4 Additional statements

2.4.1 Notes to the accounts

The main 'accounts' are the profit and loss account for a period, and the balance sheet at the end of it. But modern practice is to simplify the basic accounts; thus some detailed information appears not on the face of the accounts, but in separate **notes to the accounts.** For example, the notes will contain details of fixed assets, of changes in shareholders' funds due to capital transactions, and of long-term liabilities. Hence readers should strictly regard the notes as a part of 'the accounts', not merely as an optional extra.

2.4.2 The directors' report

Company law requires a **directors' report** with the financial statements. It contains certain details, if not mentioned elsewhere, such as the number of employees and their total pay; changes in the board of directors during the year; and an analysis of trading results by product and by geographical area.

2.4.3 The chairman's statement

The chairmen of most public companies publish a statement with the annual accounts. This is broader in scope than the directors' report; it comments on the past period, and may indicate prospects for the future. It can discuss factors which are not easily quantifiable, such as political events. Although it is not strictly a part of the accounts, anyone trying to analyse company accounts should read the chairman's statement carefully.

2.4.4 Statistical tables

Most public companies also publish a table of financial statistics at the end of their annual reports. These summarize the main accounting information over the past five or ten years. They are not subject to audit, as a rule, and need to be interpreted with some care. In particular, comparing trends over many years is difficult without proper allowance for inflation (see Chapter 8).

2.4.5 The funds flow statement

In addition to the balance sheet and profit and loss account, in recent years larger companies have published a third financial statement – the funds flow statement. As we have seen, the balance sheet sets out a company's financial position as at a particular point in time, listing its assets, liabilities, and share-holders' funds. The profit and loss account shows sales revenue and expenses for a period, and the resulting profit or loss.

The **funds flow statement** shows a company's new sources and new uses of funds for the most recent period. In its simplest form it may be regarded as a statement showing balance sheet changes between the beginning and end of a period. (In contrast, the balance sheet itself shows the *cumulative* sources and uses of funds of a business ever since it began.) Funds flow statements are discussed in more detail in Section 9.4.

2.5 The auditors' report

A company's *directors* are responsible for its published accounts. But under the Companies Act 1985, limited companies must also have their accounts 'audited'. An **audit** is an examination of accounts in order to determine whether or not they present a true and fair view of the state of the company's affairs.

A standard form of auditors' report to a set of company accounts might read as follows:

We have audited the financial statements in accordance with approved auditing standards. In our opinion the financial statements give a true and fair view of the company's state of affairs as at the (end of the financial year) and of the profit (or loss) for the year then ended, and comply with the Companies Act 1985.

The auditors are professional accountants, independent of the company's management, who are acting on behalf of a company's owners – its shareholders. They do not assert that the accounts are 'correct'; as we shall see later, preparing company accounts involves many subjective estimates and judgements. Nor do auditors *guarantee* to discover any fraud that may have occurred or any mistakes that may have been made in preparing the accounts. (A famous legal judgement once called the auditor 'a watchdog not a bloodhound'.)

In the rare instances where the auditors are unable to report that in their opinion the accounts give a true and fair view, then they must say so in their report. They must **qualify** their **audit report,** and give reasons for doing so. Where there is substantial uncertainty, the auditors may disclaim any opinion. (They would say: *'We are unable to express an opinion.'*) Where there is disagreement, the auditors may express an adverse opinion. (They would say: *'In our opinion the accounts do not give a true and fair view...'*.)

Examples of uncertainty might include:

1 lack of proper accounting records;
2 doubts about the company's ability to continue as a going concern;
3 inherent problems in relation to major litigation or long-term contracts.

Examples of disagreement might include:

1 failure to follow Statements of Standard Accounting Practice (see 3.1.3(b));
2 disagreement as to facts or amounts included in the accounts;
3 disagreement as to the matter or extent of disclosure in the accounts.

What happens where the auditors disagree with the directors' proposed treatment of certain accounting items? There is likely to be pressure on the directors to change their treatment, and on the auditors not to 'qualify' their report. Often one side or the other gives way, and the disagreement never becomes public knowledge.

Work section

A. Revision questions

A1   What two questions do business accounts try to answer?

A2   How can diverse business activities be summarized?

A3   Why did Alison Robbins need to deduct her building society mortgage in estimating her 'wealth'?

A4   Why did Alison's wealth change by a different amount to the change in her bank balance?

A5   What are the two main statements contained in a set of company accounts?

A6   What does a company 'balance sheet' show?

A7   How often must companies publish balance sheets?

A8   What does a company 'profit and loss account' show?

A9   What is the link between the profit and loss account and the balance sheet?

A10   What does the funds flow statement show?

A11   How does the funds flow statement differ from the balance sheet?

A12   What are the notes to the accounts?

A13   What is an audit?

A14   When may auditors 'qualify' their report on a company's accounts?

A15   On whose behalf are auditors acting?

B Exercises and case studies

B1   a. Make a list of all your personal possessions and liabilities as of one year ago, and value them to estimate your 'wealth'. Do the same as of now. Try to construct a statement which will show how the difference in your 'wealth' came about.

       b. Write down any problems you came across in giving values to any of your possessions or transactions. How did you resolve these problems? Do you think your solutions are completely satisfactory? If not, why not?

B2   A further year has passed for Alison Robbins (see 2.2). At the end of it, she reckons her house's value is unchanged, while the value of her furniture and household goods, and of her car, have each declined by a further £800. Her receipts and payments for the year are listed opposite.

Receipts	£
Monthly wages (*less* PAYE tax deductions)	10,800

Payments	
To building society (of which £1,200 interest)	2,600
Light, heat, etc.	2,000
Housekeeping	2,600
Car running expenses	1,400
Clothing, holiday, etc.	1,800
	10,400
Surplus of receipts over payments:	400

a. Draw up a list of Alison's 'wealth' as at the end of the second year.
b. Prepare a statement accounting for the change in Alison's wealth during the second year.

B3 Your local village grocer, knowing you are studying accounting, asks for your help. He wants to know how his company stands at the year end, and what sort of year it had. He provides you with the following information about the company, which is called **Village Traders Ltd.** All the figures refer either to the year ended 31 March, or to that date itself.

	£
Paid wages to Mrs Molloy	2,496
Value of delivery van at end of year	3,200
Cost of goods sold to customers	46,960
Salary paid to self	10,400
Sales of goods to customers	73,880
Value of shop building and land as at end of year	40,000
Cash in the till and at bank	1,400
Sundry expenses paid (such as light, telephone, etc.)	7,000
Amounts owing to suppliers at end of year	2,400

You are also told that during the year property values in the area have risen, but because the general state of repair of the shop has deteriorated, its value has, on balance, stayed the same as a year ago. The van, on the other hand, was worth £4,000 a year ago, but is now a year older, and hence has been valued at a lower figure.

B4 John Clippitt is a barber. In the year which has just ended, his records disclose the following transactions. Draw up a profit and loss account for the year ended 31 March.

	£
Wages to John Clippitt	7,200
Wages to apprentice	2,000
Cash received for haircuts	20,000
Lease of premises for year	2,400
Cost of electricity and telephone	1,000
Sundry small expenses	600
New chairs bought and installed on 30 March	1,200
Income from sub-lease of a surplus room	600
Tax paid on profits	3,400

Note: The value of the equipment has not changed much during the year.

C   Essay questions

C1   An acquaintance of yours has decided to set up in business as a butcher. What sort of information would you advise him to collect in order to prepare accounts? How might he record this information?

C2   How would you work out whether you are living within your current income? (How *do* you work it out?)

C3   You are the accountant for a small business which has recently been inherited by the son of the founder. He knows nothing of accounting, and asks you to write him a brief memo explaining what the financial accounts are intended to show him.

C4   What are the advantages and disadvantages of using money as a common denominator in accounting?

C5   The chairman of a medium-sized company is wondering whether for the first time to publish a separate statement with the company's annual report, which will be distributed to the company's 500 shareholders. As the company secretary, write him a brief memo arguing either for or against this proposal.

C6   What does the funds flow statement show that the profit and loss account and balance sheet between them do not?

C7   Why might it be desirable for company accounts to be audited, even if company law did not require it?

C8   If auditors do not guarantee either that published accounts are correct, or to discover any fraud which may have been perpetrated, how can they justify their fees?

C9   Explain why additional statements are needed in a set of company accounts, besides the balance sheet and profit and loss account.

C10 Explain to someone who knows nothing about accounting what is meant by a 'true and fair view'.

3

Foundations of accounting

Plan of the chapter:

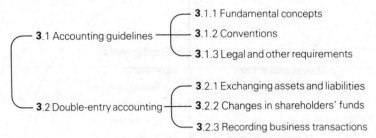

3.1 Accounting guidelines
— **3**.1.1 Fundamental concepts
— **3**.1.2 Conventions
— **3**.1.3 Legal and other requirements

3.2 Double-entry accounting
— **3**.2.1 Exchanging assets and liabilities
— **3**.2.2 Changes in shareholders' funds
— **3**.2.3 Recording business transactions

Fig.3.0

Objective: *To describe the concepts and conventions which underlie financial accounts, and to illustrate the double-entry approach in accounting.*

Synopsis: *Four fundamental concepts in accounting are: going concern, accruals, consistency and prudence. Four conventions are: separate entity, double entry, money terms, and historical cost. Conventions may change if they cease to be useful. Statements of Standard Accounting Practice (SSAPs) based on these guidelines aim to limit different approaches in preparing accounts, without suppressing independent judgement of complex businesses. In addition, there are certain legal and other requirements, but these too mostly focus on the need for accounts above all to present a 'true and fair view'.*

Each transaction has two aspects in double-entry accounting, and affects a balance sheet in one of only four possible ways (see figure 3.2). The profit and loss account summarizes for a period all the trading transactions which affect shareholders' funds. A simple example illustrates how the balance sheet shows the cumulative results of business transactions to date.

3.1 Accounting guidelines

The basic purpose of financial accounts is to show a 'true and fair view' of a business's financial position and profit or loss for a period. There are two sets of guidelines which help accountants to prepare accounts which will give a true and fair view: fundamental concepts and accounting conventions. In addition there are certain legal and other requirements.

Ideally all accountants should follow the guidelines closely enough to produce a similar picture from the same data. But as we shall see in more detail later, *judgement* is also important in preparing accounts. In complex businesses, competent independent accountants can honestly disagree. Thus often there is not only one 'true and fair view' that could be derived from a specific set of events and transactions.

Figure 3.1 summarizes the main fundamental concepts, conventions and legal and other requirements, affecting financial accounts.

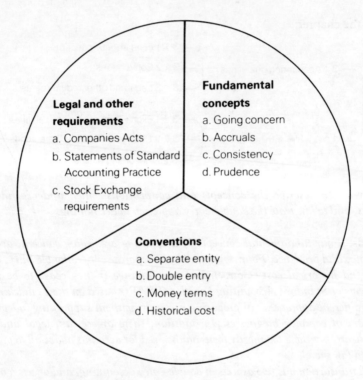

Legal and other requirements
a. Companies Acts
b. Statements of Standard Accounting Practice
c. Stock Exchange requirements

Fundamental concepts
a. Going concern
b. Accruals
c. Consistency
d. Prudence

Conventions
a. Separate entity
b. Double entry
c. Money terms
d. Historical cost

Figure 3.1 Accounting guidelines

3.1.1 Fundamental concepts

Four fundamental accounting *concepts* underlie the figures in accounts.

(a) The **going concern** concept assumes that an enterprise will continue in business for the foreseeable future. This normally means valuing assets at cost, on the assumption that they are worth at least this much. A different assumption might be that the business was soon going to be wound up (liquidated). It might then be prudent to value assets at the amount they would realize on immediate sale (which might be less than cost).

(b) The **accruals** concept tries to match expenses against revenues. It recognizes revenues as they are earned and expenses as incurred. The timing normally coincides with the delivery of goods or performance of services. An alternative approach might be to recognize transactions only on payment or receipt of cash; but this would be less relevant in a credit economy. (But some non-commercial bodies, such as government departments, still use cash accounting.)

(c) The **consistency** concept requires the same treatment for similar items. Otherwise comparing accounting results between periods and between businesses would be meaningless. (The same concept applies to all statistics.)

(d) The **prudence** concept (sometimes called 'conservatism') means that accounts include revenues (and profits) only when they are 'realized'. This may be either in cash or in the form of assets whose ultimate cash proceeds are fairly certain. In contrast, companies make full provision at once for all expected losses and expenses, even where they have to estimate the amount.

Do not worry if not all the implications of these concepts are obvious at first. Later chapters will spell them out in more detail. For example, Chapters 5 and 6 discuss the 'matching' principle, and Chapter 7 discusses the 'prudence' concept in connection with valuing stocks.

You may find it useful to refer back to this sub-section from time to time as you go through the book.

3.1.2 Conventions

As accounting has developed over the centuries, certain procedures (known as **conventions)** have become generally accepted, and accountants everywhere now take them for granted. If conditions were to change in future, they might need to be modified. As a rule the fundamental concepts and accounting conventions also apply to management accounting (though *not* the legal and other requirements). Four of the most basic conventions are:

(a) Separate entity

A company is a legal 'person' in its own right, completely separate from its promoters, managers, owners, and employees. The accounts of a company therefore deal only with the affairs of the company. This is obvious with large companies: Unilever's balance sheet does not include the personal possessions of its directors! But small companies, where the owners are also the managers, may need care to separate the personal affairs of the owners from those of the business. (And this can also affect tax.)

(b) Double entry

Section 3.2 discusses **double-entry accounting**, which Goethe called 'the finest invention of the human mind'. It means that one can look at any transaction from two points of view. Any funds a company uses (for example, to buy equipment) have to come from somewhere (for example, from a bank loan). Similarly, any funds that a company has obtained (such as share capital from the owners) must be used somewhere (even if only deposited with a bank).

(c)   Money terms

The accounting 'unit of measurement' is money (the 'language' of business). Expressing many diverse business transactions in terms of money means they can be added together. But in financial statements, as in life, not everything that matters is capable of being expressed in money. (Thus, for example, accounts ignore the state of the managing director's liver – even though it may be an important business fact!) High and varying rates of inflation in recent years have revealed another serious disadvantage of using money as the unit of account (see Chapter 8).

(d)   Historical cost

Another accounting convention is to use original cost to value assets in the balance sheet, rather than current value. This may seem odd at first sight. (For instance, Alison Robbins tried to estimate the current value of her various possessions in 2.2.) As a rule, though, accountants have preferred to use definite known historical cost figures which auditors can independently verify. In contrast, current values can only be estimated within a very wide margin of error for many assets. But in times of inflation, historical cost figures can be very different from current values (see Chapter 8).

3.1.3   Legal and other requirements

(a)   Companies Act 1985

The Companies Act 1985 (which consolidates the provisions of earlier Companies Acts) lays down legal requirements with respect to company accounts. The main requirement is that accounts (which must be audited) should show a true and fair view of the state of a company's affairs and of the profit or loss for the year.

UK company law has tended not to lay down precise rules, for example about the format of accounts. But since the UK's entry into the EC, more detailed regulations have started to apply to accounts.

(b)   Statements of Standard Accounting Practice

Since the early 1970s the accountancy bodies have issued a series of Statements of Standard Accounting Practice (SSAPs). These appear in two stages: first an **exposure draft** (ED), outlining proposals which are subject to comments and arguments; and then an SSAP, which may modify the exposure draft if necessary. SSAPs have dealt with many of the major accounting problems: depreciation, stock valuation, tax, foreign currencies, and so on. They may be revised from time to time, in the light of new conditions, or changes in professional and other views.

Companies are expected to follow SSAPs, though they do not carry the force of law. In practice companies sometimes fail to abide by an SSAP, perhaps with the agreement of their auditors if there is a good reason. There are advantages in having uniform methods for dealing with particular accounting problems;

but there are also dangers in trying to force very different kinds of business into following a single set of rules.

(c) Stock Exchange requirements

Listed companies are subject to the regulations of the Stock Exchange. (One of them is that SSAPs must be followed.) These tend to require more disclosure than the Companies Act. The penalty for failing to comply with Stock Exchange requirements, in theory, would be suspension of the company's 'quotation'. But in practice there would be a good deal of debate before taking such a drastic step for a major company.

The over-riding tenor of British rules about accounting is to insist on extensive disclosure of what has been done in trying to present a true and fair view.

3.2 Double-entry accounting

3.2.1 Exchanging assets and liabilities

We have already mentioned the double-entry principle in accounting. It is the reason why the balance sheet always 'balances'; and why, in total, the sources of funds in one part of the balance sheet always equal the uses of funds in the other part.

Each transaction has two aspects. For example, when a company buys goods on credit, it obtains the goods (an asset), but at the same time it incurs an obligation to pay for them later (a liability). Double-entry accounting records *both*: assets on the left-hand side of the account, liabilities on the right. Any simple transaction must affect the balance sheet in one of the four ways shown in figure 3.2. In each case, the two aspects exactly offset each other, so the balance sheet will continue to balance.

(a) Asset	+			
Asset	−			
(b)		Liability	+	
		Liability	−	
(c) Asset	+	Liability	+	
(d) Asset	−	Liability	−	

Figure 3.2 The four kinds of double-entry effects of transactions

Let us now look at a simple example of each kind of transaction, and the resulting changes to the balance sheet.

(a) Asset + / Asset –
A company buys stock for £100 cash.

Stocks	+	£100
Cash	–	£100

(b) Liability + / Liability –
A company increases its bank overdraft by £500 to pay a supplier (trade creditor) who is pressing for settlement. The company still owes £500, but now to the bank, not to the trade creditor concerned.

Bank overdraft	+	£500
Trade creditor	–	£500

(c) Asset + / Liability +
A firm purchases a motor vehicle, on credit, for £8,000. So it has acquired an asset in return for an obligation to pay later (a liability).

Motor vehicle	+	£8,000	Trade creditor	+	£8,000

(d) Asset – / Liability –
A company draws a cheque for £300 to pay trade creditors who supplied goods some months earlier.

Cash	–	£300	Trade creditors	–	£300

After each of the above transaction, the two parts of the balance sheet remain equal in total.

3.2.2 Changes in shareholders' funds
The four examples just used to illustrate the double-entry principle all involved a straightforward exchange of one asset or liability for another. We now look at three examples of transactions which affect shareholders' funds. They still fall within the four categories listed in figure 3.2 (where the term 'liability' means 'shareholders' funds and liabilities').

1 A company sells goods from stock. The cost of the goods was £50, and the company sells them on credit for £65. Thus there is a profit of £15. *This goes to shareholders' funds.* The changes on the balance sheet are as follows:

Stock	–	£50	*Shareholders' funds*	
Debtors	+	£65	Profit and loss account	+ £15

2 A company issues more shares to increase the funds at its disposal. In return for the new paid-up share capital of 180,000 £1 shares, the shareholders pay in £180,000 cash. From the company's point of view, this is a receipt of cash.

Cash	+ £180,000	*Shareholders' funds*	
		Paid-up share capital	+ £180,000

3 A company pays £14,000 cash on wages, an expense which reduces profit. Hence (indirectly) it reduces shareholders' funds on the balance sheet.

Cash	– £14,000	*Shareholders' funds*	
		Profit and loss account	– £14,000

Many transactions affect the amount of shareholders' funds in the balance sheet. The profit and loss account shows the success or failure of a company in making profits. It is a summary of all the trading transactions in a given period which affect the shareholders' funds. But as example 2 above showed, some transactions affecting shareholders' funds are not related to the profit and loss account. They are **capital** transactions, as opposed to **revenue** transactions (see also 5.3.2).

3.2.3 Recording business transactions

The previous two sub-sections dealt with the balance sheet changes from exchanging assets and liabilities and changes in shareholders' funds. Now we illustrate the effects of a series of business transactions on the balance sheet of a new company. To simplify the picture, suppose that each set of transactions occurs in a different month. Apart from the initial issue of shares, the first few transactions do not affect shareholders' funds.

> *Example: Keith and Ray Thompson are brothers. They decide to start their own business in the baking industry, and plan to begin by building up three good retail stores.*

The new company, called Thompson Brothers Limited, will need share capital of £60,000, and Keith and Ray agree to provide half each. Each month's transactions are set out separately below.

(a) In January the company issues share certificates to the two brothers, each for 30,000 £1 shares, in exchange for two cheques for £30,000 made payable to the company. The company opens a bank account and pays in the two cheques totalling £60,000.

Assets		Shareholders' funds	
Cash	+ £60,000	Paid-up share capital	+ £60,000

(b) In February the company buys three freehold properties costing a total of £78,000. Half is paid for by raising a mortgage bond (liability) with an insurance company. The other half is paid by cheque.

Assets		Shareholders' funds	
Freehold property	+ £78,000	Mortgage bond	+ £39,000
Cash	− £39,000		

Figure 3.3 shows the company's (**horizontal format**) balance sheet at the end of February.

	£		£
Fixed assets		Shareholders' funds	
Freehold property	78,000	Paid-up share capital	60,000
Current asset		Long-term liability	
Cash at bank	21,000	Mortgage bond	39,000
	99,000		99,000

Figure 3.3   Thompson Brothers Ltd balance sheet, end of February

(c) In March, fitting out the shops and buying the required equipment cost the company £12,000, which was paid in the same month.

Assets		
Equipment	+ £12,000	
Cash	− £12,000	

You should be able to arrive at a new balance sheet, as at the end of March, by making suitable changes to the end-of-February balance sheet (shown in figure 3.3).

(d) In April, the company began trading. In the month (i) it bought goods (bread and cake) costing £6,000 on credit, and (ii) cash sales from the three shops totalled £10,000. Each Saturday afternoon it gave unsold stocks to a local orphanage, as they would be unsaleable by Monday morning. During the month (iii) the company paid wages of £2000.

(i) Stocks	+ £6,000	Trade creditors	+ £6,000
(ii) Stocks	− £6,000	*Shareholder's fund*	
Cash	+ £10,000	Profit and loss account	+ £4,000
(iii) Cash	− £2,000	*Shareholders' funds*	
		Profit and loss account	− £2,000

*Figure 3.4 sets out the company's balance sheet at the end of April, now in the normal modern **vertical format**.*

	(£)
Fixed assets	
Freehold property	78,000
Equipment	12,000
	90,000
Current asset	
Cash at bank	17,000
	107,000
Less: *Current liabilities*	
Trade creditors	6,000
	101,000
Less: *Long-term liability*	
Mortgage bond	39,000
	62,000
Shareholders' funds	
Paid-up share capital	60,000
Profit and loss account	2,000
	62,000

Figure 3.4 Thompson Brothers Ltd balance sheet, end of April

(e) During the remaining eight months of the year to 31 December, the company undertook the following transactions in total:

1   Bought goods costing £46,000 and owed suppliers £5,000 at year-end.
2   Made cash sales totalling £80,000; had no stocks left at year-end.
3   Paid wages of £16,000
4   Paid £8,000 in respect of the mortgage bond; £4,000 in interest, and £4,000 capital repayment to reduce the size of the loan.
5   Purchased a delivery vehicle for £3,000 cash.
6   Paid £5,000 of other overhead expenses.
7   Provided for £2,000 depreciation on the equipment.

Figure 3.5 sets out the company's balance sheet as at the end of December, after all the above transactions. It now appears in £'000. You should be able to check it, stage by stage.

		(£'000)
Fixed assets		
Freehold property		78
Equipment		10
Delivery vehicle		3
		91
Current asset		
Cash at bank		18
		109
Less:	*Current liabilities*	
	Trade creditors	5
		104
Less:	*Long-term liability*	
	Mortgage bond	35
		69
Shareholders' funds		
Paid-up share capital		60
Profit and loss account		9
		69

Figure 3.5 Thompson Brothers Ltd balance sheet, end of December, Year 1

Work section

A Revision questions

A1 What is the basic purpose of financial accounts?

What do you understand by each of the following concepts:

A2 'going concern'?

A3 'accruals'?

A4 'consistency'?

A5 'prudence'?

A6 What has recently brought the 'money' convention into doubt?

A7 Explain what the 'double-entry' convention means.

A8 How does the law affect company accounts?

A9 What are Statements of Standard Accounting Practice (SSAPs)?

A10 Why are standard rules necessary in accounting? What are their possible drawbacks?

A11 List the four basic ways in which transactions can affect the balance sheet.

A12 How does the double-entry principle deal with goods being sold for more than they cost?

A13 Name two kinds of transactions which affect shareholders' funds.

A14 What does the profit and loss account for a period contain?

A15 What is the essential difference between a cash and a credit transaction?

What happens to a company's total assets when:

A16 it issues new shares to pay off a loan?

A17 it sells land to buy new machinery?

A18 it issues new shares to buy a new building?

What happens to a company's total liabilities when:

A19 cash is used to repay a loan?

A20 a long-term loan is raised to repay a short-term loan?

B Exercises and case studies

B1 Which of the following transactions will directly affect shareholders' funds?

a. The sale of goods for more than they cost.

b. The sale of goods for less than they cost.

c. A loan to the company by a shareholder.

d. The payment of last year's tax.

e. The payment of insurance premiums.

B2 Write out the appropriate double entry for each of the following transactions, in the same way as in 3.2.3.
   a. The purchase of a machine in cash for £26,000.
   b. The repayment of a loan of £10,000.
   c. The sale of a freehold property costing £5,000 for the same amount.
   d. The purchase of a motor lorry on hire purchase for £4,500, with a deposit of £500.
   e. The sale of goods costing £500 for £650 on credit.
   f. The payment of wages of £1,000.
   g. The sale of goods costing £800 for £650 in cash.
   h. The theft of an uninsured vehicle valued at £1,500.
   i. The purchase of raw materials on credit for £14,000.
   j. The provision for taxation of £800.
   k. The sale of some land, costing £6,000, for £17,000.
   l. The raising of extra capital by issuing 10,000 ordinary shares for £1 each.

B3 Refer to 3.2.3 (c). Draw up a balance sheet, in vertical format, for Thompson Brothers Ltd as at the end of March.

B4 Refer to 3.2.3 (e). Draw up a profit and loss account for the year ended 31 December. *(Hint:* Remember the trading in April.)

B5 What balance sheet items would change (and how) in each of the following transactions?
   a. A purchase of machinery for £20,000, of which 25 per cent is to be paid at once, the balance to be paid later.
   b. The issue of 50,000 £1 11½ per cent Preference Shares, fully paid up.
   c. The purchase, for 65p per share, of 10,000 25p ordinary shares in a company which has a total issued share capital of 15,000 shares.
   d. The sale of goods, which cost £15,000, for £25,000, payment to be made 30 days from the date of sale.
   e. The cash sale of a piece of equipment for £3,600, which originally cost £8,000, but which has had £5,000 provided for depreciation over the five years of its life to date.

B6 Write out the double entry for each of the following transactions undertaken by Lopsided Ltd after its formation on 1 January. Give a complete balance sheet at the end, as at 30 June, incorporating the effect of all the transactions.

	(£'000)
a. Share capital paid in on 1 January	200
b. Land purchased on 4 January	20

   c. The company built its own factory between 4 January and 16 May, incurring the following costs:

(i) Wages paid to builders	7
(ii) Building materials	4

(iii) *Subcontractors' charges:*
     Electricians   2
     Plumbers   3

d. On 12 June the company buys materials, ready to commence production   20

e. On 16 June machinery which it had ordered several months previously arrives, and is paid for   30

f. Up to 30 June expenditure is incurred on installing the machinery   6

Identify any assumptions you have had to make.

B7 In year 2, Thompson Brothers Ltd had the following transactions (in summary):

		(£'000)
1.	Freehold property bought for two more shops	53
2.	Equipment purchased for new shops	7
3.	Mortgage bond increased by	30
4.	*Payments in respect of mortgage bond:*	
	Interest	7
	Capital repayment	6
5.	Purchases of goods	140
6.	Cash sales	217
7.	Paid wages	49
8.	Purchased another delivery vehicle	4
9.	Paid various overhead expenses	16
10.	*Provided for depreciation*	
	Equipment	4
	Delivery vehicles	2

At the end of the second year, £12,000 was owed to suppliers. You are asked to provide for taxation on the second year's profits, at an estimated rate of 35 per cent of the profit for the year.

a. Prepare a balance sheet as at end of year 2 (refer back to figure 3.5).

b. Prepare a profit and loss account for year 2.

B8 Give *one* example of a business transaction which would immediately result in *each* of the following balance sheet changes:

Cash and profit

a.	Cash	+	Profit	+

Cash not profit

b.	Cash	+	Liabilities	+

Profit not cash

| c. | Assets | + | Profit | + |
| d. | Assets | – | Profit | – |

e.   Profit   −
                                                         Liabilities   −

Neither profit nor cash

f.   Assets   +   Liabilities   −

Note: 'Profit' refers to the cumulative retained profits in the shareholders' funds part of the 'shareholders' funds and liabilities' part of the balance sheet.

B9   *Seven days in May*

Clinker Ltd's balance sheet as at 1 May 1990 is set out opposite. The following events occurred on successive days in the first week of May.

2 May. 1,000 new £1 ordinary shares are issued for £1,000 cash.

3 May. A tax liability of £400 is paid.

4 May. New fixed assets costing £700 are purchased, by means of:
    (i) a new long-term loan of £500
    (ii) a cash payment of £200.

5 May. £600 is received from credit customers (debtors), and £900 is paid to creditors.

6 May. Stocks costing £1,000 are sold on credit for £1,500

a. Show, in the columns set out, the *change* to the balance sheet resulting from each event (*not* the new balance sheet amount). Each of the six columns should 'balance'.

b. Show in the righthand column the balance sheet amounts as at the end of 7 May 1990. Make sure your balance sheet balances.

B10 *Stamford Manufacturing Company Ltd*

A. On 1 January 1990 the Stamford Manufacturing Company Ltd was formed to make and sell widgets:
1. Ordinary shares were sold to provide £200,000 capital;
2. £160,000 was borrowed short-term from a bank @ 10 per cent a year interest.

B. During the year 1990 the following cash payments were made:
1. Premises rented for £12,000 (General expense);
2. Machines purchased for £240,000 (Fixed assets);
3. 6000 widget castings bought for £10 each (Stocks) – £48,000 cash paid, £12,000 still owing at year end.
4. Operator's wages of £12,000 (Stocks). During 1990 all 6,000 widget castings were machined by the operator into finished widgets.
5. Manager's salary £24,000 (General expense).

C. Depreciation on the machines is charged at 10 per cent a year (Stocks).

D. During 1990 5,000 finished widgets were sold at £40 each – £180,000 cash received, £20,000 still receivable at year end.

Clinker Ltd balance sheet

	1 May £	2 May £	3 May £	4 May £	5 May £	6 May £	7 May £
Fixed assets	3,700						
Current assets							
Stocks	2,600						
Debtors	3,000						
Cash	1,100						
	6,700						
	10,400						
Current liabilities							
Creditors	2,400						
Tax payable	900						
Dividend proposed	300						
	3,600						
Long-term loans	2,200						
Shareholders' funds							
Paid-up £1 share capital	2,000						
Retained profits	2,600						
	4,600						
	10,400						

Figure 3.6 Clinker Ltd balance sheet

E. At the end of 1990 the bank loan was repaid, plus £16,000 interest.

F. Tax for 1990 was assessed at £10,000. £4,000 was paid in cash during the year, and £6,000 remained payable at the year end.

G. An interim dividend of £16,000 was paid in cash to shareholders during 1990, and a final dividend of £20,000 was proposed in respect of the year 1990, to be paid in April 1991.

On the basis of the above information you are asked to prepare:

a. the balance sheet at 31 December 1990.

b. the profit and loss account for the year ended 31 December 1990.

C Essay questions

C1 'To give no weight to matters incapable of money valuation renders the whole basis of accounting invalid.' Support or oppose this view.

C2 Write an essay supporting Goethe's view that 'Double entry accounting is the finest invention of the human mind.'

C3 'Flexibility in financial accounting is both necessary and potentially dangerous.' Discuss.

C4 'Uniform standards for published financial accounts are both necessary and potentially misleading.' Discuss.

C5 'The concepts of consistency and prudence may conflict; if so, practical accountants prefer prudence, while academics advocate consistency.' Discuss.

C6 State the reasons why companies prepare financial statements and accounts. Comment on their usefulness.

4

The balance sheet

Plan of the chapter:

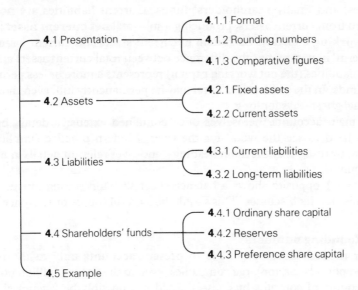

Fig 4.0

Objective: *To describe the various items in balance sheets under three headings: assets, liabilities, and shareholders' funds.*

Synopsis: *The balance sheet shows a firm's financial position at a particular date. The modern format is 'vertical', with assets, liabilities, and shareholders' funds shown underneath each other in that order.*

Fixed assets are long-term resources controlled by a business, of three kinds: tangible, intangible, and financial (investments). Current assets are expected to be turned into cash within one year from the balance sheet date. Balance sheets group them with current liabilities, and show the net difference as 'working capital'.

Current liabilities are due for payment within one year from the balance sheet date; whereas long-term liabilities are not due to be settled for more than a year, and thus form part of the firm's (long-term) 'capital employed'.

Shareholders' funds consist of paid-up ordinary share capital, reserves, and (sometimes) preference share capital. The three main kinds of reserves arise from share premiums, revaluations, and retained profits.

4.1 Presentation

A balance sheet is a statement of the financial position of a business as at a particular date. It shows the cumulative sources and uses of funds. The balance sheet does not purport to show the 'true worth' of a business: it excludes many valuable assets, especially intangible assets such as business 'know-how'.

4.1.1 Format

Balance sheets normally use a vertical format, with assets shown first, then liabilities, and finally shareholders' funds. Current liabilities are normally deducted from current assets, producing a sub-total **net current assets** (often called **working capital**). Each item in current assets and current liabilities is 'short-term' in nature; but the difference between total current assets and total current liabilities (the net working capital) represents a more or less permanent use of funds. In the same way, a hotel may be permanently full, even though no individual guest stays for long.

The main accounts themselves once contained extensive detail, but this made it hard to see the wood for the trees. Modern practice simplifies the accounts, by using only the main headings; and gives relevant details in notes to the accounts.

Figure 4.1 opposite shows a balance sheet skeleton setting out the items which this chapter discusses. This should be a useful source of reference.

4.1.2 Rounding numbers

Another modern development is to present accounts only to the nearest thousand pounds (or, for large companies, even to the nearest million pounds). The accounts of complex businesses could not possibly be 'accurate' to the nearest pound, but even if they were, it would still be a mistake to publish so much detail. That would obscure the overall view of the company's affairs which accounts aim to show. So the general rule in accounting is to ignore tiny amounts, group similar items together, and so on. The legal maxim *'de minimis non curat lex'* (the law does not bother with trifles) also applies in accounting.

In this respect British accounts are probably in advance of American practice. As recently as 1975, General Motors Corporation (the largest manufacturing company in the world) still presented its accounts to the nearest dollar! (Its sales revenue in that year was reported as $35, 724, 911, 215 and its net profit after tax as $1,253,091,965!)

4.1.3 Comparative figures

Finally, company law requires accounts to show figures not only for the most recent date, but also for the preceding period. This is to let readers compare the two years. (In analysing accounts, of course, other standards for comparison may also be useful, such as the performance of competing firms.) Separate tables of statistics often set out major accounting items over a period of five

---

Balance sheet of (name of company) at (date)

	(£'000)	
Fixed assets		
Tangible	xxx	
Intangible	xxx	
Investments	xxx	
		xxx
Current assets		
Stocks	xxx	
Debtors and prepayments	xxx	
Cash and liquid resources	xxx	
	xxx	
Less: *Current liabilities*		
Bank overdrafts and loans	xxx	
Creditors and accrued charges	xxx	
Taxation	xxx	
Dividends payable	xxx	
	xxx	
Net working capital		xxx
Total assets less current liabilities		xxx
Less: *Long-term liabilities*		
Loan capital	xxx	
Provision for liabilities and charges	xxx	
		xxx
		xxx
Shareholders' funds		
Called-up ordinary share capital		xxx
Reserves: Share premium	xxx	
Revaluation	xxx	
Other	xxx	
Retained profits	xxx	
		xxx
Ordinary shareholders' funds		xxx
Preference share capital		xxx
		xxx

Figure 4.1 Skeleton of a balance sheet

years, but these are neither part of the 'accounts' themselves, nor subject to audit. (And Chapter 8 explains how one needs to be careful about allowing for the effect of inflation in making comparisons over time.)

4.2 Assets

Assets are valuable resources which a business owns or controls. Accounts usually state assets at original cost, less deductions for **accumulated depreciation**. Chapters 6 and 7 discuss the basis for valuing fixed assets and stocks.

4.2.1 Fixed assets

Fixed assets are long-term resources of a business. They are used to provide goods or services over their life, rather than to be sold in the ordinary course of trading. Some fixed assets, like land, never 'wear out' – though they may need to be maintained in proper condition. Others have a finite limited life: either for physical reasons (like motor vehicles), or for legal reasons (like leases or patents).

The reason for acquiring assets determines whether they are 'fixed' or 'current', not their tangible form. A company which makes filing cabinets for sale would show them as current trading stocks in the balance sheet; while one simply using filing cabinets as permanent office furniture would show them as fixed assets.

Fixed assets are classified under three headings: (a) tangible; (b) intangible; (c) investments.

(a) Tangible fixed assets
1 Land and buildings.   Most businesses need land and buildings to operate from, which they may own outright or lease (rent). 'Freehold property' is shown either at cost or at a more recent valuation, less **depreciation** on buildings. Any capital sum (premium) paid for a lease appears separately as 'leasehold property', and is **amortized** over the period of the lease.
2 Plant and equipment. The heading 'plant and equipment' may cover almost all tangible fixed assets except land and buildings, in service industries as well as in manufacturing . It could include: all sorts of production machinery and tooling; motor vehicles; and office furniture, fittings, and equipment.

(b) Intangible fixed assets
Many fixed assets are tangible physical items, such as land and buildings, or plant and equipment. But others may be **intangible,** such as goodwill, patents, or development costs. Accounts show these items at original cost less amortization.
1 Goodwill. **Goodwill** appears in accounts only if a distinct *cost* can be identified: it does not refer to normal commercial 'goodwill' which has gradually built up over the years. Accounting 'goodwill' occurs if a company buys another business, and pays more than the fair value of the individual acquired assets. (The value of the whole business may be more than the sum of the identified fixed and net current assets.) Some companies eliminate

any purchased goodwill which does arise, by deducting it from reserves in the balance sheet; others amortize it against profit over time.

2 Patents, copyrights, and trade marks. Certain other intangible fixed assets may appear on the balance sheet. These include (a) patents, the sole right to make and sell a product, (b) copyrights, the sole right to publish and sell a book, and (c) the registered right to use particular trade marks or brand names. Where a company has acquired another business owning such rights, the 'goodwill' figure may include their cost. Many companies treat the cost of obtaining such legal rights as a revenue expense, even if they expect future benefits. Some companies have recently begun to **capitalize** brand names in their accounts.

3 Development costs. The cost of basic or applied research is written off at once as an ordinary business expense. But companies may carry forward the costs of specific product development and amortize it over the periods expected to benefit, if there is a good chance of enough future revenue to cover the costs. But even here, 'prudence' often prevails over 'matching', and most companies prefer to treat all development costs as an ordinary expense.

(c) Investments

A third fixed asset heading covers long-term investments in financial securities, such as holdings of ordinary shares in other companies. These may include:

1 investments in **subsidiaries,** if more than 50 per cent of the paid-up ordinary shares are owned;
2 investments in **associated (related) companies**, if between 20 per cent and 50 per cent;
3 **trade investments** if less than 20 per cent;
4 sometimes there may also be long-term investments in fixed-interest securities, such as government stocks.

The investments in 3 and 4 may give rise to a separate item, 'investment income', in the profit and loss account.

4.2.2 Current assets

Current assets are short-term resources, either already in liquid form, or expected to be used up or turned into cash within twelve months from the balance sheet date. The main current asset headings are: stocks, debtors and prepayments, cash and liquid resources.

(a) Stocks

Stocks (inventories) represent **raw materials** and processed goods which are either unfinished (**work-in-progress**) or unsold (**finished goods**) (see 7.3). Most firms also hold small supplies of stationery and maintenance stores to use in the course of business.

The level of stocks will vary with the nature of the business. A company which makes only against firm orders will hold low stocks of finished goods: it will deliver goods to customers as soon as they are ready. And stocks will tend to be low if goods are highly perishable, like bread or newspapers. But companies building ships or aircraft, with a long manufacturing cycle, may invest large amounts in work-in-progress. (And they may receive payments on account to cover some of it.)

Holding stocks can be expensive: it involves handling and storage costs, insurance, risks of decay or theft, as well as the financial cost of tying up funds. On the other hand, it can also be costly to run out of stocks and so be unable to satisfy customers at once. The art of managing stocks is to balance these conflicting costs and benefits.

(b) Debtors and prepayments

When firms sell on credit, they show the amounts which customers owe at the balance sheet date as **debtors** (or **accounts receivable**). The amount will depend both on the volume of credit sales and on the average period of credit taken. Many businesses sell almost entirely on credit, and find the average period of credit taken is about two months. This represents a substantial investment (use) of funds.

Certain expenses, by custom or law, have to be paid in advance – for example, insurance premiums. At the balance sheet date, part of the amount paid may relate to the next accounting period. This is a **prepayment,** and the balance sheet shows it as a current asset, often grouped together with debtors.

(c) Cash and liquid resources

Cash in hand (**petty cash**) consists literally of notes and coins, but **cash** in accounting also refers to balances in bank accounts. Most companies plan to keep their bank balances fairly low, since they do not normally earn much interest. On the other hand, it could be very serious to run out of cash, especially if there are no bank overdraft arrangements. Many companies now

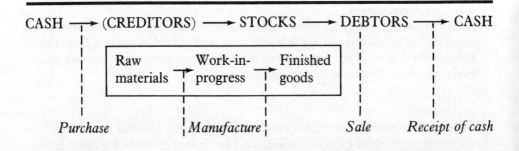

Figure 4.2 Working capital cycle of a manufacturing business

use the general term **liquid resources** to include cash in hand and at banks, together with short-term marketable securities.

Figure 4.2 shows the working capital cycle of a manufacturing business. The business first purchases raw materials on credit, then uses labour and capital equipment (in various proportions in different industries) to convert the raw materials into finished goods. When it sells and delivers the finished goods, legal title passes to the customer. He either pays cash or, if he buys on credit, owes the price to the selling company. The transaction ends when the debtor finally pays cash to settle his account.

4.3   Liabilities

A company must repay amounts borrowed when they are due, and regularly pay the agreed amount of interest. Failure to do so will entitle the lender to take immediate legal action to recover the principal and any unpaid interest. 'Current' or 'short-term' liabilities are payable within twelve months from the date of the balance sheet, while those payable later are 'long-term' (sometimes 'medium-term', between one and five years).

4.3.1 Current liabilities
There are six main kinds of **current liabilities** payable by a company within twelve months from the date of the balance sheet. Each is discussed briefly below. The order in which they appear can vary.

(a) Bank overdrafts and short-term loans
A regular source of short-term loans (for individuals as well as for companies) is the **bank overdraft**. This simply means a bank allowing its customer to spend more, by drawing cheques, than there is money in the account. Permission to borrow in this way, and the maximum amount of any such overdraft, together with a repayment date, must normally be agreed in advance with the bank. Overdrafts are legally repayable 'on demand'.

(b) Current part of long-term borrowings
Even long-term borrowings have to be repaid when the time comes; and balance sheets show as 'current' liabilities those amounts payable within twelve months.

(c) Trade creditors
Goods and services supplied by one business to another are often sold 'on credit', rather than for immediate settlement in cash. Accounting practice records the purchasing companys as owning the goods from the moment of delivery. The normal period of credit ranges from one to three months after that date. Amounts due for goods owned but not yet paid for are shown as

trade **creditors** (or **accounts payable**). In effect the suppliers have 'lent' the purchasing company, for a short period, the funds (normally interest-free) with which to buy the goods.

(d) Dividends payable
Most British companies pay an **interim dividend** out of profits during the year, with the directors recommending a **final dividend** in respect of the year. The balance sheet shows the proposed final dividend as a current liability on the assumption that shareholders will approve it at the company's Annual General Meeting (several months later).

(e) Corporation tax
Taxation based on profits – called **corporation tax** for companies – is shown as a separate liability in the balance sheet. Most of it is usually 'current'.

(f) Accrued charges
Certain expenses accrue from day to day, but a bill (invoice) may be sent only every three months (for example, for electricity or telephones). Accountants estimate the amount relating to the accounting period and include it as an expense in the profit and loss account. The balance sheet shows it as an **accrued charge** (or accrual).

Figure 4.3 shows the 'current liabilities' section of the balance sheet of Guinness plc at 31 December 1988.

Creditors (amounts falling due within one year)

	£m.	
Short-term borrowings		
Bank overdrafts	54	
Bank loans	139	
		193
Other creditors		
Trade creditors	181	
Dividends	79	
Corporation tax	125	
Social security and other taxes	54	
Other creditors	194	
Accruals and deferred income	179	
		812
		1,005

Figure 4.3 Guinness plc: group current liabilities at 31 December 1988

4.3.2 Long-term liabilities

Five aspects of **long-term liabilities** are briefly discussed below:

(a) Public quotation

Larger companies may borrow from the public, with such loans (called **debentures)** 'quoted' on the Stock Exchange rather like ordinary shares. The main influence on their price will be changes in interest rates (whereas ordinary shares will also be affected by the company's profit prospects). Smaller companies will tend to borrow from a single lender, such as an insurance company or bank.

(b) Security

Long-term borrowing may often be **secured** against particular assets. In a liquidation, the secured lender has a prior claim to the proceeds of the assets concerned. Any surplus remaining after the **secured loan** is fully repaid goes into the pool to pay unsecured creditors; while if there is any shortfall, to that extent the 'secured' creditor has to rank equally with other unsecured creditors.

(c) Interest rate

Recent large fluctuations in rates of inflation and in interest rates have made 'fixed-interest' loans unpopular. In effect they forced both lenders and borrowers to speculate about the future rate of inflation. To avoid this need, 'variable-rate' loans have developed, with the interest rate varying in line with interest rates in general. For example, a company might borrow at '2 per cent above LIBOR' (the interest rate on the London Inter-Bank market).

(d) Currency

As international business continues to grow, more companies may wish to borrow foreign currencies (rather than sterling) to finance their overseas operations. Accounts need to translate interest and principal into sterling using the **exchange rate** at the date of the balance sheet. A sharp change in the exchange rate can have a big impact on the sterling equivalent of a foreign currency loan (see Chapter 19, Problem B5, Laker Airways).

(e) Conversions into equity

Sometimes loan capital is 'convertible' into ordinary shares, at the option of the lender, on prearranged terms. The balance sheet shows such **convertible loans** as long-term liabilities until either they are converted into ordinary shares **(equity)** or they are repaid. After conversion they appear as shareholders' funds, the split between paid-up share capital and share premiums depending on the conversion price.

4.4 Shareholders' funds

Shareholders' funds are provided directly or indirectly by the owners of the business – the **shareholders. Owner's equity,** as it is sometimes called, represents permanent capital. As long as a company continues in business, amounts become legally payable to shareholders as a rule only when the company declares **dividends** out of profits.

4.4.1 Ordinary share capital

A new company issues **ordinary share capital** to its original shareholders, in return for cash (or other assets). Existing companies may issue more ordinary shares during their life, in order to increase the total funds at their disposal.

Shares can be of any amount, often either £1 or 25p units. Shareholders must legally authorize companies to issue share capital; and the total **authorized share capital** (shown in the Notes) is usually somewhat larger than the called-up (issued) share capital in the balance sheet.

Each company records its shareholders and the number of shares they own, and issues certificates of ownership. Shareholders may be individual persons, companies, or various financial institutions such as life assurance companies, pension funds, or unit trusts. The company records any change of ownership in the share register. It then issues a new share certificate in place of the old one. But the company's *total* paid-up share capital does not change as a result of such 'secondary' dealings among shareholders.

The liability of ordinary shareholders is limited to the fully-paid **nominal value** of their shares (hence the name **limited company** (Ltd) – or **public limited company** (plc) for larger companies). In contrast, the partners in a **partnership** firm have unlimited personal liability to meet the firm's debts. But if things go wrong, ordinary shareholders in a company may lose all they have invested. On a **liquidation,** they will get whatever is left over after the company has paid all amounts owing to creditors and preference shareholders. If there are not enough assets to pay creditors in full, then the ordinary shareholders get nothing. This quite often happens.

Only ordinary shareholders may normally vote at the company's general meetings, and they elect the company's directors. Ordinary shareholders may loosely be said to 'own' a company's profits, but they have no legal right to them unless the directors choose to declare dividends. So ordinary shareholders are really 'residual owners' of a company's assets. Sooner or later they can expect to receive anything left over after all other suppliers of finance have been paid their agreed *fixed* money amounts.

Shareholders obtain a 'return' from their investment in two ways: by cash dividends from the company, and by any increase in the market value of their shares ('capital gain'). If a company does well, there is no ceiling on the possible return.

4.4.2 Reserves

Three kinds of **reserves** are shown as part of ordinary shareholders' funds: share premiums, revaluations, and retained profits.

(a) Share premiums

When an existing company issues more ordinary shares, the price may exceed the nominal value per share (it must not be less). Thus a 25p share might be issued at a price of 60p. The **share premium** (35p per share) is shown separately under reserves. It is permanent, like called-up share capital, and can never be used for dividends. But only the nominal amount is shown as called-up share capital.

(b) Revaluations

Chapter 6 discusses how accounts value fixed assets. As a rule the basis is original (historical) money cost. But in times of rapid inflation, some assets may be worth much more than their original cost; and companies may wish to revalue them upwards in the balance sheet in order to give a fairer picture of their financial position. So that the balance sheet will continue to balance, the amount of any increase on a **revaluation** of assets is added to ordinary shareholders' funds under **revaluation reserve**.

(c) Retained profits

Cumulative **retained profits** are also included as part of the reserves. They are profits which directors decide *not* to distribute as cash dividends to ordinary shareholders. Thus they are 'retained' in the business, and attributed to ordinary shareholders in the balance sheet. Indeed they are the most important source of funds for most companies. In a changing and uncertain economic environment, annual retained profits may fluctuate sharply. They can even be *negative* for a period, if dividends paid exceed the current period's profits, or if losses occur.

As stated, the three kinds of reserves described above appear as part of ordinary shareholders' funds in the balance sheet. They represent *sources* of funds. But how those funds are *used* may vary. There is no reason why 'reserves' in the balance sheet should be represented on the assets side of the balance sheet by cash or liquid resources. More likely they will have been invested in other assets, such as stocks or plant and equipment. Thus it is quite wrong to suppose that 'reserves' are available to be spent in cash.

Figure 4.4 sets out the shareholders' funds part of the BOC Group's balance sheet at 30 September 1988. (It shows group reserves of £803.7 million at that date; but the group's liquid resources on that date amounted to less than a quarter as much.)

	£m.	
Called-up share capital	116.8	(a)
Share premium account	192.6	
Revaluation reserve	61.5	
Profit and loss account	549.6	
Related companies' reserves	59.6	(b)
Shareholders' funds	**980.1**	
Minority shareholders' interests	48.8	(c)
	1,028.9	

Notes
(a) Ordinary shares of 25p each   114.3
     Preference shares of £1 each   2.5

(b) Principal related companies, in which BOC's equity stake is between 35 and 50 per cent, are in: Australia, Hong Kong, India, Japan, Malaysia, Singapore, Taiwan and Turkey.

(c) Principal minority (outside) interests in BOC Group subsidiaries are in:
     The Commonwealth Industrial Gases Ltd (Australia)   13 per cent
     African Oxygen Ltd (South Africa)   42 per cent

Figure 4.4   The BOC Group plc: group capital and reserves at 30 September 1988

4.4.3 Preference share capital
In respect of both income and capital, preference shareholders rank after all other creditors, but before ordinary shareholders. For tax reasons, **preference shares** have become unpopular in recent years. Stated rates of preference dividend must be paid in full for a period *before* any ordinary dividends can be paid. On a liquidation, unless preference shareholders are repaid the full nominal amount of their shares, the ordinary shareholders will get nothing.

4.5 Example
Figure 4.5 shows an actual balance sheet for Courtaulds plc at 31 March 1989. Notice the comparative figures for 1988. At this stage, readers are strongly recommended to obtain a set of up-to-date published accounts and examine the balance sheet and notes carefully. (Most large companies are glad to send a copy of their latest annual report and accounts on request.)

Courtaulds plc: group balance sheet 31 March 1989

	1989 (£m.)	1988 (£m.)
Fixed assets		
Tangible assets	594.5	579.7
Investments	34.9	32.0
	629.4	611.7
Current assets		
Stocks	434.6	420.5
Debtors	415.5	404.0
Cash and deposits	329.1	184.8
	1,179.2	1,009.3
Creditors (amounts falling due within one year)		
Loans and overdrafts	(93.7)	(65.7)
Other	(651.1)	(596.2)
	(744.8)	(661.9)
Net current assets	434.4	347.4
Total assets less current liabilities	1,063.8	959.1
Creditors (amounts falling due after more than one year)		
Loans	(251.1)	(274.2)
Other	(25.8)	(22.2)
	(276.9)	(296.4)
Provisions for liabilities and charges	(23.5)	(23.6)
	763.4	639.1

(Continued overleaf)

Figure 4.5   Courtaulds plc: group balance sheet 31 March 1989

Courtaulds plc: group balance sheet 31 March 1989

	1989 (£m.)	1988 (£m.)
Capital and reserves		
Called-up share capital	101.3	101.1
Share premium account	118.3	117.5
Profit and loss account	535.3	395.5
	754.9	614.1
Minority interests	8.5	25.0
	763.4	639.1

Figure 4.5 Courtaulds plc: group balance sheet 31 March 1989(continued)

Work section

A Revision questions

A1   Define a 'balance sheet'.

A2   Define 'working capital'.

A3   How can there be a permanent need to finance net current assets?

A4   What is the function of notes to the accounts?

A5   Give two reasons why accounts are not presented to the nearest pound.

A6   What are 'comparative figures'?

A7   How is a balance sheet set out?

A8   Into which main categories are balance sheets classified?

A9   Define an 'asset'.

A10   How are assets normally valued in balance sheets?

A11   What are the three different 'fixed asset' headings?

A12   What are 'intangible' assets? Give two examples.

A13   Define 'goodwill' in accounting.

A14   Define a 'current asset'. What are the three main types?

A15   What are the three main kinds of stock for a manufacturing company?

A16   What is a debtor, and how does it arise?

A17   What is a prepayment? Give an example as well as a definition.

A18   What are accrued charges?

A19   Define a bank overdraft.

A20   What does the current liability item 'taxation' consist of?

A21   What appears on a balance sheet as 'dividend payable'?

A22   How do 'current' liabilities differ from 'long-term' liabilities?

A23   How does 'secured' lending differ from 'unsecured'?

A24   Why have variable-interest-rate loans become popular?

A25   How are foreign currency borrowings treated in sterling balance sheets?

A26   What is convertible loan stock?

A27   What are the two main sources of ordinary shareholders' funds?

A28   Distinguish between authorized and issued share capital.

A29   Why are 'limited' companies so called?

A30   What do ordinary shareholders receive when a company is liquidated?

A31   How can ordinary shareholders get a 'return' from their investment?

A32   What is a share premium?

A33   How does revaluing assets upwards affect the balance sheet?

A34   Define the balance sheet item 'retained profits'.

A35   Can retained profits for a period be negative?

A36   Why are balance sheet 'reserves' unlikely to be represented by cash?

A37   What are 'cumulative' preference shares?

A38 What priority do preference shares take on liquidation?
A39 Distinguish preference shares from ordinary shares.
A40 How do shareholders' funds differ from long-term liabilities?

B   Exercises and case studies

B1   The balance sheet of Millers Emporium at 30 June was as follows:

	(£)
Fixed assets	15,000
Current assets	10,000
	25,000
Share capital	10,000
Retained profits	15,000
	25,000

However, it had been forgotten that tax of £2,000 would have to be paid on the £6,000 profits for the year which had been added to retained profits, and that the shareholders were certain to approve a proposed dividend of £1,000 at the annual general meeting.

a. Make any necessary changes to the balance sheet.

b. Explain in your own words what you have done, and why.

B2   The following is the balance sheet of Acme Motors Ltd at 31 March:

	(£)
Premises	10,000
Stocks	10,000
	20,000
Share capital	15,000
Retained profits	3,500
Creditors	1,500
	20,000

a. During April the company sells half of the cars in stock for £10,000 in cash. It uses this cash to extend its premises.

   (i) How does the resulting balance sheet at 30 April differ from the one above?

(ii) What does this tell you about the nature of a reserve?

b. During May Acme Motors sells its premises for £25,000, and buys more vehicles with the cash received.

(i) How will the balance sheet at 31 May differ from that at 30 April?

(ii) Are the changes different in nature from those in April?

B3 Keram Ltd starts business as a publisher of multi-coloured economic charts in January 1990. The company's transactions during its first six months of operations are summarized below. You are asked to show how the balance sheet will appear at the end of June 1990. *(Hint:* you may find it best to prepare a rough balance sheet summary and alter the numbers month by month, to record the separate transactions.)

a. *January.* 20,000 £1 ordinary shares issued for cash at par.

b. *February.* Cash used to buy equipment for £6,000, stocks of raw materials for £3,000 and leasehold premises for £8,000.

c. *March.* Raw materials costing £4,000 bought on credit.

d. *April.* Materials which had cost £2,000 were sold, after much processing, to customers for £5,000 cash.

e. *May.* Creditors for materials were paid £4,000.

f. *June.* Materials which had cost £4,000 were sold to customers for £9,000 of which £6,000 was on credit.

How would the end of June balance sheet be changed if, in addition to the above, wages of £1,000 in cash were paid monthly?

B4 Place the items number 1 – 20 in the following categories: shareholders' funds, long-term liabilities, current liabilities, fixed assets, current assets, other.

1. Finished goods awaiting despatch
2. Money lent out at 24 hours' call
3. Convertible loan stock
4. Surplus on sale of land
5. Sales director's company car
6. Shares in subsidiary company
7. Land held for future expansion
8. Issued share capital
9. Management expertise
10. Overdraft at the bank
11. Money owed to suppliers
12. Petty cash in hand
13. Unpaid customers' accounts
14. Proposed dividend
15. Retained profits (cumulative)
16. Machinery and equipment
17. Work-in-progress
18. Loss for the year
19. Authorized share capital
20. Accrued charges

B5 From the following information, construct a balance sheet for Village Stores Ltd at 31 May 1990.

Premises £25,000; Overdraft £6,500; Goods in stock £8,900; Retained profits £10,000; Fittings £2,000; Mortgage bond £16,000; Delivery vehicle £1,000; Owed to suppliers £3,500; Owed by customers £1,700; Share capital £2,750; Cash on hand £150.

B6   The following information applies to Good Products Ltd as at 31 December 1990. Calculate the amount of shareholders' funds, and then arrange the information into a balance sheet.

	(£'000)		(£'000)
Long-term lease on factory	160	Shares in suppliers' companies	10
Owed to suppliers	28	Stocks of raw materials	15
Delivery vehicles	16	Dividend proposed	15
Loans from bank	60	Finished goods in stock	11
Owed by customers	41	Government bonds	26
Machinery in factory	110	Expenditure on new patents	5
Taxation owed	40	Debentures issued	80
Cash	2		

B7   Write out brief definitions for the following:
1. Balance sheet
2. Fixed assets
3. Current liabilities
4. Authorized share capital
5. Debtors
6. Current assets
7. Work-in-progress
8. Shareholders' funds
9. Ordinary share capital
10. Prepayments

B8   From the following information as at 31 March 1990, construct a balance sheet for Domestic Appliance Manufacturers Ltd, in vertical form with appropriate headings, sub-totals and totals:
Cash and liquid assets £70,000; Ordinary shares, four million 25p shares, fully paid up; Undistributed profit £20,000; Machinery and equipment £850,000; Trade creditors £180,000; Unfinished appliances £160,000; Patents £50,000; 200,000 50p Preference shares fully paid-up; 10 per cent mortgage bonds of £300,000, secured on property; Shares in subsidiary £100,000; Tax provision £50,000; Bank overdraft £12,000; Debtors £230,000; Freehold property £339,000; General reserves £250,000; Dividends payable £25,000; Raw materials and components £140,000; Accrued expenses £2,000.

B9   The balance sheet of J. Arthur Bloggs Ltd shown in Figure 4.6 contains ten deliberate mistakes. Please identify as many as you can, and in each case say what is wrong.

B10 From the following information (figures are in £ thousands), construct a vertical balance sheet at 30 September 1990 for Duplication Ltd:
Liquid resources 7; Creditors 59; Plant and equipment 41; Issued ordinary share capital 26; Tax 12; Goodwill —?—; Reserves 80; Land and buildings 125; Stocks 46; Long-term liabilities 62; Dividends 4; Debtors 45; Convertible loan 30.
Please insert an amount against Goodwill to balance the accounts.

B11 On 7 August 1990 a burglary took place at the head office of Francis Furniture Ltd. Among the items stolen was the only copy of the draft balance sheet as at 30 June 1990. Since the company's books of account had not appealed to the burglar(s), it would have been possible to

J. Arthur Bloggs Ltd
Balance sheet for the year ended 31 March 1990

(*£'000*)

Fixed assets		
Freehold property, at valuation		420
Plant and equipment:		
Accumulated depreciation	390	
less: Cost	140	
= Net book value		250
Stocks of finished goods		110
		780
Current assets		
Accounts payable	220	
Bank overdraft	70	
Stocks of raw materials	80	
	370	
Current liabilities		
Debtors	130	
Taxation	80	
	210	
= *Working capital*		580
Net assets		1,360
Shareholders' funds		
Issued £1 preference share capital		400
Retained profits		560
		960
Long-term liabilities		
Loans	90	
Revaluation reserve	130	
		220
Other assets		
Goodwill		180
Capital employed		1,360

Figure 4.6 J. Arthur Bloggs Ltd: balance sheet

compile the balance sheet again. But Mr Alec Smart, the assistant chief accountant, had noted on a separate piece of paper a number of balance sheet items and relationships.

See if you can reproduce the company's balance sheet at 30 June 1990, in vertical format, from Mr Smart's notes, which are shown below:

a. Stock = 2 × current liabilities
b. Long-term investments = 3 × cash
c. Issued ordinary share capital = working capital = £40,000
d. Current assets = 3 × current liabilities
e. Total liabilities + shareholders' funds = £102,000
f. Long-term liabilities = 3 × long-term investments
g. Debtors – long-term liabilities = 0
h. Net tangible fixed assets = 1 ˙ × retained profits
i. All items (in £thousands) are even whole numbers.

C   Essay questions

C1 Company chairpeople sometimes say: 'Our workforce is our most important asset.' Why is this 'asset' hardly ever shown on the balance sheet? Should it be?

C2 When a company is liquidated, will the ordinary shareholders receive the balance sheet amount of 'shareholders' funds'? Why or why not?

C3 Explain why balance sheets should always balance.

C4 Why are large business enterprises nearly always organized as limited companies and not as partnerships?

C5 How do 'reserves' arise in accounts, and what use are they?

C6 What are shareholders' funds, and why are they important?

C7 Discuss the reasons for the conventional classification of assets on the balance sheet.

C8 Why might it be risky for a UK company to borrow a loan denominated in a foreign currency?

C9 Why are accounts not precisely 'accurate'? To what extent does it matter?

C10 'Using the historical cost of items on the balance sheet makes more sense when the latter is seen as a statement of sources and uses of funds rather than as a statement of shareholders' funds.' Discuss.

5

The profit and loss account

Plan of the chapter:

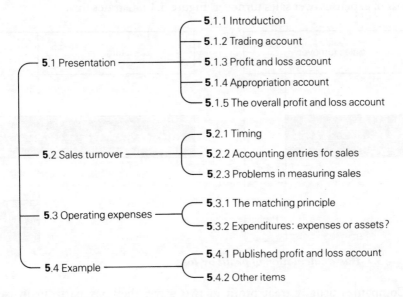

5.1 Presentation
- **5**.1.1 Introduction
- **5**.1.2 Trading account
- **5**.1.3 Profit and loss account
- **5**.1.4 Appropriation account
- **5**.1.5 The overall profit and loss account

5.2 Sales turnover
- **5**.2.1 Timing
- **5**.2.2 Accounting entries for sales
- **5**.2.3 Problems in measuring sales

5.3 Operating expenses
- **5**.3.1 The matching principle
- **5**.3.2 Expenditures: expenses or assets?

5.4 Example
- **5**.4.1 Published profit and loss account
- **5**.4.2 Other items

Fig 5.0
Objective: *To outline the format of the profit and loss account; to show how sales turnover for a period is calculated; and to describe how the 'matching' principle determines whether to treat expenditures as expenses or as assets.*

Synopsis: *The three parts of the profit and loss account are: the trading account, the profit and loss account, and the appropriation account. In practice they are often combined, with many of the trading details left out. Dividends are not an expense, but an 'appropriation' of profit.*

Companies recognize sales revenue, as a rule, when they deliver goods to customers, rather than earlier (when they complete production) or later (when they finally receive cash in respect of credit sales). The timing of sales also determines the timing of profits.

Under the matching principle, expenses incurred are deducted from related sales revenue. Balance sheets carry forward expenditures as assets only if there are expected to be future sales revenues against which to match them later. Otherwise they are written off as expenses in the current period's profit and loss account.

5.1 Presentation

5.1.1 Introduction

Many companies buy and sell goods and services. In a year there are literally millions of transactions. If company managers succeed, they satisfy customers at a profit; if not, their companies may incur losses.

A company's profit and loss account shows how much profit or loss it has made in total in a given period (often a year). A profit is the excess of sales **turnover** over expenses for a period. A loss is simply a negative profit: the excess of expenses over sales turnover. Figure 5.1 illustrates this.

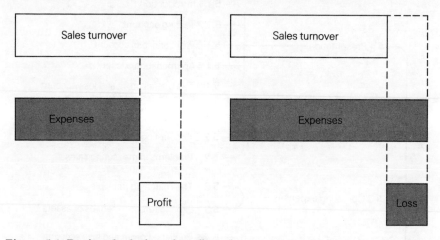

Figure 5.1 Basic calculation of profit or loss

Companies usually treat profit in two ways: they pay part out in cash dividends to shareholders, and keep ('retain') the rest. Retained profit increases the amount of shareholders' funds in the balance sheet. Thus shareholders may benefit from company profits either directly, in cash dividends they receive, or indirectly, in increased net assets owned by the company on their behalf. (Of course, a loss *reduces* the total amount attributed to shareholders' funds in the balance sheet.)

Retained profit for a period thus represents the *link* between the starting and finishing balance sheets, and the profit and loss account for that period. In Chapter 4 we saw how the balance sheet describes and classifies various items: now we look at the profit and loss account. This first section describes the form of presentation; 5.2 discusses problems in determining the amount of sales turnover in a period; 5.3 looks at the operating expenses; and finally 5.4 gives a detailed example.

5.1.2 The trading account

The **trading account** consists of sales revenue less operating expenses (cost of goods sold and distribution and administrative expenses). The final result is the trading (or 'operating') profit for the period.

Management accounts, for use by managers inside the company, would include budgets for future periods, as well as actual past results. They would also contain much more detailed analysis (see 11.3.2). For example, sales turnover, cost of goods sold, and selling and other expenses might be analysed in two kinds of ways: (a) by month; and (b) between divisions, factories, departments, or product groups. There would also be much more detail about expenses; for example, selling expenses would be split between advertising, distribution, salesmen's expenses, administration.

5.1.3 The profit and loss account

The profit and loss account starts with trading profit, includes any non-operating income (see 5.4.2 (a)), deducts interest and taxation, and ends with profit after tax for the period.

Interest expense represents the 'price of time' – the cost of borrowing money for a period. Long-term liabilities and bank overdrafts bear interest charges while other current liabilities usually don't. Accounts show interest expense separately because it relates to a company's method of financing operations (its sources of funds) rather than to the operating results themselves. The profit and loss account may show any interest receivable either as a separate item of **non-operating income** (below operating profit), or else set it off against interest payable. As we shall see in Chapter 9, analysis of company accounts often focuses on 'profit before interest and tax'.

Taxation expense in company accounts refers only to corporation tax, the tax on company profits. All other taxes – such as property taxes or pay roll taxes – come under other expense headings and are not shown separately. The tax rules are complex, and the tax charge is not simply the corporation tax rate applied to the reported profit before tax. Hence company accounts show corporation tax separately, to enable readers to look at either profit before tax or profit after tax, depending on their precise needs.

5.1.4 The appropriation account

The profit and loss **appropriation account** shows the profit after tax for a period, the amount of any dividends paid or proposed, and the amount of profit for the period retained in the company (added to reserves, under the heading 'shareholders' funds').

Ordinary dividends declared out of profits are *not an expense*. They do not affect the amount of profit actually earned during the period: they merely represent one possible way of using those profits.

The retained profit for a period is an important item: (a) in finance, because it is a major source of new funds for a business; and (b) in accounting, because it is the link between the two main financial statements – the profit and loss account and the balance sheet.

The amount of profits retained ('ploughed back') for a period is added on to the cumulative retained profits, as part of shareholders' funds in the balance sheet. Retained 'profits' for a period will be a *negative* either (a) if there is a loss for the period, or (b) if dividends happen to exceed profits after tax. (Either would *reduce* the figure for cumulative profits in the balance sheet.)

5.1.5 The overall profit and loss account

The normal published profit and loss account combines all three separate parts: the trading account, the profit and loss account, and the appropriation account. The published figures may omit details of the trading account. Figure 5.2 shows a typical skeleton layout.

	£	
Sales turnover	xxx	⎫
Cost of goods sold	xxx	
Gross profit	xxx	
Selling and distribution expenses xxx		Trading account
Administrative expenses xxx		
	xxx	⎭
Operating (trading) profit	xxx	⎫
Non-operating income	xxx	
Profit before interest and tax	xxx	
Interest payable	xxx	Profit and loss account
Profit before tax	xxx	
Taxation	xxx	⎭
Profit after tax	xxx	⎫
Ordinary dividends	xxx	Appropriation account
Retained profit for the period	xxx	⎭

Figure 5.2 Layout for the overall profit and loss account

The information in the overall profit and loss account for a period can be shown graphically, as in figure 5.3 opposite.

5.2 Sales turnover

5.2.1 Timing

Figure 4.2 set out the working capital cycle of a manufacturing business. It showed how a firm acquires materials, transforms them into finished goods, sells them to customers (often on credit), and finally gets paid in cash.

Figure 5.4 opposite shows three different points in time at which a company (in its accounts) might *recognize* that a sale has occurred:

1 when it completes the production process;
2 when it delivers the finished goods to customers;
3 when the customers pay cash.

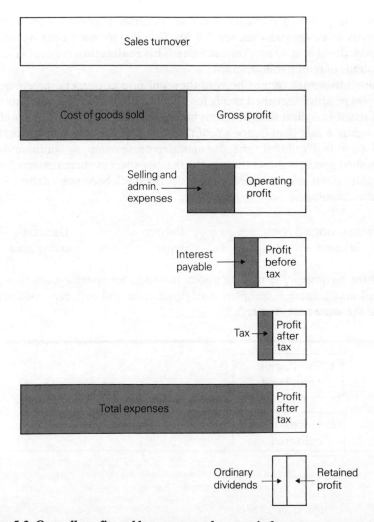

Figure 5.3 Overall profit and loss account for a period

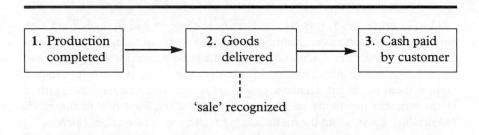

Figure 5.4 Recognition of sale in a credit transaction

Accounts generally recognize a sale as occurring at point **2** – on delivery of the goods to customers (but see 7.3.3). This is important because accounts recognize profit at the same time as sales. This **realization** concept is justified on grounds of reasonable *certainty*.

Many businesses cannot be sure they will find customers merely because they have produced finished goods for sale. Hence prudent accountants would be reluctant to 'count their chickens before they are hatched'. They prefer *not* to recognize a sale (and hence a profit) until a definite customer has agreed to buy the goods. Until that time, the manufacturing company continues to own the finished goods; it shows them in the balance sheet as current assets (stocks), and values them *at cost*. After a credit sale, the stock becomes a debtor – *and is valued at selling price.*

FINISHED GOODS STOCK	+	PROFIT	=	DEBTOR
at cost	+	*profit*	=	*selling price*

Where a company is making goods to order, for specific customers, then stages **1** and **2** above – completion of production and delivery – will occur at almost the same time (figure 5.5).

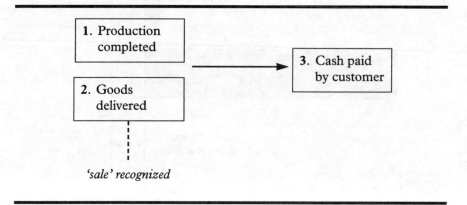

Figure 5.5 Recognition of credit sale for made-to-order goods

On the other hand, waiting until credit customers had actually paid cash would be *too* conservative. Customers who fail to pay can be legally sued for the amount of the sale price. Unless there is some good reason for non-payment in full (such as faulty manufacture, dispute over the price, etc.), the courts will compel them to pay up. Hence accountants recognize that a sale has occurred at the moment (normally on physical delivery) when legal title to the goods (ownership) passes from the manufacturer (seller) to the customer (buyer).

Where sales are for cash, rather than on credit, then on credit, then points **2** and **3** above – delivery of the goods and payment of cash – will occur at the same time (figure 5.6).

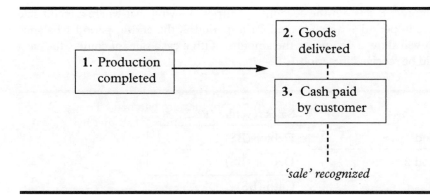

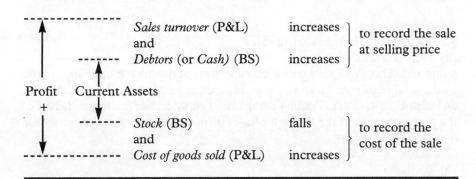

Figure 5.6 Recognition of cash sale

5.2.2 Accounting entries for sales

When a sale is recognized, two sets of changes occur in the profit and loss account (P&L) and balance sheet (BS): (a) profit is increased (and thus shareholders' funds, via retained profit); and (b) current assets are increased by the amount of the profit (figure 5.7).

Figure 5.7 Changes when accounts recognize a sale

The profit and loss account includes the sales revenue less the **cost of goods sold** (COGS), which increases profit (hence, ultimately, shareholders' funds in the balance sheet). Debtors (or cash) in the balance sheet increase by the amount of the sale, while stock is reduced by the cost of the goods sold. Hence current assets also increase by the amount of the profit.

The final result of a credit sale is the same as for a cash sale: *the amount of the sale is received in cash.* But with a credit sale, this result happens in two stages: (1) when the sale is recognized, the customer becomes a debtor for the amount; and (2) when he pays cash (which then replaces the debtor as a current asset).

Figure 5.8 sets out the accounting entries showing that where a credit sale occurs in period 1 which is paid for in period 2, the end-of-period 1 balance sheet will show a debtor for the amount. With a cash sale, of course, the cash would be received in period 1.

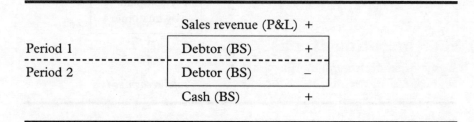

Figure 5.8 Accounting entries for a credit sale

Thus we see the three stages of figure 5.4 reflected for a credit sale in the three different kinds of current asset, at each stage becoming more 'liquid':

EVENT	Production completed	Delivery of goods	Receipt of cash
CURRENT ASSET	*stock*	*debtor*	*cash*

5.2.3 Problems in measuring sales

(a) Value added tax

Value added tax (VAT) is a tax on the supply of goods which is ultimately borne by the final customer. However, it is collected at each stage of the production and distribution chain. Trading companies simply collect the tax on behalf of the government; and the figure for 'sales turnover' in their accounts does *not* include VAT.

(b) Bad debts

Sometimes credit customers fail to pay the full amount owed for goods they have bought. The profit and loss account treats any such **bad debt** as a separate expense item, leaving the original 'sales turnover' figure as it stands. (When the selling company 'writes off' the bad debt, it also reduces debtors in the balance sheet.)

(c) Goods returned

Where a customer physically returns goods (and the selling company agrees to take them back), or where an agreed allowance is made against the original price (for example, because the goods are of poor quality), a deduction is made from 'sales turnover'. (Again, the amount the debtor owes is reduced too.)

(d) Errors on invoice

The account for goods or services, called an **invoice,** is the legal document which tells customers what the goods cost. If a sale were wrongly charged on an invoice as £315 instead of £135, the seller would issue a **credit note** for £180 to reduce the original sales turnover figure of £315 to £135.

5.3 Operating expenses

5.3.1 The matching principle

The **matching principle** deducts from sales turnover for a period those expenses incurred in earning it. This enables accounts to determine profit or loss for a period.

> *Example: Mary Mullins received £15 on her birthday, which she planned to use in a part-time business venture. She bought pictures at £3 each from her big brother, who painted them as a hobby, and planned to sell them to her friends for £5 each. During the first week she bought five pictures and sold two: but was disappointed when she calculated her trading result:*

SOLD	*2 at £5*	=	*£10*
BOUGHT	*5 at £3*	=	*£15*
	Loss for week		*£ 5*

> *Her father, an accountant in the City, explained her mistake. Since she sold only two pictures in the first week, she should deduct only the cost of those pictures (as cost of goods sold) from the week's sales revenue. The three remaining pictures she should simply record as stock in hand at the end of the week (valued at cost). Thus the week's trading actually produced a profit of £4 (£10 − £6).*
>
> *Figure 5.9 (overleaf) shows Mary's transactions for the first four weeks, including the first week's profit, and the cost of the stock held at the end of that week. The connecting lines show the week in which she sold each picture bought.*

5.3.2 Expenditure: expenses or assets?

The accrual principle means that accounts record items when they are legally incurred, rather than when cash is paid. This applies to **expenditures** as well as to sales turnover. Expenditures for which no cash has yet been paid appear in the balance sheet as current liabilities (creditors), just as sales for which no cash has yet been received appear in the balance sheet as current assets (debtors).

A more interesting question is whether to treat expenditures (a) as **(revenue) expenses** in the current period's profit and loss account, or (b) as **(capital)** assets on the balance sheet, usually valued at cost.

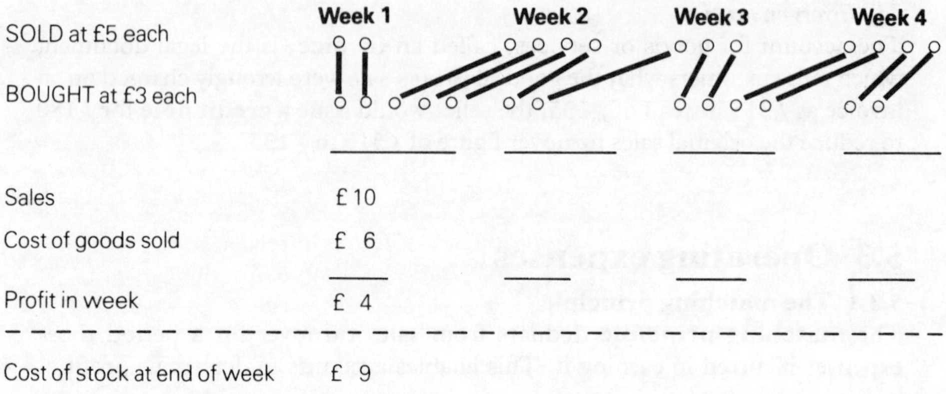

Figure 5.9   Mary Mullins, trading transactions and profit

A manufacturer of motor vehicles will deduct from sales turnover the costs of producing the cars sold. Steel, glass, and all the other materials and components, together with the wages of factory workers, can be directly identified with specific products; they are **product costs**. These also include production overheads, such as factory supervision, rent, lighting and heating, and depreciation of factory equipment.

But the company must incur other costs too, such as advertising, distribution, and office workers' salaries. These selling and other expenses are general overhead expenses of running the business which cannot easily be identified with particular products. They may be regarded as being incurred at a definite rate per period, rather than varying with the number of units produced; hence they are often called **period costs.**

Many expenditures are also expenses in the same period, either because they are product costs relating to goods sold in that period, or because they are period costs relating to that period. But two kinds of expenditures are not treated as expenses in the same period. Product costs relating to products which have not yet been sold at the end of a period are 'carried forward' as stocks on the balance sheet (like Mary Mullins's pictures). Also carried forward as assets are period costs *relating to future periods*. These may simply represent 'prepaid expenses' (such as insurance premiums paid in advance). Or they may be 'fixed assets' (such as equipment) to be used (and depreciated) by the business over several years in the future (see Chapter 6).

It should be stressed that not all expenditures *can* be 'matched' against sales turnover. This may be because they are period costs rather than product costs. Or they may, in effect, simply be losses: for example, the cost of advertising a product that nobody buys. Companies carry forward expenditures as assets only if they expect sufficient future revenues against which to match them. Expenditures which cannot be fully matched against future revenues, or product costs relating to the current period's sales turnover, are **written off** as expenses in the current period's profit and loss account.

Figure 5.10 summarizes the treatment of expenditures.

	Product costs	Period costs
Expense (P&L)	In period when product sold	If related to *current* period
Asset (BS)	If product unsold by end of period	If related to *future* period

Figure 5.10 Product costs and period costs

5.4 Example

5.4.1 Published profit and loss account
Figure 5.11 overleaf shows an example of a published profit and loss account for Pilkington plc. To keep it simple, the comparative figures for 1988 have been omitted.

5.4.2 Other items
(a) Non-operating income
Many companies hold financial fixed assets (see 4.2.1 (c)), which may give rise to income from associated (related) companies or from other investments.

(b) Minority interest
Where a company controls subsidiary companies, it must own at least 50 per cent of the ordinary shares, but it may own less than 100 per cent. Suppose a company C owns 80 per cent of the ordinary shares in its subsidiary company S. In theory C might include in its own **group** (or **consolidated**) **accounts** only 80 per cent of S's profit for the period. In practice, however, C includes all S's profits in its operating profit (and deducts all S's taxation expense in its group tax charge). A *separate* deduction from C's reported group profit after tax is then made for **minority interests** – representing a deduction of the 20 per cent of S's profit after tax which does not 'belong' to the shareholders in C.

(c) Unusual items
The profit and loss account may need to disclose separately two kinds of unusual items.

1 **Exceptional items** are unusual only on account of their size. Examples may be very large bad debts, or stock write-offs. They are deducted in arriving at operating profit; and disclosed separately.

**Pilkington plc   Group profit and loss account for the year ended
31 March 1989**

	(£ m.)	
Turnover	2,572.6	
Operating profit	349.2	(a)
Investment income and related companies	44.8	
Interest paid less received	(68.8)	
Group profit before taxation	325.2	
Taxation	98.6	
Profit on ordinary activities after taxation	226.6	
Profit attributable to minority shareholders	25.7	
Earning attributable to shareholders of Pilkington plc	200.9	
Extraordinary items	(24.4)	(b)
Profit of the group attributable to shareholders of Pilkington plc	176.5	
Dividends	70.2	
Retained profit	106.3	
Earnings per ordinary share	27.3p	(c)

Notes
(a) After charging: Cost of sales — 1,936.5; Distribution costs — 111.0; Administration expenses — 197.0
(b) Restructuring and cessation of operations
(c) £200.9 m ÷ 737.2 m. average number of ordinary shares in issue

---

*Figure 5.11 Pilkington plc: group profit and loss account for the year ended
31 March 1989*

2 **Extraordinary items** arise from events or transactions outside the ordinary
activities of the business and are not expected to recur regularly or
frequently. The published profit and loss account discloses them separately,
net of related tax, but **below the line** – that is, after the line showing profit
after tax on ordinary activities for the year (but still before deducting
dividends). Hence extraordinary items are not included in the calculation of
earnings per share (see 9.3.3).

(d) Disclosure required

Certain items of expense must be disclosed separately, in the notes to the accounts if not elsewhere. (They often appear in the report of the directors.) These items include the following:

1 Audit fee
2 Depreciation of fixed assets
3 Directors' remuneration
4 Charitable and political donations
5 The number of persons employed, and their aggregate remuneration.

Work section

A   Revision questions

A1   What does the profit and loss account try to show?

A2   Define 'loss' for a period.

A3   In what two ways may profit for a period be used?

A4   In what two ways may shareholders benefit from company profits?

A5   What is the link between the profit and loss account and the balance sheet?

A6   Into what three parts can the overall profit and loss account be split?

A7   What does the trading account show?

A8   What three main items does cost of goods sold consist of?

A9   What does the profit and loss account contain?

A10 Which liabilities do not normally bear interest? Which do?

A11 What is 'taxation expense' in accounts?

A12 Are ordinary dividends an expense? Why or why not?

A13 Name two possible reasons for retained profits for a period being negative.

A14 How do negative retained profits for a period affect shareholders' funds?

A15 Define 'minority interests'. How are they treated in the profit and loss account?

A16 Distinguish between the definition and accounting treatment of 'exceptional' and 'extraordinary' items.

A17 What does 'below the line' mean?

A18 Which three different events *might* cause recognition of a 'sale'?

A19 Which event actually causes recognition of a sale in accounting?

A20 Of the three events in A18 above, which two coincide when goods are:
(a) made to order, (b) sold for cash?

A21 When does the legal title to goods normally pass to the buyer?

A22 When is 'cost of goods sold' charged as an expense?

A23 What is the difference between a cash sale and a credit sale:
(a) in the profit and loss account, (b) in the balance sheet?

A24 How much do shareholders' funds change when a sale is recognized?

A25 How much do current assets change when a sale is recognized? Explain.

A26 What is a 'bad debt'? How does the profit and loss account treat it?

A27 Why might the original sales figure need amendment?

A28 What is the matching principle?

A29 What is the accrual principle?

A30 Distinguish between revenue expenditure and capital expenditure.

A31 Distinguish between product costs and period costs.

A32 Under what circumstances are product costs treated:
(a) as an asset, (b) as an expense?

A33 Under what circumstances are period costs treated:
(a) as an asset, (b) as an expense?

A34 Name two reasons why some expenditures may not be able to be matched against sales revenue.

A35 What is the criterion for carrying forward expenditure as an asset on the balance sheet?

B Exercises and case studies

B1 Is sales revenue recorded when:
   a. A debtor pays for an earlier purchase?
   b. A merchant signs a legal contract for goods?
   c. A nearby client takes delivery of an order placed last year?
   d. The factory completes all the goods for an order?

B2 Write out the double entries for each of the following.
   a. Purchase of goods for £500 in cash.
   b. Sale for £600 in cash of goods costing £400.
   c. Purchase of goods for £500 on credit, and the payment one month later to the supplier.
   d. Sale on credit for £600 of goods costing £400, and the receipt of cash two months later from the customer.

B3 Is a purchase recorded when:
   a. A company places a written order for goods?
   b. A deposit is paid on goods for later delivery?
   c. A supplier is paid by cheque for goods received last year?
   d. Goods ordered last year arrive at the company's premises?

B4 Refer to Mary Mullins and her trading activities.
   a. Complete the table in figure 5.9 for weeks 2, 3, and 4.
   b. Draw up Mary's balance sheet at the end of week 4.

B5 The balance sheet of Vogue Fashions Ltd at the end of 1990 is summarized below:

	(£)
Assets	15,000
Shareholders' funds	5,000
Liabilities	10,000
	15,000

The transactions for 1991 are summarized below:

	(£)
Trading expenses	46,000
Interest paid	1,000
Sales	52,000
Ordinary dividends paid	1,000
Tax	2,000

a. Draw up a profit and loss account for 1991, and a summarized balance sheet (similar to that shown above) at the end of 1991. Liabilities at the end of 1991 total £11,000.

b. Describe and explain the changes in the end-1991 balance sheet as compared with the end-1990 balance sheet.

B6   From the following list of items for Wilfred Kelly Limited in respect of the year ending 30 September 1990, prepare a summarized profit and loss account in a form suitable for publication.

	(£'000)
Ordinary dividend – interim paid	4
Ordinary dividend – final proposed	7
Operating profit	47
Retained profit for the year	?
Tax	18
Sales revenue	346
Interest expense	11

B7   In January, Brown makes an inquiry.
In February, Smith quotes a price.
In March, Brown places an order.
In April, Smith buys the materials.
In May, Smith completes production.
In June, Smith delivers the order.
In July, Brown queries the quality.
In August, Smith agrees to a small price reduction on the order.
In September, Smith reminds Brown of what is owed.
In October, Brown pays half the amount due.
In November, Smith demands the balance.
In December, Brown pays balance due to Smith.
When does Smith recognize the profit on the above transaction?
(*Hint:* You may find it difficult to answer in a single word.)

B8   Potter Trading's balance sheet at the end of March contains only the items: cash £1,000 and issued share capital £1,000. The company purchases goods for £1,000 and sells them for £1,300. Calculate the profit or loss and construct the new balance sheet at the end of April:

a. if all transactions were for cash
b. if all transactions were on credit

    c. if sales were for cash and purchases on credit

    d. if purchases were for cash and sales on credit.

B9 A friend of yours buys a small country pub. After three months of business he asks you to help him calculate his profits on beer sales. He has had 500 gallons delivered each month. When he took over the pub (on New Year's Eve) there were 50 gallons in the cellar, and at the end of March there were still 50 gallons there. Beer costs £4.00 per gallon. His monthly output was: January 400 gallons, February 500 gallons, March 600 gallons; but 5 per cent of beer is lost in spillage, etc. The beer is sold for 80 pence per pint.

    a. Calculate the total profit on beer sales per month.

    b. Calculate the profit per pint sold.

B10 Refer to figure 5.9. At the end of week 4, Mary Mullins had no pictures left. At this point she decided it would be more profitable to pay her brother a 'wage' of £1 for each picture he painted, and for her to buy the materials for him to use, rather than buying completed pictures from him. Her brother agreed to this new arrangement. Mary estimated that her other direct production costs (such as paints, paper, etc.) would be 40p per picture, and the frames £1.20 for each picture.

    In week 5, Mary purchased frames for six pictures. Her brother completed four pictures, and was paid £4 wages. The other direct production costs were in line with Mary's estimate. Mary sold three of the pictures in week 5 for £5 each.

    a. Construct a profit and loss account for week 5 (Mary's first week of 'manufacturing').

    b. Construct a balance sheet as at the end of week 5, assuming that Mary only makes deals for cash.

B11 What, if anything, should be shown on the balance sheet at 30 June 1990, and where should it be shown, in respect of each of the following items:

    a. Telephone account for quarter ended 31 May (unpaid at the end of June).

Rental (3 months in advance)	£60
Calls for 3 months to 31 May	£75
	£135

    b. Electricity account £96 for quarter ended 30 April (paid in June).

    c. Audit fee £850 in respect of year ended 30 June 1990 (not started until August 1990; invoice sent November 1990; paid December 1990).

    d. Motor insurance premiums £240, for year ended 30 September 1990, paid October 1989.

B12 Calco, which makes electronic calculators and sells them for £15.00 each, has direct production costs as follows:

Raw materials	£33.00 per dozen units
Bought-in components	£ 5.30 per unit

Direct wages   £ 2.65 per unit
Production overheads   £ 0.70 per unit

Calco's weekly performance in terms of sales and output, and its expenditure on materials and components, was as follows:

Week	1	2	3	4	5
Units sold	10,000	10,000	11,000	11,000	12,000
Units produced	12,000	12,000	8,000	12,000	15,000
Materials purchased (£)	41,250	27,500	41,250	27,500	27,500
Components purchased (£)	63,600	63,600	42,400	63,600	79,500

Calculate the gross trading profit each week.

B13 Acme Joiners Ltd produces a popular line of kitchen units. It buys several components and makes the rest of the parts itself from raw materials. Machinists perform the production operations, and assemblers put together their output plus the appropriate components bought ready-made. The units are then spray-painted and packed in cartons.

The following information is presented to the accountant by her assistant early in January 1991

                                                                             (£'000)

Stock on hand on 1.1.90:
   Materials   30
   Components   48
   Finished goods   180
Stock on hand on 31.12.90
   Materials   36
   Components   57
   Finished goods   90
Wages paid to factory personnel:
   Machinists   30
   Assemblers   15
   Painters   12
   Packers   3
Materials received   306
Components received   489
Payments made to suppliers   759
Production overheads paid   60
Sales on credit   1,050
Sales for cash   600
Received from debtors   630
Administrative overheads paid   90
Selling overheads paid   45

During 1990 the company paid a dividend of £75,000; and used most of the rest of the profits to buy new plant for a proposed expansion. Taxation is payable at 40 per cent on profits.
Construct a profit and loss account for internal use.

B14 Refer to B13

Amend the profit and loss account to take account of the following:

a. In December 1990 an advance payment of £9,000 for a market research survey to take place in January 1991 was made. This amount was included in the selling overheads for 1990.

b. On 20 January 1991 an invoice was received for £15,000 for renovations to the buildings carried out in the previous autumn. The renovators had forgotten to invoice Acme, and nobody there had noticed the omission.

c. Debtors owing a total of £17,000 are now thought unlikely to pay in full; and a provision of £11,000 is to be made for bad debts.

d. It has been decided to recommend a final ordinary dividend of £35,000 in respect of 1990, in addition to the £75,000 interim dividend already paid.

e. It is now expected that the tax rate applying to 1990 profits will be 35 per cent, not 40 per cent.

C Essay questions

C1 Should profit be recognized in accounts when extra value is created? At what stage *is* value added by a manufacturing company?

C2 'A profit and loss account merely analyses the total expenses to be deducted from sales revenue.' Comment.

C3 Discuss the view that 'matching' is essentially a *balance sheet* concept. Why may the matching principle conflict with prudence for intangible assets?

C4 'The difference between cash accounting and accrual accounting is the difference between expenditure and expense.' Discuss.

C5 Should bad debts be deducted directly from sales revenue, instead of only indirectly, as a separate item of 'expense'?

C6 Can there be any justification for treating period costs as an asset?

C7 'The profit and loss account for a period merely explains the change in one balance sheet item between dates.' Discuss.

C8 Should extraordinary items be excluded altogether from the profit and loss account? How else could they be treated?

C9 Should increases arising on revaluation of assets be regarded as profits?

C10 Why does it matter when a sale is recognized in accounts?

6

Depreciation of fixed assets

Plan of the chapter:

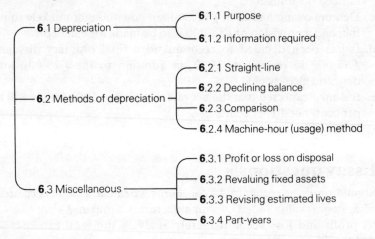

6.1 Depreciation
- **6**.1.1 Purpose
- **6**.1.2 Information required

6.2 Methods of depreciation
- **6**.2.1 Straight-line
- **6**.2.2 Declining balance
- **6**.2.3 Comparison
- **6**.2.4 Machine-hour (usage) method

6.3 Miscellaneous
- **6**.3.1 Profit or loss on disposal
- **6**.3.2 Revaluing fixed assets
- **6**.3.3 Revising estimated lives
- **6**.3.4 Part-years

Fig 6.0
Objective: *To explain the purpose of depreciation of fixed assets, to outline the information needed to determine it, and to describe the main methods.*

Synopsis: *Depreciation aims to spread a fixed asset's cost over the periods which benefit from its use. It is thus an extreme example of the 'matching principle'. A fixed asset's life may be limited by the passing of time, physical wear and tear, or technical or market obsolescence. The information needed to determine depreciation is: (1) the fixed asset's original cost; (2) its expected economic life; (3) its expected residual value (if any); and (4) the chosen method of depreciation. The many estimates required make the amount of depreciation expense somewhat subjective.*

The two main depreciation methods are: straight-line, charging an equal amount each year, which is easily the most common in the UK; and declining balance, charging a constant percentage of declining net book value.

6.1 Depreciation

6.1.1 Purpose

Fixed assets are resources lasting for several years and intended to produce goods or services, not for resale. **Depreciation** expense is charged in accounts in order to spread a fixed asset's cost over its life in the periods which benefit from its use. Depreciation of fixed assets (usually called amortization for intangible assets) is thus an extreme example of the 'matching' process in accounting.

If a business simply charged the whole cost of a new machine as an expense in the year it was bought, the accounts would understate profit in that year. The whole cost of a machine lasting several years would have been deducted from the first year's sales turnover. But in later years the accounts would *overstate* profit, with no deduction from sales turnover for the use of the machine.

On the other hand, if the business charged no depreciation expense during a machine's life, profit would have been overstated and a large loss would arise when it was finally scrapped. This treatment would be suitable only for those fixed assets – like land – which may not lose value over time.

Accounts normally show fixed assets at their original cost less the accumulated depreciation expense charged to date. Accounts charge a period's depreciation as an expense in the profit and loss account, and add it to the accumulated depreciation on the balance sheet. Thus the effect is to reduce shareholders' funds (via retained profits), and to reduce the net book value of fixed assets.

Figure 6.1 shows balance sheet **net book values** (NBV) for a fixed asset with a three-year life, costing £12,000 at the beginning of 1990. Depreciation expense is £4,000 in each of the three years.

	End 1990 (£)	End 1991 (£)	End 1992 (£)
Original cost	12,000	12,000	12,000
Less: accumulated depreciation	4,000	8,000	12,000
Net book value	8,000	4,000	0

Figure 6.1 Balance sheet amounts for fixed asset

6.1.2 Information required

To calculate depreciation we need four separate items of information:
a. the fixed asset's original cost (or later valuation);
b. its expected remaining economic life;
c. its expected residual (or scrap) value;
d. the *method* of depreciation to use.

The first three are discussed below, and the method of depreciation is covered in 6.2.

(a) Original cost

The original cost of a fixed asset may simply be the amount invoiced by a supplier. But other amounts may increase the 'cost', such as legal charges incurred in acquiring leasehold property, or costs of installing equipment, or perhaps the interest costs incurred while a large-scale fixed asset is being constructed. The cost of an improvement to an asset should be capitalized (added to the fixed asset's 'cost'); it may lengthen an asset's life, increase its physical capacity, or better the quality of its output. But major repairs to a fixed asset which merely restore the asset to its former condition should be treated as an expense.

(b)   Economic life

The useful life of an asset may be limited by whichever is shortest of:

1   the passing of time – for example, a lease for a definite number of years, or a patent which has a maximum legal life of only 20 years;
2   physical wear and tear – for example, a machine which gradually wears out;
3   technical obsolescence – for example, rapid electronic calculators have largely superseded much slower old-fashioned adding machines (even if they still work as well as ever);
4   market obsolescence – for example, clothes whose style may go out of fashion, even without any new technology.

Engineers with experience of similar assets can often estimate physical wear and tear fairly closely; and they can sometimes estimate technical obsolescence, though only roughly. Market obsolescence may be harder to guess as it depends on the subjective preferences of customers.

Accountants tend to be conservative: if in doubt they prefer to use a shorter asset life rather than a longer one. As a rule accountants try to avoid a firm having to sell or scrap an asset for much less than its net book value. (They mind less if they underestimate an asset's life, so that it continues in use long after its net book value has been written down to zero.)

(c)   Residual value

The difference between a fixed asset's original cost and its expected resale or scrap value has to be charged as depreciation expense during its economic life. For example, a car hire firm may keep its vehicles for only three years before replacing them. If each car costs £10,000 and can be sold after three years for £4,000, then the firm writes off only £6,000 in total (£2,000 a year) as depreciation. In practice a fixed asset's **residual value** may be so small, or so uncertain, that it is ignored in estimating depreciation in advance.

6.2   Methods of depreciation

6.2.1   Straight-line

The **straight-line** method of depreciation is the simplest and the most common. It writes off an *equal* expense each year, based on the asset's net cost (original cost less residual value) and estimated life. Thus if a machine costs

£10,000, and is reckoned to have a useful life of five years, with a residual value of £2,000, the depreciation expense each year would be £1,600:

$$\frac{£10,000 - £2,000}{5} \quad = \quad \frac{£8,000}{5} \quad = \quad £1,600$$

Figure 6.2 shows what would appear in the accounts each year

	Profit and loss account	End-of-year balance sheet				
	Depreciation expense	Original cost	−	Accumulated depreciation	=	Net book value
	(£)	(£)		(£)		(£)
Year 1	1,600	10,000	−	1,600	=	8,400
Year 2	1,600	10,000	−	3,200	=	6,800
Year 3	1,600	10,000	−	4,800	=	5,200
Year 4	1,600	10,000	−	6,400	=	3,600
Year 5	1,600	10,000	−	8,000	=	2,000

Figure 6.2 Fixed asset entries in accounts: straight-line depreciation

Figure 6.3 shows the same information graphically.

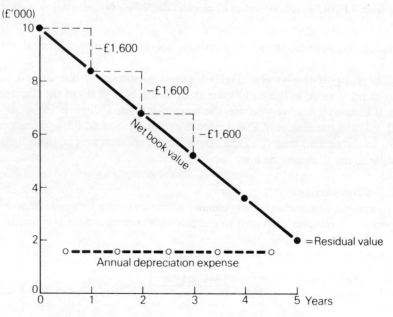

Figure 6.3 Straight-line depreciation

6.2.2 Declining balance

The **declining balance** method of 'accelerated' depreciation charges larger amounts to expense in the early years of an asset's life than in the later years. It applies to the asset's declining net book value each year a constant percentage to reduce the cost (roughly) to the expected residual value at the end of its life.

For the machine costing £10,000, lasting five years, and with an expected residual value of £2,000, the required constant declining balance percentage rate would be about $27\frac{1}{2}$ per cent a year.* Figure 6.4 shows what would appear in the accounts each year.

	Profit and loss account Depreciation expense	End-of-year balance sheet			
		Original cost	−	Accumulated depreciation	= Net book value
	(£)	(£)		(£)	(£)
Year 1	2,750	10,000	−	2,750	= 7,250
Year 2	1,994	10,000	−	4,744	= 5,256
Year 3	1,446	10,000	−	6,190	= 3,810
Year 4	1,048	10,000	−	7,238	= 2,762
Year 5	760	10,000	−	7,998	= 2,002

Figure 6.4 Fixed asset entries in accounts: declining balance depreciation

Figure 6.5 (opposite) shows the declining balance information graphically.

The **sum-of-the-years' digits** method (common in the United States) also charges more in the early years than in the later years of the fixed asset's life. If an asset has a five-year life, the sum-of-the-years' digits is 15 (= 5 + 4 + 3 + 2 + 1). In the first year, the depreciation charge would be $\frac{5}{15}$ of the original cost, in the second year $\frac{4}{15}$ of the original cost, and so on. The overall effect is similar to the declining balance method.

6.2.3 Comparison

Both straight-line and declining balance methods aim to charge as depreciation expense a fixed asset's net cost to the business over its expected economic life.

* Solving the equation below gives the exact percentage:

$$\text{Annual rate of depreciation} = \left\{ 1 - n\sqrt{\frac{\text{Residual value}}{\text{cost}}} \right\} \times 100 \text{ per cent}$$

where n = the number of years of useful life.

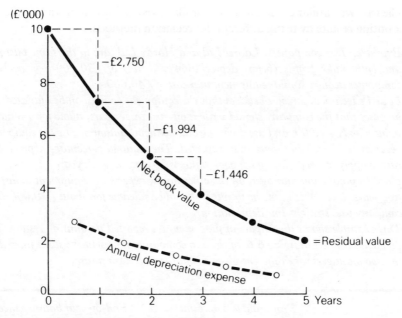

Figure 6.5 Declining balance depreciation

But the pattern of expense and net book value varies year by year. Most British companies use the straight-line method; while many American companies use declining balance. The choice between them is partly a matter of custom.

Two arguments are sometimes suggested in favour of the declining balance method. For many assets, maintenance and repair costs tend to grow as the asset becomes older. Hence using declining balance depreciation tends to result in a more equal total expense each year for fixed-asset-related expenses (maintenance plus depreciation).

A second argument is that many assets tend to lose second-hand market value faster in the early years. Thus declining balance net book values more closely reflect the pattern of decline in the market value of the assets. (But depreciation is a process of allocating a fixed asset's net cost over its economic life, on the assumption that it will be held until the end: there is no pretence that balance sheets normally show market values.)

The declining balance method needs a higher percentage rate than the straight-line method to write an asset off. This is because the declining balance percentage ($27\frac{1}{2}$ per cent for the machine) applies to the declining net book value each year, whereas the straight-line percentage (16 per cent) applies to the original cost. (For the same reason, the declining balance method will never quite reduce an asset's net book value to zero. But when the net book value becomes very small in relation to original cost, it can be written off entirely in a single year.)

85

Clearly two similar companies with similar fixed assets can produce different accounting results by using different depreciation methods.

Example: Two companies, Laurel Ltd and Hardy Ltd, are in the same business, and both make profits (before depreciation and tax) of £30,000 a year. Both companies acquire similar equipment at a cost of £40,000.

Laurel's technical director believes that the equipment could soon be outdated. He proposes that the company should write it off over three years, allow for a residual value of only £5,000, and use declining balance depreciation in case the equipment becomes obsolete even sooner than expected. The required percentage depreciation rate to apply to the declining net book value is 50 per cent each year.

Hardy's production manager, on the other hand, expects his equipment to last for five years, after which time he thinks it should be saleable for about £10,000. The company uses straight-line depreciation.

This example shows the impact of judgement on reported accounting results. The different numbers in figure 6.6 for the two companies represent the same facts. But the two managers take different views about the uncertain future.

		Profit and loss account		End-of-year balance sheet	
		Depreciation expense	Net profit	Accumulated depreciation	Net book value
		(£'000)	(£'000)	(£'000)	(£'000)
LAUREL	Year 1	20	10	20	20
	Year 2	10	20	30	10
	Year 3	5	25	35	5
	Year 4	$2\frac{1}{2}$	$27\frac{1}{2}$	$37\frac{1}{2}$	$2\frac{1}{2}$
	Year 5	$1\frac{1}{4}$	$28\frac{3}{4}$	$38\frac{3}{4}$	$1\frac{1}{4}$
HARDY	Year 1	6	24	6	34
	Year 2	6	24	12	28
	Year 3	6	24	18	22
	Year 4	6	24	24	16
	Year 5	6	24	30	10

Figure 6.6 Comparison of two depreciation methods

6.2.4 Machine hour (usage) method

If physical wear and tear is the main cause limiting an asset's life, it may make sense to relate depreciation expense to the amount of *use* in any period. Suppose that a machine which costs £22,000, and will have a residual value of about £2,000, is expected to produce 50,000 units over its life before it wears out. Then, under the **usage method**, the depreciation expense is 40p per unit produced (= £20,000/50,000 units). In the first year 14,000 units are produced, so the depreciation expense is £5,600; in the second year 8,000 units, so depreciation in that year is only £3,200; and so on. The same approach may apply to other assets, such as motor vehicles (on a mileage basis). Notice that the usage method, in effect, treats depreciation as a variable expense (see 10.2.1).

6.3 Miscellaneous

6.3.1 Profit or loss on disposal
When fixed assets are finally sold, the proceeds will differ from the balance sheet net book value unless both the economic life and the residual value have been guessed precisely right. Any profit or loss on disposal in effect represents an *adjustment* of prior years' depreciation charges, and is usually subtracted from (or added to) the current year's depreciation charge. But large profits or losses on disposal may be disclosed separately, as 'exceptional items' (see 5.4.2 (c)).

6.3.2 Revaluing fixed assets
Apart from accounting for inflation (see Chapter 8), some UK companies revalue fixed assets above original cost even in 'historical cost' accounts. For instance, many companies revalue all their freehold and leasehold property about every five years. If the valuation exceeds the previous net book value, the excess is added to revaluation reserve (see 4.4.2 (b)). *It is not regarded as a profit.* Companies rarely revalue other fixed assets, such as plant, perhaps because future depreciation would then be based on the new higher valuation. The effect would be to reduce reported profits. Comparing the results of different companies is difficult if some have revalued their fixed assets while others continue to use historical cost.

6.3.3 Revising estimated lives
When companies revise their estimates of fixed asset lives, they write down the existing net book value to residual value over the revised remaining life. Where the original estimated life was too long, there would otherwise be a loss on disposal. Where, however, the estimated life was too short, a company may continue to carry on its books fixed assets which are fully written off. (Accumulated depreciation equals original cost, and the net book value is zero.) Cost and accumulated depreciation for a specific fixed asset are removed from the books only when it is disposed of or retired from active use.

6.3.4 Part-years
Companies buy and sell fixed assets all through the year. Some companies charge a full year's depreciation in the year of purchase, and none in the year of

sale; while others do the opposite. Probably the best practice is to charge depreciation pro rata. Thus for a fixed asset bought after four months of the accounting year, $\frac{4}{12}$ of a full year's depreciation is charged in the first year. Whichever practice is used should be followed consistently.

Work section

A   Revision questions

A1   Define a fixed asset.

A2   What is the purpose of depreciation?

A3   What is the difference between depreciation and amortization?

A4   How are fixed assets normally valued in balance sheets?

A5   Distinguish between depreciation expense and accumulated depreciation.

A6   What four items of information are needed to estimate depreciation?

A7   Give two reasons why depreciation is usually only an estimate.

A8   When might 'repairs' be added to the cost of fixed assets in the balance sheet?

A9   Name three possible reasons why an asset's useful life may be limited.

A10 Why is residual value relevant in estimating depreciation?

A11 Distinguish between the two main methods of depreciation.

A12 When may the usage method of depreciation be especially suitable?

A13 How can a profit or loss arise on disposal of a fixed asset?

A14 How does the profit and loss account normally treat a profit or loss on disposal of a fixed asset?

A15 Explain in two different ways how much is charged in total as an expense in respect of a fixed asset over its whole life.

A16 How can revaluing fixed assets affect future depreciation charges?

A17 Name two possible ways to calculate first-year depreciation expense when a company buys a fixed asset in the middle of the year.

A18 What cash flows are directly associated with a fixed asset? When do they occur?

A19 Explain why increasing depreciation expense does not affect cash flow.

A20 Explain why increasing depreciation expense does not affect tax.

B   Exercises and case studies

B1   A firm of solicitors acquires a four-year lease for £24,000.

a. What depreciation expense should be charged each year?

b. How will the lease appear on the balance sheet at the end of each year?

B2   Marcel et Cie uses straight-line depreciation. It buys a new machine for weighing chemicals. The machine costs 120,000 francs at the beginning of 1990, and is expected to last for six years.

Show how the machine will appear in Marcel's balance sheet at the end of 1991:

a. if no residual value is assumed,

b. if residual value of 30,000 francs is allowed for.

B3   Kenneth Barker buys a new word processor for £600. He plans to use it for four years, after which time he anticipates it will have a trade-in value of about £150. He proposes to depreciate the machine using the declining balance method, with a percentage rate of 30 per cent.

a. What will the depreciation expense be each year?

b. What will the net book value be at the end of each year?

B4   James Carter pays £12,000 for a truck with an estimated life of four years. Residual value of £2,000 is expected, and straight-line depreciation is used. After three years the truck is sold for £4,000.

a. Calculate the profit or loss on disposal.

b. Prepare a table showing how the truck's total net cost over its whole life is charged as an expense year by year.

c. What would the profit or loss on disposal have been if residual value had been ignored in charging depreciation?

B5   Peterborough Printers Ltd buys photogravure equipment for £11,000 at the beginning of 1990. It makes £8,000 a year profit before charging depreciation. The company's manager expects the equipment will last for five years, and will then have a scrap value of £1,000.

a. Draw up a table showing the net profit year by year:

  (i) using straight-line depreciation;

  (ii) using declining balance depreciation at 35 per cent per year.

b. Comment on the magnitude of the percentage rate used for the declining balance method, compared with straight-line depreciation.

c. How might you have dealt with depreciation if the equipment had been bought halfway through 1990?

B6   Jones Car Hire Ltd purchases new cars which are kept for three years before being sold second-hand, for about one-third of the original price. In 1990, 1991 and 1992 the company buys four, two and five new vehicles respectively, for £6,000 each.

a. Construct a table showing total depreciation expense each year for these cars, using straight-line depreciation.

b. Construct a similar table using declining balance depreciation.

B7   Reliable Transport Ltd acquires a lorry for £14,000 which it expects to last for four years, at the end of which time it will be sold for about £2,000. The lorry's mileage each year is as follows:

	(*'000 miles*)
Year 1 (part)	14
Year 2	20
Year 3	24

	('000 miles)
Year 4	10*
Year 5 (part)	12

* Off the road for the second half of year 4, due to engine problems.

a. Draw up a table comparing the depreciation expense each year under:
  (i) the usage method;
  (ii) the straight-line method.
b. What information would be needed at the start of the lorry's life in order to calculate depreciation under each method?
c. Show the accounting results, under each method, if the lorry had been sold for £1,000 when it broke down in the middle of year 4.

B8 Robertson Engines plc invests £150,000 in tooling which it expects to last for five years and to have a residual value of £25,000. The company uses straight-line depreciation.
  a. Prepare a table showing year by year over the asset's expected life:
    (i)   depreciation expense;
    (ii) accumulated depreciation;
    (iii) net book value.
  b. Prepare a similar table for a competitor company, Paynter and Sutcliffe Ltd, which buys identical tooling for £150,000, but estimates only a four-year life and a residual value of £20,000, and which uses declining balance depreciation.

B9 Adam Blair & Sons use the sum-of-the-years' digits method to depreciate a machine costing £75,000 with an estimated four-year life.
  a. Prepare a schedule of the year-by-year depreciation charge and net book value of the asset.
  b. What is the accounting result if the machine is sold at the end of year 6 for £4,000?

B10 Simon Fisher Inc. buys machinery for $200,000, which is expected to last for three years and to have a residual value of $60,000.
  a. Using the formula in Section 6.2.2, calculate a suitable annual percentage rate of declining balance depreciation.
  b. Confirm your arithmetic by setting out the net book value of the machine for each year of its three-year life.

B11 George Viner Ltd depreciates its office building, which originally cost £300,000, over 20 years, using straight-line depreciation and ignoring any possible residual value. After 15 years it realizes that too short a life has been used; and the building's remaining life is re-estimated at 15 years.
  a. What is the annual depreciation expense for the early years of the building's life?
  b. What will it be for the later years?
  c. What would it have been throughout, if the life had been 'correctly' estimated to begin with?

B12 Oregon Yards acquired equipment for £30,000 which was expected to last for 10 years, and would be written off on the straight-line basis, with no residual value allowed for. After six years the company reckoned its equipment still had eight years of useful life remaining, and decided to adjust its future depreciation charges accordingly.
   a. What would the annual depreciation charge be:
      (i) in years 1 to 6?
      (ii) in years 7 to 14?
   b. What difference would it make if in each case a residual value of £6,000 was allowed for?

B13 The machine discussed in 6.2.1 and 6.2.2 was actually sold for £3000 at the end of year 4.
   Show the profit or loss on disposal:
   (i) using straight-line depreciation
   (ii) using declining balance depreciation.

B14 With £6,000 he received as a redundancy payment, James Palmer decided to start a travelling greengrocer's business. He bought a second-hand van for £4,800; and used the remaining £1,200 to buy his initial trading stock.

   Each morning he went to the wholesale market to buy vegetables and fruit for his day's sales. All his purchases and sales were for cash. Each weekend Mr Palmer threw out any remaining stock. He kept aside the £1,200 he would need to buy new stocks on Monday morning and regarded any excess over the amount as profit which he spent on living expenses (and on tax).

   After five years the van was on its last legs, and a garage offered £800 for it as a trade-in against a replacement costing £4,800. But Mr Palmer was quite unable to raise the extra £4,000 cash required, so his business collapsed.
   a. Was the cash taken for personal use really his business profit?
   b. What steps could Mr Palmer have taken to avoid the collapse of his business?

B15 In 1980 Plant Hire Ltd paid £10,000 for a crane with an estimated life of 10 years. Using the straight-line method, the company charged £1,000 a year depreciation to overheads. Plant Hire's policy was to finance all fixed asset purchases out of profits, and to distribute 50 per cent of its profits in dividends to shareholders. Operating profits were usually about 10 per cent of sales revenue.

   When the crane had to be replaced in 1990, the company found the price was £30,000.
   a. Calculate the extra volume of sales the company must make to finance the increased price of the crane if it wishes to follow its normal financing and dividend policy. (Assume that corporation tax is 35 per cent of profits before tax.)

b. How, if at all, could the company have avoided this problem caused by a trebling of plant prices over 10 years?

B16 TXW Plastics Ltd buys a computer for £800,000. It is expected to last four years, and to have a residual value of £100,000.

a. Prepare a table showing depreciation expense and net book value year by year if declining balance depreciation is used.

b. After three years, at a cost of £160,000, an improvement extends the computer's life to six years in all. The new residual value is expected to be £60,000. Prepare a revised schedule of declining balance depreciation for years 4 to 6 inclusive.

c. The computer breaks down at the end of year 5, and is sold for only £20,000. What is the profit or loss on sale? Prepare a table showing how the year-by-year expenses charged over its whole life amount in total to the net cost of the computer.

C Essay questions

C1 Why is it necessary to charge depreciation?

C2 Would it matter if a business simply charged the whole cost of fixed assets as an expense in the year of acquisition? Why or why not?

C3 How would you try to estimate a new machine's useful life, and residual value?

C4 Why does selling fixed assets usually cause profits or losses on disposal?

C5 Identify three different matters to consider when deciding whether or not to replace old machinery with a more modern equivalent.

C6 What are the main arguments for and against the usage method of depreciation?

C7 Does the method of depreciation of fixed assets have any bearing on a firm's cash position, and if so, why?

C8 Should brands be shown on balance sheets? If so, how should they be amortized?

C9 'The subjective estimates and arbitrary choices of method in calculating depreciation make reported profits or losses unreliable as measures of economic performance.' Discuss.

C10 As accountant of a plant hire firm, write a memo to the managing director of your company, putting the case for changing from straight-line to declining balance depreciation.

7

Valuing stock

Plan of the chapter:

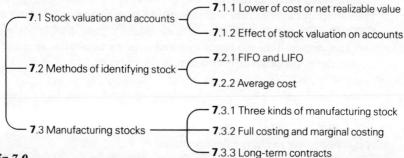

Fig. 7.0

Objective: *To describe how accounts value stocks, and to explain the effect on the measurement of profit.*

Synopsis: *Accounts normally value stocks at cost, unless net realizable value is lower. Stock valuation directly affects the amount of cost of goods sold, and therefore the amount of profit.*

The First In First Out (FIFO) method of stock valuation assumes that a business uses up the earliest purchases first, so that the stock left at the end of a period is that most recently purchased. Last In First Out (LIFO), widely used in the United States, makes the opposite assumption.

The 'cost' of partly-completed and of finished manufactured goods may not be easy to determine. UK companies use the 'full costing' approach, which allocates production overheads to products, as well as direct labour and materials costs. 'Marginal costing', which is not allowed for financial accounts, but is widely used in internal management accounting, excludes production overheads from the value of stock, treating them as 'period costs'.

7.1 Stock valuation and accounts

The problem in valuing stock for accounting purposes is to attach a money value to each item of stock physically on hand. It is simplest to begin with a trading business which buys and sells finished goods. Later we look at the more complex problems that arise where firms process raw materials into finished goods before selling them.

7.1.1 Lower of cost or net realizable value

Accountants normally value stocks at cost, or **net realizable value** (NRV) if lower. This is the estimated net selling price less (a) all further costs to completion and (b) all marketing, selling and distribution costs. The basis for the rule is prudence: accountants prefer not to recognize profit in accounts until they are fairly sure it has been earned; but to provide for losses as soon as possible. The 'lower of cost or net realizable value' rule applies to each item of stock separately. The process of noticing the possibility of loss calls for both alertness and judgement.

A profit-seeking business aims to sell each item for more than it cost. But there are two reasons why net realizable value of trading stocks might be lower than cost:

1 physical damage may have reduced the saleable value;
2 market conditions may have worsened since purchase.

Here are two examples:

(a) *Physical damage*
   Ovoids Limited buys one million eggs in April for 4p each. It has sold half of them for 6p each when the air-conditioning plant breaks down. The remaining half-million eggs in stock all go bad, so their value at the end of the month is zero. Nobody is going to buy rotten eggs at any price! So Ovoids Limited must write off the entire cost of the unsaleable eggs as an expense in April.

(b) *Market conditions worsen*
   Peregrine owns a ladies fashion boutique. He buys 100 dresses for £40 each which he hopes to sell for £80. At the end of the year, with the new season due soon, he has sold only 90 dresses. How should he value the remaining 10 out-of-fashion dresses? At cost? But if he judges that the net realizable value will probably be less than £40 each, then he should use that lower figure to value the closing stock.

7.1.2 Effect of stock valuation on accounts

Stock valuation matters in accounting because the cost of goods sold depends on the closing stock value. We know that the profit for a period depends on the cost of goods sold charged against that period's sales revenue. *So profit for a period depends on the closing stock value.* Stock valuation also, of course, affects the amount of current assets shown in the balance sheet.

We can identify the cost of goods sold in a trading business as follows:

	opening stock	£xxx	
+	purchases in period	£xxx	
=	goods available	£xxx	all at cost
−	closing stock	£xxx	
=	goods sold in period	£xxx	

There are several reasons why goods may not be in closing stock even though they have not been sold:
1 the opening stock figure may have been incorrect;
2 the closing physical count may have been wrong;
3 they may have disappeared (for example, evaporated);
4 they may have been scrapped, as obsolete or damaged;
5 they may have been lost;
6 they may have been stolen, by employees or others.

Companies need to take suitable precautions against all the above. Many companies physically check their stock from time to time against their accounting records. They may then derive their end-of-period stock at least partly from the records, if satisfied that they are accurate. That avoids the possibly troublesome need to make a physical check of all stocks at a single date.

Let us assume that a firm has correctly counted and valued its opening stock, and knows how much its purchases cost in the period. That determines the cost of the goods becoming 'available for sale' in the period; from which we deduct the cost of the goods still left in stock at the end. We then know the amount to charge as an expense against sales revenue as 'cost of goods sold' in the period.

Example: Trendy Footwear's normal 'mark-up' on cost was 50 per cent. Thus a pair of shoes purchased for £10 would normally be sold for £15 – giving a 'gross profit' of £5. The shop then had to deduct its various running expenses in order to calculate its net operating profit.

At the end of 1990, Trendy had several thousand pairs of shoes in stock, valued (at cost) at £30,000. During the year 1991 further purchases of shoes cost £270,000, and the shop's sales revenues totalled £360,000.

Obviously we can't say the shop made a gross profit of £60,000 in 1991, because (like Mary Mullins – see 5.2.1) we have not yet allowed for the closing stock. Suppose the cost of the shoes left in stock at the end of the year totalled £50,000. Then the cost of goods sold in 1991 was £250,000, and the gross profit was £110,000.

(a)   Cost of goods sold (£250,000) is made up from:

Opening stock	+	Purchases	–	Closing stock
£30,000	+	£270,000	–	£50,000

(b)   Gross profit (£110,000) consists of:

Sales revenue	–	Cost of goods sold
£360,000	–	£250,000

This is set out in figure 7.1.

When Trendy's manager looked at the closing stock he found that many pairs of shoes were slightly damaged, and that others would have to be sold at somewhat less than original cost, due to a change in fashion. He considered the closing stock of shoes item by item, in each case taking the lower of (a) cost, or (b) net realizable value. As a result, the manager valued the closing stock of shoes in total at only £40,000.

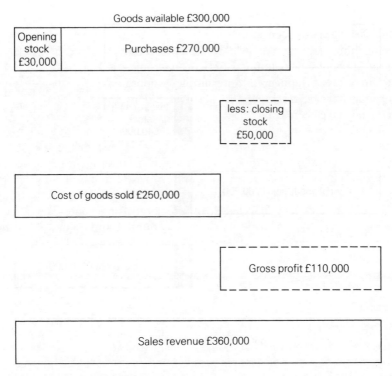

Figure 7.1 The calculation of gross profit

The reduction in value of the closing stock, from £50,000 to £40,000, also reduced the gross profit for the year by £10,000, from £110,000 to £100,000. This is set out in figure 7.2 overleaf. The reduction of £10,000 in the closing stock value (shown as the shaded area) has, in effect, been added on to the cost of goods sold. It has thus reduced 1991's gross profit to the same extent.

Changing the stock value at one moment may not affect the total profit reported over the whole life of a business. (That will be sales revenue less total expenses.) What it does is *shift* the reporting of some profit from one accounting period to another. Reducing the closing stock valuation reduced Trendy's 1991 profit. But it also reduces 1992's opening stock, which increases 1992's reported profit. (Trendy's reduced profit would probably have been discovered in 1992, when some shoes could not be sold at their normal prices.)

7.2 Methods of identifying stock

7.2.1 FIFO and LIFO
So far we have assumed that we can identify the 'cost' of goods in stock; but in practice this can present problems, especially where prices are changing. In this

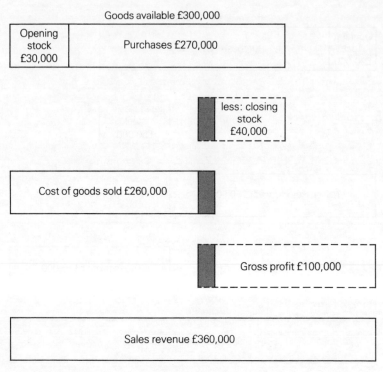

Goods available £300,000

| Opening stock £30,000 | Purchases £270,000 |

less: closing stock £40,000

Cost of goods sold £260,000

Gross profit £100,000

Sales revenue £360,000

Figure 7.2 How reducing closing stock value reduces gross profit

section we shall assume that prices are rising over time; but it should be obvious that similar problems occur if prices are falling.

The normal way to identify stocks (in the United Kingdom) is the **First In First Out** (FIFO) method. This assumes that the first items of stock purchased ('in') are the first items to be sold ('out'). Thus the earliest purchases are used up first (starting with any opening stock), leaving the most recent purchases in stock at the end of a period.

What it means to use FIFO may become clearer if we contrast it with **Last In First Out** (LIFO), a method widely used in the United States but not normally used in the United Kingdom. The LIFO method assumes that the first items to be sold are those most recently purchased. So they will have been purchased at the most recent prices.

The method used for accounting purposes need not match the physical flow of goods. Obviously FIFO should be the method actually used to move perishable goods (such as food); but for durable goods other physical patterns of flow may be suitable. For example, coal may be dumped before all existing stocks have been used up; and withdrawals from the surface may then leave a 'core' of older coal.

Example: Quickflo Pumps Ltd operates a petrol filling station. At the end of May the storage tanks contained 30,000 litres of petrol, which had cost 30p per litre. During June the company received two deliveries each of 20,000 litres, costing 40p per litre. At the end of June 30,000 litres remained in the tanks, the same amount as at the start of the month. Competitive market conditions prevented Quickflo from increasing the selling price of petrol: it remained at 50p per litre all through June. The question is: how much gross profit did Quickflo Pumps make in June? Clearly we need to make an assumption about which petrol was left at the end of June. Was it (a), the 30,000 litres in the tanks at the start of June? Or (b), part of the two deliveries of 20,000 litres each made in the month of June? These amount to using (a) LIFO and (b) FIFO. Figure 7.3 shows how the profit for June is £3,000 higher using FIFO.

	'000 litres	Price	FIFO £'000		LIFO £'000
Opening stock	30	30p	9		9
Purchases	40	40p	16		16
Petrol available	70		25		25
Less: closing stock	30	40p	12	30p	9
Cost of petrol sold	40		13		16
Sales revenue	40	50p	20		20
Gross profit			7		4

Figure 7.3   Quickflo Pumps Ltd gross profit for June

If prices are rising, using LIFO produces a lower figure for gross profit. That is because LIFO charges against sales revenue the more recent (the higher-priced) purchases. But LIFO results in a low balance sheet figure for stock which may be very out-of-date. So if the volume of stock falls, part of the cost of goods sold will consist of very out-of-date costs, thus distorting the profit and loss account.

FIFO, on the other hand, uses recent costs to value stock in the balance sheet; but somewhat out-of-date costs in the profit and loss account. Thus FIFO 'overstates' profit.

Figure 7.4 (overleaf), in summary, shows that both FIFO and LIFO have drawbacks in times of rising prices. FIFO overstates the current period's profit, while LIFO understates balance sheet stock value.

7.2.2 Average Cost
FIFO is common in the UK, while LIFO, which is common in the United States, is almost unknown in the UK. There is also a third method of identifying stock for valuation purposes, quite widely used in the UK. This is the **average cost**, which simply assumes that the average cost – recalculated on

99

	Profit and loss *account*	*End-of-period* *balance sheet*
FIFO	Out-of-date costs	Cost of most recent purchases
LIFO	Cost of most recent purchases	Very out-of-date costs

Figure 7.4 FIFO versus LIFO

every purchase – forms the basis for valuing closing stock. Of course, a company must be consistent in the method it uses. Figure 7.5 shows how Quickflo Pumps Ltd would value its petrol stock at £11,667 using the average cost method, compared with £12,000 using FIFO and £9,000 using LIFO.

	'000 *litres*	*price*	*(£)*
Opening stock	30	30p	9,000
Issued	20	30p	6,000
	10	30p	3,000
First delivery	20	40p	8,000
	30	*36.7p	11,000
Issued	20	36.7p	7,333
	10	36.7p	3,667
Second delivery	20	40p	8,000
Closing stock	30	*38.9p	11,667
* calculated			

Figure 7.5 Quickflo Pumps in June, using the average cost method

7.3 Manufacturing stocks

7.3.1 Three kinds of manufacturing stock

Until now we have been looking at the stock of a trading company which buys and sells only finished goods. Now we move on to consider manufacturing stocks. The most obvious difference is that there are three different kinds of stock held in a manufacturing company:

1 raw materials stocks;
2 work-in-progress;
3 finished goods stocks.

Figure 7.6 illustrates the relationship of these three kinds of stock showing the flow of materials through a manufacturing process.

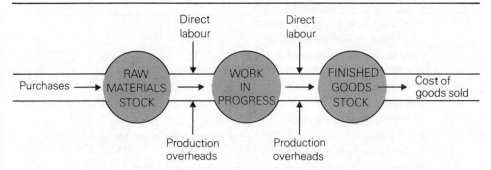

Figure 7.6 Flow of material through a production process

The shaded areas in figure 7.6 show the three kinds of manufacturing stock. Raw materials stock is valued at cost. (For simplicity we ignore the use of net realizable value if lower than cost, which applies to all kinds of stocks.) But work-in-progress and finished goods stocks are harder to value because their 'cost' includes not only raw materials but also the costs of direct labour and of production overheads (see 7.3.2).

Figure 7.7 overleaf shows how the three kinds of manufacturing stock relate to different stages of production: (A) raw materials used up; (B) cost of goods manufactured; and finally (C) cost of goods sold.

Cost of goods sold equals raw materials purchases, direct labour and production overheads in a period, plus opening stocks, minus closing stocks. Thus a net *increase* in combined stocks during a period *reduces* cost of goods sold, while a net decline in combined stocks increases cost of goods sold. (It may help to think either of starting with no stock (for an increase in stocks over the period), or of ending with no stock (for a decrease in stocks over the period).)

Opening stocks	**
Raw materials purchased	xx
Direct labour	xx
Production overheads	xx
Less: closing stocks	(**)
	—
= Cost of goods sold	xx

101

	Raw materials	Work-in-progress	Finished goods
Opening finished goods stock			★★
Opening work-in-progress		★★	
Opening raw materials stock	★★		
+ Purchases of raw materials	xx		
= Raw materials available	xx		
Less: closing raw materials stock	★★		
(A) = Raw materials used in production		xx	
Direct labour		xx	
Production overheads		xx	
		xx	
Less: closing work in progress		★★	
(B) = Cost of finished goods made			xx
= Finished goods available			xx
Less: closing finished goods stock			★★
(C) = Cost of goods sold			xx

Figure 7.7 Detailed make-up of cost of goods sold in a manufacturing company

7.3.2 Full costing and marginal costing

There are two approaches to valuing manufacturing stocks, known as full costing and marginal costing. The last section discussed LIFO, which is not used in the UK, in order to bring out more fully the implications of the FIFO method. So here we discuss marginal costing, which is not used in financial accounting, in order to bring out the implications of full costing.

Full costing values manufacturing stocks by including all costs incurred in bringing stocks into their present condition. This includes the cost of materials, plus direct labour, plus production overheads (based on the normal level of activity). In contrast, **marginal costing** values manufacturing stocks by including only material costs and direct labour. The difference between the two is that full costing includes production **overheads** as part of the cost of stocks, whereas marginal costing does not. UK companies must use full costing in published financial accounts; though some companies use marginal costing in their internal management accounts.

Example: Jones Packaging Ltd makes wooden crates from second-hand timber. The company produces 400 crates per month at a direct cost of £40 (£25 timber plus £15 direct labour); and plans to sell them for £80 each to removal firms. The company also incurs production overheads amounting to £8,000 per month. These include the production director's salary, depreciation of equipment, factory lighting, and other production expenses.

In its first three months of operations, the company sold 300, 450, and 350 crates. How much profit did it make for the quarter? What is the value of stock on hand at the end of the third month? (The answer to the first question, of course, depends on the answer to the second.) Figure 7.8 shows the different results using full costing and marginal costing.

	Full costing (£'000)	Marginal costing (£'000)
Opening stock	–	–
Raw materials (timber)	30	30
Direct labour	18	18
Production overheads	24	24
Total production costs	72	72
Less: closing stock	6	4
Cost of goods sold	66	68
Sales revenue	88	88
Gross profit	22	20

Figure 7.8 Jones Packaging Ltd results for first quarter

Marginal costing values each crate at direct cost only (£25 timber plus direct £15 labour), whereas full costing also includes £20 per crate in respect of production-overheads. This is simply the £8,000 per month divided by the 400 crates produced each month. Thus closing stock of 100 crates is valued at £6,000 using full costing (£60 each), but only at £4,000 using marginal costing (£40 each). The difference of £2,000 in the closing stock valuation, and hence in profit for the quarter, represents the 100 crates in stock times the production overheads of £20 per crate.

Full costing treats production overheads as 'product costs', and writes them off as expenses only when the goods to which they relate are sold. This is regarded as according better with the matching principle. Marginal costing, in contrast, treats production overheads, in effect, as 'period costs' (see 5.3.2), and writes them off as expenses in the period in which they are incurred. It could be argued that marginal costing is more prudent.

7.3.3 Long-term contracts

We have seen that accounts normally value stocks at 'the lower of cost or net realizable value'. The intention is clear: accounts should not recognize any profit until goods have actually been sold. This applies to all three kinds of manufacturing stock: raw materials, work-in-progress, and finished goods.

But there is an important exception, in respect of long-term contracts. Construction of buildings, or civil engineering projects such as dams, motorways, tunnels or power stations, may take two years or more. If construction work-in-progress on such long-term contracts were never valued at more than cost, none of the profit would be recognized until the date of completion. But this would be unrealistic.

Instead work-in-progress on long-term contracts is valued at cost plus attributable profit, less any foreseeable losses. If a project was two-thirds completed at the balance sheet date, with no problems expected in future, then two-thirds of the estimated total profit on the contract should be included in valuing work-in-progress.

Thus contractors recognize profits only to the extent 'earned'; but losses in full as soon as they are foreseen. Where there is a conflict, 'prudence' here outweighs the 'matching' principle.

The above approach does have certain snags:

1 A contract normally requires completion before ownership passes to the purchaser. Half a ship is not much use.

2 It may be hard to apportion profit between different parts of a project.

3 Many contracts contain uncertainties right up to the time of completion, in respect of labour problems, exchange rate fluctuations, etc.

4 It may give management more opportunities to present misleading profit figures, either in apportioning profit or in estimating future losses. Again, therefore, consistency of treatment is important.

Work section

A   Revision questions

A1   What is the general rule for valuing stock in accounts?

A2   Define 'net realizable value'.

A3   Why may net realizable value be lower than cost?

A4   Why does stock valuation matter in accounts?

A5   Name three reasons why unsold goods may not be physically on hand.

A6   Define 'cost of goods sold'.

A7   Explain carefully how the value of closing stock affects profit.

A8   If stock value falls, is the difference (a) added to or (b) deducted from the period's purchases in computing cost of goods sold? Explain why.

A9   Why may subjective value be needed in valuing stock?

A10 Define FIFO.

A11 What is the FIFO method trying to do?

A12 Define LIFO.

A13 How does FIFO differ from LIFO as regards: (a) the profit and loss account, (b) the balance sheet?

A14 If prices were falling, which method would produce a higher stock valuation: FIFO or LIFO? Explain why.

A15 What is the 'average cost' method of valuing stock?

A16 What assumption does LIFO make about the date of acquisition of closing stock?

A17 What happens under LIFO if closing stock is less than opening stock?

A18 What is the main disadvantage of (a) FIFO? (b) LIFO?

A19 What are the three different kinds of manufacturing stock?

A20 In a manufacturing company why are raw materials stocks easier to value than the other two kinds of stock?

A21 Distinguish full costing from marginal costing.

A22 Which of full costing or marginal costing will result in higher profits if the volume of stocks held is: (a) rising? (b) stable? (c) falling?

A23 Which costs does full costing include in stock valuation?

A24 Which costs does marginal costing include in stock valuation?

A25 How are long-term contracts in progress valued in accounting?

B   Exercises and case studies

B1   Non-Ferrous Metals Ltd started 1990 with £200,000 worth of stock; during the year the company purchased altogether 2,500 tonnes of copper costing £2.4 m. Sales for 1990 were £1.6 m; and at the end of the year the company had 800 tonnes of copper in stock. This was all purchased at £1,200 per tonne during a price boom late in the year. Shortly afterwards, before Non-Ferrous Metals Ltd had sold any of its stock, the market price fell to £1,000 per tonne as a result of over-supply on the market.

a. How should the company value its copper stocks at the end of 1990?

b. What was the company's gross profit for 1990?

B2   George Bull speculates in commodities. In June 1990 his purchases of platinum were as follows:

		(£'000)
Week 1.	2,000 ounces at £290 =	580
Week 2.	1,500 ounces at £280 =	420
Week 3.	1,000 ounces at £270 =	270
Week 4.	2,000 ounces at £260 =	520
	6,500	1,790

His opening stock at the beginning of June was 1,500 ounces, valued at £450,000. During the month he sold 4,500 ounces of platinum, for a total of £1,250,000.

What was George Bull's profit or loss on platinum deals for the month of June 1990 (a) using LIFO, (b) using FIFO?

B3   Simpson Eagle Equipment Ltd makes television sets. Materials amount to £80 per unit, and direct labour to £40 per unit. The production overheads total £400,000 per month. The company had no opening stock at the start of 1991 because the Christmas rush in 1990 had exhausted supplies. In January 1991 production was at the normal rate of 5,000 sets per month. During the month 3,500 sets were sold, for a total of £850,000.

a. What was the company's gross profit for January 1991:

  (i) using full costing,   (ii) using marginal costing?

b. Explain the difference between the two profit figures.

B4   During the first three years of its existence, the Libman Company's manufacturing costs, closing stocks, and sales were as follows:

Year	Manufacturing costs *(£'000)*	Closing stocks *(£'000)*	Sales revenue *(£'000)*
1	80	80	none
2	90	130	60
3	30	none	250

Ignoring all other costs and revenues, determine the company's gross profit for each of the three years.

B5 From the information below, calculate what is the profit or loss for Ecco Trading for each of the first three years:

	Year 1 (£'000)	Year 2 (£'000)	Year 3 (£'000)	Year 4 (£'000)
Sales	30	70	90	n/a
Purchases	40	80	60	n/a
Opening stock	nil	20	50	30

B6 Imperial Imports Ltd bought 5,200 tonnes of sugar in the year to 31 March, 500 tonnes at £200 and the rest at £180 per tonne. By the end of the financial year, 31 March, the market price for sugar had jumped to £400 per tonne. In the year to 31 March sales were 4,500 tonnes at an average of £230 per tonne. Stocks at the beginning of the year had been 800 tonnes valued at £170 per tonne.

a. What was the value of closing stocks of sugar at 31 March?

b. What was the profit for the year?

c. Comment on the implications of the rise in price to £400.

B7 Bernard Deel, a second-hand car trader, constructs his balance sheet and profit and loss account as follows:

End-of-year balance sheet	(£'000)	*Profit and loss account for year*		(£'000)
Stocks	30	Sales revenue		134
Debtors	22			
Cash	1	Opening stocks	28	
	—	Purchases	106	
	53		134	
Less: Creditors	3	Less: Closing stock	30	
	50			104
Shareholders' funds	20			30
Loans	30	Overhead expenses		20
	—			—
	50	Profit		10

The auditor, however, notes that a number of cars, included in closing stock at cost at a total of £18,000, have been in stock for more than six months. When he asks why, Mr Deel tells him the cars are probably priced too high. The standard mark-up of one third on cost has been applied in setting their selling prices.

a. Draw up a new set of accounts, assuming that the selling prices of the old stock have to be reduced by $33\frac{1}{3}$ per cent.

b. What difference would it make if the selling prices had to be reduced (i) by 25 per cent; (ii) by 20 per cent?

B8   Old Mistresses Ltd was started by two spinster sisters, Belinda and Caroline, to trade in pictures and antiques. The company's financial year ended on St Cecilia's Day. Details were recorded of each item dealt in, showing the date of purchase, name of supplier, and cost. When it was sold, the date and amount and (usually) the name of the customer were recorded. Thus the sisters were able to prepare a list of every item which had not yet been sold at any time, together with its original cost.

At the end of the 1990 accounting year, stock lists were prepared showing items apparently unsold with a total cost of £23,700. This figure was included as closing stock in the draft 1990 accounts. In the course of the audit (by a female chartered accountant), the following queries arose. Please identify for each one what adjustment, if any, is needed to the closing stock figure; and calculate what the total closing stock valuation should be in the final accounts.

a. A notebook containing a short story which had been thought to be by Daisy Ashford on an off-day turned out to be by Jane Austen. Its selling price was accordingly raised from £25 to £200 (which compared with a cost of £5).

b. No trace could be found of a number of small items of jewellery which, according to the records, ought to have been in stock. They had cost £215 in total, and none of them had been sold since the end of the financial year. Belinda reckoned the sales proceeds would have totalled about £430, but Caroline believed the jewellery would probably have realized closer to £500.

c. A rather dented silver coffee pot (Queen Anne), which had cost £300, had been in stock for over a year. Because of its poor condition it had been written down to £160 in the 1989 accounts. Its selling price was currently set at £360, but Caroline didn't think Old Mistresses Ltd would be able to sell it for more than £180.

d. The business had in stock a pair of Constable water colours, which together had cost £200. Unfortunately, they were now attributed to Maria not to John Constable; and as a result their selling price had to be reduced from £1,200 to £80.

B9   At 1 April 1990 Snip Snaps Ltd had 30 units of a particular type of camera in stock. They were shown as costing £16 each. In the year ended 31 March 1991, three batches of cameras were purchased. In June 1990, 40 cameras at £17 each; in October 1990, 20 cameras at £19 each; and in December 1990, 30 cameras at £20 each.

1. Calculate the closing stock valuation at 31 March 1991, when there were 60 cameras in stock.

2. Compute the cost of goods sold for the year ended 31 March 1991.

3. Verify your computation by identifying the volume of cameras and related costs per camera assumed to be sold.

Answer the above three questions:
a. using the FIFO method of stock valuation;
b. using the LIFO method.

B10 Dorchester Decorations was a wholesaler of wallpaper. It replenished its stock of a certain type of paper (known as Rainbow) at the end of each quarter. For the calendar year 1990, opening stock was 1,200 metres, and the quantities purchased were 1,800 metres in March, 2,400 metres in June, 1,200 metres in September, and 1,800 metres in December. The cost attributable to the opening stock was £4.20 per metre. Purchase prices per metre through the year 1990 were £3.60 (March), £3.00 (June), £5.00 (September), and £4.00 (December).

The quantities sold each quarter were as follows: March quarter 900 metres; June quarter 1,700 metres; September quarter 1,400 metres; and December quarter 1,900 metres. The closing stock at 31 December 1990 amounted to 2,500 metres of Rainbow wallpaper.

The company used the average cost method of valuing stock, and its practice was each quarter to deduct the issues from stock (in respect of sales during the quarter) *before* adding on the purchases for that quarter, which were made right at the end of each quarter.

Calculate:
a. the value of closing stock of Rainbow wallpaper at 31 December 1990,
b. the cost of Rainbow wallpaper sold during the year 1990.

B11 Skyline Construction Ltd signed a contract on 1 January 1990 to build an office block for White Elephant Enterprises Ltd for a total of £6.0 m. Skyline estimated that the job would take three years to complete, and that construction would cost £4.8 m. At the end of the first year, on 31 December 1990, the job is on schedule, and costs incurred, at £1.2 m, are also on target.

What profit, if any, should Skyline Construction report in its 1990 account in respect of the White Elephant contract:
a. on the basis of the information above?
b. if progress payments totalling £1.3 m have been received by 31 December 1990?
c. if, on review, the directors of Skyline conclude that unexpected delays and cost increases mean that overall the contract will show a loss of £0.5 m instead of a profit of £1.2 m?

B12 Presto Sums Ltd was formed to produce small electronic calculators. Sales were estimated at some 5,000 units per quarter, at an average price of £30 per unit; so production was set at this level. Stocks were planned to build up at the start, since the first quarter's sales were not expected to exceed 3,500 units. By the end of the first quarter it seemed that even that sales estimate was too optimistic, and production was accordingly cut back to 2,000 units for the second quarter.

Direct costs of production averaged £20 per unit, and fixed production overheads amounted to £20,000 per quarter. The company sold 2,000 units in the first quarter and 4,000 (at a price reduced by 5 per cent) in the second. When the managing director saw the company's profit and loss accounts (set out below) for the first two quarters, he was astonished.

	1st quarter (£'000)		2nd quarter (£'000)
Sales revenue		60		114
Opening stocks		–		72
Cost of production	120		60	
	120		132	
Less: closing stocks	72		30	
Cost of goods sold		48		102
Gross profit		12		12

Write a brief memo to the managing director explaining why profits were the same in each quarter despite sales volume having doubled.

B13 Fred Makepiece, a car dealer, sold a new car for £4,000 plus the value of an old car traded in by the customer. The new car had cost Fred £3,100. After repair work on the traded-in car costing £600, it was sold for £2,200.
a. How much profit did Fred make? (Ignore tax: Fred does!)
b. What information would you need if the traded-in car had been sold in a later accounting period, so that it was held in stock at the end of Fred's financial year?

B14 Kostov Sails Ltd's turnover was £120,000 in year 1; in year 2 there was a 25 per cent increase; and in year 3 sales were £20,000 higher than in year 2. Purchases in year 2 were £96,000 – 20 per cent higher than in year 1, but 20 per cent lower than in year 3. Stocks fell by £12,000 in year 1 (comparing the closing stock with the opening stock), rose by £16,000 in year 2, and rose by £12,000 in year 3.
What was the profit in each of the three years?

B15 Refer to 7.3.2 and figure 7.8.
Calculate for Jones Packaging for each of the three months *separately*;
  (i) closing stock value;
  (ii) cost of goods sold;
  (iii) gross profit;
using:
a. the full costing approach;
b. the marginal costing approach.
Confirm that the total of the profits for the three months equals the total profit for the quarter shown in the text for each method.

B16 From the following information prepare a statement of cost of goods sold for Interweave Ltd for 1990, in a format similar to that used in figure 7.7

	(£'000)
Production overheads	320
Closing WIP	65
Opening raw materials stock	50
Raw materials used in production	280
Purchases of raw materials	260
Direct labour	200

Opening finished goods stock was twice the value of the opening raw materials stock; opening work-in-progress amounted to half as much as closing raw materials stock; and closing finished goods stock was double the value of the closing raw materials stock.

a. What is the overall percentage change in stocks during 1990 ?

b. If closing raw materials stock value was reduced by 40 per cent, how, in detail, would that affect your answer?

c. What is the raw material content in closing finished goods stock?

B17 One of Keys' products is garden gnomes. The average cost of a garden gnome is £5, of which the average fixed cost is £2 at the present level of sales and output (10,000p.a.). The retail price of a gnome is £7.50. There are 250 gnomes in stock at the end of the accounting year.

a. Calculate *two* alternative valuations of the closing stock of garden gnomes.

b. Explain the implications of each method.

c. If the retail price falls to £3.50, explain how this affects the stock valuation and recorded profit.

d. Sales and output increase to 12,000 units per year. Given that the retail price is £7.50, calculate the increase in profits.

(UCLES International Examinations, 1989, GCE A level Business Studies.)

B18 A dealer selling cars has a large open space which will contain exactly 100 cars. The space was one-quarter full on 1 January 1988. Each car in stock cost the dealer $10,000.

During the following six months the dealer received three deliveries of 50 cars. Each of these cars cost the dealer $12,000.

All cars were to be sold at a standard price of $15,000. By 30 June 1988 the open space was half full of cars.

(a) Calculate the dealer's profit over the six month period 1 January 1988 to 30 June 1988, using:

(i) the First in First out method (FIFO), <u>AND</u>

(ii) the Last in First out method (LIFO).

(b) Briefly outline the advantages and disadvantages of using each method.

(International Baccalaureate, 1989, Business Studies Higher level, part question)

111

C Essay questions

C1 One period's closing stock is the next period's opening stock. What does this imply in relation to the valuation of stock?

C2 Should UK manufacturing companies be allowed to use marginal costing in valuing stock? Why or why not?

C3 Should production overheads be treated as 'product costs' or as 'period costs'? How would you try to convince someone who took the opposite view?

C4 Discuss the problems facing a producer of fashion shoes when valuing year-end stocks.

C5 What accounting principles, if any, are contravened by the rule requiring stock to be valued at 'the lower of cost or net realizable value'? Might it be better always to value stocks either (a) at cost, or (b) at net realizable value? Why or why not?

C6 In a period of rising prices, management performance often appears better using FIFO stock valuation rather than LIFO. Yet it makes more sense to base selling prices on the unit costs of the latest purchases. Try to explain this apparent paradox.

C7 Should LIFO be permitted as a method of valuing stock? Why or why not?

C8 Write a memo to the managing director of a construction company arguing against a proposal to account for profit on long-term projects year by year.

C9 How can professional accountants be expected to audit estimates by company directors, who have to exercise their own special expertise and judgement in valuing stocks?

C10 Should companies ever be allowed to *change* their methods of valuing stocks, in order to substitute better methods for poorer methods? If so, under what conditions? If not, how can accounting practice improve?

8

Accounting for inflation

Plan of the chapter:

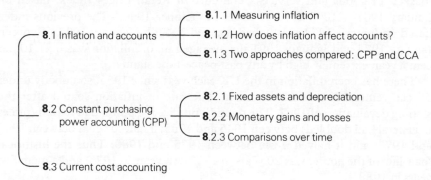

Fig.8.0

Objective: *To explain how inflation affects accounts, and briefly to describe two proposed ways of dealing with the problem.*

Synopsis: *The pound has lost more than 80 per cent of its purchasing power since 1972. As a result, two different methods of 'inflation accounting' have been proposed.*

Constant Purchasing Power (CPP) accounting challenges the convention of using money as the unit of account. It treats money of different dates in effect as 'foreign currencies', and uses the Retail Prices Index as a measure of general inflation to translate all money amounts into units of constant purchasing power of a particular date.

Current Cost Accounting (CCA) challenges the convention of using historical costs as the basis for valuing assets and expenses, and instead uses estimated current replacement costs. It continues to use money as the unit of account, and is thus not a method of adjusting accounts for general inflation.

8.1 Inflation and accounts

8.1.1 Measuring inflation

From an accounting point of view **inflation** means a general increase in the money prices of most goods and services. Another name for the same thing is **currency debasement**: this refers not to the increase in money prices, but to the fall in the value (**purchasing power**) of money.

Inflation is a modern disease: apart from the period around the Napoleonic Wars, the UK suffered almost no prolonged inflation between 1660 and 1914. Thus the general level of prices on the outbreak of the First World War was about the same as it had been on the restoration of Charles II! Prices rose from time to time, of course, during those two and a half centuries, but they *fell* too. There was no persistent *cumulative* increase in the general level of prices.

The usual measure of inflation in the UK is the **Retail Prices Index** (RPI). This monthly index represents a weighted average of the prices of a typical 'basket' of goods and services. The current Retail Prices Index, based on January 1987 = 100, stood at 130.3 in October 1990. (The previous index based on January 1974 = 100, had reached 394.5 by January 1987.) Between January 1974 and January 1991 the average rate of inflation was over 10 per cent a year, extremely high by any past peace-time standard.

There has been inflation in the UK each year since 1935, so nobody under 55 can remember a year without it. The rate of inflation soared after the sterling devaluation of 1967. The pound's purchasing power had halved (prices in general had doubled) between 1945 and 1965; it halved again between 1965 and 1975; and it halved *again* between 1975 and 1980. Thus the historical 'half-life' of the pound was 20 years in 1965, ten years in 1975, and a mere five years in 1980.

In the ten years between 1972 and 1981 the annual rate of inflation averaged 14 per cent; while in the nine years between 1982 and 1990 the rate averaged 'only' 5 per cent per year. Even so, as figure 8.1 shows, by 1990 the pound had lost more than 85 per cent of its purchasing power in 1968, only twenty-two years earlier.

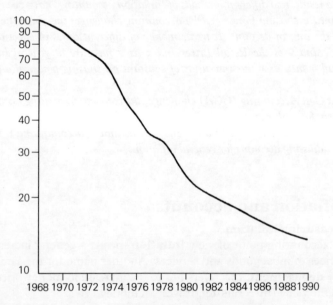

Figure 8.1 Purchasing power of the pound, 1968 to 1990

8.1.2 How does inflation affect accounts?

For accounting, inflation has caused serious problems, which have proved unexpectedly difficult to solve. There has been much debate (in the United States as well as in the United Kingdom) over which of the traditional accounting conventions to change in order to allow for inflation. As a result, two distinct systems of **'inflation accounting'** have developed: constant purchasing power (CPP) accounting and current cost accounting (CCA).

Constant purchasing power accounting challenges the convention of accounting in money terms. When the value of money is falling rapidly, it is argued, the monetary unit no longer serves as an adequate unit of accounting measurement. Hence CPP uses an index of general purchasing power (the Retail Prices Index) to translate all money amounts in accounts into 'units of constant purchasing power', depending on the date when they occurred. In effect, CPP regards money of different dates as 'foreign' currencies, and uses the RPI as a sort of 'exchange rate over time'. All the other concepts and conventions which we have been using until now (summarized in 3.1.1 and 3.1.2) continue to apply.

Current cost accounting challenges the convention of accounting in historical cost terms. Even when there is no general inflation, it is argued, the **current values** of a company's assets are likely to be different from their original cost. This is because in ever-changing markets, the specific prices of goods and services vary as conditions of supply and demand fluctuate over time. CCA therefore continues to use money as the unit of measurement, but substitutes current values ('current costs') for historical costs in accounts.

8.1.3 Two approaches compared: CPP and CCA

Figure 8.2 summarizes the two approaches to inflation accounting. It shows traditional historical cost (HC) accounting in the top lefthand quadrant, using money as the unit of account and historical costs. CPP is in the bottom left-hand quadrant, using a CPP unit of account and historical costs. CCA is in the top righthand quadrant, using money as the unit of account and current costs.

	Basis of valuing assets and expenses	
Unit of account	Historical cost	Current cost
Money	Historical cost (HC)	Current cost accounting (CCA)
Unit of constant purchasing power	Constant purchasing power (CPP)	CCA/CPP combination

Figure 8.2 Different kinds of inflation accounting

Finally, the bottom righthand quadrant shows a possible *combination* of CPP and CCA. This would change two of the accounting conventions at the same time, preparing accounts in terms of constant purchasing power units (like CPP) rather than money, but also using current costs (like CCA) rather than historical costs.

Throughout the book we have been measuring a company's profit for a period by deducting expenses from sales turnover. An alternative approach would be to ask: ignoring dividends and all capital transactions, how much have shareholders' funds changed during the period? In other words, after maintaining the amount of 'capital' attributable to shareholders at the start of a period, how much increase (or decrease) has resulted from profit-and-loss-account transactions during the period?

In HC accounting the definition of the 'capital' to be maintained is the money amount of shareholders' funds. In CPP accounting it is the purchasing power amount of shareholders' funds. Thus until shareholders' funds have been maintained *in terms of constant purchasing power*, the business has not made any CPP profit. Essentially both HC and CPP use a *financial* concept of capital. In contrast, the CCA definition of 'capital' is a physical one; until a company has maintained the *physical productive capacity of its business*, it has not made a CCA profit. Which of these definitions of 'capital' is thought more useful ultimately depends on what one believes the economic purpose of a business enterprise to be.

Both the proposed methods of inflation accounting have pros and cons. CPP has the advantage of using the same readily available 'general' index of inflation (the Retail Prices Index) to apply to all items in accounts; and it also allows proper comparisons of financial statements and amounts over time (see 8.2.3). On the other hand, its 'CPP unit of account' is artificial, and may be difficult for some readers of accounts to understand. Also not everyone believes the Retail Prices Index is an adequate measure of general inflation.

CCA has the advantage of continuing to use the familiar monetary unit as the unit of accounting measurement; but as a result it is not strictly a method of accounting for general inflation. Current costs may be more relevant for assessing business performance than historical costs; but because it is not always easy to tell which is the best specific index of cost changes to use, CCA is more subjective than CPP. CCA is also more complicated to apply in practice than CPP: it brings a number of difficult technical problems which could be hard for smaller businesses to deal with.

8.2 Constant purchasing power accounting

8.2.1 Fixed assets and depreciation
For CPP accounts, the historical cost of a fixed asset acquired some years ago must be translated into purchasing power units of the latest year's accounts; and the appropriate rate of depreciation is then applied to the new amount.

The 'restatement' of the fixed asset's HC opening net book value in the balance sheet is exactly 'balanced' by a similar restatement of shareholders' funds (which CPP accounts do *not* regard as a 'profit').

Example: Alan Hampton Ltd writes off all equipment over 15 years, using straight-line depreciation and assuming no residual value. The company buys a machine in 1974 for £90,000, on which it charges £6,000 HC depreciation expense each year. In the 1974 HC balance sheet the machine's net book value appears at £84,000; by the end of 1987, after 14 years of use, the HC net book value is only £6,000.

The Retail Prices Index quadruples between 1974 and 1987. How will Hampton's CPP accounts treat the machine? The cost, which was actually £90,000 in 1974, must be thought of in CPP terms as being $_{74}$ £90,000, because CPP accounts date all money amounts.

Since the RPI has quadrupled, in Hampton's 1987 CPP accounts the machine's original cost will appear as $_{87}$ £360,000; and the depreciation expense will be based on that amount. Figure 8.3 shows how Alan Hampton Ltd will treat the machine in the 1987 CPP accounts.

Year	Cost	Depreciation expense	Accumulated depreciation	Net book value
	(£'000)	(£'000)	(£'000)	(£'000)
1974	$_{74}$£ 90 × $\frac{1}{15}$ = $_{74}$£6	× 1 = $_{74}$£ 6		$_{74}$£84
......	....	......	......	......
1987	$_{87}$£360 × $\frac{1}{15}$ = $_{87}$£24	× 14 = $_{87}$£336		$_{87}$£24

Figure 8.3 The machine in Hampton's CPP accounts

In this case conventional (HC) accounts would charge only £6,000 depreciation expense (= $_{74}$£6,000) in the 1987 accounts, although the 'correct' (CPP) inflation-adjusted charge is $_{87}$£24,000. This is a big difference, which would evidently produce a smaller reported profit for Alan Hampton Ltd in the CPP accounts, as compared with the HC accounts.

The extent of the depreciation understatement in HC accounts varies with the asset life, the depreciation method, and of course the rate of inflation. Over a 15-year life with straight-line depreciation, an average inflation rate of 10 per cent a year would give an understatement of 97 per cent of HC depreciation. In other words, CPP depreciation on average would need to be about *double* the HC depreciation expense!

It should be noted that inflation adjustments, whether to depreciation or to other items, are disallowed for tax purposes. Thus in effect they are all adjustments to 'after-tax' profit.

8.2.2 Monetary gains and losses

We now come to an unfamiliar item: gains and losses on monetary liabilities and assets. It is unfamiliar because we are used to historical cost accounts where money is the unit of account. But in CPP accounts we are reckoning in terms of units of constant purchasing power. If the purchasing power of money is falling (as it will be in times of inflation), a company which holds money will be *losing purchasing power*. CPP accounts record this loss as an expense in the profit and loss account. Obviously there is no equivalent item in HC accounts.

> *Example: Graham Nash holds £20,000 in cash at the end of 1980, and continues to hold the same amount of money all through 1981. During the year the Retail Prices Index rises by 12 per cent. Figure 8.4 shows how in Nash's 1981 CPP accounts there will be a **monetary loss** of $_{81}$£2,400.*
>
> *Although Nash holds the same amount of money at the end of 1981 as at the beginning of the year, he holds less purchasing power.*

	HC Accounts		*CPP Accounts*
Start of year	£20,000	(= $_{80}$£20,000)	$_{81}$£22,400
End of year	£20,000	(= $_{81}$£20,000)	$_{81}$£20,000
Monetary loss	–		$_{81}$ £2,400

Figure 8.4 Calculation of Graham Nash's monetary loss in 1981

In times of rapid inflation this point is obvious. If Rip Van Winkle had put £1,000 in £1 notes into a sock under his bed in 1974, when he woke up in 1987 he would have found his £1,000 still there. But with the Retail Prices Index four times as high in 1987 as in 1974, his money would have lost 75 per cent of its purchasing power. The amount of money is the same, the amount of its purchasing power is not.

Where the amount of money – or **monetary assets,** such as debtors – varies during the year (as it normally will), the actual calculation is somewhat more complicated. Then we have to use averages. But the principle is the same. And if a company happens to have net **monetary liabilities,** by *owing* more money than it is owed or possesses, then in CPP accounts its profits (in terms of constant purchasing power) will be *increased* by a **monetary gain**. (Everybody who borrows a mortgage on his house benefits from this; but of course that is why nominal (money) rates of interest are so high!)

For simplicity, one can normally treat opening and closing stocks as if they were 'monetary' assets for the purposes of CPP accounts. Thus all current assets and all current liabilities are normally treated as being 'monetary'. To determine the amount of net monetary assets (or liabilities), one simply deducts long-term monetary borrowings from net working capital.

8.2.3 Comparisons over time

Two different kinds of CPP adjustments are needed to financial statements to allow for inflation. So far we have been discussing the first kind, the CPP adjustments to the current year's HC accounts: in respect of fixed assets and depreciation, and the inclusion of constant purchasing power gains or losses on monetary liabilities or assets.

The effect is usually *both* to reduce the amount of profit reported and to increase the amount of assets and shareholders' funds. Thus in both respects inflation adjustments tend to worsen the HC ratio of profit to assets (or 'return on investment', see 9.3.1 and 9.3.3).

The second kind of CPP adjustment, which we consider now, is needed to allow a proper comparison of financial amounts between *different years*.

Example: Gordon Mitchell's salary was £12,000 in 1980, £17,000 in 1984, and £20,000 in 1988. Obviously it has been increasing in money terms: but he wants to know whether he is better off in 'real' terms, after allowing for inflation. (For simplicity, he decides to ignore tax.)

Gordon Mitchell can use the CPP approach and adjust his money salary by reference to the Retail Prices Index for the year concerned. The index, based on January 1987 = 100, averaged 67 in 1980, 89 in 1984, and 107 in 1988. Gordon wants to translate the money amount of his salary for the three years into terms of 'constant purchasing power units' which he can compare directly with each other. So he adjusts the earlier years' figures into terms of the purchasing power of the most recent year, 1988, as in figure 8.5.

Year	Money salary £		Adjustment	'Real' salary (1988 CPP units) 1988 £
1980	12,000	×	107/67	= 19,164
1984	17,000	×	107/89	= 20,438
1988	20,000	×	107/107	= 20,000

Figure 8.5 Restating Gordon Mitchell's salary: 1980, 1984 and 1988

These CPP adjustments show that Gordon's salary in 'real' terms increased by about $6\frac{1}{2}$ per cent between 1980 and 1984, but that it actually fell in real terms by just over 2 per cent between 1984 and 1988. This is not obvious from the money salaries for the three years. Figure 8.5 doesn't need to change the amount of the 1988 salary, since it is already expressed in terms of 1988 pounds.

In times of rapid inflation, this kind of adjustment is needed to allow comparisons over time in **'real' terms**. It is used in many published economic statistics, such as the Gross National Product, and it can be very useful in compiling trends of figures from company accounts.

In accounting, we make such adjustments to different years' CPP accounts in order to translate all the different years' CPP figures into terms of the same CPP units (normally, though not necessarily, those of the most recent year being looked at). Then we can calculate proper trends, and make comparisons over time. Pictures, graphs, and other comparisons over time which do *not* allow for inflation are very likely to mislead the reader, whether deliberately or not.

8.3 Current cost accounting

Current cost accounting (CCA) continues to use money as the unit of account, but translates historical costs into *current* costs, both in the profit and loss account and in the balance sheet. To do so CCA uses a variety of specific indices for fixed assets.

The CCA depreciation adjustment is rather similar to CPP's (see 8.2.1). But instead of using the Retail Prices Index for all items, CCA uses a variety of specific indices for different fixed assets, depending on how their own replacement costs have changed since the date of original acquisition. Any increase (or decrease) to fixed assets resulting from applying such specific indices is added to (or subtracted from) shareholders' funds as a separate revaluation reserve. In general, CCA aims to use the current **replacement cost** for each fixed asset, in place of its actual historical cost; and this then forms the basis for CCA depreciation. The CCA 'depreciation adjustment' is simply CCA depreciation less the HC depreciation already charged in calculating HC operating profit.

Clearly not all prices change at exactly the same rate. If the general rate of inflation (as measured by the Retail Prices Index) is 10 per cent in a given period, some prices of assets will rise by 10 per cent, others by 15 per cent, and others by 5 per cent; and some asset prices may double, while others actually fall. Even when prices-in-general are stable - when there is no general 'inflation' - the specific prices of particular goods and services will still fluctuate. *So CCA accounts will differ from HC accounts even when there is no general inflation.* Thus the numbers used for CCA will differ from those used for CPP: but the nature of the adjustment for fixed assets and depreciation is similar.

The second main CCA adjustment is to cost of goods sold, in respect of price changes affecting opening and closing stocks. Without going into the precise details, the effect on the profit and loss account in respect of this **'cost of sales adjustment'** is rather like valuing cost of goods sold on a LIFO basis (rather than average cost or FIFO), as described in 7.2.1. The effect on the profit and loss account can be significant, but there is usually not much change to the HC balance sheet amount shown for closing stocks.

Work section

A Revision questions

A1 What do you understand 'inflation' to mean?

A2 How is inflation measured in the UK?

A3 How is the Retail Prices Index calculated?

A4 What annual rate has UK inflation averaged since 1974?

A5 What does the 'half-life' of the pound mean?

A6 What is the rate of currency debasement if prices triple?

A7 Which accounting convention is challenged by CPP?

A8 Which accounting convention is challenged by CCA?

A9 What briefly are the essential differences between CPP and CCA?

A10 What definition of the 'capital' to be maintained before reckoning profit or loss is used:
(a) by HC; (b) by CPP; (c) by CCA?

A11 Name two advantages of CPP and two disadvantages.

A12 Name two advantages of CCA and two disadvantages.

A13 Name two variables which affect the size of the depreciation adjustment in the inflation-adjusted profit and loss account.

A14 Why are inflation adjustments to the profit and loss account 'after-tax'?

A15 What is meant in CPP accounting by a 'monetary loss'?

A16 Explain in words how an employee could compare his salary in 'real' terms over the past five years.

A17 Why may a graph showing financial information over time be misleading?

A18 How does CCA value assets on the balance sheet?

A19 When a CCA adjustment increases the net book value of fixed assets, how does the CCA balance sheet still balance?

A20 Why do all prices not change at exactly the same rate?

B Exercises and case studies

B1 You are left £25,000 by an aunt. Assuming that inflation will average 6 per cent a year in future, which of the following investment strategies would you choose (ignoring the problem of tax)? Explain why.
a. Keep the cash in a safe place.
b. Use the cash to purchase a fixed-interest government security returning 3 per cent a year.
c. Buy a piece of land which will appreciate on average at 10 per cent a year, but will give no cash return meanwhile.

   d. Buy a country cottage which will appreciate in line with inflation and which will also yield an annual rental of £500.

B2   Refer to figure 8.5. Restate Gordon Mitchell's money salary for 1980, 1984, and 1988 into terms of constant 1980 pounds.

B3   Reed Water Ltd acquires a machine in April 1990 for £50,000 when the Retail Prices Index (January 1987 = 100) stands at 125. The machine is expected to last 10 years and to have no residual value. The company uses straight-line depreciation, and charges a full year's depreciation in the year of acquisition.

   a. What will the CPP depreciation expense be for the year ending 31 December 1992 if the Retail Prices Index stands at 150 in December 1992?

   b. What will the machine's CPP net book value be at 31 December 1992? What will the machine's HC net book value be on that date?

B4   A company begins life with a share capital of £100 which it immediately uses to purchase a £100 machine. Using historical cost accounting, it then makes a profit of £20 in the first year, £24 in the second, £28.80 in the third, etc. (that is, the profits rise in line with inflation which is considered to be 20 per cent a year). There is no taxation, and all profits are immediately paid out at the end of each year in cash dividends; depreciation is calculated on the straight-line basis at £10 a year.

   a. Illustrate what happens to the shareholders' funds year by year, and to the assets.

   b. Are shareholders receiving a constant, falling, or rising real return through their dividends?

   c. Comment on the shareholders' situation as reflected in shareholders' funds in the balance sheet.

   d. What problems is the company creating for itself by its method of accounting?

   e. Describe the sort of changes you would wish to make to overcome the problems you have described in (d).

C   Essay questions

C1   How might inflation distort the annual accounts of a company? Briefly propose a way of overcoming these problems.

C2   Write a memo to the manager of a medium-sized business arguing for a change from historical cost to current cost accounting.

C3   Write a memo to the manager of a medium-sized business arguing for a change from historical cost to constant purchasing power accounting.

C4   Would the best solution to the problem of accounting for inflation be a combination of CPP and CCA?

C5   Write an essay defending the continuing use of historical cost accounting, as opposed to either CPP or CCA.

C6 If there is no inflation will there be no need for inflation accounting?

C7 'It is just common sense that when the value of money is falling fast enough the monetary unit becomes useless and irrelevant as a unit of account. CPP accepts and builds on this obvious point: CCA denies it.' Discuss.

C8 Comment on the following statement in the Sandilands Report: 'In determining a change in the 'purchasing power' of money it is necessary to know on what it is spent...a general index of the 'purchasing power' of money is unlikely to be helpful.'

C9 'The index method (CPP) is not strictly a proposal for a change from accounting based on historical cost.' Institute of Chartered Accountants in England and Wales, 1952. Discuss.

C10 Who should decide how best to account for inflation: the government, the accountancy profession, or some other group?

9

Analysing accounts

Plan of the Chapter:

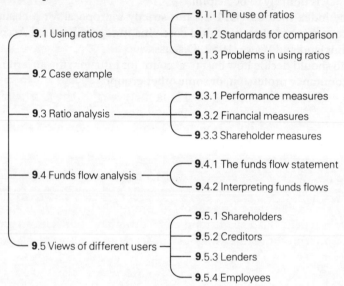

Fig 9.0

Objective: *To explain the purpose of ratio analysis and funds flow analysis in interpreting financial accounts, and to describe accounting ratios and their use.*

Synopsis: *Accounting ratios summarize financial relationships. They allow comparisons over time, with other firms, and with internal budgets. There are problems in using ratios: they raise questions rather than providing definite answers.*

Ratios can be split into three groups: performance measures, financial measures and shareholder measures.

Funds flow analysis identifies a company's sources and uses of funds over one or more periods. It may also help in forecasting future financial needs.

A case example illustrates the kinds of questions which may be of interest to different users of accounts: shareholders, creditors, lenders and employees.

9.1 Using ratios

9.1.1 The use of ratios
Much of Chapters 3 to 8 has dealt with *preparing* accounts: the basic accounting concepts and conventions (Chapter 3); the detailed formats of

balance sheets (Chapter 4) and profit and loss accounts (Chapter 5); and key problem areas in depreciation of fixed assets (Chapter 6), in valuing stocks (Chapter 7), and in allowing for inflation (Chapter 8).

Now we move on to consider how to interpret and analyse the accounting information in published financial statements.

One piece of information by itself may not mean much. A 'ratio' is simply a method of *comparing* one number with another. An accounting ratio has meaning only if there is some reason to expect a definite relationship between the two. There is some reason to expect profit for a period to be related to total assets, or to sales turnover. But if, for example, we were to divide accumulated depreciation by the interest payable, the result would be meaningless. There is no reason to expect the two numbers to be related.

Using a common format, by expressing two numbers as a ratio or as a percentage, makes comparisons with a particular standard much easier (see 9.1.2). The 'ratio' may simply be one number as a percentage of another. Or we might divide one number directly by another.

The value of accounting ratios must partly depend on the accuracy of the underlying data. Thus HC 'return on investment' ratios may be misleading because inflation distorts *both* parts of the ratio (see Chapter 8).

Ratios need not consist only of financial information. We can calculate 'fixed assets per employee' for a manufacturing company; or 'sales per square metre of space' for a retail store. In schools a commonly used ratio is 'number of pupils per teacher'. But a single ratio on its own may not tell us very much. In order to interpret the meaning of most ratios, we need *standards* for comparison.

9.1.2 Standards for comparison

(a) Over time

One obvious way to compare ratios is over time, between years. Figures for past periods are likely to be available on a consistent basis (though inflation adjustments may be needed). Suitable comparisons over time enable us to detect *trends,* to see whether things are getting 'better' or 'worse', or staying much the same. This can help us to interpret financial (and other) information, though we should not assume that the future need be like the past. In other words, trends go on until they stop!

(b) Inter-firm comparisons

Another useful standard is the performance or position of other firms in the same industry. A company's rate of profit to assets employed, for example, may be increasing over time. But it may still be much lower than the rate of return which other companies in the same industry are earning. That is useful to know, because it provides an *external* standard by which to judge performance. If other companies in the same industry can do much better, we would like to know the *reasons*. They may give us some clues as to possible improvements in our own performance (see 11.3.2).

(c) Inter-firm comparisons over time

A natural extension is to *combine* these two standards: inter-firm comparisons over a period of years. Figure 9.1 compares the profit margin on sales of three food retailing companies over a five-year period.

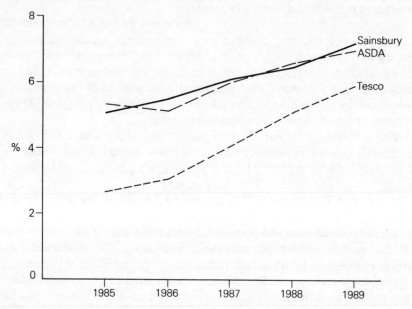

Figure 9.1 Profit margins on sales of three food retailers (1985 to 1989)

What does figure 9.1 show?

All the profit margins increased every year, except for ASDA in 1986. Tesco's margins, which in 1985 were more than two percentage points less than ASDA or Sainsbury, have doubled since 1986, and by 1989 were only one percentage point less.

In terms of constant purchasing power, Sainsbury's sales volume increased by 56 per cent between 1985 and 1989, Tesco's by 30 per cent, and ASDA's by 18 per cent. The effect is that ASDA's real profit increased over the period by about 60 per cent, Sainsbury's by 120 per cent, and Tesco's by 180 per cent.

(d) Internal budgets

For management accounting purposes, another useful standard for comparison is the company's own internal budgets. Unlike published financial accounts, they should be available in great detail; thus enabling the internal analyst to interpret performance much more thoroughly than is possible with aggregate accounting information. (Figure 1.3 lists the essential differences between financial and management accounting.)

The more care is spent on preparing budgets, the more confidently they can be relied on as standards, though one still needs to allow for changes in conditions since the budgets were prepared and agreed. Chapter 12 discusses budgets in detail; in particular, how variance analysis compares 'actual' with 'budgeted' performance, and tries to explain reasons for any significant differences.

9.1.3 Problems in using ratios

Ratios can be useful in suggesting questions to look into; but they are unlikely on their own to provide complete answers. Some of the main problems in using ratios to interpret published accounts are listed below:

(a) Comparisons over time
1 Inflation may need to be allowed for (see Chapter 8).
2 If accounting methods or product groupings change, figures on the new basis may not be available for earlier periods.
3 We cannot assume the future will be like the past. Business conditions can change in unpredictable ways.

(b) Inter-firm comparisons
1 Individual firms, even in a single 'industry', may differ in product mix, cost structure, or in business objectives and strategies.
2 Financial years may end on different dates.
3 Accounting methods and definitions may vary, especially between different countries.

(c) General
1 Accounts record only matters which can be expressed in financial terms. This may exclude vital business information. Hence in interpreting accounts, it is always important to use other sources, such as the directors' report, chairman's statement, etc. (see 2.4).
2 Not all relevant information is published. Sales revenue consists of volume times price; but published accounts (unlike internal budgets) hardly ever split the sales turnover figure between the two.
3 Most accounting figures are not precisely 'correct'; they often include an element of personal judgement.

9.2 Case example

Hamilton Pumps Ltd had been in business for more than 25 years. In 1987 Lewis Jack, the company's founder, retired in favour of his son David, who decided to expand production capacity and move into overseas markets. In March 1988 he arranged for the company's shares to be quoted on the Unlisted Securities Market (USM); and at the same time the Jack family sold to the public $1\frac{1}{2}$ million of the 4 million shares in issue.

By the beginning of 1990 there were rumblings of discontent. Shareholders complained of being kept in the dark about the company's plans; and the share price fell steadily throughout 1990. At the same time, two major suppliers had shown reluctance to allow any further trade credit; the company's bank, refusing to extend the overdraft as much as requested, had insisted on some of the necessary funds being raised by medium-term loans; and there were signs of discontent about wage levels from employees.

The company published its 1990 accounts in mid-April 1991, with the AGM due at the end of May. Around the same time, David Jack had arranged three other important meetings: (a) to see the company's major supplier; (b) to visit the company's bank manager; and (c) to meet representatives of the employees.

Hamilton Pumps Ltd's 1990 profit and loss account and balance sheet are shown in figures 9.2 and 9.3. In Section 9.3 we calculate some accounting ratios arising

Hamilton Pumps Limited
Profit and loss account for the year 1990

1989 (£'000)			1990 (£'000)
6,500	Sales		6,750
4,440	Cost of sales		4,820
1,110	Selling and administrative expenses		1,205
950	Operating profit*		725
75	Interest payable		175
875	Profit before tax		550
300	Taxation		200
575	Profit after tax		350
	Ordinary dividends:		
50	Interim, 1.25p (1.25p)	50	
100	Final, 1.25p (2.50p)	50	
150			100
425	Retained profit for the year		250

*After charging depreciation £375,000 (£250,000).

Figure 9.2 Hamilton Pumps Ltd: profit and loss account for the year 1990

Hamilton Pumps Ltd
Balance Sheet at 31 December 1990

1989 (£'000)		1990 (£'000)
	Fixed assets	
600	Freehold property	750
1,350	Plant and equipment	2,250
1,950		3,000
	Current assets	
1,050	Stocks	1,350
1,300	Debtors	1,850
250	Liquid resources	100
2,600		3,300
	Less: Current liabilities	
1,450	Creditors	1,600
–	Bank overdraft	900
300	Taxation	200
100	Dividends payable	50
1,850		2,750
750	*Net working capital*	550
2,700	*Net assets*	3,550
	Shareholders' funds	
1,000	Issued ordinary 25p shares	1,000
1,200	Retained profits	1,450
2,200		2,450
	Long-term liabilities	
500	Mortgage debenture	500
–	Other loans	600
		1,100
2,700	*Capital employed*	3,550

Figure 9.3 Hamilton Pumps Ltd: balance sheet at 31 December 1990

from them. In Section 9.4 we return to see how David Jack's various meetings turned out.

9.3 Ratio Analysis

We now consider the main ratios for Hamilton Pumps Ltd. (See also 11.3.)

Performance measures

Performance measures try to show how well the business is being run. These key ratios are of interest to nearly all readers of accounts. The main two measures are both to do with profits; they relate profit for a period (i) to the amount a company has invested in assets, and (ii) to its sales turnover. In general, the higher both of these ratios are the better.

		1990		1989	

1 **Return on net assets** $= \dfrac{\text{Operating profit}}{\text{Net assets}}$ $\dfrac{725}{3,550} = 20.4\%$ $\dfrac{950}{2,700} = 35.2\%$

This basic measure of operating return on investment ignores taxes, which are also affected by non-operating factors. It also ignores interest paid on loan capital, being concerned with the total amount invested, whether financed by equity capital or by loans. 1990's rate of return on net assets is significantly down on 1989.

2 **Profit margin** $= \dfrac{\text{Operating profit}}{\text{Sales turnover}}$ $\dfrac{725}{6,750} = 10.7\%$ $\dfrac{950}{6,500} = 14.6\%$

This is another basic performance measure relating operating profit (as before) to sales turnover. Again there is a definite reduction in 1990 compared with 1989.

3 **Net asset turnover** $= \dfrac{\text{Sales turnover}}{\text{Net assets}}$ $\dfrac{6,750}{3,550} = 1.90$ $\dfrac{6,500}{2,700} = 2.41$

The number of times that net assets are 'turned over' in a year in sales revenue (turnover) is one measure of the 'productivity' of assets. Once again the 1990 figure is much lower than 1989's.

Notice the link between the above three ratios:

	Profit margin	×	Net asset turnover	=	Return on net assets
1990	10.7%	×	1.90 times	=	20.4%
1989	14.6%	×	2.41 times	=	35.2%

		1990		1989	

4 **Stock turnover** $= \dfrac{\text{Cost of sales}}{\text{Stocks}}$ $\dfrac{4,820}{1,350} = 3.6$ $\dfrac{4,440}{1,050} = 4.2$

A high rate of stock turnover is normally better than a low one, though if it is too high there may be a risk of running out of stock. This ratio can also be expressed as 'number of days' sales' in stock:

$$\frac{365}{3.6} = 101 \text{ days} \qquad \frac{365}{4.2} = 89 \text{ days}$$

		1990		1989	
5 **Days' sales in debtors** =	$\dfrac{\text{Debtors}}{\text{Sales}/365}$	$\dfrac{1,850}{6,750/365}$ =	$\begin{array}{c}100\\ \text{days}\end{array}$	$\dfrac{1,300}{6,500/365}$ =	$\begin{array}{c}73\\ \text{days}\end{array}$

This measure, like stock turnover, helps to show how well a company is managing its current assets. If debtors take too long to pay it can cause financial problems; so the big increase in 1990 is worrying.

9.3.2 Financial measures

Financial measures look at a company's financial position. The gearing measures look at the long-term capital structure of a business. The larger the proportion of total capital coming from outside lenders, rather than from shareholders, the 'riskier' the financial structure of the business (see Chapter 18). The liquidity measures relate a company's short-term assets to its short-term liabilities. Profit and cash are both important to a business, but they are different (see Chapter 13). Hence even a profitable business may experience liquidity problems.

			1990		1989	
6 **Gearing ratio**	=	$\dfrac{\text{Long-term liabilities}}{\text{Capital employed}}$	$\dfrac{1,100}{3,550}$ =	31.0%	$\dfrac{500}{2,700}$ =	18.5%

The gearing ratio (**debt ratio**) reflects the risk a company runs in the way it finances the business, as between equity and debt. Including short-term bank overdrafts would increase the 1990 gearing ratio to 44.9% (2000/4450).

			1990		1989	
7 **Interest cover**	=	$\dfrac{\text{Operating profit}}{\text{Interest payable}}$	$\dfrac{725}{175}$ =	4.1	$\dfrac{950}{75}$ =	12.7

The gearing ratio is a balance sheet measure of financial risk, while the interest cover is a profit and loss account measure. It shows how many times operating profit 'covers' the fixed interest payments.

			1990		1989	
8 **Current ratio**	=	$\dfrac{\text{Current assets}}{\text{Current liabilities}}$	$\dfrac{3,300}{2,750}$ =	1.20	$\dfrac{2,600}{1,850}$ =	1.41

The current ratio reflects liquidity, that is, how well a company's short-term assets cover its short-term obligations. The current ratio should normally be between $1\frac{1}{2}$ and 2. If it is too low, there is a danger of running out of cash;

while if it is too high, then money may be tied up unprofitably in excess current assets.

		1990		1989	

$$\textbf{9 Acid test ratio} = \frac{\text{Liquid assets}}{\text{Current liabilities}} \quad \frac{1{,}950}{2{,}750} = 0.71 \quad \frac{1{,}550}{1{,}850} = 0.84$$

The acid test ratio is an even more severe test of liquidity than the current ratio. It compares liquid assets (cash plus debtors) to current liabilities. Both debtors and cash should become cash fairly soon after the balance sheet date (hence they are sometimes called **quick assets**), while stocks may be much less liquid. As a rule of thumb, the acid test ratio should not be much below 1.0.

9.3.3 Shareholder measures

Shareholder measures are of special concern to equity shareholders and the stock market generally. They deal not only with total profitability and financial position, but with how well the *shareholders* are doing on their investment in the company. Hence the measures are concerned not only with the numbers in the published accounts, but also with the market value of the equity shares in the company.

$$\textbf{10 Return on equity} = \frac{\text{Profit after tax}}{\text{Shareholders' funds}} \quad \frac{350}{2{,}450} = 14.3\% \quad \frac{575}{2{,}200} = 26.1\%$$

This 'return on investment' measure relates to the ordinary shareholders. It divides profit after interest and after tax (the profit 'available' for ordinary shareholders) by the amount of the shareholders' funds (owners' equity) shown in the balance sheet. The 1990 ratio is only just over half the 1989 level.

$$\textbf{11 Earnings per share (EPS)} = \frac{\text{Profit after tax}}{\text{No. of shares}} \quad \frac{350}{4{,}000} = 8.75\text{p} \quad \frac{575}{4{,}000} = 14.38\text{p}$$

This measure means little on its own, but we shall use it later to compare with the stock market price per share. Also the rate of *growth* in earnings per share may be of interest. Notice that the number of shares issued is 4 million not 1 million. The balance sheet shows £1 million issued share capital; but each share has a nominal value of only 25p.

$$\textbf{12 Dividend cover} = \frac{\text{Profit after tax}}{\text{Dividends}} \quad \frac{350}{100} = 3.5 \quad \frac{575}{150} = 3.8$$

This measure shows how many times more dividend could have been paid out of current earnings. (Earnings per share/dividend per share = 8.75p/2.50p = 3.5 times.) A shareholder's total 'return' on investment consists of dividends plus any capital gains in the share price. So if a company can re-invest its earnings profitably, a shareholder may be content not to get a higher dividend in the current period.

		1990			1989	
13 Price/earnings ratio $= \dfrac{\text{Market price}}{\text{Earnings per share}}$		$\dfrac{50}{8.75}$	= 5.7		$\dfrac{150}{14.38}$	= 10.4

The market price per share (in pence), which fluctuates from day to day, is not published in the annual report; it can be found in the financial section of a newspaper. The price/earnings ratio may be taken as an indicator of confidence in the future prosperity of a company: the higher the ratio the better.

		1990			1989	
14 Dividend yield $= \dfrac{\text{Dividend per share}}{\text{Market price}}$		$\dfrac{2.50}{50}$	= 5.0%		$\dfrac{3.75}{150}$	= 2.5%

This measure is often complicated by tax (which we ignore here). The dividend yield has doubled because the share price has fallen by two thirds while the dividend per share has fallen by 'only' one third.

9.4   Funds flow analysis

9.4.1 The funds flow statement

After studying the accounting ratios (in 9.3), another important step in analysing Hamilton Pumps Ltd's 1990 accounts is to look at the flow of funds during the year. This shows where (from what sources) the company obtained funds during the year to finance its business, and how the company invested (used) those funds.

The funds flow statement in figure 9.4 overleaf shows profit before tax as the starting point. Strictly speaking, the source of the funds is sales to customers; but all the costs of sales and other operating expenses (apart from depreciation – see below) have to be deducted as uses of funds. So figure 9.4 shows only the net amount for the source of funds from operations.

9.4.2 Interpreting funds flows

Figure 9.4 makes it clear that Hamilton Pumps has used funds in 1990 in three main ways: (a) in paying tax and dividends; (b) in building up stocks and debtors, the main components in working capital; and (c) in investing in new fixed assets. The three main sources of funds were: (d) internally-generated funds from operations (profits plus depreciation); (e) bank overdraft; and (f) long-term loans. The simple pie-charts in figure 9.5 overleaf show this general overall view.

In trying to forecast the company's future need for funds, we have to predict each of the main sources and uses of funds. We may assume no more long-term loans; and depreciation should be about £400,000. Working capital should be kept to a modest increase, say £100,000; and spending on fixed assets may now fall back to around £600,000 next year. So unless the return on net assets reaches about 20 per cent (leaving, say, £625,000 profit before tax, after charging long-term interest, and perhaps £300,000 after tax and dividends), it will not be possible to reduce the bank overdraft.

Hamilton Pumps Ltd
Funds flow statement for the year 1990

			1990 *(£'000)*
	SOURCES OF FUNDS		
Internal	Profit before tax	550	
	Add: Depreciation (see 13.2.2)	375	
			925
External	Bank overdraft	900	
	Long-term loans	600	
			1,500
			2,425
	USES OF FUNDS		
	Taxation paid	300	
	Dividends	150	
			450
	New fixed assets acquired		1,425
	Net increase in working capital:		
	Stocks	300	
	Debtors	550	
	Creditors	(150)	
	Reduction in liquid resources	(150)	
			550
			2,425

Figure 9.4   Hamilton Pumps Ltd: funds flow statement for the year 1990

Indeed there is probably a need for more long-term capital to replace the bank overdraft and finance future expansion unless profits recover very sharply, or the investment in working capital can actually be cut (which may be possible).

Obviously the assumptions above may be questioned; but they show the sort of approach to estimating future funds flows that can be taken. One of the keys is to make one's assumptions explicit; another is to quantify them.

9.5 Views of different users

9.5.1 Shareholders

At the AGM David Jack, as Chairman of the Company, spoke about the 1990 results. He explained that the fall in profits was largely due to inflationary pressures, and the smaller final dividend to the need for cash to expand

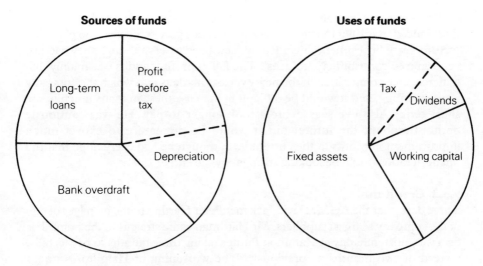

Figure 9.5 Hamilton Pumps Ltd: sources and uses of funds 1990

production capacity. He ended on an optimistic note, expecting only a polite question or two. But in this he was mistaken.

The investment manager of a life assurance company, which owned 100,000 shares in Hamilton Pumps Ltd, spoke first. He was unhappy that the company had halved the final dividend (from 2.50p per share to 1.25p). It was also worrying that the return on equity for the year had virtually halved from 26 per cent to 14 per cent. No wonder the share price had dropped from 150p to only 50p, with the price earnings (P/E) ratio down from 10 to less than 6. Nearly half the net assets were now financed by borrowing; and the high rates of interest on this debt meant the interest cover was now dangerously low, at four times. Even apart from the question of financing, the operating performance had got much worse with the return on net assets down from 35 per cent to 20 per cent.

Subsequent questioners, emboldened by this outspoken criticism, raised a number of other matters. Why were profit margins down from nearly 15 per cent to just over 10 per cent? How much of the increase in sales revenue was due to higher prices rather than increased volume? Was the rise in costs due to higher wages, increased materials prices, or what?

In reply, David Jack agreed that not enough thought had been given to the company's short-term cash needs. There had been an unexpected increase in materials prices towards the end of 1990, which had partly caused the increase in the level of end-year stocks. Although some of the borrowing needed to finance the expansion had been arranged on a medium-term (five-year) basis, the bank overdraft had risen faster, and higher, than expected. A major effort in the early months of 1991 to hold down working capital needs for funds (in respect of stocks and debtors) was now beginning to yield worthwhile results.

135

There was no question of postponing the expansion: it was much too late for that. Indeed, the 1990 return on investment ratios gave somewhat too gloomy a picture, since 'investment' included the new fixed assets although they had not yet begun to contribute to 'returns'. The fall in profit margins was mainly due to fierce price competition in the new overseas markets into which the company was expanding; and it would be difficult to increase these margins much in the short term. Also overseas debtors took longer to pay. He was cautiously optimistic about the future; but it would be premature to expect much improvement in profits in the current year, though he had every hope that the financial ratios would be looking stronger by the end of 1991.

9.5.2 Creditors

Three days after the AGM, David Jack met Peter Hardman, the manager of one of the company's largest suppliers. Mr Hardman came straight to the point. His firm was most unhappy at Hamilton Pumps taking three months to pay its bills, instead of two months as previously. The worsening of Hamilton's liquid position was shown by the current ratio having fallen from 1.4 to 1.2, and the acid test ratio from 0.84 to 0.71; and these suggested that Hamilton was under-capitalized. He feared that matters could get worse, especially if the bank was not prepared to increase the overdraft. Mr Hardman felt he had to insist that Hamilton Pumps settle all his firm's accounts within at most two months; failing which they would supply future orders only against cash payments.

David Jack explained that the company's practice had been to take about as long to pay suppliers as Hamilton's own customers took to pay. In 1990, both as a result of increased competition, and because more business was now being done abroad, they had been forced to allow customers a longer period of credit. Hamilton would certainly monitor debtors closely over the rest of 1991, and he expected no net increase in total debtors in the next few months.

Mr Hardman repeated that the overdue payment of accounts must be corrected. In order to avoid serious disruption to Hamilton's cash planning, he would accept this being done over the next three months.

9.5.3 Lenders

After lunch the same day, David Jack visited the bank, where he had arranged to discuss matters with the new branch manager, Christopher Blackburn. He explained that Hamilton was in the middle of a major expansion; and that at the same time higher prices were requiring a larger investment in trading stocks. In addition, it was now clear that Hamilton would have to reduce the amount of trade credit it had been taking from suppliers. As a result, the company would need to increase its bank overdraft – still around the December 1990 level of £1.0 million – to about £1.5 million.

Mr Blackburn expressed surprise, and said he had asked for the meeting because his head office had instructed him to arrange for Hamilton Pumps to cut back the overdraft to under £0.5 million by the end of 1991. From his viewpoint the signs for the immediate future were not encouraging, and even maintaining the present overdraft level, let alone increasing it, could be justified only if clear plans to overcome the company's problems were agreed.

In particular, Mr Blackburn was concerned that a major expansion was being so largely financed by short-term borrowing; and he was critical of the level of both stocks and debtors. These suggested some lack of management control, which needed to be speedily put right. It was also worrying that the expansion seemed to be into overseas markets where profit margins were lower and trade credit periods longer. The combination would continue to cause liquidity problems.

With hindsight, it appeared that the long-term loans totalling £600,000, which the bank had insisted on, had not been enough to relieve the pressure on short-term overdraft facilities. Given the poor profit record, however, and the high level of overall gearing, it seemed unlikely that more long-term borrowing could be arranged on acceptable terms. Since the expansion programme was nearly completed, the only solution now seemed to be a new issue of ordinary shares, though this would be difficult after the last 12 months' trading performance.

David Jack thanked Mr Blackburn for being so frank, but admitted that his refusal to permit any increase in the overdraft was rather a shock. He would have to consult his fellow-directors, and other members of the family. He knew members of the family would be reluctant to see an equity issue which would dilute their own holdings; since it would be impossible for them to put up any significant amount of new capital.

9.5.4 Employees

Later that week, David Jack met three representatives of the company's employees to talk about wage levels. The employees' representatives produced figures showing a 20 per cent increase in labour productivity in 1990:

	1989	1990
Total sales turnover	£6,500,000	£6,750,000
Total number of employees	260	225
Sales revenue per employee	£25,000	£30,000

They then put forward a claim for a wage increase of 20 per cent. This comprised three parts: (a) compensation for ten per cent inflation in 1990; (b) compensation for anticipated inflation of five per cent in 1991; and (c) a modest share of the 20 per cent increase in labour productivity, as evidenced by the above figures.

David Jack was unable to negotiate without discussing the claim with his senior managers, but he felt he ought to point out straightaway some of the problems with a wage claim of such a size. Total wages, together with associated costs (such as social security and pension contributions) had amounted to £2,250,000 in 1990. Thus a 20 per cent rise would cost nearly half a million pounds a year. This equalled almost the entire 1990 profit before tax. The 1990 dividend had to be cut; and the price had already fallen by two-thirds from its 1989 level. The effect of conceding the proposed wage increase would not only alarm the Stock Market, but probably cause the bank to call in the overdraft. Obviously it would not be in anyone's interest for the company to be driven into liquidation.

The employees' representatives, however, felt there was room for increasing the selling prices of Hamilton's products in order to provide for increased wages. They also believed that the fall in profits, and the increase in the bank overdraft, had been largely due to management's mistakes, for which they did not expect the employees to suffer.

Work section

A   Revision questions

A1   Give an example of a 'performance' ratio that might be useful for:
(a) a church; (b) an army; (c) a football team.

A2   Name one external and one internal standard for comparison.

A3   Name the three main groups of accounting ratios.

A4   What two different items in accounts do performance ratios compare profit to?

A5   Why does the return on net assets ratio use profit *before* interest?

A6   Define 'return on net assets'. Identify and define the two ratios into which it can be split.

A7   If a company had as much long-term borrowing as equity capital, what would its gearing ratio be?

A8   Identify and define one liquidity ratio. How does it differ from the other liquidity ratio?

A9   What are the possible consequences if the current ratio is:
(a) too high; (b) too low?

A10   Why does the acid test ratio leave out stocks?

A11   Could a company's dividend ratio ever be:
(a) exactly 1.0? (b) less than 1.0? (c) negative? Why in each case?

A12   Why might a company with an issued ordinary share capital of £1.0 m. not have 1 m. ordinary shares in issue?

A13   What steps do you need to take to calculate the price/earnings ratio?

A14   Distinguish between 'return on net assets' and 'return on equity'.

A15   Identify and define separately the numerator (top line) and the denominator (bottom line) in the following ratios: (a) gearing ratio; (b)price/earnings ratio; (c) current ratio.

A16   What are three problems in making comparisons over time?

A17   What are three problems in making comparisons with other firms?

A18   Why is depreciation added to profit before tax, in order to calculate 'internally-generated funds'?

A19   Name four sources of funds for a business firm.

A20   If the average number of days' credit taken by a firm's customers falls from 80 to 60, does that represent a source or a use of funds? Why?

A21   If a company owes more to its suppliers at the end of a period than at the beginning, is that a source or a use of funds? Why?

A22   What is the difference between a balance sheet and a funds flow statement?

A23   Can a company have a positive generation of funds from operations if it makes a loss before tax? Why or why not?

A24 Why must sources of funds for a period always exactly equal uses of funds?

A25 Name four different potential users of published financial accounts.

B Exercises and case studies

B1 Refer to Pilkington plc's group profit and loss account for the year ended 31 March 1989 in figure 5.11. Calculate as many as possible of the 14 financial ratios listed in Section 9.3.

B2 Refer to Courtaulds plc's group balance sheet at 31 March 1989, in figure 4.5. Calculate as many as possible of the 14 financial ratios listed in Section 9.3.

B3 Refer to the Hamilton Pumps' accounts (Section 9.2) and financial ratios (Section 9.3). If the net book value of the company's fixed assets were to be revalued upwards at 31 December, 1990, from £3.0 m. to £5.0 m., which of the 14 accounting ratios would be affected? How?

B4 Refer to 3.2.3 (e).
Draw up a funds flow statement for Thompson Brothers Ltd for the year ended 31 December.

B5 Super Traders Ltd's accounts for the calendar year 1990 contain the following information as at 31 December 1990:
There were:
(i) No current assets other than stocks, debtors and bank balance.
(ii) No liabilities other than shareholders' funds and current liabilities.
(iii) No assets other than fixed assets and current assets.

Current ratio (current assets : current liabilities)	$1\frac{3}{4} : 1$
Acid test ratio (debtors and bank : current liabilities)	$1\frac{1}{4} : 1$
Net current assets	£75,000
Issued share capital in ordinary shares	£100,000
Fixed assets as a percentage of share capital	60 per cent
Stock turnover (based on year-end stock)	4.16 times
Debtor turnover based on a 52-week year	7 weeks

a. Calculate the value of each of the current assets

b. Ignoring taxation, construct in as much detail as possible the balance sheet of Super Traders Ltd as at 31 December 1990.

B6 College Printers Ltd's accounts for 1990 are given opposite. Comment on the company's performance and prospects.

B7 Arrange to get the latest accounts of any public quoted company. Analyse them from the point of view of:
a. a shareholder;
b. the company's bank manager;
c. an employee;
d. a student of accounting.

College Printers Ltd
Balance sheet at 30 June 1990

1989 (£'000)			1990 (£'000)
	Fixed assets		
48	Plant at cost	74	
16	Less: accumulated depreciation	24	
	32		50
	Current assets		
22	Stocks	30	
56	Debtors	60	
2	Cash	—	
	80		90
	112		140
	Less: current liabilities		
–	Bank overdraft	9	
77	Creditors	86	
3	Taxation	5	
	80		100
	32		40
	8 *Long-term loan*		10
	24		30
	Shareholders' funds		
10	Called-up share capital	10	
14	Retained profits	20	
24		30	

Profit and loss account for year ended 30 June 1990

160	Sales turnover	200	
14	Profit, before charging:	25	
4	Depreciation	8	
1	Interest payable	2	
3	Taxation	5	
8		15	
6	Net profit	10	
4	Dividend paid	4	
2	Profit retained	6	

Figure 9.6 College Printers Ltd: balance sheet and profit and loss account

B8   The accounts of Hamilton Pumps Ltd for the year ended 31 December
1991 are set out in figures 9.7 and 9.8.

Hamilton Pumps Ltd: balance sheet at 31 December 1991

(£'000)

Fixed assets		
Freehold property		800
Plant and equipment		2,400
		3,200
Current assets		
Stocks	1,250	
Debtors	1,750	
Liquid resources	200	
	3,200	
Less: current liabilities		
Creditors	1,600	
Bank overdraft	550	
Taxation	250	
Dividends payable	100	
	2,500	
Net working capital		700
Net assets		3,900
Shareholders' funds		
Issued ordinary 25p shares		1,000
Retained profits		1,800
		2,800
Long-term liabilities		
Mortgage debenture	500	
Other loans	600	
		1,100
Capital employed		3,900

Figure 9.7 Hamilton Pumps Ltd: balance sheet

Calculate the following financial ratios for 1991:

a. Performance measures.

b. Gearing and liquidity measures.

c. Shareholder measures (share price at 31.12.91 = 100p).

B9   Refer to B8.

a. Prepare a funds flow statement for Hamilton Pumps for 1991.

b. Prepare your own estimate of possible funds flows in 1992 - making and stating explicitly what you think are reasonable assumptions.

B10 Refer to B8 and B9.

From your analysis of the 1991 results for Hamilton Pumps Ltd, what are the key comments you would make and the questions you would ask of the managing director:

a. as a shareholder?

b. as Mr Blackburn, his bank manager?

c. as a representative of the employees?

Hamilton Pumps Ltd:profit and loss account for the year 1991

		(£'000)
Sales		7,500
Operating profit*		925
Interest payable		175
Profit before tax		750
Taxation		250
Profit after tax		500
Ordinary dividends:		
Interim, 1.25p	50	
Final, 2.50p	100	
		150
Retained profit for the year		350

*After charging depreciation £400,000.

Figure 9.8 Hamilton Pumps Ltd: profit and loss account

B11 Identify, with a brief explanation, how adjusting historical cost accounts to allow for inflation would affect:

a. performance measures

b. gearing and liquidity measures

c. shareholder measures.

143

B12 **Farley Components Limited**

After their new company, Farley Components Ltd, had been going for six months, George Farrell and Andrew Leyton met to decide what to do next. The company seemed to be off to a good start, and they were thinking of devoting their full time to it.

Mr Farrell, 29, was a production engineer with Godfrey Machines, a large Midlands firm, for whom Mr Leyton, 32, worked on the sales staff. Each earned a salary of £15,000 a year. In 1989 Mr Farrell had invented a new type of stepping switch (an electrical device used in product testing). In his own time he developed a working model and applied for a patent. After tests and discussion, the quality control department of Godfrey Machines agreed to purchase 20 stepping switch units for £900 each.

Messrs Farrell and Leyton thereupon formed Farley Components Ltd on 1 March 1990. Each took 6,000 shares in the company, in exchange for £6,000 cash, a large fraction of their savings. Mr Farrell assigned all his rights in the invention to the new company in exchange for a non-interest-bearing 10-year debenture for £12,000.

Making the stepping switch involved mainly assembly and wiring, which the two men did themselves in Mr Leyton's basement, working evenings and weekends. They completed the twenty units for Godfrey Machines, and received payment, by July 1990. During the six months from March to August, the company also sold five more stepping switches to different customers.

Throughout the period, Messrs Farrell and Leyton each worked about ten hours a week, making stepping switches, answering enquiries, and handling other Farley problems. They chose not to pay themselves any salary, since the company needed its limited cash to buy components and to pay for their specially-designed equipment.

Meanwhile Mr Leyton wrote and placed free 'product announcements' and a small amount of paid advertising in trade journals. These resulted in a number of enquiries from other companies, which encouraged the two owners to seek sales more actively. In July they placed larger advertisements costing a total of £3,000.

In order to be able to fill promptly the orders expected as a result, they continued to assemble stepping switches in July and August. By the end of August they had in stock six completed units and also a sizeable supply of printed circuits and other component parts.

Early in September 1990, Mr Leyton prepared the financial statements shown in figures 9.9 and 9.10. In addition to the parts and components shown in the balance sheet, Farley Components had also ordered £5,000 worth of other components, to be delivered in late September. Upon seeing the statements Mr Farrell commented as follows: 'Not bad for a starter. Even after deducting all our advertising costs, we still show a nice profit, and a splendid rate of return on our investment.'

	(£)
Sales turnover	22,500
Cost of sales	11,800
Gross profit	10,700
Advertising	4,400
Other expenses	1,500
	5,900
Net profit	4,800

Figure 9.9 Farley Components Ltd: profit and loss account for the six months ended 31 August 1990

	(£)	(£)
Fixed assets		
Equipment at cost	7,900	
Patent rights	12,000	
		19,900
Current assets		
Completed switches	2,900	
Stock of parts and components	6,200	
Debtors	1,800	
Cash	700	
		11,600
		31,500
Liabilities		
Creditors	2,700	
10-year debenture	12,000	
		14,700
Shareholders' funds		
Paid-up share capital	12,000	
Retained profits	4,800	
		16,800
		31,500

Figure 9.10 Farley Components Ltd: balance sheet at 31 August 1990

a. How well are they doing?

b. What advice, if any, would you give?

B13 Set out in figure 9.11 are 'balance sheet percentages' of six companies in different industries: distilling; mail order; motor vehicle manufacturing; pharmaceuticals; retail store; tobacco. Identify each column of figures with a particular industry. The percentages relate each of the balance sheet items (and annual sales revenue) to net assets (= to long-term capital employed).

	A	B	C	D	E	F
Fixed Assets						
Cost or valuation	101	24	104	26	55	66
Less: accum. depreciation	45	6	3	9	20	33
Net book value	56	18	101	17	35	33
Goodwill and other assets			1	8	23	25
Current Assets						
Stocks	61	63	18	72	30	72
Debtors	53	102	4	21	31	35
Cash	32	–	12	9	16	15
	146	165	34	102	77	122
Less: current liabilities						
Bank loans	20	26	5	6	2	23
Creditors	75	52	14	11	23	54
Dividends payable	–	3	4	3	3	1
Taxation	7	2	13	7	7	2
	102	83	36	27	35	80
=Working capital (CA – CL)	44	82	(2)	75	42	42
Net assets	100	100	100	100	100	100
Long-term debt	12	22	8	13	23	39
Deferred tax	4	2				3
Minority interests						17
Shareholders' funds	84	76	92	87	77	41
Capital employed	100	100	100	100	100	100
Sales turnover (annual)	318	310	278	111	151	149

Figure 9.11 Balance sheet percentages

B14 Keys Ltd makes and sells metal castings. In 1986 and 1987 its sales were £1,000,000 and £1,400,000 respectively. The balance sheet is shown in figure 9.12.
a. Calculate, for each year, the following ratios:
(i) current
(ii) stock turnover
(iii) debtors turnover
(iv) asset turnover
b.On the basis of the information available, do you feel that Keys Ltd was run more efficiently in 1987 than in 1986 ? Explain your view.
What further information would you wish to have in order to judge Keys Ltd's performance?

Balance Sheet of Keys Ltd at 31 December 1987

1986 (£'000)		1987 (£'000)	1986 (£'000)		1987 (£'000)
400	Shareholders Funds	420	150	Land and buildings	150
50	Long term liabilities	50	200	Machinery	150
100	Creditors	120	200	Stocks	150
100	Bank	60	100	Debtors	200
650		650	650		650

Figure 9.12 Keys Ltd: balance sheet at 31 December 1987

(UCLES International Examinations, 1989, GCE A level Business Studies)

B15   The balances in the books of account of XY Limited after the
preparation of the Profit and Loss Account for the year ended 31
December, 1985 were as follows:

Share Capital (authorised and issued)	
200,000 Ordinary Shares	100,000
Capital Reserve Account	10,000
Balance of undistributed profit	6,000
General Reserve	35,000
9% Debentures (secured on Freehold Property)	20,000
Freehold Property (at cost)	110,000
Equipment (at cost)	30,000
Vehicles (at cost)	18,000
Provision for Depreciation:	
Equipment	11,000
Vehicles	16,800
Stock of goods	48,200
Debtors	19,000
Bank Overdraft	800
Creditors	9,600
Proposed Dividend	16,000

Sales for the year amounted to £152,000 and purchases to £115,200. All
are on a credit basis.

Required:

(a) Prepare the balance sheet as at 31 December, 1985.
(b) On the basis of the above figures calculate:
   1. the average period of credit allowed to debtors
   2. the par value of an ordinary share
(c) Outline the difference between a Capital Reserve Account and a
     General Reserve
(d) Calculate the current assets ratio and the liquid ratio and comment
     on the liquid position of XY Limited at 31 December, 1985.

(International Baccalaureate, 1986, Business Studies Higher Level)

C Essay questions

C1 In analysing a company's business position, what information would you want to examine apart from the company's latest accounts? Why?

C2 What are the most serious problems likely to be met in trying to make comparisons (a) over time and (b) between companies?

C3 Should employees be given access to more accounting information about their company? Consider the arguments for and against.

C4 A correspondent to the *Financial Times* once suggested that, to help readers of accounts, each company's annual report should print in bold type on its front cover the statement: 'The profit per cent on capital employed is *x* per cent.' Discuss this view.

C5 Comment on the following statement by a leading American accountant: 'Perhaps comparability among companies and industries is unattainable – perhaps it is not even desirable. Much of the demand for uniformity in accounting is based on a wish for unattainable certainty in man's financial affairs, and on a desire that the extremely complicated elements reflected in financial reports be made simple of understanding, even by the uninformed and ignorant.'

C6 'Ratios extracted from one company's accounts are virtually useless without additional information'. What other information would you need in order to make them valuable ?

C7 A shareholder finds certain aspects of a company's activities recorded in the annual report and accounts. To what extent do the details supplied allow him to make an assessment of the state of his investment?

C8 What are the limitations on the use of ratios to determine a company's liquidity position from its final accounts? How might these limitations be overcome and what other sources are available?

C9 Outline the objectives of funds flow statements and discuss the usefulness of such statements to a business.

C10 'Company directors are ultimately responsible to one group alone – the shareholders'. Critically evaluate this statement.

10

Costs

Plan of the chapter:

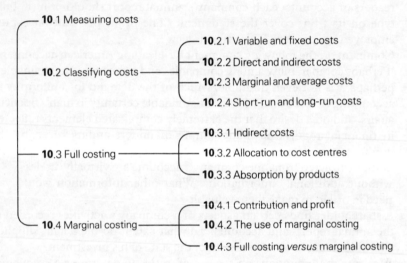

Fig.10.0
Objective: *To describe the main ways of classifying and of measuring costs in business.*

Synopsis: *There are four basic ways to classify costs in business: between (1) variable and fixed, (2) direct and indirect, (3) marginal and average, and (4) short-run and long-run. Full costing allocates all costs to products, by making assumptions about indirect costs. Marginal costing does not try to allocate indirect costs to products. Each approach has pros and cons.*

10.1 Measuring 'cost'

The **cost** of something is what one must give up to get it. This is often money – the generally accepted 'medium of exchange' – though it need not be: it might be time, or some other scarce resource.

But 'cost' is not the same as 'value'. Oscar Wilde said a cynic knows the price of everything and the value of nothing. Someone who buys a book for £5 is presumably 'valuing' it at *more than* £5 (he prefers having the book to having £5): he might have been willing to pay twice as much for the book.

Why does a business measure its costs?

1   To measure profit, by comparing costs with revenues.
2   To help control costs, by comparing them with pre-set standards.

It may be possible to find data for costs that have already been incurred. But estimating future costs is not so easy. Past costs may not reflect present, let alone future, conditions. The past period may not have been typical; or some costs may have changed since then.

An alternative is to use standard costs as a basis for forecasting the future. Actual past results can be modified to allow for expected changes, so that standard costs genuinely become a useful 'standard'.

A firm estimates standard costs per unit of production:

1   to compare actual costs against;
2   to value stock in hand at the end of a period (see Chapter 7);
3   to help set selling prices;
4   to establish transfer prices between different parts of a business.

One should beware of spurious accuracy! It is more important to get a rough idea of relevant costs than to make supposedly precise calculations to the nearest fraction of a penny. Most costs can only be estimates, which often depend heavily on the underlying assumptions. Indeed, some accountants are reluctant to provide cost figures unless they know for what purpose managers want to use them!

10.2 Classifying costs

Example: Gilbert Ltd keeps a four-year-old car in a garage with three other cars. The annual garage rent is £2,400, insurance costs £240 a year, and the annual

	Direct (£)	+	Indirect (£)	=	Total (£)
Variable costs					
Petrol (5p per mile)	600				840
Maintenance (2p per mile)	240				
Fixed costs					
Insurance	240				2,460
Licence fee	120				
Depreciation	1,500				
Garage rent			600		
Total costs	2,700	+	600	=	3,300

Figure 10.1 Car operating costs for next year

151

licence fee is £120. The car does eight miles to the litre, petrol costs 40p per litre, and maintenance is reckoned to cost 2p per mile. Depreciation is £1,500 per year, and the car is expected to travel 12,000 miles next year. Figure 10.1 (on previous page) classifies the expected operating costs for next year between variable and fixed (Section 10.2.1) and between direct and indirect (Section 10.2.2).

10.2.1 Variable and fixed costs

The expressions 'variable' and 'fixed' in relation to costs refer to the volume of activity or output. Thus a **variable cost** changes in proportion to output, while a **fixed cost** remains unchanged whatever the volume of output.

Example: Gilbert's variable costs (petrol and maintenance) are 7p per mile; while fixed costs (licence fee, insurance, depreciation and garage rent) are £2,460 a year however many miles the car travels. Figure 10.2 charts the two different kinds of costs.

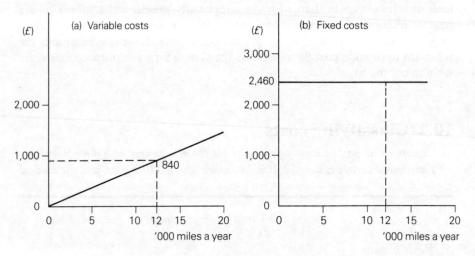

Figure 10.2 Variable costs and fixed costs

The distinction is not always clear-cut. Some expenses may be semi-variable: telephone costs and other utility bills often consist of a basic fixed charge plus an extra rate varying with usage (a 'two-part tariff'). And direct labour costs are often partly or wholly fixed.

Fixed costs are fixed *over a given range of activity*. Outside that range they may alter as a result of changes in the scale of the business. Some firms also distinguish **non-variable costs,** such as advertising or research. These may change over time; but as a result of management's 'discretionary' decisions, rather than simply because of a change in volume. If sales volume fell, for example, outlays on advertising might well be *increased*.

10.2.2 Direct and indirect costs

Most variable costs, and some fixed costs, are **direct costs** which can be directly identified with a unit or product. Gilbert's only **indirect cost** is garage rent. To estimate this, we have to use some reasonable basis of allocating the total garage rent cost between the four cars, perhaps the relative floor space occupied.

Some indirect ('overhead') costs may vary more or less with output even though they cannot be directly identified with particular units of production. On the other hand, it may be possible to identify certain fixed costs directly with products. Thus there are four possible combinations:

1 direct and variable, for example, raw materials;
2 direct and fixed, for example, depreciation;
3 indirect and variable, for example, energy costs;
4 indirect and fixed, for example, factory rent.

Whether a cost is direct or indirect may often be a matter of convenience. With enough effort it might be possible to identify nearly all costs with specific operations. But a management accountant must always ask: is the resulting 'accuracy' worth the cost of getting the information?

10.2.3 Marginal and average costs

The **marginal cost** is the extra cost incurred by producing one more unit of output. Gilbert's marginal cost of running a car is 7p per mile. Where costs are being related to sales revenue, the difference between selling price and marginal cost is called the **contribution** per unit. (This is the 'contribution' to fixed costs and profit (see Chapter 11).) Thus if Gilbert were hiring out its car at 30p per mile, the contribution would be 23p per mile.

The **average cost** is total costs divided by the total number of units of output. So Gilbert's average cost per mile, assuming the car travels the expected 12,000 miles a year, is 27.5p per mile (= £3,300/12,000 miles). For many short-term business decisions it is marginal, not average, costs which matter. One of the most important aspects of management accounting is deciding which costs are relevant for a particular decision.

> *Example: A nice example of the difference between average and marginal costs is given by the story of the office worker who went to have a haircut. When he returned, his boss asked him where he'd been.*
> *Worker: To have a haircut.*
> *Boss: In office hours?*
> *Worker: Well, it grew in office hours.*
> *Boss: Not all of it surely?*
> *Worker: No; but then I didn't have it all cut off!*

Economists often regard marginal costs per unit of production as falling at first, due to economies of scale. Later marginal per-unit costs start to rise, due to diminishing returns, overtime premiums, etc. Unlike economists, accountants usually assume that marginal per-unit costs are constant (flat), at least throughout the 'relevant range' of output (see Chapter 11).

10.2.4 Short-run and long-run costs

So far we have been discussing costs without much reference to time. But in the 'long run' a firm can change the scale of its operations. The **short run** is a period of time during which the inputs of some factors of production cannot be changed. The factor which is 'fixed' is often capital equipment, but it might be land or labour or materials. It follows that in the **long run** inputs of all factors of production can be varied. A producer can alter plant capacity, a distributor can increase warehouse size, and so on. Thus in the long run, nothing is ultimately 'fixed'. This is another way of saying that *in the long run even so-called 'fixed' costs are variable.*

As we all know, another thing that takes time is learning. A firm's workers are likely to know more about how to make a product after they have been doing so for some months than on the first day. This may enable a firm to reduce its average costs per unit. The learning may relate more to the volume of output produced than to the amount of time elapsed. If so, the firm with the largest market share, and therefore the largest output per unit of time, will be learning at a faster rate than its competitors. If this does result in lower costs, a firm which is 'further along the learning curve' can either reduce its selling price, or make a larger contribution margin on each unit sold. *Being the lowest cost producer can provide an important competitive advantage.*

10.3 Full costing

10.3.1 Indirect costs

Full costing aims to assign all business costs to particular products. Direct costs can be identified with products; but not indirect ('overhead') costs. Hence full costing first allocates indirect costs to cost centres; and then attributes the total costs of each cost centre to various products. The process of assigning indirect costs to individual products can only be approximate. The question is whether the product costs are accurate enough to be useful in running the business. Figure 10.3 outlines the full costing approach.

10.3.2 Allocation to cost centres

A cost centre is part of a business for which costs can be identified. It may be a whole factory, part of a factory, or even a single machine. Different cost centres may be suitable for different levels of management decision. For example, figure 10.4 shows possible cost centres for a company producing vehicles.

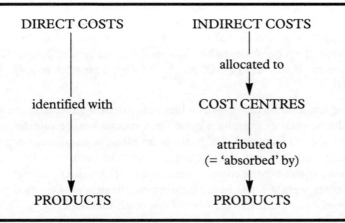

Figure 10.3 *Full ('absorption') costing*

Level of decision	Possible cost centres
1 Group directors	Operating divisions: cars, buses, trucks
2 Truck division directors	Truck factories A, B, C
3 Factory director	Truck assembly lines 1, 2, 3
4 Works manager	Welding machines, presses, lathes
5 Press shop foreman	100-tonne presses, 50-tonne presses, etc.

Figure 10.4 *Cost centres at various levels*

10.3.3 Absorption by products
Once all indirect overhead costs have been allocated to cost centres, they can be charged to individual products by sharing them out among all the units passing through each cost centre. The accounting term for this is **absorption** (the products 'absorb' the overhead costs).

In order for products to absorb indirect overhead costs, there needs to be an overhead absorption rate (or 'recovery rate'). The calculations for this are based on standard, or 'normal', volume. The pre-determined rate of overhead absorption for each product is then applied to actual volume in order to determine 'actual' full costs for each product.

The rate of overhead absorption may vary for different products. The most usual bases for the calculations are:

1 direct labour hours;
2 direct labour costs;
3 machine hours;
4 units of output.

155

Example: Suppose a business expects total indirect overheads allocated to a cost centre next year to be £480,000; and the cost centre to operate at 80 per cent of its full 'capacity' of 100,000 direct labour hours per year. Then for the purpose of product costing, overheads will be 'absorbed' by each product passing through that cost centre, at the rate of £6.00 per direct labour hour (that is, £48,000/80,000 hours).

There are several reasons why a business might wish to estimate the cost of its products, such as quoting a price for a special job, or valuing products in stock at the end of a period. To do so, it can estimate the direct costs (materials and direct labour costs), and then simply add on the estimated indirect overheads, often expressed as a percentage of the direct labour cost. So if labour costs were £4 per hour, indirect overheads (@ £6 per direct labour hour) would represent 150 per cent of direct labour costs.

10.4 Marginal costing

10.4.1 Contribution and profit

Direct costs can be identified with particular products, while indirect costs ('overheads') cannot. So any allocation of indirect costs to products, such as full costing attempts, is subject to a large margin of error.

In relating costs to sales revenues, therefore, it may be best to attribute *only* direct costs to products. This approach, known as **marginal costing** (or 'contribution costing'), avoids arbitrary guesses about how much of the indirect costs 'belong' to any particular product.

The excess of sales revenues over the direct costs is the **contribution** (towards covering indirect costs and profit). Of course contribution is *not the same* as profit. In order to determine profit, total indirect costs must be deducted from the total contributions of all the firm's products.

Contributions	=	Indirect costs	+	Profit
Profit	=	Contributions	–	Indirect costs

In estimating each individual product's contribution under marginal costing, there are three simple steps:
(a) for each cost centre, identify direct costs with the proper product;
(b) for each product, total the direct costs from the various cost centres;
(c) for each product, deduct total direct costs from sales revenue, to determine the contribution.

These three steps are illustrated in figure 10.5 with some hypothetical numbers. The final stage, for the firm as a whole, is then:
(d) add together all the products' contributions, and deduct total indirect costs in order to determine total profit. This is also shown in figure 10.5.

(a) *For each cost centre, identify direct costs with the right product:*

(£'000)	Cost centre 1	Cost centre 2	Cost centre 3
Product A	5	3	8
Product B	4	2	6
Product C	3	1	4
Total	12	6	18

(b) *For each product, total the direct costs from the various cost centres:*

(£'000)	Product A	Product B	Product C
Cost centre 1	5	4	3
Cost centre 2	3	2	1
Cost centre 3	8	6	4
Total	16	12	8

(c) *For each product, deduct total direct costs from sales revenue, to give contribution:*

(£'000)	Product A	Product B	Product C		TOTAL
Sales revenue	30	20	10	=	60
Direct costs	16	12	8	=	36
= Contribution	14	8	2	=	24

(d) *Finally, for the firm as a whole, add together all the products' contributions, and deduct total indirect costs, in order to determine total profit:*

(£'000)	Product A	Product B	Product C		TOTAL
Contribution	14	8	2	=	24
Indirect costs	NOT ALLOCATED				18
= Profit					6

Figure 10.5 Direct costs, product contribution, and total profit

10.4.2 The use of marginal costing

Marginal costing does not try to allocate all overheads to particular products where accurate data is lacking. It can apply to the future as well as the past. Marginal costing can compare actual current performance with planned performance budgets. This kind of variance analysis is helpful in seeing which aspects of the business may need corrective action.

Marginal costing can include new information quickly. This may not be possible for more complex methods, which soon tend to become out of date. It is relatively simple. Since managers who are not expert accountants will need to use regular management reports, the simpler the analysis is to understand the better.

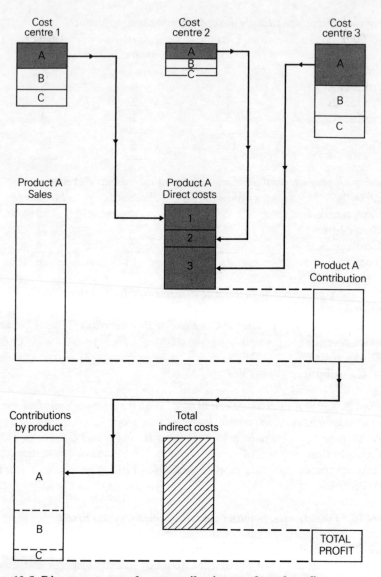

Figure 10.5 Direct costs, product contribution, and total profit

It focusses attention on products which appear to be making only small contributions. There may be good reasons for this (though a negative contribution would be unusual in most firms). A new product, for example, may take time for sales to develop; or an old product may be about to be phased out.

There are certain disadvantages with marginal costing. Perhaps the most important is that some people may tend to confuse contribution with profit.

Thus they may regard even a small positive contribution as adequate. Since a firm must cover indirect overheads before it makes any profit, however, the positive contributions from all the firm's products need in total to be at least large enough to cover the indirect overheads.

Marginal costing tends to be looking at fairly short-term aspects of a business, where the scale of operations is already fixed. Decisions about changing the scale of the business will need a good deal more information. It is not always easy to tell what is 'marginal' in a longer-term context.

It may be difficult to tell how much contribution to require from any particular product. But this problem should be resolved at the budgeting stage. The state of the market for each product is critical. For example, if costs increase it may be difficult to raise selling prices, at least in the short term. This will partly depend on the firm's competitors. It is true that some firms try to set their selling prices on the basis of direct costs plus a 'mark-up'. But this 'mark-up' percentage may not be the same for all products, and it may not be possible to maintain a product's level of mark-up if selling conditions change.

10.4.3 Full costing versus marginal costing

Both full costing and marginal costing are widely used in practice. If indirect overheads form a high proportion of total costs, management may be keen to try to allocate them between products. And the extent to which some overheads can be identified with particular products is often a matter of degree.

For example, factory rent may be allocated on the basis of floor space, even though this is not the only possible basis. Or indirect supervision may be split between products on the basis of the direct labour hours worked on each product, even if actual supervision is not split in exactly the same proportions.

Full costing does arrive at a 'profit' (or 'loss', of course) for each product; but only after more or less arbitrary allocations of indirect overheads. The accounting calculations and management reports can be difficult to understand; especially since changes in stock levels can seriously affect the results (see problem B12 in Chapter 7).

Marginal costing is simpler to apply and easier to understand. But it does risk pressure to 'shave' margins as long as a product shows any positive contribution. If this is not carefully watched, the total of the contributions of all a firm's products may not be large enough to cover the total indirect overheads. The result, of course, will then be an overall loss.

Work section

A   Revision questions

A1   What is the 'cost' of something?

A2   Why is someone who pays £20 for a pair of shoes not 'valuing' the shoes at £20?

A3   What are two main purposes of measuring business costs?

A4   What is a standard cost?

A5   Define (a) a variable cost, (b) a fixed cost. Give an example of each.

A6   Define (a) a semi-variable cost, (b) a non-variable cost. Give an example of each.

A7   Define (a) a direct cost, (b) an indirect cost. Give an example of each.

A8   Why is it sometimes a matter of *convenience* whether a particular cost is classified as direct or indirect?

A9   Define (a) marginal cost, (b) average cost.

A10   Define the 'short run'.

A11   What is a cost centre?

A12   Why are cost centres needed for full costing?

A13   What are the two stages by which full costing assigns indirect overheads to particular products?

A14   Suggest three different bases for allocating indirect overheads to cost centres.

A15   What criteria should be used to decide which basis is most appropriate for allocating indirect overheads to cost centres?

A16   What does 'absorption' mean in costing?

A17   Name three possible bases for overhead absorption by products.

A18   What is meant by the 'overhead recovery rate'?

A19   What volume of activity is an overhead absorption ('recovery') rate based on? Why?

A20   Under full costing, why is the calculation of product cost likely to be only approximate?

A21   What is the difference between contribution and profit?

A22   What are the key steps in determining a product's contribution?

A23   If you know the contribution for each of a firm's products, how can you calculate the firm's total profit?

A24   Name two advantages and two disadvantages of full (absorption) costing.

A25   Name two advantages and two disadvantages of marginal (contribution) costing.

B Exercises and case studies

B1   Ring-a-Ding produces an iron and glass telephone shelf. There are three main processes: machining, painting and assembly. The direct costs are expressed as costs per unit of output:

	Machining	Painting	Assembly
Direct labour	20p	10p	30p
Direct materials	40p	10p	20p

The firm is currently making 10,000 shelves a year; sales turnover is £35,000; and related overheads amount to £14,000 a year.
  a. Allocate the overheads on the basis of direct labour, and draw up a table showing the cost allocation between the three processes.
  b. What is the profit per shelf?
  c. What would be the effect of an increase in Ring-a-Ding's production and sales of telephone shelves?

B2   Refer to B1. Ring-a-Ding has adopted a system of allocating costs to cost centres which yields the following total annual costs:

	Machining (£)	Painting (£)	Assembly (£)
Direct labour	10,000	12,000	6,000
Direct materials	20,000	10,000	4,500
Variable overheads	12,500	12,000	8,000
Fixed overheads (at 60% of factory cost*)	25,500	20,400	11,100

*Factory cost = Direct costs + Variable overheads

The telephone shelf passes through all three cost centres, and is allocated a proportion of each centre's costs (since several products pass through each cost centre). The shelf's costs are allocated on the following bases for each cost centre:
Direct labour: 20 per cent, 25 per cent and 15 per cent of direct labour respectively for machining, painting and assembly.
Direct materials: 20 per cent of the direct materials in each case.
Variable overheads: according to each cost centre's proportion of total direct labour for telephone shelves (i.e. 20, 25 and 15 per cent respectively.)

Fixed overheads: 60 per cent of factory cost.

The shelf sells for £3.50, and production and sales are currently running at 10,000 units a year.

a. Draw up a full costing statement for the telephone shelf, showing the costs per unit.

b. What is the profit per item?

c. What profit would you expect if selling price remained the same, but the sales volume and the total variable costs increased by 10 per cent?

B3 Sansom Ltd, a light engineering firm, has received an enquiry for 10,000 components, which would need to be turned, milled and ground. Each 100 components will require 10 metres of 12 mm diameter steel bar, at a cost of 90p per metre. Turning output is 30 pieces per minute, milling 60 pieces per minute, and grinding 15 pieces per minute. Only one machine of each type is available, each staffed by a skilled machinist paid £3.00 per hour.

At the machine outputs above, works fixed overheads would correspond to 45p per 100 components. The variable overheads can be allocated as 100 per cent of direct labour costs.

Sansom's company policy is to charge a selling price which is 20 per cent above total standard costs.

a. Calculate the standard cost for the order.

b. Calculate the proposed selling price per 100 units.

c. What are the main advantages and disadvantages of this system of determining (i) product cost and (ii) selling price?

B4 The managing director of Tapir Trousers Ltd has decided to abandon production of one of the company's four lines. This decision was based on a costing statement (reproduced below) which showed Style III as losing £2 500 a year.

(£'000 per year)	Style	I	II	III	IV
Direct labour		10	7	5	8
Direct materials		10	8	6	6
Variable overheads		10	10	4	6
		30	25	15	20
Fixed overheads		15	$12\frac{1}{2}$	$7\frac{1}{2}$	10
Total cost		45	$37\frac{1}{2}$	$22\frac{1}{2}$	30
Sales revenue		47	55	20	38
Profit (loss)		2	$17\frac{1}{2}$	$(2\frac{1}{2})$	8

a. Was the decision justified on the basis of the information shown?
b. Suggest an alternative presentation of the data. What recommendations for action does this new presentation suggest?
c. On the original basis for the decision, suppose the fixed overheads are re-allocated in the same proportions as now between the remaining styles. What new decision is implied? What is the ultimate result of following this approach?

B5 Fraser and Dixon Ltd sell portable radios. Different price and marketing strategies are used in the three national sales territories (North and Midlands, South-East and South-West). The table below shows the results, together with transport costs, for each territory:

	North and Midlands	South-East	South-West
Number of sales p.a.	40,000	50,000	30,000
Price per radio (£)	45	40	50
Marketing expenditure (£'000)	400	600	500
Transport cost (£'000)	100	50	100

The variable cost of production per radio (that is, direct labour, direct materials, and indirect overheads) is £25. Fixed overheads are running at £600,000 per year.
a. What is the present contribution of each sales territory?
b. What is the firm's present profit?
c. What would be the effect of raising the price by £4.00 in each area, assuming that this would not reduce the sales volume?

B6 Broadleaze Ltd, makers of ornamental household and garden goods, had recently diversified into car accessories. There were four main reasons:
1 The car accessory market was an area of rapid expansion.
2 The firm had a good working knowledge of the local car industry.
3 The existing plant could be readily adapted to the new products.
4 The labour force was both skilled and adaptable.
After some product rationalization, the firm was struggling to achieve the right balance between products, and also to overcome the problem of unused capacity. The main problem, however, was how fast and how much extra production they could squeeze out of the factory without drastically altering the firm's cost structure.
At present the firm's fixed overheads were £720,000 a year. The present level of budgeted sales was £275,000 per month, but market expansion could raise this figure to £395,000 per month. As a result of such a rise in sales, direct material costs would rise from £30,000 to £44,000 per month, while the monthly wage bill would rise from £44,000 to £85,000.

The above increase in plant utilization (to its maximum capacity) would cause estimated indirect overheads to rise as follows:

	At present volume (£/month)	At increased volume (£/month)
Maintenance	22,000	43,000
Stores	20,000	30,000
Factory admin.	18,000	26,000
	60,000	99,000

As the firm's accountant, you are asked to:

a. Prepare a contribution cost statement from the data given, in order to allow the Board to make a rapid assessment of the possibilities.

b. Prepare a statement for the Board, explaining (with reasons) the course of action you would suggest.

c. What misgivings might you have about your analysis in (b) above?

B7 'Business is getting worse!', said the Managing Director of Lite-Rite Ltd, a firm which made adjustable reading lamps. The reason for the remark was the latest profit and loss statement for the period January to September of the current year (figure 10.6–see opposite).The sales manager had just received a special order for 5,000 lamps at a contract price of £13.00 each. He put this proposal to the managing director, who said: 'This really is the limit! A special order at less than the cost price of £14.60 per lamp, as well as an extra £2,000 fixed overhead cost for a special design!'

a. Should the firm make the special order? Give your reasons.

b. Should the firm accept orders of this type in the future?

c. What is the firm's monthly breakeven sales revenue?

B8 A public utility operates at 100 per cent of capacity for only four hours out of every 24 hours, at 50 per cent of capacity for a further four hours, and at only 25 per cent of capacity for the remaining 16 hours each day. Total operating costs are £96,000 per day. How should costs be allocated? (Capacity used is shown below.)

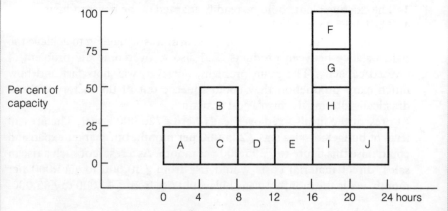

Figure 10.7 Usage of capacity

Lite-Rite Ltd
Profit and loss statement January to September

	(£)	(£)
Sales revenue (15,000 units @ £25 each)		375,000
Less costs:		
Materials (15,000 units @ £1.70)	25,500	
Labour (15,000 units @ £7.50)	112,500	
Manufacturing overheads:		
Variable (15,000 units @ £0.90)	13,500	
Fixed ($\frac{9}{12}$ of £180,000)	135,000	
Admin. selling and distribution overhead		
at £10,500 per month	94,500	
		381,000
Net profit (loss)		(6,000)

A unit cost statement is set out below:

	Cost per unit
	(£)
Direct materials	1.70
Direct labour	7.50
Manufacturing overheads:	
Variable	0.90
Fixed (based on 40,000 units a year)	4.50
= Total production cost	14.60

Figure 10.6 Lite-Rite profit and loss statement

B9 Gulls Ltd makes components for the motor industry. There are four
departments, milling (M), manufacturing (N), packing (P) and
administration (A). The following cost information is available:

	M	N	P	A
Number of workers	20	15	8	4
Wages per worker/hour	£4.50	£4.00	£3.75	£5.00
Materials per unit	50p	40p	20p	–
Capital used at cost	£120,000	£150,000	£140,000	£50,000
Working hours/week	40	40	40	40
Indirect overheads/week	£200	£250	£100	£40

On average 2,000 units are produced per week. Assume that there are 50
weeks per year. Gulls pays £18,000 rent per annum. A weekly budget for

each department is required. Note that the costs of the administration department (A) are to be allocated to the other three productive departments in accordance with direct labour costs. Ten per cent of the rent is to be charged to A and the rest allocated to the other departments in line with labour costs. Gulls' cost of capital is 15% per year.

a. Prepare a cost statement showing:
   (i) A's total costs for an average week
   (ii) the required allocation of A's costs to the other three departments
   (iii) the weekly total costs of these three departments and of the firm
      in total.
b. Calculate (stating your assumptions):
   (i) the average variable cost of a finished product
   (ii) the average total cost of a finished product.
c. Gulls Ltd has just been approached by Sharp Motors Ltd with a special order to buy 15,000 components at a total price of £82,500. Under what assumptions would you advise Gulls Ltd to:
   (i) accept the order
   (ii) reject the order?

(UCLES International Examinations, 1989, GCE A level Business Studies)

C   Essay questions

C1   Why do managers need to understand how their firm's costs vary with changes in output?

C2   'In the long run, fixed costs are variable.' Discuss.

C3   Defend the use of full (absorption) costing in internal management reports, as opposed to marginal costing.

C4   Why is it not always possible to set selling prices on the basis of 'cost' plus a mark-up?

C5   The Governors of a boarding school are considering taking on day boys. One group argues that the fees should be high in order to spread the overhead cost. Another group argues that the marginal cost of a day boy is minimal, and therefore that any fees are virtually all profit. How would you approach the problem?

C6   Distinguish between 'contribution' and 'profit'. Under what circumstances would 'contribution' be used as an indicator of the value of a cost centre to a firm?

11

Costs and revenues

Plan of the chapter:

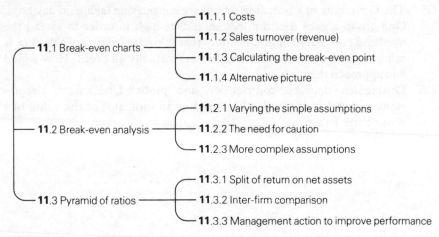

Fig.11.0

Objective: *To show how to combine costs and sales revenues on a single 'break-even chart' at various volumes of output; how to calculate the break-even point by simple algebra; how to use break-even charts; and how to use the pyramid of ratios to analyse the basic return on net assets ratio between sales revenues, expenses, and assets employed.*

Synopsis: *If a firm can split its total costs between 'fixed' and 'variable', they can be shown on a graph relating money costs and volume of output. Adding sales revenues (assumed to equal output volume times selling price per unit) produces a 'break-even chart'; this shows the 'break-even point' where sales revenues exactly equal total costs. One can also calculate the break-even point by dividing fixed costs by the variable profit (contribution) per unit.*

Break-even charts can help to estimate the profit impact of changes in fixed costs, variable cost per unit, and selling price per unit. Caution is needed in using break-even charts based on simple assumptions; but more realistic assumptions may produce too complex a picture.

11.1 Break-even charts

A **break-even** chart shows the volume of output at which a firm's sales turnover (revenue) equals its total costs, either in total or in respect of a part of the business. The firm ' breaks even' when it makes neither profit nor loss.

11.1.1 Costs

To start with, we shall assume that all a firm's costs are either 'variable' or 'fixed'. Variable costs are those which vary in line with output; while fixed costs remain the same even when output changes. We can now draw a picture of the firm's total costs at different levels of output.

Suppose that variable costs amount to £0.80 per unit produced, and fixed costs to £30,000 per year. Figure 11.1 shows how total costs vary as output changes. At a volume of 50,000 units of output a year, total costs are £70,000: this consists of £30,000 fixed costs, plus £40,000 variable costs (= 50,000 units @ £0.80). Normal practice is to show money amounts on the vertical axis and volume of output on the horizontal axis.

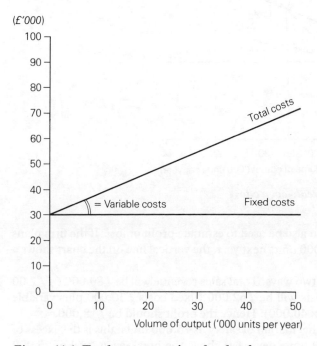

Figure 11.1 Total costs at various levels of output

11.1.2 Sales turnover (revenue)

To complete the break-even chart, we must include sales turnover (revenue) as well as costs. Assuming selling price is £2.00 per unit, figure 11.2 adds the dashed line to show sales revenue at various levels of output.

The chart shows the 'break-even point' at an output of 25,000 units a year. At this level of output, sales revenue of £50,000 exactly equals £30,000 fixed costs plus £20,000 variable costs (= 25,000 units @ £0.80). Above 25,000 units a year, sales revenue exceeds total costs and the firm makes a profit; while below 25,000 units a year the firm loses money.

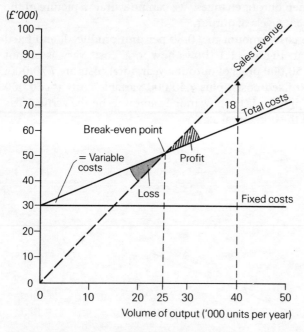

Figure 11.2 A simple break-even chart

Break-even charts can also be used to estimate profit or loss. If the firm plans to produce and sell 40,000 units next year, the vertical line on the chart shows a profit of £18,000.

We can check this in two ways. Total sales revenue will be £80,000 (= £2.00 × 40,000), and total costs will be £62,000 (fixed costs £30,000 plus variable costs £32,000 = £0.80 × 40,000). Hence the profit should be £18,000.

Or we can note that the 'margin of safety' is 15,000 units: this is the excess of planned sales of 40,000 units next year above the break-even level of 25,000 units. Since each unit sold above the break-even point yields a 'variable profit' (= contribution) of £1.20 (= £2.00 – £0.80), total profit should be £18,000 (= £1.20 × 15,000).

11.1.3 Calculating the break-even point

The estimates needed to draw a break-even chart also enable us to calculate the break-even point by simple algebra. We know that at the break-even level (call it x units), profit is zero (by definition); so that total costs must exactly equal sales revenue. But if we can split total costs between fixed and variable we can calculate the 'variable profit' (= contribution) per unit (in our example, £2.00 – £1.20 = £0.80).

To calculate the break-even point, we simply divide total fixed costs by the variable profit (contribution) per unit.

At the break-even point (x units)

Sales revenue	$=$ Total costs	
Sales revenue	$=$ Fixed costs + Variable costs	$S = F + V$
Sales revenue – Variable costs	$=$ Fixed costs	$S - V = F$
So: £2.00x – £0.80x	$=$ £30,000	$x(S - V) = F$
£1.20x	$=$ £30,000	
x	$= \dfrac{£30,000}{£1.20} = 25{,}000$ units	
	$= \dfrac{\text{Fixed costs}}{\text{Contribution per unit}}$	$x = \dfrac{F}{S - V}$

Where: x is the break-even level of output,
s is the selling price per unit,
S is total sales,
v is the variable cost per unit,
V is total variable costs, and
F is total fixed costs.

It is worth being able to handle the simple algebra: it is usually much quicker and more accurate to calculate the break-even point (and other aspects) than to draw a break-even chart and read off a rough estimate of the answers.

11.1.4 Alternative picture

Figure 11.2 showed a line for fixed costs which was horizontal and parallel to the base, and added variable costs on top of them, to give a diagonal line for total costs. Another way of drawing a break-even chart is to show variable costs at the base, and fixed costs as a line parallel to the variable costs line. Of course the line showing total costs remains unchanged.

Figure 11.3 overleaf shows this alternative way of drawing the chart. The angle between the sales revenue line and the variable costs line represents 'variable profit' (contribution). The break-even point is reached when total variable profit (£1.20 × 25,000) exactly equals fixed costs (£30,000).

Choosing the right scale to adopt when drawing break-even charts is not difficult. On most charts there will be some level of output at which sales revenues exceed costs. So it makes sense to use sales revenue (not costs) as the basis for the scale.

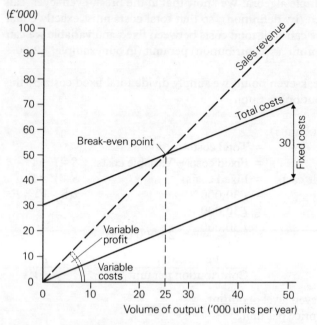

Figure 11.3 *Alternative way to draw a break-even chart*

Three steps are needed:
1 identify the maximum likely level of output;
2 identify the maximum likely selling price per unit;
3 from these, calculate the maximum likely total sales revenue.

Step **1** gives the scale for the horizontal axis, and step **3** the scale for the vertical axis.

11.2 Break-even analysis

11.2.1 Varying the simple assumptions

One of the main uses of break-even charts is to aid profit-planning. The charts allow managers to see the effects on profit estimates of simple cost/revenue/volume variations.

A change in assumptions about volume alone, of course, can be read straight off the chart. For example, refer back to figure 11.2. Suppose that planned volume of output (and sales) was 45,000 units next year, instead of 40,000 units as before. If other assumptions remained the same, the profit can be read off the chart as just under £25,000. (The precise amount is £24,000 = £1.20 × 20,000.)

Now suppose the firm reduces the selling price from £2.00 to £1.80 per unit, in order to boost sales volume. In figure 11.4 the thick dashed line shows the original selling price of £2.00 per unit, while the thinner dashed line just below it shows the revised selling price of £1.80 per unit.

The break-even point shifts from point A to B, from 25,000 units to 30,000 units; as the new variable profit per unit would be £1.00 (= £1.80 – £0.80), while the fixed costs remain at £30,000.

We can also see that to make as much profit as before, we would now need sales volume of 48,000 units instead of 40,000 units. (£18,000 profit requires the firm to sell 18,000 units (@ £1.00 contribution per unit) above the new higher break-even point of 30,000 units.) Thus a 10 per cent reduction in selling price requires a 20 per cent increase in sales volume. (We must remember that a given percentage change in selling price per unit will result in a larger percentage change in the amount of contribution per unit. This can work 'in our favour' when increasing the selling price.)

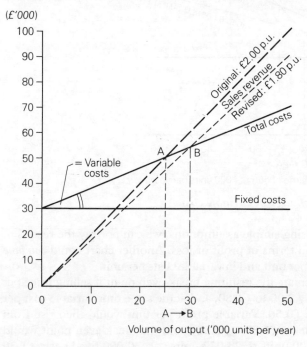

Figure 11.4 A possible change in selling price

Now suppose the firm retains the original selling price of £2.00 per unit, but manages to reduce the variable cost from £0.80 to £0.50 per unit. This increases the contribution per unit from £1.20 to £1.50 (a large change, which is easy to see on the chart).

Figure 11.5 overleaf shows original total costs as a solid line, and revised total costs as a dashed line just below it. The break-even point moves from point A to point C, falling from 25,000 units to 20,000 units (= £30,000 fixed costs/£1.50 contribution per unit).

In order to make the same £18,000 profit as before, the firm now needs to sell only 32,000 units (the break-even point of 20,000 units plus 12,000 units @ the new contribution of £1.50 per unit).

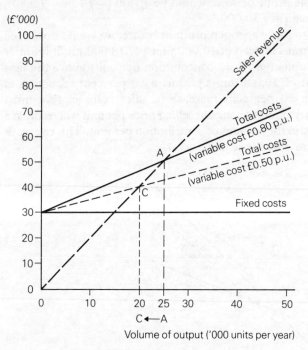

Figure 11.5 A possible change in variable costs

We have seen that, using simple assumptions, we can portray the results of any given output level in terms of profit or loss. Another chart could *combine* changes in selling price per unit and in variable costs per unit.

Or we can easily calculate the resulting break-even point if selling price per unit were reduced from £2.00 to £1.80, and at the same time variable cost per unit fell from £0.80 to £0.50. Variable profit per unit would then rise from £1.20 to £1.30 per unit (= £1.80 – £0.50); and the break-even point would therefore fall from 25,000 units to 23,077 units (= £30,000 fixed costs/£1.30 contribution per unit).

11.2.2 The need for caution

We have seen how to draw a break-even chart; and how to read off the break-even point, and the profit or loss at any given level of output. But the assumptions we have been making, taken together, may be over-simple, so we need to interpret any conclusions with caution.

The break-even chart depends on the accuracy of the data on which it is based. Information may be out of date, or estimates may be subject to a significant margin of error. In addition, we have been assuming:

1   a single selling price per unit (for a single product company), or an unchanging sales mix of products;
2   a single unchanging variable cost per unit (unchanging *per unit*, hence varying in total in line with output);
3   no changes in the level of stock, with all output sold;
4   fixed costs which remain the same at all levels of output.

In practice, selling prices may change, and the mix of products sold may well vary over time. Variable costs per unit may not remain exactly the same throughout the entire range of output: at higher levels of output they may tend to fall because of quantity discounts on materials, or to rise because of labour overtime. (It would be a happy chance if these effects cancelled out.)

Unless production output equals sales in each period, stock levels will change. Because accounting rules require firms to include some **period** ('fixed') **costs** in valuing stocks (see 7.3.2), any change in stock levels affects cost of goods sold, and hence profit or loss reported. Fixed costs will often increase in a 'step-function' as output rises, since they are usually 'fixed' only for a limited range of output.

The terms 'direct' and 'indirect' refer to how closely costs can be identified with particular products, not to whether or not they vary with output. For example, depreciation may relate to a specific product, even if it is calculated on a time basis and does not vary with output. On the other hand, some indirect overheads, such as production supervision costs, may be hard to identify with particular products, but may still be regarded as varying more or less in line with output. Allocating indirect overheads between products is often difficult (see Chapter 10); hence break-even analysis for a single product of a multi-product firm tends to be unreliable.

11.2.3 More complex assumptions

Figure 11.6 shows a break-even chart with more complex assumptions:

1   sales price per unit falls slightly as volume increases, so that the sales revenue curve slopes down to the right;
2   variable costs per unit fall at first, but then increase as overtime costs outweigh the effect of quantity discounts;
3   fixed costs increase in a step function as output increases.

One conclusion seems evident. Figure 11.6 overleaf is worth using only between output levels of 15,000 and 40,000 units a year; that is, over the range of output for which fixed costs are £30,000. No profit is possible below an output of 15,000 units; and above 40,000 units, because fixed costs jump up by £12,500 to £42,500, total costs exceed sales revenue. The position gets worse as output increases further: sales revenue per unit starts declining, and variable costs per unit start increasing.

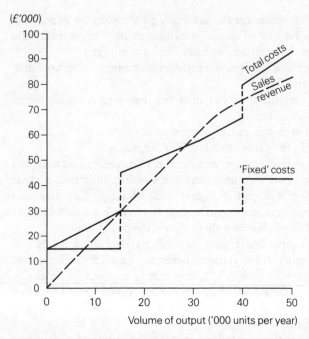

Figure 11.6 A break-even chart with more complex assumptions

Indeed, figure 11.6 shows no fewer than *three* 'break-even' points: at 15,000 units, at just under 28,000 units, and a transition from profit into loss at 40,000 units. This is probably more realistic than the earlier charts, but much harder to interpret.

It may often be difficult to get accurate information for break-even charts:

1 precise cost estimates at various different volumes, even if possible, might be expensive to obtain;
2 the market's response to price changes may be almost impossible to guess, since both consumers' behaviour and competitors' reaction are hard to forecast;
3 costs and markets are continually changing.

11.3 Pyramid of ratios

11.3.1 Split of return on net assets

In planning, controlling and reviewing operations, internal managers use financial ratios to help them analyse performance, in the same way as external users (see Chapter 9). The main difference is that managers can have any information they care to collect: in particular they can get non-financial information, as well as financial data which is both (a) more detailed and (b) more frequent than in the annual published accounts for the whole company.

This additional information is especially useful with the performance ratios. We saw earlier (9.3.1) how to combine the profit margin and the net asset turnover ratios to form the 'return on net assets' ratio. Now figure 11.7 shows how to extend this approach into a **pyramid of ratios**.

One can compare the results in detail with:

1 past periods;
2 budgets;
3 other firms.

The ratios can also be further analysed between (i) products. (ii) geographical areas, and (iii) different types of costs within each heading.

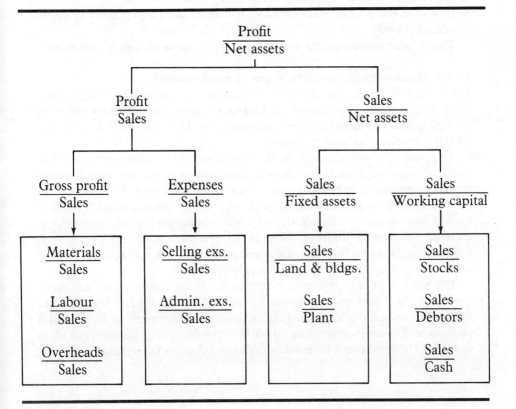

Figure 11.7 A pyramid of ratios

11.3.2 Inter-firm comparisons

Comparing a firm's ratios with those of other firms in the same industry can be extremely useful. They may show up long-standing weaknesses of which nobody is aware. Published accounts may contain too little detail, and different accounting conventions often make comparisons with foreign companies unreliable.

Different firms may have different accounting methods and costing systems even in their management accounts. So inter-firm comparison schemes, which exchange ratios anonymously between firms in the same industry, standardize the results for all firms taking part. This makes the comparisons much more useful.

Some examples of the type of questions which inter-firm comparisons can help answer are:

1 Is our return on net assets high or low for the industry?
2 Are selling costs higher than for other firms of similar size?
3 Is stock turnover out of line with comparable firms?
4 Is working capital management adequate by industry standards?
5 How does the industry leader manage to achieve such high returns on equity year after year?

Trends over time for each ratio, or set of ratios, can add to their usefulness.

11.3.3 Management action to improve performance

Figure 11.8 shows another approach to the pyramid of ratios. The diagram sets out how a company could increase its rate of return on net assets either by increasing profit or by reducing net assets employed for each £ of sales turnover (that is increasing net asset turnover).

The management accountant is a member of the management team. Accounting information is vital in helping managers to take action to improve business performance; but of course many other skills must be combined to earn maximum profits. In marketing (in addition to pricing policy), product quality and design, packaging, delivery, advertising, and so on, may help to increase sales or to improve margins. In production, skilful purchasing, engineering, factory scheduling, industrial relations, stock management, and so on, may help to minimize expenses for a given output.

The same applies to trying to minimize net assets employed for any given level of profit. Fixed asset costs can be reduced by better plant layout, more intensive use, careful maintenance, efficient management of new capital projects, and so on. And working capital is important: good managers can often reduce the large amounts invested in stocks and debtors fairly quickly.

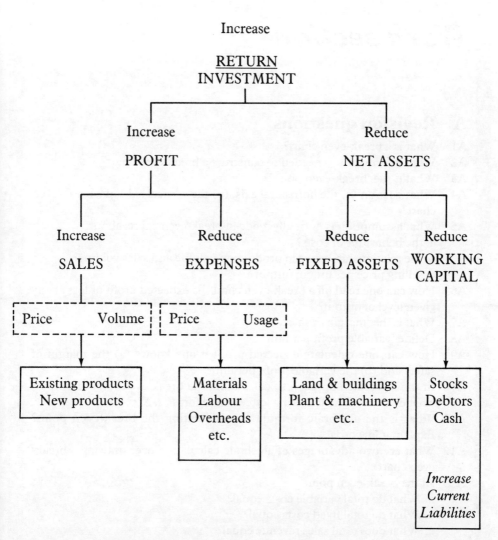

Figure 11.8 Management action to improve performance

Work section

A   Revision questions

A1   What is a break-even chart?

A2   What information is needed to construct a break-even chart?

A3   What is the 'break-even point'?

A4   What goes on (a) the horizontal axis, (b) the vertical axis, of a break-even chart?

A5   What assumption is normally made in break-even charts about:
a. the behaviour of costs?
b. the relationship between production volume and sales volume?
c. selling price per unit of output?

A6   How can one read off a break-even chart the expected profit or loss at any given level of output?

A7   What is the 'margin of safety'?

A8   Define 'variable profit per unit'.

A9   How can one calculate expected profit if one knows (a) the margin of safety and (b) the variable profit per unit?

A10   In the algebraic approach to calculating the break-even level of output, what do each of the following letters stand for: F, s, S, v, V?

A11   What is the algebraic formula for calculating the break-even point? Explain it in words.

A12   What are two advantages of algebraic calculation over drawing a break-even chart?

A13   At the break-even point:
a. What do total variable costs equal?
b. What do total fixed costs equal?
c. What does total sales revenue equal?

A14   What is the break-even point for a firm whose costs are:
(a) all fixed; (b) all variable?

A15   How do the two methods of drawing break-even charts differ?

A16   In drawing a break-even chart, how would you determine a suitable scale for (a) the vertical axis; (b) the horizontal axis?

A17   What will happen to the break-even point (and why):
a. if variable costs per unit rise?
b. if fixed costs fall?
c. if sales volume increases?
d. if selling price per unit rises?
e. if variable profit per unit falls?

A18 Name four simplifying assumptions usually made in break-even analysis.

A19 Explain how each of the simplifying assumptions usually made in break-even analysis may be unrealistic.

A20 How can there be more than one break-even point?

A21 Why may accurate information for break-even calculations be hard to obtain?

A22 Into what four main sets of ratios can a firm's return on net assets ratio be subdivided by the pyramid of ratios?

A23 Why may it be useful to study the pyramid of ratios even if the return on net assets ratio appears to be satisfactory?

A24 Why is inter-firm comparison useful?

A25 Give three examples of questions which inter-firm comparison may help to answer.

A26 Name three potential difficulties with inter-firm comparisons.

A27 Name two basic ways in which a firm could try to increase its return on net assets.

A28 Name three aspects of marketing which may help to increase sales.

A29 Name three aspects of production management which may help to reduce expenses.

A30 Name two reasons why management of working capital may be important.

B Exercises and case studies

B1   Biggin Ltd's fixed costs are £300,000 a year. Contribution is £10 per unit. Sales price is £25 per unit. Can you tell what the break-even point is?
   a. If yes; what *is* the break-even point?
   b. If not; what additional information do you need, and why?

B2   Fixed costs are £30,000 a year. Variable costs are £0.50 per unit. Selling price is £1.80 per unit.
   a. Draw a break-even chart showing the position.
   b. What is the break-even point?
   c. Compare the break-even chart with figures 11.2, 11.4, and 11.5. Identify the differences in each case.

B3   Sales revenue is £840,000 per year. Variable costs are £10 per unit. Fixed costs are £350,000 a year. Present output is 30,000 units a year.
   a. Draw a break-even chart. What is the break-even level?
   b. Confirm your graphical derivation from the chart, *both*:
      (i) by algebra; (ii) by arithmetic.
   c. Draw a second break-even chart based on the same facts, but using the alternative method.

181

B4   Refer to the facts in B3.
    a. What happens to the break-even point if (separately):
      (i) fixed costs fall to £300,000 a year?
      (ii) variable costs per unit fall to £8?
      (iii) sales price per unit increases by £5?
    b. What happens to the break-even point if all three of the changes in (a) happen together?

B5   Juxton Ltd has fixed overheads of £100,000 per annum. Direct costs and variable indirect overheads taken together average £2 per unit, and the firm's plant can make up to 50,000 units p.a. The finished product sells for £6.
    a. Draw a break-even chart showing Juxton's present position.
    b. What is the break-even output?
    c. What is the margin of safety at 45,000 units p.a. production?
    d. What is the amount of profit at 90 per cent of capacity?

B6   C's annual break-even output is 45,000 units. If sales volume is 20 per cent above that level, profit is £36,000. Variable costs per unit are one third of selling price. Draw a break-even chart showing the position. What is the break-even point?

B7   Dahren Ltd's variable costs are $6 per unit. Sales volume is currently 40,000 units a year. Fixed costs are $100,000 a year.
    a. Would you recommend an improvement in product quality which would increase variable costs to $8 per unit, if that would enable Dahren to sell 15 per cent more units at the present selling price of $15?
    b. Draw a break-even chart showing both the present position, and the position if the changes in (a) take place. In particular, identify both the old and the new break-even level of output.
    c. How could your break-even chart incorporate a required before-tax rate of return of 12 per cent on equity capital of $200,000?

B8   Fixed costs are £300,000 a year. Sales price per unit is £18. Variable costs in a year total £240,000. Present annual output is 40,000 units.
    a. What is the break-even level of output?
    b. What will the break-even level of output be if (separately):
      (i) fixed costs increase to £400,000 a year?
      (ii) variable costs in total increase by £2 per unit?
      (iii) sales price per unit falls to £16?
    c. What will the break-even level of output be if inflation increases all costs by one third, but selling prices can only be raised to £20 per unit?

B9   Porterland Ltd's fixed costs are £400,000 a year. Sales revenue is £1.2 million a year. Variable costs, at £8 per unit, currently total £480,000 a year. How would the margin of safety change if labour-saving equipment were installed which reduced variable costs by £2 per unit, but which increased fixed costs by £100,000 a year?

B10 Granham-Hill Ltd had just completed its third year of trading. The maximum capacity of the firm now stood at 80,000 units of production a year. At this level, direct material and labour costs totalled £255,000; fixed overheads amounted to £60,000 for production, £50,000 for general administration, and £40,000 for selling and distribution. Variable overheads, which had fluctuated to begin with, had now settled at a level of £145,000 a year at capacity. Finished products were sold at £10 per unit. Unfortunately, in the year just ended (to which the above figures apply), Granham-Hill had only been able to produce and sell 50 per cent of its total capacity. The market position was now beginning to improve, and next year the firm hopes to increase its output and sales to 75 per cent of capacity.

From a break-even chart determine:
a. the break-even volume;
b. the margin of safety at 50 per cent of capacity;
c. the increase in profit if the firm moves from 50 per cent of capacity to 75 per cent;
d. the new margin of safety at 75 per cent of capacity.

B11 Hicks and Marshall produce briefcases which sell for £20 each. Fixed costs amount to £24,000 a year. Variable costs per unit are: materials £5; direct labour £4; variable overheads £3.
a. What is the annual break-even level of sales?
b. Normal sales volume has been about 3,600 units a year. If the sales price per unit were reduced to £18, it is estimated that the number of briefcases sold would increase by 25 per cent.
   (i) What would the break-even level of sales then be?
   (ii) What would it be if the sales volume rose by 33 per cent?
c. Increased automation could reduce direct labour per unit to £2, but would increase fixed costs by £4,000 a year. At what sales price per unit would the break-even sales volume be 250 per month?

B12 Neve Ltd makes and sells two products, A and B. Because of the nature of the production process, two As are made for each B; and all planning is done on the basis that the number of units sold will also be in the proportion 2 to 1. Costs are as follows: Variable costs per unit: A £4, B £6; fixed costs £300,000 a year. Each A sells for £12, each B for £10.
a. Counting 2 As + 1 B as one 'unit', on an aggregate basis, what is the break-even number of 'units'?
b. If fixed costs are split £160,000 to A and £140,000 to B, what is the break-even number of units for A and for B?
c. How would fixed costs have to be split between A and B in order for the break-even number of units for A to be the same as for B?

B13 Boris Overcoats Ltd makes fashionable men's clothing. Its current product is a fur-trimmed coat which retails at £21. Variable costs of production amount to £10 per unit, and the overheads exhibit the following pattern:

Output in units	Overhead costs (£)
Up to 100	1,000
101 to 200	1,500
201 to 300	2,500
301 to 400	3,000

a. What is the minimum number of coats the company must sell to ensure a profit of 10 per cent on costs?
b. From market research the company knows it cannot expect to sell more than 350 coats a year. How many should be made in order to maximize profits?

B14 *'Sparkle' Electric Toothbrushes*

Electrics Ltd makes small electrical goods. One of its relatively news lines, 'Sparkle' electric toothbrushes, has been selling better than expected (at £5.00 each). In fact it has been so successful that the firm recently had to turn away a large French order because the factory was already fully extended. The department concerned has already reached its present capacity of 40,000 units a year, at an annual fixed cost of £45,000. The variable costs of production per unit are: direct labour £1.50; material and components £0.50; and other variable costs £0.50.

The company has been investing heavily in developing a completely new type of electric toothbrush. In about three years this should provide as good a product at a reduced price; but would probably require a new production process. The company has also been spending money to improve its distribution and marketing, in order to take advantage of the evident potential for growth in the market.

The Managing Director sees three possible courses of action open to him:

1 To continue as at present, producing under great strain.
2 To increase production by going over to a two-shift system. Recruiting extra labour would not be a problem, and instead of the present 8-hour day there could be two 8-hour shifts. The trade unions would insist that the workers' take-home pay be improved; and direct labour costs per unit would probably rise by 20 per cent. It is hoped that the 100 per cent increase in hours worked would increase output by at least 50 per cent.
3 To build a new plant on available nearby space, and so allow capacity to expand by at least 50 per cent. Such a venture would increase annual fixed costs by £30,000, but total variable costs in the new plant would be only £1.80 per unit.

a. Draw the three alternatives on a break-even chart.
b. What should be done? Why?
c. What assumptions are you making?
d. What other courses of action might you consider?

B15 The following equations represent the relationships between costs and revenues for a particular mass-produced product. You may assume that production volume equals sales volume (that is, that there are no changes in levels of stocks held).

Total costs $\quad = \quad C \quad = \quad 4 + \dfrac{w}{3}$

Total revenue $\quad = \quad R \quad = \quad \dfrac{w}{2}$

C and R are money amounts in thousands of pounds, and w is the volume of production in thousands of units.

Calculate:
a. the selling price of a unit,
b. the break-even level of production,
c. profits at a production level of 30,000 units,
d. the 'contribution' of each unit sold (to cover fixed costs and profit),
e. the extra production required to maintain profits if fixed costs rose by 50 per cent,
f. the change in the break-even level of production (as in (b) above) if the selling price could be raised by one-sixth.

B16 After several very competitive years in the domestic electric appliances field, Rolls Plugs Ltd was finding it more and more difficult to compete. The firm was operating at its present capacity of 60,000 units p.a. Variable costs were as low as they could possibly be, at £6.00 per unit; and in the short run it was impossible to trim the fixed overheads below £60,000 a year. The Managing Director wanted to know how best to increase profitability, hoping that in the short run there would be no other change in the variables involved. He was considering three alternatives:

1 To try to squeeze another 20 per cent of capacity out of the firm, by working overtime. This would add another 30p per unit to direct labour costs as a result of overtime premiums.
2 To raise the existing selling price of £7.50 per unit by 10 per cent.
3 To drop the selling price by 10 per cent to stimulate sales. In this third case, the firm would have to determine how much more output would be required to maintain its present profit level.

a. Examine the three alternatives listed above and plot them on a break-even chart, together with the firm's original position.
b. Which alternative do you think would be best for the firm? Why?
c. Explain any weaknesses which you believe exist in the analysis.

B17 Dinsdale Developments Ltd is currently operating at 75 per cent of capacity, and making an annual profit of £3 million, which is 10 per cent of its total costs. The firm's fixed overheads are £5 m. p.a. The production director has suggested modernizing the firm's production processes and buying new machinery. This would increase fixed overheads by £10 m. a year, but would reduce the variable costs in such a way that the profit at 75 per cent of capacity would remain unchanged.

185

a. Construct a break-even chart to show the present situation and the proposed alternative.
b. At what per cent of capacity is the new break-even point?
c. What is the effect of the new proposal on the firm's range of profitable operation?
d. What other factors would you consider before deciding whether to modernize as proposed?

B18 A, B and C are small producers of plastic containers who take part in an inter-firm comparison scheme. You are a member of firm A's management. In the light of the information given, suggest, with reasons, areas where your firm might usefully examine its affairs. (*Hint:* Employ a few key ratios where necessary.)

End of year balance sheets (*£'000*)

	A		B		C	
Fixed assets						
Freehold property	178		146		166	
Plant and machinery	110		206		167	
Motor vehicles	210		96		83	
		498		448		416
Current assets						
Stocks*	517		313		244	
Debtors	232		185		128	
Cash at bank	378		74		62	
		1,127		572		434
		1,625		1,020		850
Shareholders' funds						
Ordinary issued shares		700		500		500
Reserves		112		225		110
		812		725		610
Debentures		300		20		10
Current liabilities						
Bank overdraft	250		–		–	
Trade creditors	170		160		140	
Tax	33		75		50	
Dividends	60		40		40	
		513		275		230
		1,625		1,020		850

*Including work-in-progress: A £100,000; B £95,000; C £82,000.

Profit and loss accounts

	A (£'000)	(%)	B (£'000)	(%)	C (£'000)	(%)
Sales revenue	1,052	100	1,373	100	1,040	100
Cost of goods sold:						
Direct labour	200	19	192	14	156	15
Direct materials	210	20	333	24	208	20
Variable overheads	126	12	164	12	125	12
Fixed factory overheads	179	17	164	12	145	14
Marketing expenses	95	9	163	12	156	15
Admin. expenses*	158	15	165	12	125	12
	968	92	1,181	86	915	88
Net profit before tax	84	8	192	14	125	12
	1,052	100	1373	100	1,040	100

*Including interest charges: A £27,000; B £2000; C £1000

Figure 11.9 Balance sheets and profit and loss accounts for firms A, B and C

B19 PT Ltd produces three products (X, Y and Z). The relevant data is shown below:

	£ Per Unit		
	X	Y	Z
Sales price	2.00	2.50	3.25
Direct materials used (at 10p per kg)	0.30	0.40	0.50
Direct labour used	0.90	1.00	1.00
Variable overheads	0.40	0.60	0.85

The company's fixed costs amount to £10,000 a month. The raw material used is in short supply and may limit the output of PT Ltd.
a. State which product the company should concentrate on, assuming that there are no marketing constraints on the products. Support your answer with appropriate figures.
b. It is anticipated that 200,000 kg of raw materials will be obtained in each month. Showing your calculations, calculate the most profitable

187

product mix and expected profit if the projected monthly demand for X, Y and Z is 5,000, 16, 000 and 30,000 units respectively.
(*UCLES International Examinations, 1985, GCE A Level Business Studies*)

C   Essay questions

C1   'The simple break-even model provides an easily understood and effective aid to decision making.' Discuss limitations to its usefulness, and evaluate possible modifications that might be made to overcome them.

C2   'Social trends are causing break-even points to rise, hence margins of safety to fall.' Is this true? If so, why? Does it matter?

C3   'A simple break-even chart is too simple to be realistic; while a realistic one is too complicated to be usable.' Discuss.

C4   If British Rail is operating at a loss, shouldn't taxpayers be glad when there's a strike? Won't they *save* money? Explain fully.

C5   Write a brief memo, as a management accountant, to persuade your firm's managing director that participating in an inter-firm comparison scheme would be worthwhile. Discuss in your memo the main potential difficulties in inter-firm comparisons.

C6   How far can break-even analysis help to determine the price at which a product should be sold?

12

Budgets

Plan of the chapter:

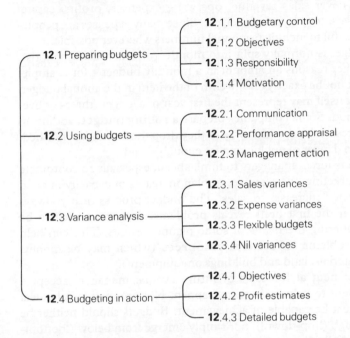

- **12**.1 Preparing budgets
  - **12**.1.1 Budgetary control
  - **12**.1.2 Objectives
  - **12**.1.3 Responsibility
  - **12**.1.4 Motivation
- **12**.2 Using budgets
  - **12**.2.1 Communication
  - **12**.2.2 Performance appraisal
  - **12**.2.3 Management action
- **12**.3 Variance analysis
  - **12**.3.1 Sales variances
  - **12**.3.2 Expense variances
  - **12**.3.3 Flexible budgets
  - **12**.3.4 Nil variances
- **12**.4 Budgeting in action
  - **12**.4.1 Objectives
  - **12**.4.2 Profit estimates
  - **12**.4.3 Detailed budgets

Fig 12.0
Objective: *To explain how to prepare and use budgets, and how to analyse variances between actual performance and budget.*

Synopsis: *Budgets are financial plans for a period, agreed in advance for (part of) a firm's operations. They help set objectives and coordinate responsibilities. After the event, budgets communicate information and help appraise the performance of managers and of business units.*

Variance analysis compares actual performance with budget. The reasons for variances should be analysed, and action taken, if necessary, to improve profits.

An example is given of preparing a budget and using it to look into variances.

12.1 Preparing budgets

12.1.1 Budgetary control

Budgets are formal business plans consisting of:

1 quantitative statements;
2 usually in financial terms;
3 covering a specific period;
4 for (part of) a firm's operations;
5 which managers have prepared and agreed in advance.

A budget may cover sales revenue, operating expenses, profits, capital spending, cash, assets, output, personnel, etc. Since many expenses are people-related, it can be useful to include personnel numbers wherever possible.

A one-year budget is normally split into months (or four-weekly periods). For seasonal or other reasons an amount in a monthly budget – for example, for heating – might not be exactly one-twelfth of the item in the annual budget. The annual budget itself may represent the first year of a longer (three- or five-year) planning period. Some companies prepare a **rolling budget,** adding an extra month's figures twelve months away as they drop the month just finished. Otherwise there is a danger of not looking far enough ahead.

Preparing budgets forces managers to think ahead, especially to coordinate production and marketing; for example, to plan increases in capacity in good time to meet expected increases in sales. The budget process nearly always contains *feedback;* if the first draft reveals problems, there may need to be changes, such as altering the *timing* of some planned events. This can help avoid bunching problems for **critical resources** (which may be money, manpower, raw materials, land and buildings or equipment).

Budgets are not neutral forecasts of future events: managers accept a personal commitment to help *make* them happen. Nor are they merely ideal targets: budgets must be capable of achievement. Budgets should neither be imposed from on high ('top-down'), nor simply emerge from below ('bottom-up'); managers normally discuss (or negotiate) the details with their bosses.

Even humble authors have 'budgets' for the number of pages and deadlines for delivering manuscripts. Students, too, have been known to *plan* their revision before exams: budgeting is part of the general process of *management,* not merely a technical aspect of money accounting.

The annual budget cycle in a business involves a number of steps:

1 forecasting general economic and industry conditions;
2 stating basic assumptions;
3 setting company objectives;
4 preparing detailed sales budgets, suitably analysed (for example, between products, regions, customers, time periods);
5 preparing suitably analysed budgets for: production, expenses, capital spending and cash;

6 translating the various budgets into the **master budget** – the overall profit and loss account, funds flow, and balance sheet budgets.

In advance budgetary control sets objectives, allocates responsibilities, and motivates managers. After the event, it communicates information, appraises performance, and assists effective management action. The next few pages discuss each of these six functions separately.

12.1.2 Objectives

Businesses do not usually think in terms of a single objective for the budget period, such as 'maximizing profits'. This is partly because many business decisions have effects lasting well beyond the current budget period.

For example, the American General Electric Company identified the eight 'key result areas' listed in figure 12.1. They might not all suit other firms and clearly some pose measurement problems. But most companies need to emphasize their long-term objectives; otherwise short-term goals may absorb too much attention.

---

1 Profit
2 Market share
3 Productivity
4 Product leadership
5 Employee attitudes
6 Public responsibility
7 Staff development
8 Balance between short-term and long-term

Figure 12.1 General Electric (US), eight key result areas

Budgetary control can also assist managers of 'non-profit' entities, such as schools, churches, the armed services. Organizations which do not sell their products on the market may find it useful to budget output in physical rather than financial terms. Of course, they need to pay attention to *quality* as well as quantity of output. They can probably budget expenditure in money terms in the usual way.

12.1.3 Responsibility

Someone must be in charge of each unit, and every manager needs to be clear exactly what he or she is responsible for. But a manager may not be able to control everything affecting his unit's results. In practice, distinguishing between *controllable* and *non-controllable* items may not be easy.

191

Not all business units can measure their output in money terms. A research unit manager, for example, should expect to keep to agreed levels of spending, neither much more *nor much less*. But it may be hard to measure the quantity and quality of his unit's output.

Three different kinds of 'responsibility centre' are: (a) revenue centres; (b) cost centres and (c) profit centres. A **revenue centre**, such as a sales department, generates revenue but doesn't spend much. More commonly, a **cost centre** is responsible for spending money, but not directly for earning revenue.

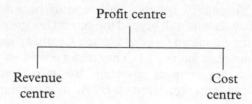

Profit centre

Revenue centre   Cost centre

A **profit centre** sells its output, and controls both revenue and expenses. Its manager is responsible for *profit,* the excess of sales revenues over expenses. Thus he decides on 'trade-offs' between them, such as whether to spend more on promotion to boost sales, or whether he can reduce design costs without affecting quality. A profit centre which sells some of its output to another part of the same firm uses internal 'transfer prices'. It is best to base these, if possible, on the outside market price for similar goods.

Finally, an **investment centre** is responsible not only for profit but also for control over a significant amount of assets. In practice, managing a firm's resources is often critically important, even if not all of them appear on the balance sheet (see 4.1).

12.1.4 Motivation

Most students work with more purpose if they know their work will be tested. It is normally sensible for people to participate in setting their own budgets; but it is for top managers to judge whether a proposed budget represents an adequate performance. Business managers whose unit's performance is going to be compared with an agreed budget will feel less commitment to achieve results if they think the standard is not fair. A budget that is either 'too easy' or 'too hard' will often be less effective than one which is 'difficult but achievable'.

There is danger in judging a unit's performance entirely by *current* profits, if some decisions have longer-term effects. For example, a manager might be able to improve current profits by spending less on research; but it could be disastrous in the long run. In practice managers are normally judged on their 'track record' over a period of years. Business success has many aspects (see figure 12.1); and using several criteria is wiser than judging managers or business units by any single accounting figure, however cunningly devised.

12.2 Using budgets

12.2.1 Communication

Budgets should be simple and easy to read. Businessmen nearly always prefer rough figures soon to 'exact' ones later. And filling reports with trivial items obscures what really matters.

Sending weekly reports is pointless if action is taken only once a month. On the other hand, timing *can* be important: small businesses, for example, may gain (compared with large firms) by being able to react *quickly* to changing events.

Signalling only important *exceptions* from an agreed standard can restrict needless detail, but requires judgement. If conditions have changed, deviation from budget may not be 'bad', nor exactly attaining it 'good'. There can be sound *reasons* for a variance from budget.

Figure 12.2 shows an example of a monthly profit and loss summary (monthly balance sheet summaries may also be useful). Attached schedules can give more details where necessary. In addition a brief report can summarize certain ratios (see Chapter 9) and point out key aspects of the results. And charts of past and projected future trends (adjusted for inflation) may be valuable.

If conditions change, the budget figures may not represent a good estimate of the current year's results. Monthly reports may then include, as in figure 12.2, a column for the 'latest estimate for the current year', updated each month. This can help show whether a variance in one month is merely a *timing*

	Latest month *October*		*Cumulative to date* *10 months*		*Current year*	
	Budget (£'000 %)	Actual (£'000 %)	Budget (£'000 %)	Actual (£'000 %)	Budget (£'000 %)	Latest estimate (£'000 %)
Sales turnover						
Variable cost of sales:						
Materials						
Direct labour						
Production overheads						
Other variable expenses						
Contribution						
Fixed production expenses						
Other fixed expenses						
Operating profit (loss)						

Figure 12.2 Monthly profit and loss report

difference, which will reverse itself next month, or the start of a trend resulting in large cumulative variances by the year-end. Clearly these could have very different meanings for management.

12.2.2 Performance appraisal

In appraising performance one needs a *standard* against which to judge actual results (see 9.1.2). If the budget is properly set, most management reports should not need to include last year's actual figures. The current budget should take them into account, together with expected changes, in setting the current year's standards.

Various methods of **flexible budgeting** (see 12.3.3) can often allow for changes in business conditions. Major changes may make it desirable to *revise* budgets, despite the time and effort involved. Otherwise managers may become demoralized by comparing actual results with budgets which are now unattainable, or else complacent if budgets are too easily achieved.

One must distinguish between appraising the performance of managers and the performance of a business unit. For example, managers may be doing well to improve the position of a loss-making business unit but the unit's performance may not yet be adequate. Ignoring the distinction could make competent managers reluctant to take on the challenge of improving poor business units.

12.2.3 Management action

Budgets should help managers to manage: they are not rigid targets to be achieved at all costs, whatever has changed since they were agreed. There can be good reasons for actual results to differ from budgets, especially if the budgets were prepared a year or more earlier. Managers may not be able to control every item in their budgets, at least in the short run; but they are expected to react to changed conditions.

Budgetary control with monthly reporting may help managers to answer the following kinds of questions:

1 What has been happening recently? How does it differ from budget? Why?
2 How if at all will these events cause latest estimates of current year results to differ from budget *if no action is taken?*
3 What if anything can be done to counter unfavourable variances from budget, *or to increase favourable ones?* (Successful managers are always alert to cash in on good luck!)
4 How soon will such action be effective? How much difference will it make? Are there any side effects we should be aware of?
5 After all proposed actions, what is now the latest estimate of current year results? Are they acceptable?

12.3 Variance analysis

12.3.1 Sales variances

It can be useful in internal reports to separate prices from the quantity of physical units. Suppose that actual sales revenue is £420, compared with a budget of £500. Figure 12.3 shows two different ways in which the **variance** of £80 could have arisen, with quite different implications for management action. In each case the overall variance (–£80) between actual and budget sales revenue is analysed into a **volume variance** and a **price variance.**

	Units	×	*Price*	=	*Revenue*
Budget	50	×	£10	=	£500
Actual - A	60	×	£ 7	=	£420
Actual - B	35	×	£12	=	£420
Actual - A					
Volume variance	+10	×	£10	=	+£100
Price variance	60	×	–£ 3	=	–£180
Total variance				=	–£ 80
Actual - B					
Volume variance	–15	×	£10	=	–£150
Price variance	35	×	+£ 2	=	+£ 70
Total variance				=	–£ 80

Figure 12.3 Analysis of sales variance

By convention, variance analysis multiples the difference in volume by the *budget price* (£10 here); and multiplies the difference in price per unit by *actual volume.* Managers are thought more likely to be able to control volume than to control price; so using budgeted price per unit isolates the effect of a presumed controllable variance in volume.

12.3.2 Expense variances

In looking at variances between actual and budgeted expenses, let us return to the Gilbert example (see 10.2.1). To keep it simple, we shall consider only the spending on petrol.

Example: The 'budgeted' cost of petrol (see 10.2) was 12,000 miles at 5.0p per mile = £600. Suppose that Gilbert's car actually travelled 15,000 miles in the year, and petrol actually cost 44p per litre (at 8 miles per litre = 5.5p per mile). Then the actual cost of petrol in the year would be £825 (15,000 miles at 5.5p). How is this 'unfavourable' total variance of £225 on petrol to be split between volume and price?

Clearly at least 3,000 miles at 5.0p per mile (= £150) is a volume variance, and at least 0.5p × 12,000 miles (= £60) is a price variance. But what should we call the balance of £15 (= 3,000 miles at 0.5p)?

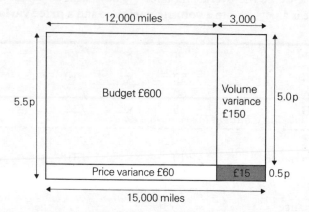

Figure 12.4 Analysis of an expense variance

Again we use the budget *cost per mile to analyse the volume variance (giving 3,000 miles at 5.0p = £150); and again we use the* actual *volume to determine the* price *variance (giving 0.5p ×15,000 miles = £75). Thus the shaded area in the bottom righthand corner of figure 12.4 is regarded as part of the* price *variance.*

12.3.3 Flexible budgets

When sales volume varies from budget, those expenses which are expected to change in line with sales volume ('variable expenses') are – *for that reason alone* – likely to differ from budget too. So when it comes to profit (= sales revenue minus expenses) it can be useful to tackle the review of actual versus budgeted profit in three stages:

1 examine the change in contribution (sales revenue less variable expenses) due to any change in sales volume alone;

2 examine the change in contribution due to any change in selling prices;

3 examine the change in expenses compared with what would have been expected at *actual* sales volume.

Example: Matlock plc's budgeted sales revenue was £30,000 for June (15,000 units at £2.00 each); variable expenses £18,000 (= 15,000 units at £1.20 per unit); and fixed expenses £7,200. Actual sales revenue was £22,800 (12,000 units at £1.90); variable expenses £16,000; and fixed expenses £6,900. Figure 12.5 analyses the £4,900 difference between Matlock's budgeted profit of £4,800 and the actual loss of £100, by using a flexible budget.

196

	Original budget		Flexible budget		Actual	
	(£)	(%)	(£)	(%)	(£)	(%)
Sales revenue	30,000	100	24,000	100 ②	22,800	100
Variable expenses	18,000	60	14,400	60 ③ⓐ	16,000	70
Contribution	12,000	40 ①	9,600	40	6,800	30
Fixed expenses	7,200	24	7,200	30 ③ⓑ	6,900	30
Profit (loss)	4,800	16	2,400	10	(100)	–

Figure 12.5 Flexing a budget for variance analysis

The total profit variance of –£4,900 between the original £4,800 budget profit and the actual £100 loss is now split into three parts (–£2,400, –£1,200, and –£1,300), which can be analysed separately:

1 The variance of –£2,400 in contribution, between the original budget (£12,000) and the flexible budget (£9,600), due to the decline in sales volume:

Sales revenue	–3,000	× £2.00	= –£6,000
Variable expenses	–3,000	× £1.20	= –£3,600
Contribution	–3,000	× £0.80	= –£2,400

2 There is a further negative variance of –£1,200 in sales revenue (and therefore in contribution) due to the 5 per cent decline in selling price per unit (from £2.00 to £1.90).

3 The total variance of –£1,300 in expenses, between the flexible budget and actual, can be split between variable and fixed expenses:

	Flexible budget	Actual	Variance
Variable expenses	£14,400	£16,000	–£1,600
Fixed expenses	£7,200	£6,900	+£300
			–£1,300

The convention is to use a + sign for a 'favourable' variance which increases actual profit over budget, and a – sign for an 'unfavourable' variance which reduces actual profit compared with budget. Thus if actual expenses are higher than budget, that is an unfavourable variance and has a – sign.

Thus we see that using a flexible budget is a convenient way to break down the analysis of variances step by step: in particular distinguishing between variances due to (a) changes in sales volume, (b) changes in selling price per unit, and (c) expenses being different from expected at the actual sales volume. In practice this is helpful because different managers are likely to be responsible. Clearly it is essential to split the apparent £2,000 favourable variance on variable expenses (between the original budget's £18,000 and the actual £16,000) between the £3,600 favourable variance due to the decline in sales volume and the £1,600 unfavourable variance due to spending too much at the actual sales volume.

12.3.4 Nil variances

If the management accountant comparing actual with budget can identify actual amounts or ratios varying from expectations, he can inform the managers responsible. If they have not already done so, they can try to find out *why.* They may then be able to take action to improve matters, to at least alter their estimates of likely future results.

Even if the overall amounts or ratios seem satisfactory, there may still be important variances at lower levels which *cancel each other out.* So analysis may be worthwhile even if the overall result seems to give no cause for alarm. And one should always remember that much drama may lie hidden behind the 'nil' variance.

Example: Financial accountants have their own targets for how long it takes them to complete the final accounts. Nobsil Ltd's financial year ends on 31 March. But in March the computer breaks down, and one of the chief accountant's key assistants is away ill; then in April another key person is getting married and a postal strike delays the receipt of important information. Furthermore the stocktaking turns out to be unusually complicated; as does the tax calculation.

Despite these problems, the financial accounting team work late most nights in order to meet their deadline. And when they achieve it, after outstanding efforts, they may feel that simply to report a 'nil' variance is hardly a complete description of what has happened. The point is that commitment can make a big difference!

12.4 Budgeting in action

Some aspects of the budgeting process may become clearer if we look in some detail at an example of a business over the whole budget cycle. This cycle lasts from the start of budget preparations for next year until after the end of that year, more than twelve months in total.

In practice the processes of planning, controlling and reviewing business operations overlap with each other. Managers are in the middle of controlling the current year's operations at the same time as they are reviewing last year's performance, and starting to plan next year's. For the sake of clarity our example omits this overlap with the previous year.

Example: Woodcraft Ltd was established in the mid 1980s to manufacture and sell three products (tables, cupboards and desks) for the medium-priced market. Early in November 1989, senior managers met to consider plans for the next financial year, running from 1 April 1990 to 31 March 1991.

12.4.1 Objectives

The chairman, Mr Carstairs, began the meeting by reminding everyone that Woodcraft's main financial objective was to earn at least 10 per cent a year return on net assets, while avoiding undue risks. A second objective was controlled expansion.

The sales manager, Mr Sidney, thought the total market would grow in volume by about 5 per cent. He estimated £1,500 sales revenue* for 1990–91, a 10 per cent increase over the current year.

	'000 Units	Price	Revenue		
Tables	30	£15	£450		
Cupboards	15	£20	£300	=	£1,500
Desks	30	£25	£750		

He also estimated £170 for selling expenses: salaries £110; promotion £35; and commissions £25.

According to Mr Potter, the production manager, the existing plant and labour force could cope with this projected increase in sales, subject to more plant in the sanding department. They would also need extra storage space; but the labour force would be sufficient, given overtime at peak periods. Mr Carstairs asked the accountant, Mr Addison, for a profit estimate and cash forecast at the next meeting.

12.4.2 Profit estimates

Mr Addison calculated the direct costs of producing the planned quantities of goods at £900, using standard cost data for each product. The figures were based partly on past results and partly on expected changes in conditions.

	'000 Units	Standard cost	Total cost		
Tables	30	£ 9.10	£273		
Cupboards	15	£13.20	£198	=	£900
Desks	30	£14.30	£429		

* All figures are in £'000; that is, sales would be £1,500,000.

After estimating administrative expenses at £280, Mr Addison prepared an overall estimate of net profit for next year (figure 12.6).

	Tables (£'000)	Cupboards (£'000)	Desks (£'000)	Total (£'000)
Sales revenue	450	300	750	1500
Cost of sales	273	198	429	900
Gross profit	177	102	321	600
Selling expenses				170
Administrative expenses				280
				450
Net profit before tax				150

Figure 12.6 Woodcraft: profit estimates, 1990/91

Mr Addison needed more information for his cash budget. First he asked Mr Potter what the new plant would cost, and how much would be needed for extra stocks of materials. Then he asked Mr Sidney what increase in finished goods stocks he expected. After confirming that there would be no change in trade credit terms, he estimated the year-end debtors by using the past number of 40 days' sales in debtors. As a result he reckoned Woodcraft would require £240 extra finance by March 1991.

At their next meeting at the end of November the managers agreed on the standard cost figures and expenses. But the estimates showed an increase in 1990/91 of £240 on the expected March 1990 net assets of £1,450. Thus the return on net assets in 1990/91 would be only 8.9 per cent (= £150/£1,690), which was less than the 10 per cent required minimum.

Mr Carstairs asked whether they could charge higher prices without losing sales volume, or whether cutting prices might be a better policy. Mr Sidney suggested raising prices slightly, and increasing spending on promotion by £60 to maintain volume. He suggested increasing prices for tables and desks by £1 each, and for cupboards by £2. Mr Addison then quickly worked out a revised profit estimate (figure 12.7) based on the new figures.

With debtors up by £10, the return on net assets then worked out better, at 10.6 per cent (£180/£1,700). The managers agreed to adopt the plan, and arranged another meeting for the end of January to look at the detailed operating budget.

12.4.3 Detailed budgets

Mr Addison knew the problems of preparing a detailed operating budget. It was always hard to get the people responsible for each part to agree; yet this was

	Tables (£'000)	Cupboards (£'000)	Desks (£'000)	Total (£'000)
Sales revenue	480	330	780	1590
Cost of sales	273	198	429	900
Gross profit	207	132	351	690
Selling expenses				230
Administrative expenses				280
				510
Net profit before tax				180

Figure 12.7 Woodcraft: revised profit estimates, 1990/91

essential. At last, however, the budgets were prepared for each of the twelve months. The cash budget showed that Woodcraft would have to raise much of the extra finance by April 1990. Mr Addison recognized that both profit budgets and cash budgets were vital for successful planning.

The January meeting approved the operating details, after discussion; and then looked at the financing decision. A large cash deficit was expected in the early months, but later in the new year the net cash inflow from sales would exceed costs and reduce the deficit. The managers decided to ask the bank to increase Woodcraft's overdraft to cover the short-term cash deficit. They also agreed on a new share issue later in the year, to finance the planned permanent increase in net assets. This decision was influenced by the need to maintain adequate liquidity ratios and low gearing, since a primary objective was to minimize risks.

Mr Addison was then left to produce detailed operating budgets for department heads to issue to each responsibility centre. Each salesman had to be given his sales target, along with the expenses he could incur; each machine operator had to be informed of the planned throughput and his allowed machine hours; and so on. Those chiefly responsible for that part of the plan would already have agreed to these figures.

As 1990/91 began, the managers watched closely each stage of implementing the plan, to make sure that unforeseen snags did not interfere with its achievement. Once more, accounting information was required. (In some cases, control reports were produced weekly or even daily.)

Mr Addison's information system recorded the key performance figures at the end of each month. He then arranged them into the same format as the detailed budget, to make it easy to compare the two. The differences between budget and actual were thus highlighted, allowing suitable corrective action to be taken on the basis of 'management by exception'.

Work section

A Revision questions

A1 Name three characteristics of budgets.

A2 How does a budget differ from a neutral forecast?

A3 Why is discussion an important part of preparing budgets?

A4 What is a rolling budget?

A5 Why should a manager's performance be distinguished from that of the business unit for which he is responsible?

A6 Name three different kinds of 'responsibility centre'.

A7 What is a profit centre?

A8 Name three possible useful supplements to monthly budget reports.

A9 How might reporting less often perhaps improve a budget system?

A10 Why may including a 'latest estimate for the current year' be helpful in monthly budget reports?

A11 Name one advantage and one disadvantage of revising annual budgets during the year.

A12 Why may a deviation from budget be acceptable?

A13 Name three kinds of question on which budgetary control may help to focus managers' attention.

A14 What is a variance?

A15 Into what two kinds of variance can an overall sales variance be analysed?

A16 Why are volume variances calculated by using budget prices (rather than actual prices)?

A17 What is a flexible budget? What is its purpose?

A18 What two adjustments were proposed by Woodcraft managers to raise the budgeted return on net assets from 8.9 per cent to 10.7 per cent in 1990/91?

A19 Why did Mr Addison expect problems in putting together a detailed operating budget?

A20 What two sorts of budgets did Mr Addison recognize were both vital for successful planning?

A21 What ratios were the managers concerned about from the point of view of minimizing risk?

A22 Why might control reports be needed more often than once a month?

A23 In what respects may internal management accounts be of more help to managers than external financial accounts?

A24 What are three basic standards of comparison for a firm's ratios?

A25 Suggest two respects in which each of the following may, in effect, have 'budgets':
   a. doctors;
   b. airline pilots;
   c. cooks;
   d. teachers.

B Exercises and case studies

B1 Shortfellows Ltd budget to sell 3,000 units in March, at an average price per unit of £2.40. Actual sales revenue in March, from 3,200 units, is £7,040.
   a. What is the total sales variance for March?
   b. Analyse the total variance between volume variance and price variance.

B2 Winslow and Terry Ltd budgeted total expenses in June at £14,400, on a sales volume of 1,400 units (of which fixed expenses represented £6,000). Actual expenses in June were £15,200 (variable £8,800 and fixed £6,400), on actual sales volume of 1,500 units.
   Account in detail for the total difference of £800.

B3 Jason Escombe Ltd budgeted sales revenue in 1990 of £360,000, variable expenses of £240,000, and operating profit of £35,000. Actual sales revenue was £295,000, at selling prices 10 per cent higher than budgeted.
   a. Prepare the flexible budget figures for 1990.
   b. What could they used for?

B4 Assume that Woodcraft Ltd's net assets at 31 March, 1989 amounted to £1300,000, and that 1989/90 profit was £150,000.
   a. Calculate and compare the 1990/91 budget with the 1989/90 actual return on net assets ratio, using 'average' not 'end-of-year' net assets.
   b. Do you regard the change brought about by this different method of calculation as significant? Why or why not?

B5 Refer to figures 12.6 and 12.7.
   a. Calculate what revised profit estimate would have resulted if Mr Sidney had proposed to reduce selling prices by 10 per cent and expected as a result to increase sales volume by one third for all three product lines (with no change in selling expenses).
   b. Comment on your answer, with special reference to the distinction between total sales revenue and total contribution.

B6 The adjustment to selling policy as a result of Mr Sidney's suggestions for 1990/91 affected the budgeted profit as well as the budgeted net assets. Why might you have expected net assets to be affected by the change? Try to quantify your answer.

B7   Refer to the inter-firm comparison in figure 12.8.
 a. Which aspects of Woodcraft Ltd's operations seem to call for special
    further examination? Why?
 b. What accounts for firm C's high return on net assets?
 c. Why do you suppose that firm B's asset turnover ratio is lower than
    Woodcraft's? *(Hint:* look at ratios 9 and 10.)
 d. If you could obtain *two* further pieces of information about the five
    companies whose ratios are listed, what would you ask for? Why?

		Woodcraft	A	B	C	D
1. Return on net assets	%	8.3	11.6	8.1	16.3	14.9
2. Profit margin	%	9.0	9.2	9.8	8.9	11.0
3. Asset turnover		0.92	1.26	0.83	1.83	1.35
4. Direct costs/sales	%	58.7	58.1	55.8	54.2	53.4
5. Selling exs./sales	%	14.5	14.8	16.4	19.1	18.4
6. Admin. exs./sales	%	17.6	17.9	18.0	17.8	17.2
7. Sales/fixed assets		2.1	2.4	2.1	2.3	2.5
8. Sales/current assets		1.4	2.0	1.3	3.4	3.1
9. Stock turnover		2.8	3.1	4.3	6.1	5.8
10. Days sales in debtors		60	45	43	41	42

*Figure 12.8 The main ratios from Woodcraft Ltd's 1990/91 accounts
alongside the equivalent ratios for four comparable firms in the same
industry*

B8   Education Tapes Ltd imports taped lectures and sells them to schools
    and colleges. At the end of 1989 the company's balance sheet was as
    shown on the opposite page (figure 12.9).
    The accountant is given the following information to enable him to draw
    up budgets for 1990
    1 *Sales.* 7,000 tapes per month at £7 each (the price was £6 last year).
    Company policy is to keep one month's sales in stock. The price of
    imported tapes is expected to rise on 1.1.90 from £5 to £6.
    2 *Expenditure.* Sales overheads   £20,000
                         Administrative overheads   £31,000
                         New equipment (to be bought on 1.1.90)   £15,000
    3 *Depreciation.* At a rate of 10 per cent, using the straight-line method.
    4 *Tax and dividends.* Tax is expected to amount to 35 per cent of net
    profit, and is payable in the following year. The intention is to pay a
    dividend of 10p per share during the year.

	(£'000)		
Fixed assets			
Equipment and vehicles, at cost		100	
Less: accumulated depreciation		25	
			75
Current assets			
Stocks	25		
Debtors	30		
Cash	10		
		65	
Less: current liabilities			
Creditors	40		
Taxation	10		
		50	
			15
Net assets			90
Ordinary share capital (£1 shares)			50
Retained profits			40
Shareholders' funds			90

Figure 12.9 Education Tapes Ltd: balance sheet

5 *Credit.* It is expected that the average collection period for debtors will be one and a half months instead of the current one month. On the other hand, the suppliers have decided to enforce strictly one month's credit to the company. All other transactions, except tax, are for cash.
   a. As accountant prepare: (1) a cash budget for 1990; (2) a profit and loss account budget for 1990; (3) an estimated balance sheet as at 31 December 1990.
   b. Use key ratios to comment on the figures you have prepared.
B9   Design an outline monthly management report for the financial results of a school. *(Hint:* remember it will have to be used by people who are not financial experts!)
B10 Mr Zebedee has a small workshop at the back of his house, where he employs three people making bedside cabinets. They each work for 40 hours a week, at a wage of £2.50 per hour. It takes four working hours to produce a cabinet, which sells for £20.00 and contains £4.00 worth of timber. Heating, rent, rates, etc. normally average £60.00 per week.
   One Sunday one of the workers catches a cold and is away for the whole of the next week. He receives no pay for that week. The other two workers

work six hours' overtime each, for which they are paid at 'time and a half'. They manage to produce 25 cabinets between them, but due to haste they use 10 per cent more material than usual. Also the timber price has risen by 20 per cent. The weather is extremely cold that week, so the bill for overheads rises to £68.00 because of additional heating for longer hours.

a. Calculate the budgeted profit or loss for the week.

b. Calculate the actual profit or loss for the week.

c. Prepare a statement explaining the difference between the actual financial result for the week and the 'budget'. Distinguish between (i) quantity differences and (ii) price differences.

B11 Alpine Novelties (Colorado) Inc produces two models of cuckoo clock. The company's budget for 1990 was as follows:

	Monster	*Baby*	*TOTAL*
Selling price each	$60	$25	
Sales quantities	2,000	8,000	
	($'000)	($'000)	($'000)
Sales revenue	120	200	320
Variable cost of sales	60	160	220
Contribution	60	40	100

The actual figures for 1990 were as follows:

Sales quantities	1,800	9,000	
	($'000)	($'000)	($'000)
Sales revenue	90	240	330
Variable cost of sales	50	185	235
Contribution	40	55	95

Figure 12.10 Alpine Novelties Inc: budget for 1990

Account for the drop in contribution between budget and actual.

B12 Household Industries Ltd make, amongst other products, a holder for toilet rolls. The manufacturing process is in three parts: (1) stamping out; (2) painting; (3) fitting with a centre rolling pin, and a bracket and screws for easy attachment to a door. The standard cost of a holder is £2.00, processing 90p, plus materials £1.10, analysed as follows:

Processing 90p	*Stamping* 500 per hour *Hourly cost*	*Painting* 500 per hour *Hourly cost*	*Fitting* 400 per hour *Hourly cost*
Wages	£160	£120	£60
Power	30	20	5
Depreciation	10	10	–
Overtime premium★	–	–	15
	£200	£150	£80

★Shortages of personnel force this department to work regular overtime, meaning higher wage rates for those hours.

The materials cost of £1.10 consists of: metal 65p; paint 15p; sundries 30p.

The management accountant makes a weekly comparison of actual with standard (or budgeted) costs and output. One week the actual performance figures were as follows:

Output of holders; 20,000.

Hours worked on holders, by departments: stamping 55; painting 49; fitting 40.

Expenses incurred in running departments:

	Stamping (£)	*Painting* (£)	*Fitting* (£)
Wages★	9,680	5,880	2,640
Power	1,650	980	200
Depreciation	550	490	–
Overtime premiums	–	–	720
	11,880	7,350	3,560

★ A wage rise for some workers had caused some departments to experience increased costs.

Materials:	Metal	£13,800
	Paint	2,900
	Sundries	6,100
		£22,800

    a. Calculate the actual cost per holder.

    b. Analyse the difference between standard cost and actual cost.

    c. Prepare a report setting out and discussing your main findings.

B13 Edison Ltd operates two small factories at Dudley and Walsall in the West Midlands, each employing 100 people in production of bicycle chains. All employees work for 150 hours a month, at a wage rate of £4.00 per hour, each producing on average 10 chains per hour. Material costs amount to 25p per chain, and Edison normally sells 300,000 chains a month, for £1.00 each, mainly to bicycle manufacturers. Fixed costs are budgeted at £80,000 a month.

A dispute about working conditions closes the Dudley factory for the month of October, and all 100 Dudley production workers are laid off and receive no pay for that month. Fixed costs, however, fall by only £8,000. The 100 Walsall workers are able to increase their productivity so that in October they actually produce 200,000 chains, all of which are sold at the usual price. They are rewarded by a productivity bonus amounting to 25 per cent of their normal wages. Thanks to a nearby metal manufacturer going bankrupt, Edison Ltd is able to buy materials for the month at a discount of 20 per cent off the normal cost.

    a. Calculate Edison's actual profit or loss for October.

    b. Prepare a table showing the difference between the actual result and the original budgeted contribution and profit for the month.

    c. Compare the actual result with a flexed budget, showing what the expenses 'should have been' at the actual volume of sales.

    d. Split the total labour cost variance for October between the difference due to efficiency (volume) and that due to rates of pay (price).

    e. Summarize all the variances to explain the difference between the originally budgeted profit and actual profit or loss.

C   Essay questions

C1   Why does business planning require attention to both cash and profit?

C2   Explain how changing the sales budget for a year may affect the cash budget.

C3   Discuss the pros and cons of using 'rolling budgets'.

C4   How can the budgeting process allow for unknown future rates of general inflation?

C5   'We prepare our annual budgets about ten months through the previous year; but conditions change so fast in our industry that the budgets are already out of date before the budget year even begins'. What kind of solution, if any, might be appropriate; and what do you see as its main advantages and disadvantages?

C6   What problems would you expect to find in preparing and using a budget for a research and development department?

C7   Explain to someone who knows nothing about accounting what is meant by 'variance analysis', and what are its benefits.

C8   Explain the purpose of flexible budgeting.

C9   How does a budgeting system make use of feedback?

C10 'Our internal management accounting reports take far too long to tell me what I already knew.' How might a competent management accountant respond to this (very common) criticism?

13

Managing cash

Plan of the chapter

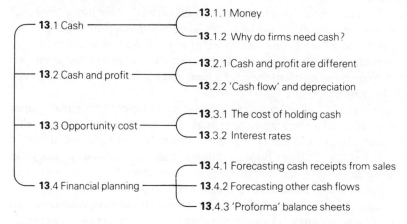

Fig.13.0

Objective: *To identify the functions of money in the economy and of cash (which includes bank balances) in a business; to distinguish between cash and profit; to analyse what comprises the rate of interest on money lent and borrowed; and to explain the process of cash forecasting within a firm.*

Synopsis: *Cash and profit are both important to business firms, but they are different. Firms hold cash to settle business transactions and to provide a margin of safety. But they must balance these benefits against the 'opportunity cost' of holding cash – what else could they do with the money? This is normally related to the current rate of interest, which comprises: pure time preference, an inflation premium, and a risk premium.*

In financial planning a company may try to forecast cash receipts and cash payments month by month, or it may try to estimate the end of period balance sheet. In either case, business forecasts are likely to be subject to a wide margin of error.

13.1 Cash

13.1.1 Money

Money is any generally accepted medium of exchange. Its main function is to act as a means of payment. If there were no money, people would have to exchange goods and services by means of barter. This is a cumbersome process, where two people must each want precisely what the other has got.

Centuries ago, gold or silver came to serve as money, being relatively scarce, stable, durable, divisible, and easy to recognize. The ruler's seal on a coin stated and guaranteed its weight (and implied its fineness); this avoided the need to assay or weigh the metal at each payment, and made such coins acceptable 'at face value'. Eventually milled edges prevented coin-clipping; but rulers of nations themselves often 'debased' coins by adding base metal to the precious metal.

Bankers held money (gold) in safe-keeping and issued paper notes (receipts) to the owners (depositors). These bank notes represented a promise to pay the holder on demand a certain amount (weight) of gold, and most people found them convenient to use for payments. In practice a bank could issue about ten times more 'paper money' than the gold it held and lend out the extra money at interest to borrowers.

Some loans would be for long periods; so if every holder of a bank's paper notes were to demand instant repayment in gold (a 'run on the bank'), the bank would be unable to meet its legal obligations. Hence prudent banks had to take great care to avoid any loss of public confidence in their **solvency.** They did this partly by **matching the maturities** of their assets and liabilities. But paper notes of a reliable bank were reckoned to be 'as good as gold'.

In time central banks evolved, to serve as banker to the government as well as to the commercial banks. They often became the sole issuer of paper notes, and 'lenders of last resort'. Eventually governments nationalized most central banks, and withdrew people's right to convert paper bank notes into gold. That made it easy (and tempting) for governments to go on printing more and more notes, thus inflating the supply of paper ('fiat') currency. The quantity theory of money, in its simplest form, says that the larger the money supply, the less the value (purchasing power) of each unit of currency.

A stable money can represent a store of wealth. More important, as long as the purchasing power of money is reasonably stable, it can represent a **unit of account**. This allows economic calculation in terms of money. If money loses purchasing power fast, however, (as in modern times) it becomes less useful as a unit of account; hence pressures for a system of inflation accounting (see Chapter 8).

In a prisoner of war camp, machine-made cigarettes served quite well as money; though subject to massive inflation when new supplies arrived, and to regular deflation as people smoked part of the money supply! People were prepared to trust the currency; though hand-rolled cigarettes were liable to be rejected, or valued at a discount.

13.1.2 Why do firms need cash?
The three main reasons for holding cash are sometimes expressed as: the transactions motive, the precautionary motive, and the speculative motive.

Most people carry some cash around with them to cover various day-to-day transactions, such as paying for a haircut or a bus fare. In the same way, firms may need large sums of cash, for example, to pay weekly wages, or, from time to time, to pay for new equipment, to settle tax bills, or to repay long-term borrowing.

Many retail shops hold large sums of cash in their tills. This is not needed for cash purchases (which would be made from other sources); nor is it merely a result of cash takings from sales (which are promptly banked). The main function of till cash is to enable shops to offer change to customers. An old *Punch* joke shows a passenger apologizing to a bus conductor as he offers a £50 note in payment for a 50p fare: 'I'm afraid I haven't got any change.' The conductor pours 495 10p pieces into his lap and replies: 'Well you have now!'

In most businesses the precise pattern of weekly cash receipts and payments will fluctuate. For example, bad weather may reduce cash sales of a department store. A business may choose to hold an extra cash balance for precautionary reasons, so that even if things go slightly wrong it will still be able to make ends meet. The amount of the cash 'safety margin' will depend on how business managers feel about the risks of running out of cash (both how likely it is, and how much it matters). A business, or individual, may also happen to hold cash because of errors in forecasts of the timing or amount of cash receipts or payments.

Strictly speaking, what is needed is not so much cash itself as the 'ability to pay'. Thus many people now carry credit cards to let them make day-to-day purchases for which they might once have needed cash. Similarly a business which has arranged bank overdraft facilities (see 14.4.5) may not need to hold any positive cash balance with its bank: it can simply continue to draw cheques up to the extent of the agreed borrowing limit.

Finally, the speculative motive is ever-present in business. A stock exchange investor may increase his cash holding by selling shares whose price he expects to fall. To be successful (make a profit) he must guess not just the *direction* in which the market is going to move, but also the *timing*. Similar motives may underlie changes in cash holdings in many businesses; for example, where raw material prices are expected to change.

13.2 Cash and profit

13.2.1 Cash and profit are different
Cash and profit are two of the main concerns of the financial manager. Both are important, but they are different. Figure 13.1 overleaf classifies some of the main differences.

Cash is a liquid asset owned by a business, enabling it to buy goods or services. A firm's cash balance can be too *large*, as well as too small.

	Balance sheet effect
1 P & L income not cash receipt	**Profit UP**
a. Sale on credit	Debtors UP
2 Cash payment not P & L expense	**Cash DOWN**
a. Purchase of long-term asset	Fixed assets UP
b. Increase in stock	Stock UP
c. Dividend paid	Equity DOWN
d. Reduction of creditor	Liability DOWN
e. Payment of tax	Liability DOWN
f. Repayment of long-term loan	Liability DOWN
3 P & L expense not cash payment	**Profit DOWN**
a. Depreciation of fixed asset	Fixed assets DOWN
b. Write off bad debt	Debtors DOWN
c. Write off stock	Stock DOWN
d. Purchase on credit	Creditors UP
e. Tax charge not yet paid	Tax liability UP
4 Cash receipt not P & L income	**Cash UP**
a. Issue new share capital for cash	Equity UP
b. Borrow long-term loan	Loans UP
c. Sale of long-term asset	Fixed assets DOWN

Figure 13.1 Why profit and cash may differ

Profit is the surplus earned in respect of a period's trading, after deducting all business expenses from sales turnover and other income. Profit is an accounting measurement, not an asset owned by a business. Other things being equal, the larger the profit earned the better.

If a business sells goods for more than they cost, it has made a profit. But if the customers have not yet paid for the goods, the business may have no cash. Similarly the amount of expenses in a period will usually not equal the amount of cash paid out.

There are obvious examples of the difference between profit and cash. When a company borrows money, the immediate result is to increase the cash balance. But no business would dream of treating the amount borrowed as a profit! It will have to be repaid in due course. Another example would be the accounting treatment of fixed assets, such as a new machine or an extension to a firm's factory. Where a firm acquires these for cash, it does not deduct the whole cost from profit in the same period in which payment was made. Instead the company's accounts charge only a fraction of the cost as depreciation expense in each period of the asset's life (see Chapter 6).

13.2.2 'Cash flow' and depreciation

The financial press often uses the term **'cash flow'** to mean 'retained profits plus depreciation' for a period. The point is that depreciation does not represent a use of funds in the period in which it is charged as an expense: it is merely an accounting entry. No cash is paid out in respect of depreciation: the only cash payment is for the original purchase of a fixed asset, at the start of its life. So since depreciation expense has been charged against (deducted from) sales turnover in measuring net profit in accounts, it needs to be 'added back' in order to convert the figure for profit in that period into (an estimate of) cash flow. (Depreciation is not the only item in the profit and loss account which may not represent cash, but it is often the single most important item.)

If depreciation were literally a source of funds, it would be possible for a company to increase its cash balance merely by increasing its charge for depreciation expense in the profit and loss account. But doing this, of course, would then reduce the reported profit to exactly the same extent! The net effect on cash flow (= profit plus depreciation) would be precisely zero.

Example: Suppose Hamilton Pumps Ltd increased its £375,000 depreciation expense in 1990 (see 9.2) to £500,000, the figure for 'cash flow' would remain unchanged at £625,000:

	Original accounts (£'000)	*Depreciation up by $\frac{1}{3}$* (£'000)
Profit before depreciation	925	925
Depreciation expense	375	500
Profit before tax	550	425
Corporation tax (unchanged)	200	200
Profit after tax	350	225
Dividends paid	100	100
Retained profits	250	125
'Add back' depreciation	375	500
= Internally-generated cash flow	625	625

Figure 13.2 Cash flow and depreciation

215

13.3 Opportunity cost

13.3.1 The cost of holding cash

There are sometimes reports of mysterious Nigerians carrying £250,000 around London in used notes who stop for a cup of coffee and when they emerge find their taxi has disappeared with their cash in a bag on the back seat. Bank notes – being anonymous – are subject to the risk of loss; but this does not apply to cash held in a bank account.

The main 'cost' of holding cash is the loss of the interest which could otherwise have been earned on it. For instance, suppose one could invest money to earn an interest rate of 10 per cent a year. Then by choosing to hold cash instead, one is giving up the potential interest yield. That **opportunity cost** is the real economic cost of holding non-interest-bearing cash.

Clearly there may be a conflict between cash and profit. A business with too little cash may be taking too much risk of running out. On the other hand, one with too much cash may be sacrificing profit.

Opportunity cost is not just some vague abstraction: it is a real, often significant, economic cost. Business managers should always be asking: 'What else could we be doing with our resources? What alternatives are open to us?' This question applies not merely to cash, but to other assets, employees, and so on.

13.3.2 Interest rates

The **interest rate** consists of three component parts: time preference, inflation premium, and risk premium.

1. Time preference

Pure **time preference** refers to the ratio between consumers' valuations of present goods as against otherwise identical goods in the future. If in general consumers did not prefer present goods to future goods, they would never consume anything. The convention is to quote the ratio as an annual rate. In effect, a pure interest rate may be regarded as the 'price of time'.

The British government recently started issuing securities which are **index-linked** (guaranteed against inflation). Since British government securities are normally regarded as **risk-free,** the yield on such index-linked securities provides a direct market measure of the rate of 'pure' time preference. In January 1990 index-linked gilts yielded about $3\frac{1}{2}$ per cent a year.

2. Inflation premium

The second component in rates of interest on loans of money is an **inflation premium.** This is needed to allow for the anticipated rate of future inflation. British government securities yield about 10 per cent a year now, compared with only about $2\frac{1}{2}$ per cent a year in Victorian times, because there was virtually no inflation then. For the same reason, money interest rates are much higher in Brazil than in Switzerland, because people expect more inflation in Brazil.

If the interest rate on a one-year loan would be 4 per cent in the absence of inflation, and if both borrower and lender expect inflation of 6 per cent in the next year, then the actual money rate of interest will be about 10 per cent a year. (Strictly it will be $1.06 \times 1.04 = 1.1024$ or 10.24 per cent.) But, of course, people may guess wrong about the future rate of inflation.

3. Risk premium

The third component in most business interest rates is a **risk premium**. This is why smaller businesses often have to pay higher rates of interest than large well-established companies: lending to them is usually 'riskier', in that smaller firms are more likely to default on interest or principal repayments. (If the risk is thought too large, a bank may simply refuse to lend at all, at any interest rate.)

Financial theory suggests a straight-line relationship between 'risk' and a lender's required rate of 'return', as shown by the capital market line in figure 13.3. Even at zero risk there is still a positive interest rate, to represent pure time preference plus an inflation premium. Thereafter as risk increases, moving to the right along the horizontal axis, so does the return required on the vertical axis.

Thus for an investment in Project α (figure 13.3), the required rate of return consists of:

1. pure time preference;
2. inflation premium;
3 (medium-high) risk premium.

These are set out, starting from zero, on the vertical axis in figure 13.3.

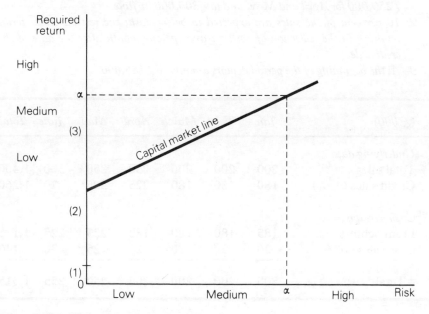

Figure 13.3 Risk and required return

13.4 Financial planning

13.4.1 Forecasting cash receipts from sales

A company's cash balance should ideally be high enough to protect the business against any serious chance of running out, but not so high as to tie up excess funds in low-yielding uses. Financial managers of a business must decide what cash levels they are aiming at. Then they need to forecast the amount and timing of the likely sources and uses of cash in future periods.

It is obviously crucial for a company to avoid running out of cash. Otherwise it might be forced into liquidation by creditors it was unable to pay; or at least funds might have to be raised at a very high cost; and subject to conditions which might be most burdensome.

Careful forecasting of the amount and timing of future cash receipts and payments has several benefits:

1   it tests the financial results of plans before making definite commitments;
2   it reveals possible future needs to raise more capital, which may take several months to arrange;
3   it avoids undesired accumulation of non-interest-bearing cash.

The most critical single estimate in cash flow forecasting for a business is very often the forecast of sales turnover. This nearly always represents the main source of cash receipts for the firm.

> *Example: Glo-lamp Ltd's financial manager is preparing a six-month cash forecast beginning in January. He decides to start by estimating cash receipts from sales, with the following basic assumptions:*
>
> 1   *Sales revenue will be £200,000 a month for the first three months rising to £250,000 for April and May, and to £300,000 in June.*
> 2   *10 per cent of the sales are expected to be for cash; the rest on credit terms resulting in the collection of cash on average one month after the date of the credit sale.*
> 3   *At the beginning of the period debtors amount to £185,000.*

(£'000)	Jan.	Feb.	March	April	May	June	Total
Underlying data							
Total sales	200	200	200	250	250	300	1,400
Credit sales (90%)	180	180	180	225	225	270	1,260
Cash receipts							
From debtors	185	180	180	180	225	225	1,175
Cash sales (10%)	20	20	20	25	25	30	140
= Total	205	200	200	205	250	255	1,315

Figure 13.4 Cash receipts from sales

Figure 13.4 translates these assumptions into a schedule of expected cash receipts from sales month by month.

The value of goods sold in the period does not at once produce the same amount of cash. Over the whole six months the Glo-lamp totals can be reconciled as follows:

	(£'000)
Opening debtors	185
Add: total sales in period	1,400
	1,585
Less: closing debtors	270
= Cash received in period	1,315

The £85,000 shortfall of cash received, as compared with sales, is reflected in the £85,000 increase in debtors between the start and end of the period.

It is worth stressing that the forecast of cash receipts from sales is often subject to a large margin of error since it depends on three different estimates, each of which may vary unexpectedly:

1 the physical volume of sales;
2 the average selling price per unit;
3 the average delay in payment (credit period taken).

13.4.2 Forecasting other cash flows

Most businesses find that cash payments in respect of operating expenses are often related fairly closely to sales volume. In particular, purchases of materials will normally be variable; though stock levels may fluctuate for a number of reasons (see 14.2.2).

Other expenses may be less affected by short-term fluctuations in the level of sales. The labour force, for example, is often virtually fixed in the short term. And there will be a number of overhead expenses whose amount can be predicted fairly accurately, such as office rents. It may be more difficult to forecast certain 'discretionary' expenses, such as research or advertising.

Various other cash receipts and payments need to be included in any overall cash forecast, even if there is no direct link with day-to-day operations. Receipts other than from sales may comprise: proceeds from disposing of old equipment; receipts from issues of share capital, or from borrowing; income on investments.

Payments other than for operating expenses may include: taxation; dividend payments; purchases of investments; acquisition of fixed assets. Cash payments to acquire fixed assets will show up in operating expenses only as a result of charging depreciation expense (a non-cash item) over the useful life of the asset (see Chapter 6).

Many of these forecasts are not easy to make. A sobering definition of forecasting is: a pretence of knowing what would have happened if what did happen hadn't.

13.4.3 'Proforma' balance sheets

The projected (proforma) balance sheet method of forecasting funds requirements is based on a forecast of *all* balance sheet items (not just cash) at a particular future date. It involves four major steps:

1   Forecasting the net total amount for each of the assets.

2   Listing the liabilities:

(a) that can be counted on without special negotiation, such as trade creditors and taxation;

(b) which do have to be negotiated, such as bank overdrafts.

3   Estimating the expected profits for the period, less dividend payments. Since profit is a residual between two much larger amounts (sales turnover less total expenses), this may be subject to a wide margin of error.

4   Total the expected assets, liabilities, and shareholders' funds, to reveal whether there is expected to be a surplus or shortage of funds on the date chosen. Further action may be needed, either to invest any anticipated surplus of funds, or to raise money to cover any shortage.

The projected balance sheet method forecasts all the balance sheet items, not just cash. It can therefore be used to forecast certain financial ratios, such as return on net assets. It can quickly make rough – yet often very helpful – forecasts where forward plans may not yet exist in sufficient detail to allow cash flow forecasting.

The method shows expected balance sheet amounts only at the *end* of the particular period selected – not during the interim period. It will therefore reveal maximum needs for funds only if dates are carefully chosen to show the balance sheet at times of maximum strain. (If there is doubt about the most suitable date to choose, then several projections at different dates may be required.)

It is often a good idea to note *in writing* the key assumptions underlying the forecasts; and it can be useful to try to identify the rough margin of error in the key items. It may also be worth preparing several alternative forecasts based on different assumptions. (Computers make it possible to prepare detailed forecasts, month by month, and to test plans in advance by varying the assumptions and seeing what difference they make.)

If the same assumptions are made for the projected balance sheet method as for a cash flow forecast, then the two methods should, of course, produce an identical forecast of the end-of-period cash balance. The projected balance sheet method forces management to make explicit assumptions about fixed assets and working capital. These are surprisingly easy to overlook in a cash flow forecast; yet they can be critical for many businesses. In Chapter 14 we go on to look in more detail at working capital.

Work section

A   Revision questions

A1   What are the three main functions of money?

A2   How does rapid inflation affect the functions of money?

A3   Why is money unsatisfactory as a unit of accounting measurement in times of rapid inflation?

A4   Name three reasons for individuals (or firms) to hold cash.

A5   How can a profitable company run out of cash?

A6   How can a company hold 'too much' cash?

A7   Why does increasing depreciation not increase cash flow?

A8   Define 'opportunity cost' in the context of cash.

A9   What three constituent parts make up the rate of interest?

A10 Why are interest rates higher in Brazil than in Switzerland?

A11 Why do smaller businesses usually have to pay higher interest rates on borrowed money than larger companies?

A12 Why does even a government security which is both 'risk-free' and 'index-linked' provide a positive interest yield?

A13 Identify as many advantages as you can of regular cash forecasting.

A14 What is likely to be the most critical estimate in cash flow forecasts?

A15 What is a 'discretionary expense'? Give an example.

A16 How will inflation affect a firm's needs for cash?

A17 What are the main difficulties in forecasting a company's cash needs?

A18 How would you forecast how much cash a company will need to provide for its working capital requirements in five years' time?

A19 Why is it often difficult to forecast retained profits for a period?

A20 Explain the main differences between a detailed month-by-month cash flow forecast and the proforma balance sheet method of forecasting.

B   Exercises and case studies

B1   The owner of a small research agency is discussing the company's future with a friend. 'We're not doing badly', he says, 'we should make a profit this year, after paying our salaries, of about £12,000. We're lucky to own our own offices; if we had to rent similar ones it would cost us another £30,000 a year.'
Discuss, using the concept of opportunity cost, whether or not the company should continue in business.

B2   An extract from the annual report of a small company runs as follows:
'We are pleased to report that the company has made an operating profit

221

which, as a proportion of the funds invested in the business, is 10 per cent this year. It is as well we have kept up our profit, since it would cost us 16 per cent interest if we had to borrow from the bank.'

Comment on this, illustrating how using the idea of opportunity cost may give a different view of the company's position.

B3   The longer the interval between cash payments and receipts, the larger an enterprise's financing needs in relation to sales revenue.

Comment on the cash flows (and thus the needs for finance) of:
(a) a farmer; (b) a food manufacturer; (c) a grocer; (d) a shipbuilder;
(e) a school.

B4   How would a food manufacturing company's forecast of its cash needs for the next year probably be affected by each of the following unexpected events? (a) Higher inflation than expected; (b) a poor crop; (c) introduction by competitors of synthetic foods; (d) rise in interest rates; (e) enforced closure of all factories for two days each week?

B5   Roughly what might be the net amount of money needed to finance the running expenses of:

a. A barrow boy who buys 250 kg of apples each morning in the wholesale market for cash?

b. A barrow boy who buys 250 kg of apples each morning in the wholesale market on one week's credit?

c. A pawnbroker who lends £500 daily, and is repaid on average after three months?

d. A supermarket chain which buys goods on one month's credit and sells them in two weeks for cash?

e. A manufacturing company with annual sales of £300,000, 20 per cent of which is profit; materials amount to half of total costs, are purchased on one month's credit, take two months to process and dispatch, and are sold on two months' credit?

f. A private house builder building 120 £40,000 houses each year?

List the six in order of the amount of money required as a percentage of sales.

B6   A company is set up with £20,000 cash, and during its first year the following takes place:

12 Jan.	: machinery bought for £10,000 cash
24 Feb.	: goods bought for £5,000 cash
12 May	: the same goods sold for £15,000 cash
16 June	: further goods bought for £20,000 cash
12 Nov.	: the goods are sold, on two months's credit, for £30,000
5 Dec.	: independent valuers put the present value of the machinery at £8,000.

Calculate: (a) profit for the year; (b) 'cash flow' for the year. As financial director, write a short report to the managing director, explaining the significance of each of these figures.

B7 A firm buys a machine for £200,000, expecting it to last for 10 years.
   a. What depreciation would you recommend is charged each year as an expense against profits?
   b. Assuming that the annual pre-depreciation profits are £50,000, what would the annual post-depreciation profits amount to?
   c. Would your answer to (a) above change if annual pre-depreciation profits of only £15,000 were expected next year? Why or why not?
   d. Soon after buying the machine, the firm decides it would be sensible to rely on only five years' useful life from the machine. What effect would this decision have on:
   (i) the annual depreciation charge? (ii) profits? (iii) cash flow?

B8 Assuming that everyone is agreed in their expectation of the future rate of inflation, what would you expect to be the effect of introducing 'usury' laws putting a ceiling on the maximum rate of interest which could lawfully be charged to borrowers? What sort of borrowers would be affected, and what sort would not?

B9 A 20-year indexed gilt yields 4.0 per cent a year, while a 20-year ordinary (non-indexed) gilt yields 10.0 per cent a year.
   a. What is the implied annual inflation premium over the period?
   b. What conclusion can be drawn if a similar calculation in respect of five-year gilts produces a figure considerably higher than your answer to (a)?
   c. If people's expectations of inflation in future increase, what would you expect to happen to the yields:
   (i) on indexed gilts? (ii) on non-indexed gilts? Why?

B10 *'It's enough to drive you off the rails for good'*
   'These costs are based on British Rail second class single tickets. And on the energy-saving Sunderland Supersnarl which averages 54.3 m.p.g. at a steady 56 m.p.h., with the cost of petrol at £1.59 per gallon. We appreciate you have to buy an SS in the first place, but at least you can run it when you want, and take four more adults at no extra cost. Just try that with BR'

   Advertisement in Sunday newspapers,
   7 February 1982.

   There followed a list of 45 destinations from London, with cost figures under two columns headed 'BR' and 'SS', and with mileage figures. A representative selection of four destinations is shown below:

	Mileage	BR (£)	SS (£)
Aberdeen	503	39.00	14.73
Birmingham	105	11.30	3.07
Bradford	195	19.60	5.71
Cambridge	54	5.40	1.58

   a. How have the SS figures been calculated?

b. Is the comparison being made a fair one? If not, why not?

c. Roughly what would you reckon is a fair comparison for the Aberdeen to London journey? How have you calculated it?

d. What would be a fair Aberdeen-London comparison for a husband and wife with their 17-year-old son?

B11 Fenton Ltd was recently formed to buy and sell wimpoles. At the end of 1991 the balance sheet simply consists of: Debtors £12,000, Stocks £27,000, and Issued Share Capital £39,000. The cash balance was zero, and there were no retained profits. The company owns no fixed assets, and has no current liabilities.

In the first quarter of 1992, the company sold 3,000 wimpoles, an increase of 1,000 on the previous quarter. These cost the company £9 each and sell for £12 each. The company expects to increase its volume of sales by 1,000 units each quarter for the next two years. Thus sales in the second quarter of 1992 are expected to be 4,000 wimpoles, in the third quarter 5,000, and so on.

Purchases are paid for in the same month as they occur, while customers (debtors) pay on average $1\frac{1}{2}$ months after the date of sale. You may assume that both purchases and sales are made evenly throughout each quarter. (For example, assume sales of 1,000 wimpoles a month in each of the first three months of 1992, then 1,333 a month in each of the next three months, and so on.) The stock level held is equivalent to predicted sales volume for the next three months; so at the end of 1991 3,000 wimpoles were held in stock.

a. Forecast the quarter-by-quarter profit and loss account and balance sheet figures for the rest of 1992 and for the first half of 1993.

b. How does the expected cumulative cash balance differ from the expected cumulative balance of retained profits? (No dividend payments are planned.) Draw a graph comparing the two.

c. What is likely to be the maximum borrowing requirement? When will it be needed?

d. If the maximum amount that can be borrowed is *less* than your projections suggest will be needed, what can Fenton Ltd do to reduce its need for funds?

B12 Spanner Ltd, a civil engineering company, accepts a government contract to build a road bridge for £8 million. The job should take two years. Earth-moving machinery must be purchased for £1.2 million, which can be sold for £200,000 at the end of the contract. Labour costs will be £300,000 quarterly in the first year and £400,000 quarterly in the second year. After three months materials will be needed, and over the next four quarters weekly deliveries will be made at a rate of £500,000 worth per quarter. Other costs (administration, petrol, etc.) are expected to be about £200,000 each quarter over the whole contract. Assuming progress accords with an agreed plan, 'progress' payments will be made on the contract, starting from the second quarter, amounting to £700,000 per quarter. The balance of the £8 million outstanding will then be payable on completion of the contract.

Making (and stating) any further assumptions you think necessary:

a. prepare a quarter-by-quarter table of cash receipts and payments for the two years of the contract;

b. show what is the maximum cash 'investment' the project requires.

c. what is the expected overall profit or loss on the contract?

B13 In 1990 Newman Machines Ltd wanted to replace an old turret lathe. It cost £20,000 in 1975; and had been depreciated over 15 years. The company had £20,000 (provided out of depreciation) to buy a new lathe, plus £5,000, the re-sale value of the old lathe.

But the replacement cost in 1990 was £70,000 for a lathe that would perform the same functions as the old machine, or £90,000 for a new improved model with special accessories. So Newman had only £25,000 to buy a £90,000 machine. The difference of £65,000 had to come out of profits.

To get that amount, the company needed to earn a profit of £100,000 before tax, because only £65,000 would be left after the government took corporation tax of 35 per cent. And to earn £100,000 profit, the company had to sell more than £1,000,000 worth of products to customers. Thus while £100,000 might sound like a lot of profit, in this case the owners of the business would get none of it. The government would take more han one third, and the rest would go to replace a single machine.

This story explains why only a relatively small amount of profit is paid out in dividends to the shareholders. A large proportion must be retained in the business to finance expansion and replacement so that a firm can carry on and the employees continue working.

Comment on the story of the 'million pound lathe'. Is it the truth, the whole truth, and nothing but the truth?

B14 Examine a recent set of published accounts.

a. Draw up a list of changes in each item in the balance sheet between the end of the latest year and the end of the previous year. Your list of 'balance sheet changes' should itself balance.

b. Classify and rearrange your list of balance sheet changes into the form of a funds flow statement.

c. Compare your version with the company's published funds flow statement. What are the main differences in presentation? Are any of the money amounts different in the two statements? If so, can you identify why?

B15 A certain company, wishing to improve its profits, is considering three alternative strategies:

a. It may raise the price of its product, thus reducing sales but increasing the profit per item.

225

b. It may aim for a larger market share, increasing advertising expenditure and lowering its price.

c. It may undertake research, aiming to produce a better product which could sell at a higher price than at present, but in the same quantities and at the same production cost.

As financial director, you are asked to write a short report setting out the impact on the company's cash position of the early stages of each policy.

B16   Mr James has asked for overdraft facilities to start up a new business and the bank has asked for information to assist them in assessing his requirements.

Assuming that the business commences on 1st July 1985 and that Mr James provides £6,000 initial cash capital on 1st July and a further £4,000 on 1st October, it is expected that:

1. Rent will be £100 per month, payable on the first day of each month in arrear.

2. Materials will be bought during July to a value of £2,400. In subsequent months purchases will be such as to maintain the stock of materials at £1,600. Payment for these materials will be made at the end of the month following that of purchase.

3. Wages will be £500 in July and £2,500 per month from August onwards.

4. It is anticipated that a salesman will be engaged from 1st August at a salary of £600 per month.

5. Production will be 100 units in July and 500 units per month thereafter. Each unit uses £4 of raw material and £5 of labour.

6. Sales will be nil in July and August but are expected to be 200 units in September, 400 in October and then 500 units each month. The selling price will be £18 per unit, payable at the end of the second following month.

7. Sundry expenses will be £300 per month and Mr James expects to draw £200 per month for private purposes.

8. Machinery costing £10,000 will be bought on hire purchase; a deposit of £1,000 will be paid in July and instalments of £500 in each month thereafter.

Required:

A cash budget showing the likely bank overdraft at the end of each month.

(International Baccalaureate, 1986, Business Studies Higher level)

B17   Mrs Khan decides to start a business selling soft toys. She has $2,000 only to invest. This sum of money she places in the business account at the bank on 1 January 1988.

She also finds a small workshop which she rents at $80 a month payable on the last day of each month.

She employs one person to work for her at the beginning. That employee is paid $200 a month. As sales begin to improve she employs a second person at the same salary from 1 April 1988. That second person helps to double output and sales.

Other costs are

Materials - $500 in January and thereafter $200 a month.

Other production costs - $50 a month.

Delivery van - on hire purchase at $500 payable in January. Thereafter at $100 a month.

The soft toys are sold for cash at a standard price of $20 each.

The number of toys sold during the first six months was:

January	- None
February	- 5
March	- 20
April	- 30
May	- 60
June	- 60

(a) Prepare a cash flow statement for the six months from January to June 1988 inclusive. Show the amount of money in hand or requiring overdraft facilities at the end of each month.

(b) Calculate whether:

   (i) the business made a profit or loss over the first six months of operation.

   (ii) the business should continue in operation.

(International Baccalaureate, 1989, Business Studies Higher level)

B18 Micro Ltd is a small private electronics company run by Anne Little, who owns 60% of the equity. It is a fast growing profitable business with sales of £800,000 over the year ending 30 April 1986, giving a post tax profit of £60,000. The company is anxious to expand, as the market demand for its product is growing fast. It needs finance, however, to do this.

a. (i) What are the main external sources of finance available to Micro Ltd?

   (ii) What factors should Anne Little consider in choosing which to use?

b. Over the next two years, Micro is planning rapid expansion and it expects sales and profits to increase each year by 25% of the present level. It also aims for:

stocks	=	3 months's sales
debtors	=	2 months's sales
creditors	=	1 month's sales

As no new capital equipment has been bought during the last year, Micro plans to spend £100,000 on replacing existing machines during the next two years and the same again on new machinery.

The present situation of the company is shown on the balance sheet below.

Balance sheet for Micro Ltd
as at 30 April 1986

1985 (£'000)		1986 (£'000)	1985 (£'000)		1986 (£'000)
410	Shareholders' funds	430	150	Land and buildings	150
120	Long term loan	120	220	Machinery	200
110	Creditors	120	245	Stock	250
170	Bank overdraft	130	195	Debtors	200
810		800	810		800

Figure 13.5 Micro Ltd: balance sheet at 30 April 1986

Stating clearly any assumptions made, calculate the following:
  (i) the cash required to support this expansion
  (ii) the extent to which internal funds will contribute.
 c. Using the information given in the balance sheet above, calculate the following ratios: (i) current, (ii) acid test and (iii) gearing. On the basis of these ratios, make recommendations as to how the company should raise any external finance necessary for its expansion.
 d. If it cannot raise the necessary cash, what alternatives are open to the company?
(UCLES International Examinations, 1986, GCE A level Business Studies)

C Essay questions

C1   What does an accountant understand by the term 'liquidity'? Outline a method by which a firm might predict future liquidity problems and explain how these may be averted.

C2   In a film called *The Million Pound Note*, Gregory Peck was able to go shopping in London without ever having to spend any cash because he could show he possessed a bank note for £1 million. Explain.

C3   'Within the next generation credit cards will almost completely replace cash.' Do you agree? Why or why not? What would the consequences be?

C4   How is it possible for a profitable firm to run out of cash, or for a cash-rich firm to be unprofitable?

C5   How do some firms survive, often for quite considerable lengths of time, when they are making a loss?

C6 Explain how you would set about forecasting your firm's cash needs for the next five years, showing the main kinds of assumption you would need to make.
C7 Cash is essentially a short-term concept, whereas profit is a longer-term one. Do you agree? Why or why not?
C8 If there were no inflation interest rates would be zero. Discuss
C9 'The principle of index-linking has revolutionary implications in nearly all areas of business finance.' Discuss.
C10 How is inflation likely to affect a company's cash position, if it wishes to continue at the same 'real' level of activity?

14

Managing working capital

Plan of the chapter:

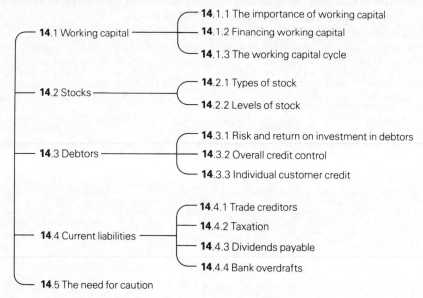

14.1 Working capital
- **14**.1.1 The importance of working capital
- **14**.1.2 Financing working capital
- **14**.1.3 The working capital cycle

14.2 Stocks
- **14**.2.1 Types of stock
- **14**.2.2 Levels of stock

14.3 Debtors
- **14**.3.1 Risk and return on investment in debtors
- **14**.3.2 Overall credit control
- **14**.3.3 Individual customer credit

14.4 Current liabilities
- **14**.4.1 Trade creditors
- **14**.4.2 Taxation
- **14**.4.3 Dividends payable
- **14**.4.4 Bank overdrafts

14.5 The need for caution

Fig.14.0

Objective: *To identify the financial importance of working capital, and the stages of the working capital cycle; to examine what determines levels of investments in stocks and debtors; and to describe the various kinds of current liability.*

Synopsis: *Long-term funds are needed to finance investment in net working capital. The main factors affecting stocks (raw materials, work-in-progress, and finished goods) are: sales volume, the relationship of production to sales, and the cost of holding stock. The amount invested in debtors depends on sales volume, and the average period of credit taken by customers. There are several components of current liabilities, of which trade creditors are often the most important.*

14.1 Working capital

14.1.1 The importance of working capital

Working capital is the excess of current assets over current liabilities. The two main items are stocks and debtors: they represent a firm's investment in goods which are unfinished, unsold, or unpaid for. Together these amount to about half the total assets of UK listed companies.

In view of its size, working capital is clearly important to many firms. (A useful ratio to calculate is working capital as a percentage of annual sales turnover.) A firm needs to determine a suitable level of investment in working capital. Finally, a firm's managers need to see that their policy on working capital is actually carried out. (A firm may 'decide', for example, that debtors should average one month's sales but someone still needs to make sure that the customers owe no more than that.)

14.1.2 Financing working capital
A hotel may be permanently full even though no individual person is always resident. In the same way there is a *permanent* need to finance working capital, even though the individual items are continually turning into cash. Each item in working capital may be 'current', but the net total may in effect be a long-term asset.

Some companies find that their working capital needs fluctuate during the year, perhaps because of seasonal sales or production patterns. How should they finance short-term seasonal working capital peaks?

Figure 14.1 shows two approaches to this problem. A company may aim to finance its *maximum* level of working capital by long-term funds, which will leave surplus cash during the off-peak period. Or it may finance only its *minimum* level of working capital with long-term funds, which will leave it needing short-term finance during the seasonal peak.

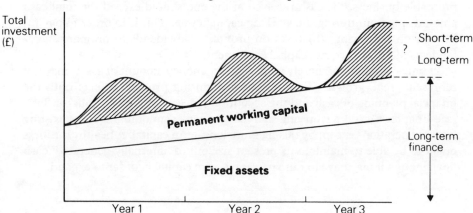

Figure 14.1 Financing seasonal working capital

14.1.3 The working capital cycle
Figure 14.2 overleaf shows the working capital cycle of a manufacturing business.

The business first purchases raw materials on credit, then uses labour and capital equipment, in various proportions in different industries, to convert the

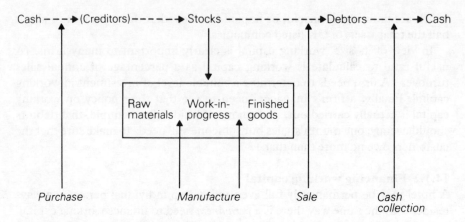

Figure 14.2 The working capital cycle

raw materials into finished goods. (Often there are intermediate stages of partly-completed goods, known as work-in-progress.) On sale of the finished goods, legal title passes to the purchaser, who either pays cash, or, if he buys on credit, owes the price to the selling company. The debtor finally pays cash to settle his account and complete the transaction.

Thus the working capital cycle comprises: cash being used to acquire raw materials and to pay labour wages to convert the materials over time into finished goods, which are then sold to customers and finally paid for. In a profitable business, the cash received at the end should exceed the total cash amounts paid out during the working capital cycle. This is in order to pay (a) interest on borrowing, (b) taxes on profits, (c) dividends to ordinary share-holders, and (d) to acquire capital equipment.

In times of inflation, merely increasing the money amount of assets may not represent 'real' growth. This serious accounting problem affects both the financial planning of cash and the accounting measurement of 'profit' or 'loss' (see Chapter 8). It is a worrying sign if a company cannot maintain its existing level of operations except by raising more long-term capital. A healthy business ought to be able to maintain its present size out of 'internally-generated' cash flow; though it may have to raise new long-term capital in order to expand.

14.2 Stocks

14.2.1 Types of stock

The three main types of stock in a manufacturing company are: raw materials, work-in-progress, and finished goods. Nearly all firms also hold stocks of supplies, such as stationery and maintenance materials, for use in the course of operations. The cumulative effect of all these stocks is to tie up part of the firm's financial resources, which could otherwise have been put to use elsewhere in the organization. Thus the investment in stocks has a real cost.

Stocks are normally stated 'at cost', or (if lower) at 'net realizable value'. 'Cost' comprises expenditure incurred in bringing a product to its present location and condition: it includes all related production overheads, based on the normal level of activity, even if these accrue on a time basis, such as factory rent (see Chapter 7).

Service industries naturally tend to have low stocks because their products usually cannot be 'stored' in finished form. The same is true of some manufacturing companies, such as newspaper publishers or bakeries.

14.2.2 Levels of stock

What determines stock levels? In general, the level of sales; the relationship between production and sales; the nature of the production process; and the cost of investment in stocks. To take the latter first, costs of holding stocks will vary for different industries, and may include handling, storage, insurance, and obsolescence, as well as interest on the money amount tied up. Average stock-holding costs may total as much as 25 to 35 per cent of book value a year; hence there is a clear need to *balance* the benefits from holding stocks at any given level against the costs.

Raw materials stocks represent a buffer between outside suppliers and the 'demands' of the manufacturing or assembly process. The level depends mainly on *buying* aspects: the nature of the goods (for example, whether they are perishable, bulky, expensive); possible interruptions to supplies (for example, from strikes or crop failures); how quickly suppliers can deliver more goods (some Japanese car makers, for example, fly in supplies of components several times a day); the economics of bulk purchasing; and expected changes in future prices, and in sales volume.

Work in progress depends largely on the method of production (such as batch versus flow); the length of the production process (bakeries will have lower work-in-progress than shipyards); the importance of set-up costs; and the possibility of sub-contracting.

Finished goods stocks represent a buffer between customer demand and intermittent supply, maybe from the manufacturing side of a business. The level depends mainly on *selling* aspects: whether goods are being made to order; the reliability of sales forecasts; policy on the risk of stock-outs; and expected changes in sales volume.

Forecasting whether a change in sales volume is temporary or more permanent can be crucial in deciding whether to change the rate of production. A wrong decision could mean either piling up unwanted stocks, or else running out of stock and thus losing potential sales. Either could be very expensive. The essence of business is judging the direction, extent, and timing of changes in market conditions in the uncertain future.

In managing stocks, as in many other areas of management, a useful control device can be 'ABC analysis' (figure 14.3). This is based on the 'rule' that a

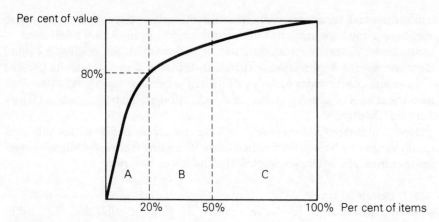

Figure 14.3 ABC analysis

small proportion (say 20 per cent) of the total *number* of items will usually account for a large proportion (say 80 per cent) of the total *value* of all items. The implication is obvious: rather than pay equal attention to all items, it makes better commercial sense to look first at the few items which account for most of the investment, starting with Class A items, then Class B, and only at the end considering the many small Class C items.

14.3 Debtors

14.3.1 Risk and return on investment in debtors
Selling for cash avoids any need to 'invest' in debtors, but most companies want to offer credit terms as attractive as their competitors. The two main risks in extending trade credit are that the customer will either take too long to pay, or else fail to pay at all (bad debts). In practice, losses due to debtors taking too long to pay tend to be far more important than losses due to bad debts. The 'return' from extending credit to customers consists of the marginal contribution to profit from the extra sales made. Trade credit policy has to balance the possible return against the risk.

One of the main determinants of the amount invested in debtors (accounts receivable) is the *volume of sales*. Since increasing sales volume is usually desirable, the main way of trying to control total credit extended is to limit the average *period of credit* taken by customers. This depends both on the credit terms offered and on the seller's collection procedures. The gain from controlling credit can be large.

Example: One company's average credit period of 137 days was reduced (over four years) to 92 days. With sales of £500 million a month, the 'saving' of 45 days' credit amounted to £750 million. The interest saved at a rate of 14 per cent a year would have been more than £100 million a year.

Another way of viewing the cost of credit is to recognize the true cost of offering a **cash discount** to customers who pay promptly. If customers on average take 45 days after invoice date before paying, then offering a $2\frac{1}{2}$ per cent cash discount for payment within 10 days would cost $2\frac{1}{2}$ per cent for 35 days. This is an annual rate of over 25 per cent. (What matters is the 45 days' credit actually taken, not the company's official credit terms of, say, 30 days.) An alternative approach is to *charge* interest on overdue accounts, but this is not popular.

In the end, a seller may prefer not to do business with a customer who takes too long to pay. In August 1989 Maxwell Communication Corporation, one of the UK's biggest book publishers, closed the credit account of Dillon's, the third biggest book retailer in the UK, 'because of persistent late payments over an extended period'. Publishers obviously need retail outlets for their books; but the outlets also need supplies.

Incurring *no* bad debts at all suggests that a firm is probably taking *too few* credit risks. In view of the likely returns foregone, it makes little sense to refrain from making sales on credit to 99 customers on the off-chance that one may fail to pay the whole amount due.

14.3.2 Overall credit control

One of the most powerful tools for controlling debtors is simply to calculate the average number of days' sales still owing at the end of a period.

Example: Sales for the past calendar year amounted to £180,000, and debtors at the end of December totalled £30,000. So 61 days' sales were outstanding:

$$\frac{30,000}{180,000} \times 365 = 61 \ days$$

Or we could do the sum in two stages:

a. *Daily sales:* $\quad \dfrac{£180,000}{365} \ = \ £493$

b. *Outstanding:* $\quad \dfrac{£30,000}{£493} \ = \ 61 \ days$

But a more accurate estimate, identifying debtors with sales in particular months, could suggest an average credit period of 41 days (or $1\frac{1}{3}$ months), if December sales were £25,000 and November sales £15,000 and we simply assume that customers pay in chronological order. Then total debtors of £30,000 at the end of December include all of December's sales (that is 31 days), plus $\frac{5}{15}$ of November's sales (that is, 10 days).

Good credit managers are quick to respond to changes in the overall pattern of debtors: they also tend to operate with specific targets, either in absolute amounts or (preferably) in terms of average days' sales outstanding.

If the average credit period allowed to customers is increasing, or too high, management should find out why. Has trade credit policy changed? Or the mix of customers? Is the company giving the largest customers suitable priority? Sending out invoices and statements promptly? Chasing up slow payers vigorously enough?

14.3.3 Individual customer credit

There are normally two decisions to make about individual credit customers: whether to extend credit at all: and, if so, up to what maximum amount? There are several ways to check the credit-worthiness of a potential new customer: trade references from other suppliers, bank references, credit bureau reports, past financial statements, and the view of the firm's own salesman.

A business may refuse to supply more goods if customers ignore credit terms too blatantly, either the total amount of credit, or the period of credit taken. Ultimately there is an implied threat of legal action against customers who do not pay amounts due according to the credit terms agreed. But it is better to avoid this if possible: the supplier wants his money, but dislikes the trouble and expense of taking formal legal action against debtors. On the other hand, in the end one has to show that one means business.

The credit control system should include a regular review of all customers, to ensure that they are not exceeding their maximum credit limits. (But people will tend to ignore unrealistically low credit limits, like speed limits on roads.) One surprisingly useful way to get money from debtors is simply to telephone and ask why they haven't paid! Some companies even telephone customers *during* the credit period to confirm that they can expect the amount involved to be paid on the due date. This also enables them to sort out any queries in good time.

14.4 Current liabilities

The extent to which net working capital needs to be financed by long-term capital depends both on the amount of the various current assets, and on the amount of the current liabilities. These are amounts owing to suppliers, banks, the tax authorities, and others.

14.4.1 Trade creditors

Goods transferred from one business to another are often sold 'on credit' (rather than for immediate settlement in cash). The time lag between supply and payment is usually between one and three months. In total, trade credit can be a very important source of finance for many businesses; and just as there is a need for a 'permanent' investment in debtors (credit extended to customers), so most firms can expect to rely on a 'permanent' source of finance from trade creditors.

An example of a typical credit transaction in manufacturing industry is set out in figure 14.4:

A delivers raw materials to B	B works on goods	B delivers finished goods to C		
3	13–20 May 15 22	25	June 18	July 2
	B pays wages		B pays A for materials	C pays B for goods

Figure 14.4 A typical credit transaction

In firm B's end-of-May balance sheet, the amount owing to Firm A will appear under Creditors (accounts payable) as a current liability; while the amount owing from Firm C will appear under Debtors (accounts receivable) as a current asset. Of course, in Firm C's end-of-May balance sheet, the amount owing to Firm B will appear as a current liability.

The average period of credit given to customers is often similar to the average period of credit received from suppliers. But the total *amount* of debtors, for firms which sell on credit, is usually larger than the total amount of creditors. The differences comes not only from the profit margin, but also from certain expenses, paid in cash (such as wages to employees), and other expenses not reflected in trade creditors (such as depreciation of fixed assets). Firms whose 'added value' is high will tend to have low trade creditors, since much of their cost of goods sold will consist of wages rather than raw materials or bought-in parts.

14.4.2 Taxation
Taxes due on profits (corporation tax for companies) are shown separately both in the profit and loss account and in the balance sheet. There are special rules for calculating the liability to tax on profits, which mean that 'taxable profit' is not the same as reported profit before tax in accounts. In particular, the depreciation expense charged in accounts is replaced, for tax purposes, by special tax 'capital allowances', calculated according to Inland Revenue rules. Thus a company cannot reduce its tax bill by increasing its book depreciation charge. Moreover, some expenses may be altogether 'disallowed' for tax purposes, and there may be certain differences of timing for revenues or expenses. Other taxes (such as national insurance, Value Added Tax, PAYE, etc.) are not included with tax on profits.

14.4.3 Dividends payable
Normal UK practice is to pay an interim dividend during the year, and to propose a final dividend which is paid after the year-end. So the balance sheet

shows only the final dividend as a current liability, while the profit and loss (appropriation) account shows the total of the interim and final dividends. In all cases dividends are shown net of basic rate income tax.

14.4.4 Bank overdrafts

In the British banking system, customers (by agreement) may have negative balances ('overdrafts') on current account with banks. The amount borrowed depends on exactly how much is required at any time. Apart from a possible small 'commitment fee' (payable on the maximum limit of the agreed overdraft facility), only the actual amount overdrawn bears interest. This is calculated from day to day, at a rate which varies with money market conditions.

Bank overdrafts are legally repayable 'on demand' (that is, without any notice), and are shown on the balance sheet as current liabilities. The overdraft system is convenient for customers; but it makes it hard for banks to know how much of their total agreed overdraft limits with customers will actually be required at any time.

14.5 The need for caution

Accounting ratios based on aggregates need to be interpreted with caution. Marks and Spencer plc's working capital figures, for example, give ratios which at first sight seem alarming (figure 14.5).

Current assets	*(£ m.)*
Stocks	364
Debtors	193
Investments	14
Cash at bank and in hand	88
	659
Current liabilities	
Bank loans	67
Trade creditors	153
Other creditors and accruals	224
Taxation	195
Proposed final dividend	104
	743

Figure 14.5 Marks and Spencer plc, working capital 31 March 1989

The current ratio is 0.9 (compared with a 'rule of thumb' 1.5) and the acid test ratio is only 0.4 ('rule of thumb' 1.0). Thus current liabilities exceed current assets, and net working capital is actually negative! What is going on? Is Marks and Spencer going bankrupt, despite 1989 sales of £5,122 million?

In all financial and accounting work, an essential rule to bear in mind is: don't panic! If a particular figure looks odd, it is worth spending a little time thinking *why* the number works out as it does.

The £364 million stock at 31 March 1989 (nearly all available for sale in retail stores) represents about one month's sales. So we could expect most of it to have turned into cash by the end of April. Indeed Marks and Spencer's *stock* is a good deal more 'liquid' than most companies' debtors! Clearly the acid test ratio (which omits stock) gives much too gloomy a view.

Marks and Spencer's 'debtors' of £193 million represent mainly prepayments and other items. (Trade debtors of £289 million appear, oddly enough, under fixed assets, as part of the net investment in financial activities.)

Not all the current liabilities are due for payment within the next month or so. The proposed final dividend of £104 million will not be paid until after the annual general meeting in mid-July. And the £195 million corporation tax liability is mostly due on 1 January 1990, nine months after the year end.

So even if we assumed that all other creditors (totalling £444 million) were due within the next 30 days, we could expect the company to have about that much cash available from the £88 million cash plus, say, £364 million from one month's sales of stock. Thus the liquidity position actually seems fairly comfortable.

The truth is that a balance sheet gives only a very crude idea of the real position; and we need to know a good deal about a particular business before we can begin to draw conclusions. Accounting ratios may raise questions which need to be considered - but they rarely provide the answers.

Work section

A   Revision questions

A1   Why is managing working capital important?

A2   Why is there a permanent need for most companies to finance working capital even though the individual items are all 'current'?

A3   What are the main types of current assets?

A4   What is the working capital cycle of a manufacturing business?

A5   What are the three main categories of stock in a manufacturing firm?

A6   Why might expectations about future prices lead a business to hold low stocks of raw materials?

A7   Identify four different kinds of costs of holding stocks.

A8   Why may the nature of the production process affect the amount of stock held?

A9   How can one assess whether a company's levels of stock are, or are not, reasonable?

A10   What is the 'opportunity cost' of high stock levels?

A11   What is the 'opportunity cost' of low stock levels?

A12   On what basis are stocks valued in a balance sheet?

A13   What is ABC analysis? Why is it useful?

A14   What are the two main risks in extending trade credit to customers?

A15   What are the two most important factors in determining the amount of debtors (accounts receivable) outstanding at any time?

A16   How can a $2\frac{1}{2}$ per cent discount represent an annual interest rate of   25 per cent?

A17   How can one assess whether a company's level of debtors is, or is not, reasonable?

A18   Why may it be undesirable for a company which sells on credit to have no bad debts at all?

A19   Will a company whose 'added value' is low tend to have (a) a high or (b) a low level of trade creditors? Why?

A20   Why is trade credit an important source of finance for many firms?

A21   Why is the amount of trade credit received likely for most companies to be less than the amount of trade credit given?

A22   Why does a balance sheet normally show only the final dividend as a current liability, while the profit and loss account shows both the interim and final dividends?

A23   On what basis is interest calculated on bank overdrafts?

A24   How would you calculate the number of days' sales in debtors?

A25   In what circumstances may it be acceptable for working capital to be negative?

B   Exercises and case studies

B1   A company with annual sales of £120,000 physically 'turns over' its stocks once every three months. Its cost of goods sold percentage (to sales revenue) is 60 per cent. What average level of investment in stocks (at cost) is held?

B2   A newsagent sells £500 worth of newspapers on credit each week. He sends out bills to credit customers once a quarter; and on average they take two weeks to pay.
   a. What is his average level of debtors? (Assume one month = four and one-third weeks.)
   b. What will his average level of debtors amount to if he changes to sending out bills once a month? (Assume customers still take two weeks to pay.)
   c. How much would such a change save him per year, if interest rates are 18 per cent a year?

B3   A company with current liabilities of £120,000 has the following current assets: stock £80,000; debtors £60,000; cash £40,000.
   a. What is its current ratio?
   b. What is its acid test ratio?
   c. What is its working capital?

B4   From the following balance sheet, calculate:
   (a) working capital to sales; (b) current ratio; (c) return on net assets.

		(£ m.)
Fixed assets, net		6.0
Current assets	7.5	
Less: Current liabilities	4.0	
		3.5
		9.5
Long-term debt (15%)		2.0
Shareholders' funds		7.5
		9.5

Note: Sales = £8.0 million in the last year.
         Profit before tax = £1.6 million in the last year.

B5   It is suggested that your firm encourage prompt payment by customers by offering a 2 per cent cash discount off the price of any order which is paid within one month of delivery. At present the average period of delay before settlement is two-and-a-half months after delivery.

a. As the finance director, and bearing in mind that your bank charges 15 per cent a year on the company's overdraft, comment on this suggestion.

b. Would it be more attractive to offer a 3 per cent cash discount for settlement within 10 days after delivery? Why or why not?

B6 Refer to 14.3.2. Suppose that the £45,000 sales in the last quarter of the year represented sales of £25,000 in October, £15,000 in November, and £5,000 in December. Using the method of calculation shown, estimate how many days' sales are still owing at the end of December, if debtors then amount to £30,000.

B7 A company's credit sales in a year are £150,000; and end-of-year debtors amount to £40,000. Terms are settlement within one month after invoice. Sales in the last four months of the year are as follows: September £20,000; October £15,000; November £12,000; December £8,000.

How many days' sales are outstanding in debtors:

a. Using the annual sales figures?

b. Using the monthly sales figures?

c. Using the monthly sales figures, but assuming the pattern of sales for the last four months of the year was: September £8,000; October £12,000; November £15,000; December £20,000?

B8 Refer to B7. Assuming that nobody has paid before the due date, both for parts (b) and (c) above, what proportion of total debtors at 31 December represents amounts that are:

a. Overdue?

b. At least one month overdue?

c. More than two months overdue?

B9 Centaur Ltd's balance sheet contains the following items: stocks £55,000 (raw materials £15,000, work in progress £15,000, finished goods £25,000); debtors £48,000; creditors (for materials) £18,000.

Annual sales amount to £180,000; and cost of goods sold represents $66\frac{2}{3}$ per cent of sales (of which materials amount to $33\frac{1}{3}$ per cent of sales).

Assuming that work in progress represents on average goods which are half-finished, how many days' operations does net working capital represent (ignoring liquid resources and current liabilities other than creditors)?

B10 'How will our big companies with weakened balance sheets find the cash to pull out of recession without doing themselves further damage?... At GKN, where they have shifted a third of the work force in two years... they reckon they have an answer. Chairman Sir Trevor Holdsworth calculates that the company can put on more business without going to the banks. An extra £100 of sales at the margin will need another £21 in working capital – but will earn £30 in extra profits. On sums like that, who needs a rights issue (of ordinary shares, to raise more equity capital)?'

The Standard, 22 March 1982.

Assume that GKN is not liable to UK corporation tax on marginal profits; and that its *average* position is the same as its *marginal* position outlined above. Assume further:

(i) sales are £2,000 million a year; (ii) fixed expenses are £500 million a year, and all other operating expenses are variable with sales; (iii) net asset turnover is 2.0.

On the above assumptions, calculate:

a. Variable expenses for a year.
b. Operating profit (before interest and tax).
c. Working capital.
d. Fixed assets.
e. Return on net assets.

C Essay questions

C1   In what respects do the financial implications of investment in working capital differ from those relating to fixed assets?

C2   How would inflation affect a company's working capital?

C3   Describe two alternative approaches for financing seasonal working capital needs. What are the pros and cons of each?

C4   'Stocks are the link between production and selling.' Discuss, with special reference to the financial implications.

C5   How can stocks (a) damp down and (b) accentuate business fluctuations?

C6   What are the main principles on which a company should aim to control the total amount of trade credit granted to customers?

C7   '*No* bad debts is too few'. Comment.

C8   What are the advantages and disadvantages of a high level of trade creditors?

C9   What effect would the abolition of trade credit have on the financing of different industries?

C10 Why is caution necessary before drawing conclusions from comparing a company's current ratio with the rule of thumb of 2.0 to 1?

15

Long-term investment projects

Plan of the chapter:

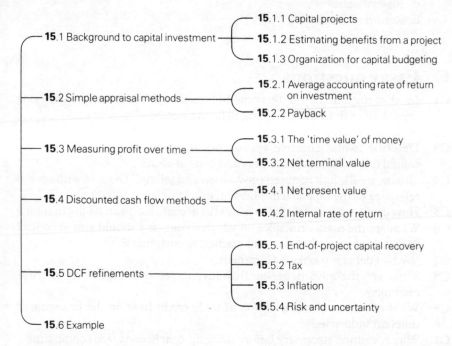

Fig.15.0

Objective: *To describe the background to capital investment decisions; to outline the two main 'traditional' appraisal methods; to discuss the time value of money; and to outline the two main discounted cash flow (DCF) methods, together with ways of allowing for capital recovery, tax, inflation, and uncertainty.*

Synopsis: *The most important thing is finding good projects. Of the traditional appraisal methods, average accounting rate of return ignores the timing of returns, while payback ignores profit. The opportunity cost of capital (interest rate) can be used as an 'exchange rate over time' to compare a payment now with receipts in future. The two main DCF methods estimate both the amount and the timing of a capital project's expected future cash flows. Net Present Value (NPV) discounts the cash flows, using a criterion discount rate, to see if the project's 'value' exceeds its cost.*

Internal Rate of Return (IRR) compares the discount rate which produces a zero NPV with the criterion rate. But financial appraisal of capital projects is by no means the only thing that matters.

15.1 Background to capital investment

15.1.1 Capital projects

Capital **investment** means spending money now in the hope of getting sufficient returns later. Investment as such is not 'good': companies invest money in order to make a *profit*.

Three main kinds of capital investment are: replacing equipment, to reduce costs or improve quality; expanding productive capacity, to meet growing demand; or providing new facilities, to make new products.

A capital investment 'project' in a company involves a number of steps, which can be portrayed in terms of a decision framework (figure 15.1). In this chapter we shall be dealing mainly with the two shaded sections of the chart, on planning and decision.

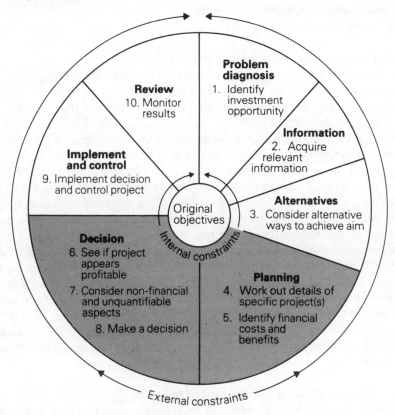

Figure 15.1 Capital investment decision framework

Easily the most important stage is the first: finding good projects. That requires imagination and alertness to spot the investment opportunity. It is also worth remembering that business success usually requires a certain amount of *luck!* The techniques for analysis in this chapter merely enable us to tell (very roughly) how good a project promises to be, once it has been thought of. Probably some firms spend too much time and effort appraising projects, and not enough *searching* for new business opportunities. To gather information, market research is often needed.

Army men say: 'Time spent in reconnaissance is never wasted'. The same is true of many large capital projects. Once started, they may be impossible to abandon, except at a significant loss. Before diving into detailed analysis, it is nearly always worth double-checking that one has looked at all practical alternatives. (If there is literally 'no alternative' to a proposed course of action, then there is *no decision* to make!)

Reaching a sensible answer may depend on asking the right questions. For example, for a capital investment the choices may be:

1 *whether or not* to buy machine H;
2 whether to buy *machine H or machine J;*
3 whether to buy machine H *now or later*;
4 whether to *buy or lease* machine H.

15.1.2 Estimated benefits from a project

It can be hard to estimate a project's future net benefits. What consumers will want in a few years' time, what competitors will be up to, how production methods may change – all are uncertain. Yet they may affect the project's life, sales volume, selling prices, costs.

In trying to tell how much net *improvement* will result from a project, the forecast of sales revenue is often critical. For example, publishers may be able to calculate production costs quite closely, with a fixed selling price, but sales *volume* may be very uncertain; or petrol companies may be fairly sure how much petrol they will sell, but not what the selling *prices* will be. On the other hand, ship-building on a fixed-price contract would provide certain sales revenue, but uncertain costs and timing.

An 'expansion' or 'new product' project will be expected to increase sales revenue by more than operating costs. A 'cost reduction' project, in contrast, may not affect sales revenue at all: reduced future operating costs are the net 'benefits' of the project (compared to what would happen without it). In figure 15.2, the shaded areas represent the incremental benefits resulting from (a) an expansion project, and (b) a cost reduction project. In Section 15.2 we discuss methods for comparing a project's future expected net benefits with the initial investment.

15.1.3 Organization for capital budgeting

In addition to a method of looking at each capital project's expected profit, companies must have a system of **capital budgeting**. This involves planning

246

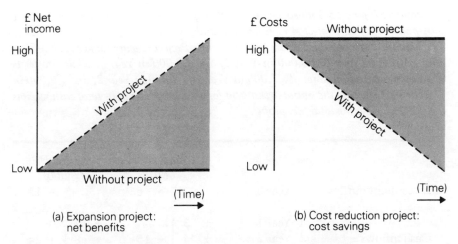

Figure 15.2 Incremental benefits for different kinds of projects

the *total* amount of capital spending over the next year or two, and its phasing over time, in order to arrange suitable financing. Such plans are often updated quarterly, since both the amounts and the timing of payments for capital projects can change quickly.

After looking at possible alternatives to each project, detailed engineering estimates, market forecasts, etc. will need to be prepared. Capital investment projects may often cover the whole range of business: production, marketing, organization, strategy. Hence large projects involve groups of people from many parts of a business, and often cover quite long periods of time.

In most organizations, what goes on informally is at least as important as the formal system. The internal 'politics' of capital budgeting are often crucial. In any case, the financial estimates may not be the most critical aspects of capital investment projects.

Even after the final decision to invest, there remains the vital process of *implementing* the decision. This process cannot simply be taken for granted: it may take many months (or even years); and mistakes here can be very costly.

Finally, after the event some companies have a system of post-project audit. This may involve checking the amount and timing of the capital investment outlay. Or it may involve a full-scale reappraisal to check on the accuracy of the original estimates of operating cash flows as well as capital spending. The purpose is not so much to apportion blame if things have gone wrong, as to learn how to do better in future.

15.2 Simple appraisal methods

15.2.1 Average accounting rate of return on investment
Profitability is often expressed as an annual rate of return on investment.

Example: Figure 15.3 illustrates two rival proposals for capital investment, Project A and Project B. Project A requires an initial investment of £6,000, Project B of £12,000. Each project will last for three years. Project A will produce cash inflows of £3,000 in Year 1, £4,000 in Year 2, and £8,000 in Year 3; while Project B will produce cash inflows of £7,000 in Year 1, £8,000 in Year 2, and £9,000 in Year 3. Deducting the initial investment for each project from its total cash receipts (inflows) gives the total 'net profit'.

		Project A (£'000)		Project B (£'000)	
Investment outflow	Year 0	− 6		− 12	
Cash inflows	Year 1	+ 3		+ 7	
	Year 2	+ 4	+ 15	+ 8	+ 24
	Year 3	+ 8		+ 9	
Net profit (3 years)			+ 9		+ 12
Average annual profit			+ 3		+ 4
$\dfrac{\text{Average annual profit}}{\text{Initial investment}}$			$\dfrac{3}{6} = 50\%$		$\dfrac{4}{12} = 33\%$

Figure 15.3   Project A versus Project B

Project B produces higher total cash inflows than Project A (24 versus 15). If we deduct the initial investment from total cash inflows, Project B also produces a higher total net profit over the three years (12 versus 9). Accountants would call this charging 'depreciation'. Because the projects have the same life (three years), Project B also produces a higher average annual profit ('return') than Project A (4 versus 3).

But if we divide the average annual profit by the initial amount invested, Project A produces a higher rate of return on investment than Project B (50 per cent versus 33 per cent). Hence using the 'rate of return on investment' approach, Project A is better than Project B.

In using accounting figures to derive the average rate of return on investment, some tricky questions arise. What do we mean by 'return'? (Is it before or after tax? What about depreciation?) What do we mean by 'investment'? (Should we use initial or average investment? Should we include assets at original cost, or net of depreciation?)

The average rate of return on investment (expressed as an annual percentage) does tell us something about a capital project's profitability. But the averaging process eliminates relevant information about the *timing* of the returns.

Example: Suppose we now compare Project A (as before) with Project C. Project A's profits (note: not its cash inflows) are £1,000, £2,000 and £6,000 in Years 1, 2 and 3 respectively; while Project C's, let us suppose, are £6,000, £2,000 and £1,000. The order is reversed.

The average rate of return on investment is the same for both projects: 50 per cent a year (£3,000/£6,000). The only difference is that Project C gives a return £5,000 higher than Project A in Year 1, but £5,000 lower in Year 3. In total this difference 'averages out'; but the extra £5,000 received in Year 1 under Project C can, of course, be invested for two years, to yield a positive return. Thus, taking this 'opportunity cost' into account (see 12.3), Project C is better than Project A.

But the average rate of return calculation does not reveal this conclusion, since it ignores the timing of the returns.

15.2.2 Payback

Probably even more widely used than 'rate of return on investment' is the **payback** method. This shows how many years it will take before a capital project 'pays back' the original amount invested, that is, before the cumulative cash returns exceed the initial investment. The shorter the payback period the better.

For the payback period, it is usual to look at cash receipts from a project rather than accounting profits. (We already know from 13.2 that they may differ.) Thus in calculating a project's net cash inflows, only cash expenses should be deducted from sales revenues, not depreciation.

Let us now use again the figures for Project A and Project C, each costing £6,000, assuming that cash is received evenly throughout the year (figure 15.4).

		Project A (£'000)	Project C (£'000)
Investment	Year 0	− 6	− 6
Cash inflows	Year 1	+ 3	+ 8
	Year 2	+ 4	+ 4
	Year 3	+ 8	+ 3

Figure 15.4 Cash inflows for Project A and Project C

Example: The 'payback period' for Project A can easily be calculated. £3,000 is 'repaid' in Year 1, and £4,000 in Year 2. Thus Project A's payback period is one-and-three-quarter years. (One year at £3,000 plus three-quarters of a year at £4,000 equals the initial investment of £6,000.) Similarly we can calculate

Project C's payback period as nine months. Only three-quarters of the £8,000 cash inflow in Year 1 is needed to recover the initial investment of £6,000.

Figure 15.5 shows these results graphically.

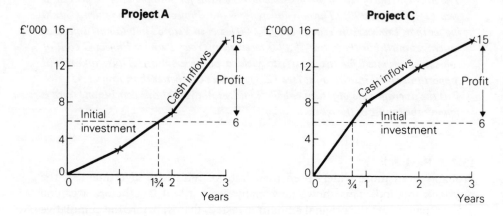

Figure 15.5 Payback periods for Project A and Project C

The payback method of project appraisal does have one clear advantage over the average rate of return on investment method: it takes timing into account. It is also simple to calculate and easy to understand. But the payback method ignores cash receipts *after* payback. This is vital: there can be no profit unless we get back *more* than the original investment.

Example: Suppose that in Year 4, Project A produced a cash inflow of £20,000, while Project C produced only £1,000. According to the payback method, that would not change the relative attractiveness of the two projects: Project C would still look 'better' than Project A. This clearly doesn't make business sense!

Thus while it may be a useful measure of *risk* (the sooner the payback, the less the risk), the payback method does not measure profit.

In practice payback is often used as a rough 'screening' device. But there are better ways to estimate the profitability of capital projects

15.3 Measuring profit over time

15.3.1 The 'time value' of money
Investment means spending money now in the hope of getting returns later. To tell whether the returns are large enough to produce a profit, we need a way to compare returns in the *future* with investment *now*.

A given amount of money now is worth *more* than the same amount of money in future. Why? Because it can be invested today to yield a return in the meantime.

The rate of interest on money does *not* merely represent inflation: it also allows for time preference and risk (see 13.3.2).

Let us suppose that we can invest money today to yield 10 per cent a year, so that £100 invested today will accumulate (compounding once a year) to the amounts below:

In 1 year's time, to £100 × 1.10   = £100 × 1.100 = £110.00.
In 2 years' time, to £100 × (1.10)^2 = £100 × 1.210 = £121.00.
In 3 years' time, to £100 × (1.10)^3 = £100 × 1.331 = £133.10

Thus, using an interest rate of 10 per cent a year, the *future value* of '£100 now' is '£133.10 at the end of three years'. We can say the same thing the other way round: the **present value** of '£133.10 receivable at the end of 3 years' is '£100 now'. In figure 15.6 which sets this out, the 'End of Year 0' is 'the present', or simply 'now'.

	End of Year 0 (£)	End of Year 1 (£)	End of Year 2 (£)	End of Year 3 (£)
Future values	100.00 ⟶	110.00 ⟶	121.00 ⟶	133.10
Present values	100.00 ⟵	110.00		
	100.00 ⟵		121.00	
	100.00 ⟵			133.10

Figure 15.6 Future values of '£100 now', at 10 per cent a year

What, then, is the present value of '£100 receivable at the end of three years'? Clearly it must be £75.13:

$$\frac{£100.00}{(1.10)^3} = \frac{£100.00}{1.331} \left[\text{or} \; \frac{£100.00}{£133.10} \times £100.00 \right] = £75.13$$

We can prove this by showing what would happen if we invested £75.13 at 10 per cent a year. Each year the effect of compound interest is to add 10 per cent of the start-of-year cumulative amount invested:

After 1 year the amount becomes: £75.13 + £7.51 = £82.64

After 2 years the amount becomes: £82.64 + £8.27 = £90.91

After 3 years the amount becomes: £90.91 + £9.09 = £100.00

Figure 15.7 shows the present value of £100.00 receivable at the end of Years 1, 2 and 3:

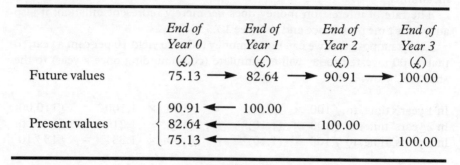

	End of Year 0 (£)	End of Year 1 (£)	End of Year 2 (£)	End of Year 3 (£)
Future values	75.13 →	82.64 →	90.91 →	100.00
Present values	90.91 ←	100.00		
	82.64 ←		100.00	
	75.13 ←			100.00

Figure 15.7 Present values of '£100 in future' at 10 per cent a year

Assuming an interest rate of 10 per cent a year, the present value of any amount (call it *x*) receivable at the end of three years is £0.7513*x*. (The **discount factor** for three years at 10 per cent a year is 0.7513: it is equivalent to $1 \div (1.10)^3$.

In effect this gives us an 'exchange rate over time'. Just as compound factors tell us the future values of present-day money amounts, so discount factors tell us the present values of future money amounts. (See Appendix 3 for tables of discount factors.)

We have been assuming that we can always invest any sum of money now (say with a bank) to yield an annual return of 10 per cent. In practice it is not always easy to estimate the rate of interest (the 'opportunity cost' of capital), as we shall discuss in more detail in Chapter 18.

15.3.2 Net terminal value

If the relevant opportunity cost of capital is 10 per cent a year, then that is also the **required rate of return** on a capital investment project. (This is sometimes called the **criterion rate**, or 'hurdle rate', or 'cut-off rate'.) If you can get 10 per cent a year by depositing money with a bank, why invest in any capital project expected to yield less than 10 per cent a year? We need to get a higher return from any particular capital project for it to be worth investing in.

Example: A (non-returnable) investment now of £10,000 in Project D is expected to produce cash receipts of £3,000 at the end of Year 1, £4,000 at the end of Year 2, and £5,000 at the end of Year 3. Should the firm invest in Project D or not, assuming that it could otherwise invest the money to earn 10 per cent a year?

Figure 15.8 sets out the amount and timing of Project D's expected cash flows, both the initial investment of £10,000, and the subsequent cash inflows. Using the interest rate of 10 per cent a year enables us to calculate how much money will have accumulated by the end of Project D's three-year life:

a. if the firm invests in Project D (£13,030);

b. *if the firm doesn't invest in Project D, but merely earns the 'going rate' of 10 per cent a year (£13,310).*

The £3,000 *cash receipt at the end of Year 1 can be re-invested for two years (until the end of Year 3), at 10 per cent a year when it will amount to* £3,630; *while the* £4,000 *cash receipt at the end of Year 2 can be invested for only one year.*

End of year (EOY)	Cash flow	×	Compound factor		=	'Terminal' EOY 3 value
	(£)					(£)
0	−10,000	×	1.331		=	−13,310 (b)
1	+ 3,000	×	1.210	= + 3,630		
2	+ 4,000	×	1.100	= + 4,400 } =		+13,030 (a)
3	+ 5,000	×	1.000	= + 5,000		
	Net Terminal Value				=	− 280

Figure 15.8 Net terminal value of Project D

Clearly Project D is not *worthwhile. Its* **net terminal value (NTV)** *is negative (−£280). That means the firm would be better off investing with a bank at the 'going rate' of 10 per cent a year, rather than investing* £10,000 *in Project D.*

15.4 Discounted cash flow methods

15.4.1 Net present value

The **net present value** (NPV) method of investment appraisal (like the net terminal value method we saw in 15.3.2) calculates a project's profit by comparing cash payments and cash receipts at the *same* point in time. Rather than looking at the *end* of a project's life, however, it looks at the start. It does so by discounting expected future cash flows back to the present (that is, back to the end of year 0); and then comparing the total present value of the future cash receipts with the initial capital investment in the project.

The NPV method multiplies future cash flows by a suitable discounting factor (this is equivalent to dividing by the appropriate compounding factor). The discounting factor depends on two things: the discount rate being used, and the number of years in future that the cash flow arises.

Example: Looking again at Project D, we see that its net present value is negative. Hence the project is not financially worthwhile. The 'cost' of investing in Project D is £10,000 *now, while the present value of the cash receipts in future is* £9,790. *Thus Project D amounts to a proposal to pay out* £10,000 *now in order to acquire the rights to future cash flows which have a (present) value of £9,790. That is hardly smart business: it represents a* loss *(in present value terms) of £210.*

End of year EOY	Cash flows (£)		Discount factor (at 10%)	'Present' EOY 0 value (£)	(£)
0	−10,000	[÷ $(1.10)^0$] × 1.000 =		−10,000	= −10,000
1	+ 3,000	[÷ $(1.10)^1$] × 0.909 =		+ 2,727	
2	+ 4,000	[÷ $(1.10)^2$] × 0.827 =		+ 3,308	= + 9,790
3	+ 5,000	[÷ $(1.10)^3$] × 0.751 =		+ 3,755	
			Net present value		= − 210

Figure 15.9 Net present value of Project D

Note that we round off all amounts to the nearest pound. There is absolutely no advantage in seeking more accuracy. Our figures for cash flows are usually no more than estimates; and the discount rate used is nearly always only a rough approximation (see Chapter 18).

The principles used to calculate Net Present Value are exactly the same as those used for Net Terminal Value. Hence both methods always give the *same* signal about whether or not a project is worthwhile. The only difference is that NPV compares amounts at the start of the project, NTV at the end.

The numbers from Project D show that NPV is precisely equivalent to NTV:

$$\text{NPV (EOY 0)} \quad - £210 \times 1.331 = \text{NTV (EOY 3)} - £280$$

or

$$\text{NTV (EOY 3)} \quad - £280 \times 0.751 = \text{NPV (EOY 0)} - £210$$

In practice firms use the Net Present Value method, rather than the Net Terminal Value method, for two reasons. NPV enables us to compare different projects as at the same point in time (EOY 0); whereas different projects might last for a different number of years, hence, with NTV, have different 'terminal' dates. Also managers prefer to think in terms of 'present values', rather than in terms of 'future values'.

The great advantage of the Net Terminal Value method, at least in a textbook, is to clarify the precise *meaning* of the interest rate used in discounted cash flow methods. The 'compounding' approach of the NTV method makes the 'opportunity cost' nature of the interest rate quite explicit.

The net present value (NPV) method, as we have seen, compares cash receipts and payments expected to result from a capital project. It multiplies them by discounting factors to translate all the expected cash flows from a project into 'present values' (that is, into end-of-year 0 money terms).

Figure 15.10 shows this approach graphically:

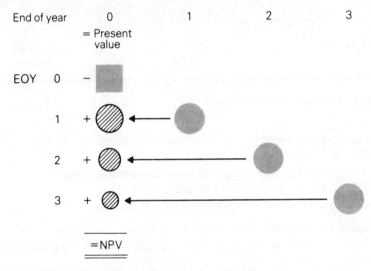

Figure 15.10 The discounting process in net present value

Discounted cash flow (DCF) methods involve forecasting both the *amount* and the *timing* of **incremental cash flows** which are expected to result if a particular project is undertaken, but not otherwise. Note that DCF methods deal with *cash flows* and *not* with accounting profits, income and expenses. Hence non-cash expenses such as depreciation should be ignored in estimating future cash flows. To tell whether a project is expected to be profitable, we simply see whether or not the present value of the project's discounted cash inflows exceeds (the present value of) the cash investment involved.

In other words, we first 'value' the project, and then compare that amount with the project's *cost*. This may simply be the initial amount of the cash investment, though sometimes projects consist of several cash payments spread out over time, which themselves need to be discounted back to 'present value' terms. If the project's value is more than its cost (that is, if it has a positive net present value), then it is worth undertaking on financial grounds; it will increase the owner's wealth.

Figure 15.11 shows a way of picturing this valuation process:

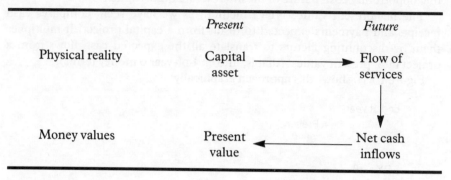

Figure 15.11 Valuing a capital asset

The net present value method, in theory, will always give the 'correct' answer – if one assumes that:

1 the amounts and timing of the cash flows are correctly forecast;
2 the opportunity cost of capital is correctly estimated;
3 there are no non-financial aspects to a capital project.

The sweeping and unrealistic nature of these necessary qualifications makes it clear that in practice no method of analysis can be guaranteed to give a precisely 'correct' answer.

15.4.2 Internal rate of return

Another method of discounting cash flows is often used instead of the net present value method. This is the **internal rate of return** (IRR) method (also called the DCF yield method).

The net present value method lists the amount and timing of all the expected future cash flows from a project; and the internal rate of return method does the same. The NPV method then applies a pre-selected (criterion) discount rate, to see whether the net total of all the discounted cash flows is positive or negative. If the NPV is positive, then the project is worthwhile (from a financial point of view); if the NPV is negative, then it is not.

In contrast, the internal rate of return method determines, by trial and error, what is the (initially unknown) discount rate which when applied to the same cash flows, will produce a net present value of exactly zero. That discount rate is the project's 'internal rate of return': it must then be compared with the criterion rate, to see whether or not the project is worthwhile.

Example: In Project D, a 10 per cent discount rate produced an NPV of –£210. We know that a zero discount rate would produce an NPV of +£2,000 (simply by adding up the undiscounted cash flows). Therefore, since the sign changes, the IRR (which has to produce an NPV of zero) must lie between 0 and 10 per cent. And since −£210 is much closer to zero than +£2,000 is, the IRR will lie much closer to 10 per cent than to zero.

Using the 'trial and error' method of finding the internal rate of return, suppose we first try a discount rate of 9 per cent (figure 15.12).

End of year EOY	Cash flows (£)	Discount factor (at 9%)	'Present' value (£)	(£)
0	−10,000	× 1.000 =	−10,000	= −10,000
1	+ 3,000 $[÷(1.09)^1] = × 0.917 =$		+ 2,751	
2	+ 4,000 $[÷(1.09)^2] = × 0.842 =$		+ 3,368	= + 9,979
3	+ 5,000 $[÷(1.09)^3] = × 0.772 =$		+ 3,860	
			Net present value =	−21

Figure 15.12 Internal rate of return of Project D

The net present value of −£21 is close enough to zero; so in practice we would reckon the internal rate of return as being (just under) 9 per cent a year. (The 'actual' figure is 8.9 per cent.) Since the required rate of return is 10 per cent, Project D's internal rate of return is not quite high enough to justify investing in it. In fact we can plot the net present value of Project D for a whole range of different discount rates (figure 15.13).

Three values in particular are worth noting:
1. Using a 0 per cent discount rate, the NPV is +£2,000.
2. Using a 10 per cent discount rate (the criterion rate), the NPV is −£210.
3. The net present value is zero at a discount rate of 8.9 per cent. This is the internal rate of return.

A project with a higher internal rate of return may not always be better than a project with a lower IRR, for two main reasons. First, the amount invested may be different. Is a 50 per cent IRR better than 25 per cent? Not if the 50 per cent is earned on an investment of £100, while the 25 per cent is earned on an investment of £10,000.

The second reason is that IRR in effect assumes **re-investment** at the project's own ('internal') rate of return. But this may not be the actual 'opportunity cost' of capital; which makes it hard to compare two different projects, especially if they have different lives.

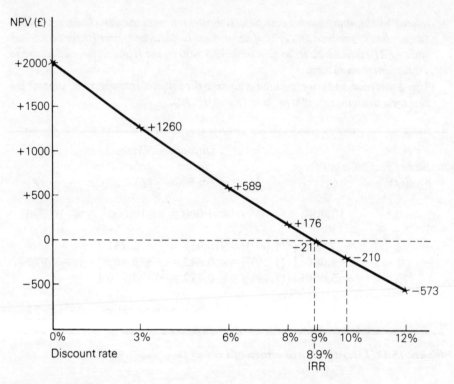

Figure 15.13 Net present value of Project D at various discount rates

Even where one of the DCF methods (NPV or IRR) appears to show that a project will be profitable, it is still important for managers to identify the general economic reasons for the project. In other words, *why* can a particular project make a profit? If no specific reason can be identified, then the apparent result of the financial evaluation must be doubtful. All experienced managers know how easy it is to include very optimistic assumptions to make a project 'look' good!

15.5 DCF refinements

15.5.1 End-of-project capital recovery
Many capital projects consist of two parts:
1 Fixed capital investment (for example, factory buildings, machines, etc).
2 Working capital investment (for example, in stocks to support an expansion project). This is usually assumed to be recovered at the end of a project.
   Possible limitations to a project's economic life include:
1 Physical exhaustion of equipment.
2 Technical obsolescence of equipment or process.

3 Market factors, such as changing consumer tastes.
4 An arbitrary **horizon** date.
Amounts recoverable at the end of a project's life may stem from:
1 Value of land or buildings.
2 Scrap or second-hand value of equipment.
3 Working capital.

Even where a firm recovers part (or all) of the original investment at the end of a project, the time value money is still relevant. Capital has an opportunity cost as long as it is invested in a project; so any amount recoverable must be discounted back to present value.

For long projects it is common to use an arbitrary 'horizon' period of 10, or perhaps 15, years beyond which no cash flows are included even if the project is actually expected to last longer. With a fairly high discount rate this may not make much difference. (For example, with a 20 per cent discount rate, extending the horizon from 15 to 30 years for a project with equal annual cash inflows would increase the present value of all cash inflows only by about 7 per cent. The discount factor would increase from 4.675 to 4.979.)

15.5.2 Tax

As we shall see in Chapter 18, the appropriate criterion rate is an after-tax discount rate. Hence after-tax cash flows should be used in capital project appraisal. Larger companies are subject to a corporation rate tax of 35 per cent on profits, but the rate for small companies is only 25 per cent. Tax is payable about one year after **taxable profits** are earned, but for simplicity this time lag is often ignored.

In place of depreciation charged by companies, the tax authorities allow statutory **'capital allowances'**. For industrial buildings these amount to 4 per cent on cost; for most plant and equipment the tax capital allowances are 25 per cent of the written down value (declining balance).

The simplest assumption is to take it that all cash inflows and outflows will be subject to tax, except for cash flows relating to working capital.

15.5.3 Inflation

The likelihood of future inflation at varying rates makes it difficult to forecast cash flows more than a year or two ahead. It may also be necessary to forecast specific price changes: for example, if one expected general inflation of 7 per cent a year in future, one might still forecast wage costs to rise at 11 per cent a year, or raw material costs at only 4 per cent a year.

Two methods of allowing for inflation are possible:
1 Use actual money amounts expected year by year, with a criterion rate of return which *includes* an allowance for expected inflation. Thus if the 'real' criterion rate (excluding inflation) were 8 per cent a year, then the discount rate including inflation would need to be about 15 per cent.
2 Use present-day (Year 0) constant purchasing power for all forecast amounts, with a 'real' discount rate *excluding* inflation. Any money amounts

expected to rise in future by less than the general rate of inflation will appear to *fall* in terms of constant Year 0 purchasing power (for example, lease payments, tax capital allowances).

In principle either approach can work, but consistency is essential. If you use money cash flows, discount them at a money interest rate, including an inflation premium (see 13.3.2). If you use 'real' cash flows, discount them at a 'real' interest rate, excluding inflation.

15.5.4 Risk and uncertainty

Allowing for risk and uncertainty in capital investment project appraisal is difficult, and there really is no perfect 'answer' to the problem. Strictly, **risk** means outcomes whose probability of occurrence is known (for example, the odds against the number 5 coming up at roulette); whereas **uncertainty** refers to events whose probability of occurrence is unknown (for example, the chances of the basic rate of income tax being below 20 per cent in 1996). Business events are usually 'uncertain', rather than 'risky'; and many large capital projects are unique. Thus frequency probabilities (of the sort used by life assurance companies) do not apply: one simply doesn't know the odds.

No single approach is foolproof, but here are six different ways of trying to allow for risk and/or uncertainty:

(a) Conservatism

Simply making 'conservative' estimates of future net cash flows may lead to rejection of potentially profitable projects. A widely-used variant is to use a deliberately short estimate of a project's life (which may imply a low terminal value).

(b) Payback

Payback does not measure a project's profit (see 15.2.2), since it ignores cash inflows expected to occur after payback. But it may be a useful indicator of risk: the sooner the payback, the lower the risk.

(c) 'Best'/'Worst' forecasts

Making more than one set of cash flow estimates may give some idea of the spread of possible outcomes. It requires a consistent approach to the parameters (for example, is 'best' likely to happen once in ten occasions, or once in ten thousand?); it is often difficult to estimate inter-dependencies (for example, what is the relationship, if any, between advertising and sales, or between research spending and new products?). Finally, it may be subject to bias, especially to over-optimism in projecting the 'worst' outcome.

(d) Sensitivity analysis

If one can identify critical assumptions in forecasting future cash flows, one can also test how much it changes a project's outcome to vary them. A (difficult) further step would be to estimate how likely it is that critical assumptions will vary by specific amounts.

(e) Adjusted discount rates
If one can classify the 'riskiness' of difference types of project, the criterion discount rate can be adjusted by allowing for different 'risk premiums' (see 18.2).

(f) Expected values
Guessing the likelihood of various possible future events, using 'subjective probability estimates', enables one to compute **expected values** for future cash flows, from which an 'expected' net present value can be derived.

One must remember, of course, that managers are not merely trying to *measure* levels of risk and return: they are also trying to *manage* projects, either by increasing the return or by reducing the risk (see 18.1.4).

15.6 Example

It may now be helpful to bring together in a single example much of the detail in this chapter relating to discounted cash flow analysis of capital projects. (The exercises and case studies in section B of the work section following this chapter deal with many of the detailed topics separately.)

Example: Ancastle Ltd, a small food company, is considering whether to introduce a new beverage called GULP. For appraisal purposes, the life of the GULP project is to be taken as 10 years (though the company hopes it will, if introduced, last much longer).
Ancastle is subject to corporation tax at 25 per cent on profits, and requires 20 per cent a year after-tax as the minimum acceptable rate of return on new product proposals.
All the figures set out below relate to the GULP project. They represent the best estimates that Ancastle's managers can make; but obviously they are all subject to a margin of error.

1 Fixed capital assets

	Buildings (£'000)	Plant and equipment (£'000)
Cost (all payable at start)	800	1,200
Residual value	480	120
Book depreciation on cost (straight line)	$2\frac{1}{2}\%$	10%
Tax capital allowances	4% on cost	25% on WDV*

* Written Down Value (=declining balance).

2 Operating cash flows

Sales revenue (£'000): Year 1 600; Year 2 1,200; Year 3 2,000; Year 4 (and later years) 3,000.

Cost of goods sold (including book depreciation) : 60 per cent of sales revenue. In addition, special promotion expenses of £200,000 a year for Years 1 to 5, and £100,000 a year thereafter.

3 Working capital

20 per cent of sales revenue (assumed payable at the end of the year to which it relates). All recoverable at the end of the project.

Required:

a. Prepare a statement showing the amount and timing of the cash flows expected to result from the GULP project.

b. Calculate the net present value of the GULP project; and recommend whether the company should go ahead with it.

An answer is shown in figure 15.14

(£'000)	EOY 0	EOY 1	EOY 2	EOY 3	EOY 4	EOY 5	EOY $\frac{6}{10}$ per year	EOY 10
FIXED CAPITAL								
Cost								
Buildings	−800							
Plant & Equipment	−1,200							
Capital allowances								
Buildings		8	8	8	8	8	8	
Plant & Equipment		75	56	42	32	24	8*	
Residual values								
Buildings								480
Plant & Equipment								120
	−2,000	83	64	50	40	32	16	600
WORKING CAPITAL		−120	−120	−160	−200	–	–	600
CAPITAL CASH FLOWS	−2,000	−37	−56	−110	−160	32	16	1,200
OPERATING CASH FLOWS								
Sales revenue		600	1,200	2,000	3,000	3,000	3,000	
Cost of goods sold		−220	−580	−1,060	−1,660	−1,660	−1,660	
Promotion expenses		−200	−200	−200	−200	−200	−100	
		180	420	740	1,140	1,140	1,240	
Tax @ 25%		−45	−105	−185	−285	−285	−310	
OPERATING CASH FLOWS		135	315	555	855	855	930	
TOTAL NET CASH FLOWS	−2,000	98	259	445	695	887	946	1,200
20% discount factors:	1.000	0.833	0.694	0.579	0.482	0.402	1.201	0.162
Present values	−2,000	82	180	258	335	357	1,136	194
NET PRESENT VALUE	+542							

Recommendation: On the basis of the above figures, showing a positive net present value of £542,000, Ancastle Ltd should go ahead with the GULP project.

* Capital allowances on plant calculated on straight-line basis for year 6–10.

Figure 15.14 Net present value calculation for the GULP project

Work section

A   Revision questions

A1   Is capital investment desirable? Why or why not?

A2   What was suggested as the most important stage in capital investment?

A3   Why may it be hard to forecast a project's future cash flows?

A4   Why may financial estimates not be the most critical aspects of capital investment projects?

A5   What are the two main kinds of post-project audit?

A6   What is the average rate of return on investment method?

A7   What is the main disadvantage of the average rate of return on investment method?

A8   What is the payback method?

A9   What is the main disadvantage of the payback method?

A10 Name two advantages of the payback method.

A11 Why does money have a 'time value'?

A12 Why is the timing of cash flows on an investment project important?

A13 How can a rate of interest provide an 'exchange rate over time'?

A14 Explain the net terminal value method of investment appraisal.

A15 What is the meaning of the interest rate used in the net terminal value method?

A16 How does the net present value method translate expected future cash flows into terms of 'End of Year 0' money?

A17 What assumption does the net present value method make about the 'opportunity cost' of capital?

A18 What is the difference between present value and *net* present value?

A19 Explain the net present value method of investment appraisal.

A20 What basic financial information about a capital project is needed in order to use the net present value method?

A21 Explain how the internal rate of return method works.

A22 What basic financial information about a capital project is needed in order to use the internal rate of return method?

A23 Why is the internal rate of return method sometimes called the 'trial and error' method?

A24 What 'reinvestment assumption' is made under the internal rate of return method? Under the net present value method?

A25 Describe the main difference(s) between the net present value method and the internal rate of return method.

A26 Name two reasons why a project with a lower internal rate of return may be better than one with a higher internal rate of return.

A27 What might cause a project's life to end?

A28 Name two items which may constitute capital recovery inflows at the end of a project's life?

A29 What is a 'horizon'?

A30 Why must working capital be allowed for in project appraisal even if it will be fully recovered at the end of the project's life?

A31 What rate(s) of corporation tax do UK companies pay on their profits?

A32 What is the difference between 'specific' price changes and 'general' price changes?

A33 What are the two main methods of allowing for inflation in project appraisal? (Describe them in sufficient detail.)

A34 What are some limitations of the DCF approach to project appraisal?

A35 Name three ways of allowing for uncertainty in capital projects.

A36 Why might a cost reduction project be less risky than a new product project?

A37 What does sensitivity analysis involve?

A38 What is the difference between 'risk' and 'uncertainty'?

A39 Suggest two ways in which a manager might try to reduce the riskiness of a capital project.

A40 If DCF methods are better, why is payback still widely used?

B Exercises and case studies

B1 Write down a brief description of:
   a. The criterion rate
   b. The net present value of a project.
   c. Incremental cash flows.
   d. Sensitivity analysis.
   e. Horizon date.
   f. The re-investment assumption.

B2 a. Calculate the compound interest owing at the end of a three-year period if £100 is borrowed at an annual interest rate of 12 per cent.
   b. If you employed *simple* interest, how much less would the total interest amount to?
   c. What would be the advantage to a bank of charging interest at 1 per cent a month rather than at 12 per cent a year, over the three-year period?

B3 a. What amount will compound to £2,700 after six years at an interest rate of 20 per cent a year?
   b. At what interest rate will £1,500 compound to £2,500 over eight years?
   c. What compound interest rate is required to double a sum of money in five years?

  d. The Retail Prices Index, based on January 1974 = 100, reached 395 in January 1987, when a new series was started. What annual average rate of inflation does this imply?

B4 Calculate the present value of the following future cash flows at the given annual rate of interest (r):

  a. £550 1 year away, $r = 10\%$. b. £1,728 3 years away, $r = 20\%$.

  c. £251 2 years away, $r = 12\%$. d. £2,000 9 years away, $r = 8\%$.

B5 At 12 per cent a year, what is the present value of an 'annuity' of £200: (a) for 8 years; (b) for 20 years; (c) for 50 years?

B6 Which would you rather have (starting at the end of Year 1):

  a. £3,000 a year for the next 20 years, discounted at 20 per cent a year?

  b. £2,000 a year for the next 20 years, discounted at 12 per cent a year?

  c. £1,000 a year for the next 20 years, discounted at 3 per cent a year?

B7 A project requires an outlay of £1,500, and is expected to produce net receipts of £2,000 at the end of Year 5 and £2,000 at the end of Year 10. Should it be undertaken if the firm's cost of capital is: (a) 12 per cent; (b) 16 per cent?

B8 Which would you prefer:

  (a) £500 a year for seven years; or (b) £700 a year for five years?

B9 A new machine can reduce operating costs (excluding depreciation) by £12,000 a year, and its life is expected to be eight years. Is it worth paying £50,000 for the machine if the firm's criterion rate is 12 per cent?

B10 A project is expected to yield £1 million at the end of Year 10. The initial outlay is £410,000. What rate of return does it offer?

B11 A project requiring an initial outlay of £5,400 will yield returns of £1,000 a year for 10 years. (a) What is the rate of return? (b) What annual returns would be needed to yield a 20 per cent internal rate of return?

B12 A project requires an initial investment of £6,000. Its expected cash receipts amount to £2,000 a year.

  a. If its life is five years, what is the highest cost of capital the company can have and still find the project worthwhile?

  b. If the cost of capital is 25 per cent a year, for how many years (at least) must the project last to be worthwhile?

B13 What is the present value of:

  a. £1,200 a year receivable from the end of Year 3 to the end of Year 7 at an interest rate of 20 per cent a year?

  b. £4,000 a year payable from the end of Year 5 to the end of Year 10 at an interest rate of 15 per cent a year?

  c. £800 a year receivable from the beginning of Year 4 to the end of Year 8 at an interest rate of 12 per cent a year?

  d. A pension of £5,000 a year receivable from the end of Year 30 to the end of Year 50 at an interest rate of 15 per cent a year?

B14 Four projects costing £4,200 each produce a net present value of zero discounting at 6 per cent a year:

a. 5-year annuity of £997   b. 10-year annuity of £571

c. 20-year annuity of £366   d. 50-annuity of £266.

What happens to *each* project if the rate of interest falls to 4 per cent?

B15 Assuming an interest rate of 12 per cent a year, if a first-class letter (costing 22p postage) takes one day to reach its destination, while a second-class letter (costing 17p postage) takes four days, how large does a cheque which you intend to post to your bank manager to reduce your overdraft need to be to justify sending it first class?

B16 A car licence for 12 months costs £100. For six months, a licence costs £55. How should a motorist who expects to drive throughout the next year decide whether to buy his licence in a 12-monthly payment rather than in two six-monthly instalments? (Assume he can borrow from a bank, if necessary.)

B17 A new toll road is expected to produce net cash receipts of £3.0 m. a year when it is completed. Assume that the road will be operational for 25 years. The road will take five years to complete; and the cash outflows are expected to be: £8.0 m. at the end of year 0, and £5.0 m. a year for years 1 to 5.

What is the project's internal rate of return?

B18 You purchased, five years ago, a vase for £800.

    a. If you accept £1,000 for it, have you made a 'real' profit, with inflation at five per cent a year during the past five years?

    b. With inflation at 10 per cent a year during the past five years, what offer price would you need now in order to break even, in 'real' terms?

B19 H. Stephenson Ltd is considering an investment project requiring the investment of £50,000 in new fixed assets and £12,000 in additional stocks. The annual sales revenue for the project is forecast to be £80,000, and the annual running costs £60,000 (including S/L depreciation of £10,000). The project's life is expected to be five years. Ignoring tax:

    a. Show the cash flows year by year.

    b. Should the project be accepted if the firm's cut-off rate is 20 per cent?

B20 Refer to B19. Additional information is as follows:

    1. Existing assets (being replaced) can be sold for £2,000.

    2. Tax at 35 per cent is assumed payable on profits on the last day of the year in which they are earned.

    3. For tax purposes, S/L depreciation is to be ignored; but capital allowances of 25 per cent a year on the declining balance are given on the investment in new fixed assets.

    Assume that these can be used to reduce tax on the firm's overall profits.

    a. Show the net cash flows year by year.

    b. Should the project be accepted if the firm's cut-off rate is 15 per cent?

B21

End of year:	0	1	2	3	4
H cash flows (£)	−1,000	+500	+400	+350	+300
J cash flows (£)	−1,000	+400	+400	+400	+400

    a. Which of these two projects has the higher net present value at a discounting rate of 15 per cent a year? By how much?

    b. What is the payback period of each project?

    c. Chart the net present value of project J at discount rates of 6 per cent, 12 per cent, 18 per cent, 24 per cent and 30 per cent. Estimate the internal rate of return from the chart.

B22 Project T requires an initial investment of £2,000 (which is non-returnable), and is expected to produce cash inflows of £700 a year for five years. Is it worth investing in if the opportunity cost of capital is 15 per cent a year? Calculate your answer using:

    a. Net present value method.

    b. Internal rate of return method.

    c. Graph the project's NPV at discount rates of 6 per cent, 12 per cent, 18 per cent, 24 per cent and 30 per cent. Estimate the IRR from the graph.

B23 Project X requires a cash investment in a new machine of £36,000, which is to be completely depreciated in equal instalments over its expected four-year life. The project's accounting profits are expected to amount to £4,000 a year in Years 1 and 2, and to £7,000 a year in Years 3 and 4.

    a. What is the average accounting rate of return on investment?

    b. Draw up a schedule of the amount and timing of cash flows for Project X.

    c. What is the payback period?

    d. If the discount rate is 20 per cent a year, what is the net present value?

    e. What is Project X's internal rate of return?

B24 Project Y is expected to produce accounting profits of £24,000 a year over its eight-year life. The initial investment in fixed capital equipment is £120,000, and the firm uses straight-line depreciation.

    a. What is the average accounting rate of return on investment?

    b. Draw up a schedule showing the amount and timing of Project Y's cash flow.

    c. What is the payback period?

    d. Chart Project Y's net present value, using discount rates from 0 to 30 per cent inclusive, at 10 per cent intervals.

    e. From the chart, what is Project Y's internal rate of return?

    f. Check your estimated IRR by calculation from the tables.

B25 A company expects to reduce labour costs by £20,000 a year if it invests £50,000 in new equipment which will last five years. Ignoring tax:

    a. What is the annual increase in accounting profit?

    b. What is the average rate of return on investment?

    c. What is the annual net cash inflow?

    d. What is the payback period?

    e. What is the NPV at 15 per cent a year?

    f. What is the IRR?

B26 Colin Park is enthusiastic about a new German machine, which he thinks would enable Park Products to reduce operating costs by £20,000 a year (before tax). The machine costs £60,000. For tax purposes, capital allowances of 25 per cent a year on the declining balance are available. (Ignore any tax time-lags.) At the end of its expected five-year life the machine could probably be sold for about £5,000. The company normally requires a return of at least 15 per cent a year (after tax) on this kind of investment.

Should the German machine be bought? (The tax rate is 35 per cent.)

B27 Park Products did go ahead and buy the German machine (G) (see B26); but a month later Colin Park visited Japan in order to keep abreast of the latest technical developments. While he was in Tokyo he learned about an even better machine, (J), which would cut Park's operating costs by a further £12,000 a year by replacing machine (G). Machine (J) would last five years, with not much salvage value at the end, and would cost £60,000. Unfortunately machine (G) would have to be sold, and would realize only £25,000.

a. Should machine (J) be purchased?

b. If machine (J) *is* purchased, presumably it was a mistake to buy machine (G) in the first place. How much did this mistake cost? How did it come about?

B28 Globe Gears Ltd is about to choose between three projects. Project A is for the purchase of a new machine; Project B is for a promotional campaign to boost sales; and Project C is for the rationalization of part of the production department. The cost and expected returns for each project are set out below:

End of year	Project A (£)	Project B (£)	Project C (£)
0 (Initial outlay)	10,000	10,000	10,000
Cash inflows			
1	1,000	4,000	3,000
2	2,000	3,000	3,000
3	3,000	3,000	3,000
4	3,000	2,000	3,000
5	3,000	–	2,000
6	3,400	–	1,000
Total	15,400	12,000	15,000

a. Ignoring tax: calculate for each project:
   (i) average rate of return on investment,
   (ii) payback period,
   (iii) DCF rate of return.

b. State with reasons the projects you would rank as of greatest value to the firm, on purely financial grounds.

c. What other factors might you consider before a final choice?

B29 New Supa-calc requires investment in a factory of £2.0 million, in equipment of £1.5 million, and in working capital of £1.0 million. Assume that all cash outflows occur at the same time; that after eight years working capital will be recovered in full, the equipment will be sold for £200,000, and that the factory will then have a value of £500,000. What is the net present value of the capital investment cash flows:

a. Ignoring tax, and assuming a discount rate of 20 per cent?

b. Assuming a tax rate of 35 per cent, an after-tax discount rate of 12 per cent, 25 per cent annual tax capital allowances on the equipment's declining balance and 4 per cent on cost annual allowance on the factory.

B30 Sales volume of new Supa-calc is expected to be 100,000 units in Year 1, 250,000 units in Year 2, and 500,000 units a year for each of the next six years. The selling price per unit will be £6.00 for Years 1 to 4 and £5.00 for Years 5 to 8. Variable costs are expected to amount to (a) production costs of £2.40 per unit in Years 1 and 2, and £2.00 per unit in Years 3 to 8, and (b) selling costs equal to 5 per cent of sales revenue.

Advertising costs will be £100,000 in Year 1, £60,000 in Year 2 and £40,000 per year thereafter.

a. Ignoring tax, set out a schedule of the amount and timing of the operating cash flows, assuming all receipts and payments are for cash (not on credit), and that all cash flows take place at the end of the year to which they relate.

b. What is the net present value of the cash flows, assuming a discount rate of 20 per cent a year?

c. What is the net present value of the after-tax cash flows, assuming a tax rate of 35 per cent and after-tax discount rate of 12 per cent a year?

B31 Refer to B29 and B30. Using a tax rate of 35 per cent and a discount rate of 12 per cent a year:

a. What is the Supa-calc project's net present value?

b. What is the payback period?

c. What is the internal rate of return?

B32 A hospital X-ray department has a machine which cost £250,000 five years ago, when it still had an expected life of ten years. It costs £2,500 a year to maintain and, in addition, a new special part costing £6,600 is needed, on average, every 18 months. The life of this part is directly related to the number of investigations carried out by the machine, which averages 400 per year. In order to reduce film costs the X-ray department is considering the purchase of a camera at a cost of £35,000 to replace the existing X-ray film unit. This camera will cost £200 per year to maintain and is estimated to have a residual value of £2,000 in five years time. The direct costs per investigation under both systems are given in the table below:

	Machine with X-ray film unit	Machine with camera
Film costs:		
average number of pictures	35	50
fixed cost	–	£1
cost per picture	£1	10p
Drugs	£5	£5
Minor equipment	£30	£30
Contrast injections		
(@ £14 per bottle)	2 bottles	2 bottles - 75% of the time
		3 bottles - 25% of the time

Labour (@ £5 per hour)		
Day	Not applicable as it can be regarded as a fixed cost	
Night	2 hours	2 hours

(i) On the assumption that the X-ray film unit is in use, calculate the marginal cost of an investigation, both during the day and as a night-time emergency.

(ii) What additional costs should be included if you were calculating the total cost of an investigation in order to charge the patient?

b. (i) Show that the annual cash flow can be reduced by £10,000 per year if the camera is bought.

(ii) Calculate the pay-back period for the purchase of the camera.

(iii) If the camera is bought, the net present value of the *change* in cash flow over the next five years is £4,100, using a discount rate of 10%. You are required to undertake the same calculation using a discount rate of 16%.

c. (i) Discuss the relative merits of the methods of investment appraisal used in (b)(ii) and (b)(iii). On numerical grounds, would you recommend that the camera be bought?

(ii) What other factors should be taken into consideration before a final decision is made?

(*UCLES International Examinations, 1987, GCE A level Business Studies*)

C Essay questions

C1 'Choosing the criterion discount rate for use in DCF investment appraisal is not the most important aspect of the capital investment process.' Discuss.

C2   How, if at all, should a local authority's approach to capital project appraisal differ from that of a commercial business?

C3   How should a firm using DCF select the discount rate?

C4   What are the quantitative techniques of investment appraisal? Assess the extent to which they should be used by firms to plan future capital investment.

C5   A large well-known company uses the payback method of investment appraisal. It is apparently fairly successful. Assuming that it is prepared only to use a single method of investment appraisal, write a paper to convince its finance director that the company should change *either* to net present value *or* to internal rate of return. (Choose whichever of these two DCF methods you prefer.)

C6   A firm which changed from payback to net present value a few years ago is now thinking of changing back. It complains that not many of its managers seem to understand NPV, and that anyway its cash flow forecasts are so unreliable that the extra sophistication of DCF hardly seems worthwhile. Try to persuade the company's managing director to stay with NPV.

C7   A firm is thinking of reducing its horizon period from 15 years to 5 years, in view of the apparently increasing uncertainty in the business environment. Write a paper supporting (or opposing) this proposal.

C8   What are the advantages and disadvantages of post-project audits?

C9   How should a medium-sized manufacturing business try to allow for risk and uncertainty in capital investment project decisions?

C10   A company's finance manager has asked you how his company should allow for inflation in capital investment appraisal. His firm currently uses both payback (mainly to assess risk) and the internal rate of return method. Write an answer which he can circulate to the departmental managers who will have to put your advice into effect.

C11   'When interest rates are fluctuating wildly a discounted cash flow method of capital investment appraisal becomes no more than an academic exercise'. To what extent do you agree with this comment?

C12   What advantages and disadvantages would the discounted cash flow technique have over other methods when evaluating investment projects?

16

Debt

Plan of the chapter:

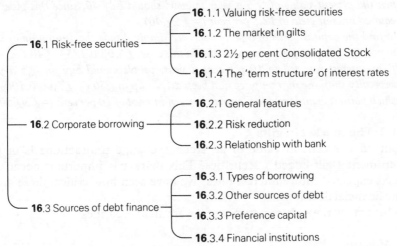

Fig.16.0

Objective: *To describe how risk-free securities are valued and traded; and to describe the main features and the main sources of corporate borrowing.*

Synopsis: *The present value model (Chapter 15) can be used to value risk-free securities; though the market in gilts has a number of complications, such as level of coupon, and index-linking against inflation.*

Business loans usually contain restrictions, many of which reflect lenders' attempts to reduce their risks.

There is a whole spectrum of borrowing possibilities, with some of the variables being: (a) the term of the loan; (b) the extent of security; (c) whether the rate of interest is fixed or floating; (d) the currency; (e) conversion options. Other forms of 'debt' include: hire purchase, leasing, and factoring. Another way for a company to increase its financial gearing is through preference share capital.

16.1 Risk-free securities

16.1.1 Valuing risk-free securities

In Chapter 15 we saw how to 'value' future cash flows expected from a capital investment project, by discounting them back to 'present value'. The same approach can also be used to value shares or other assets.

Imagine a risk-free government **security** guaranteeing an interest payment of £5 a year forever (a **perpetuity**). Ignoring tax, what would we expect its market price (that is, its present value) to be? We know the amount and timing of future cash receipts, so all we need to determine is the appropriate interest rate to use when discounting them back to present value. This should be the 'opportunity cost' - the rate of return which could be earned on similar-risk **investments**.

Example: If the current interest yield on risk-free securities is 12.5 per cent a year, then the present value of '£5 a year forever' should be £40, since this gives the required interest yield of 12.5 per cent (= £5/£40).

To find the capital value of a perpetuity, we simply divide the annual amount of interest by the appropriate interest rate. In this case, £5.00/0.125 = £40.00.

If the interest rate fell to 10 per cent a year, people would buy our £5-a-year perpetuity until the market price had been driven up to £50 (= £5,00/0.100), at which point it would yield the 'current' rate of interest of 10 per cent (=£5/£50).

16.1.2 The market in gilts

About 75 per cent in value of all stock exchange transactions is in UK government ('gilt-edged') securities. This market is important because it reflects expected future interest rates. We have seen how critical these are in many financial decisions.

There are various characteristics of government securities:

(a) Maturity

New government securities are issued with maturity periods varying from three months to more than 25 years. 'Shorts' have less than five years to run until final maturity, 'mediums' from five to 15 years, and 'longs' over 15 years (including **irredeemables** which need *never* be repaid).

(b) Coupon rate

To suit higher-rate tax-payers, the government issues some securities with very low coupons (nominal rates of interest paid per £100 of stock). They are issued at a large discount from par (£100), thus providing a large element of tax-free 'capital gain' to anyone holding them until maturity. The capital gain is counted as part of the overall **yield to redemption**, in addition to the regular interest (the **flat yield**).

(c) Index-linking

Since 1981 the UK government has issued low-coupon gilts with interest and principal index-linked (adjustable by reference to the Retail Prices Index). By eliminating the risk of inflation, the government is enabled to offer only a low 'real' interest rate – currently about $3\frac{1}{2}$ per cent a year. The difference between the yield on index-linked gilts and the yield on ordinary gilts provides an estimate of expected future inflation.

16.1.3 $2\frac{1}{2}$ per cent Consolidated Stock

Certain UK government securities have no redemption date: they simply promise to pay a stated coupon rate each year. Some of these 'perpetuities' have been in issue for more than 100 years, so they allow long-term comparisons of gilt-edged prices and interest yields.

In the years after the Second World War, interest rates, by modern standards, were low. Indeed in 1946, $2\frac{1}{2}$ per cent Consolidated Stock was quoted at par (£100), implying interest rates of $2\frac{1}{2}$ per cent a year. Figure 16.1 shows the market price of £100 nominal of $2\frac{1}{2}$ per cent Consolidated Stock for each year between 1946 and 1989 – adjusted (by the RPI) into constant January 1987 pounds. This chart dramatically illustrates the single most important financial phenomenon of the post-war years in the UK– continuous and rapid government-created **currency debasement**. In 43 years since 1946, the real value of $2\frac{1}{2}$ per cent Consolidated Stock fell by more than 98 per cent!

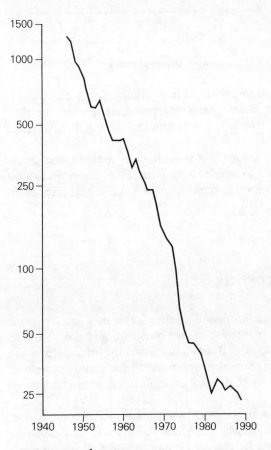

Figure 16.1 $2\frac{1}{2}$ Consolidated Stock: market price of £100 nominal, 1946-89 (in January 1987 pounds)

275

16.1.4 The 'term structure' of interest rates

The different maturity dates of UK government securities reveal the **term structure of interest rates.** Charting interest yields against the time to maturity (or 'term') of risk-free government securities may show three different shapes (figure 16.2):

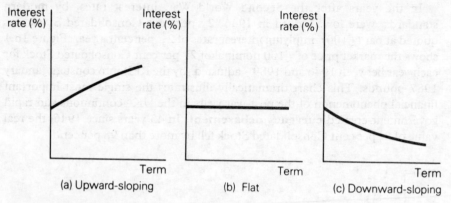

Figure 16.2 Three kinds of 'term structure' of interest rates

According to the *expectations theory,* the term structure will be upward-sloping if investors expect that interest rates will rise (perhaps because they expect the rate of inflation to increase), but downward-sloping if they expect interest rates to fall.

The *liquidity preference theory* argues that most lenders want to lend short-term, while most borrowers want to borrow long-term. Hence borrowers have to offer lenders a premium, to induce them to lend long; which implies an upward-sloping term structure.

16.2 Corporate borrowing

16.2.1 General features

A company must repay amounts borrowed **(debt)** when they are due, and regularly pay the agreed amount of interest on debt outstanding. Failure to do so entitles the lender to take immediate legal action to recover the principal and any unpaid interest. Both lender and borrower will want to see a good margin of safety, to enable a company to meet its legal commitments even if things go wrong.

A lender will be concerned with the borrower's honesty and competence. The borrower will have to explain why he needs the money, how much he requires, for how long, and how he plans to repay the loan. Cash forecasts covering the period of the proposed loan can help answer many of these questions (see 13.4). It may be useful to prepare more than one set of forecasts, based on different assumptions.

Term loans are normally now variable-rate (instead of fixed-rate); and bank overdraft interest rates too change as market rates vary. Longer-term loans often carry higher interest rates than short-term borrowing (see 16.1.4), and smaller or riskier firms will have to pay a higher rate of interest than larger or more secure companies.

The 1980 Wilson Committee, in respect of large and medium-sized companies, 'could not find a single example of an investment project which had not gone ahead because of the inability to raise external finance ... '. It reached no conclusion on the criticism that, regarding small firms, banks tended to be over-cautious with respect to gearing and security conditions.

16.2.2 Risk reduction

(a) Personal guarantee

In a limited company the liability of ordinary shareholders is limited. In contrast, creditors of partnerships or sole traders can, if need be, look for repayment to the private assets of the individual owners. *Their* potential liability is unlimited. Given the risk of loss if the business fails, anyone lending money to a small limited company may want to get a personal **guarantee** of repayment from the main shareholders. This will put the lender in the same position as if the small limited company were a sole trader or partnership.

> *The reverse side of this coin is that giving a personal guarantee is a major step. At the time it may seem almost a 'free' way of improving a small company's credit rating, but giving a personal guarantee* fundamentally *changes the legal position of the controlling owner of a limited company. If things go wrong, the consequences can be extremely serious.*

(b) Security

Another way for a lender to reduce his risk of loss is to arrange for certain assets to serve as formal security for his loan. On liquidation this gives him priority: the proceeds from selling those assets will go first to repay his loan. Anything left over will go into the company's general pool of funds to pay off unsecured creditors. If the proceeds from assets serving as collateral do not cover the full amount of a secured loan, then the creditor will rank as 'unsecured' in respect of the shortfall.

Debtors, some stocks, and general (not specialized) equipment can serve as collateral for loans, as well as land, buildings and marketable securities. Legal title to the asset needs to be easily transferable; and the asset's value should be fairly stable and easy to determine.

Instead of securing a loan on particular assets, a lender may obtain a **floating charge** on all a borrower's assets. This comes into effect ('crystallizes') only when a company goes into liquidation – thus permitting normal selling of assets in the ordinary course of business. But debts which come before the claims of unsecured creditors (for example, certain wages and taxes) also have priority over any floating charges, though *not* over a fixed charge on a specific asset (see 19.4.1).

(c) Covenants
Corporate lenders usually insist on certain conditions **(covenants):**
1. to prevent the sale of substantial parts of the business, or the granting of prior claims to other subsequent lenders;
2. to require the maintenance of certain financial ratios at stated levels or the maintenance of physical assets in good condition;
3. to require the provision of regular up-to-date financial information;
4. for smaller companies, there might be covenants restricting dividend payments or directors' salaries.

Breach of covenant (like failure to pay interest when due) can lead to the lender being entitled to require immediate repayment of the loan. But the breach may simply act as a 'trigger', alerting the lender to the need to talk to the borrower about the current state of the business.

16.2.3 Relationship with bank
Unpredictable events may cause any business, however well run, to need to borrow money from its bank from time to time. The precise dates and amounts of such unexpected borrowing requirements are, of course, impossible to forecast.

There may be a grain of truth in the definition of a banker as 'someone who will lend you money only when you don't need it'. It makes sense, therefore, for a business (especially a small one) to be on good terms with the bank, so that if an unexpected need does arise, there is a reasonable chance of being able to borrow the amount required on acceptable terms. It is in the good times, when you don't need money, that you can lay the foundations for borrowing money later if you should need to.

A firm's financial director (or, in a small business, the managing director) should be sure to talk to his bank manager regularly (at least once a year). If everything is going well, the meeting may simply consist of a friendly chat, keeping the bank informed of general trends, challenges and opportunities currently facing the business. If there are financial problems, of course, longer and more detailed meetings may be required.

In addition, the bank manager should be kept informed of the detailed financial progress of the business. At a minimum this means sending the bank manager the firm's annual accounts. It might also be desirable to send him a copy of the cash forecasts for the ensuing year. Unfortunately some businesses do not prepare such forecasts on any formal basis even for their own internal use. Needless to say, *they* are the ones most likely to find themselves suddenly in need of 'unexpected' bank borrowing!

16.3 Sources of debt finance

16.3.1 Types of borrowing

Business loans for less than one year are regarded as 'short-term'. 'Medium-term' means from one to five years; and 'long-term' means more than five years. (But for *government* borrowing, any period less than five years is 'short-term' – see 16.1.2.)

(a) Short-term borrowing

Bank overdrafts are the best-known form of short-term borrowing. Only the amount actually overdrawn bears interest, though there may be a small 'commitment fee' on the agreed maximum limit. Interest accrues from day to day, at a rate which varies with market conditions. The bank overdraft is convenient and flexible for borrowers: its main drawback is that it is legally repayable 'on demand'.

(b) Term loans

Term loans are arranged for stated periods of less than a year to more than five years. Sometimes the timing of repayment may be partly related to a project's profitability. Term loans may be more expensive than bank overdrafts, and there will usually be a penalty on early repayment, which can limit flexibility.

(c) Long-term borrowing

The whole of a long-term loan is repayable on the maturity date. Where a company's financial position has worsened since the original borrowing, it may be difficult and expensive to meet the repayment by new borrowing ('re-financing'). **Project finance,** relating to a specific project rather than to the company's business as a whole, may provide for partial repayment at regular intervals.

Long-term loans may be either secured or unsecured (see 16.2.2 (b)), and may be listed on the stock exchange. Such listing means that an original lender can be 'repaid', not by the corporate borrower, but by the sale of his **loan stock** to another investor. At the **maturity** date (on **redemption)** the borrowing company will repay the principal (nominal) amount to the then-registered holders of the loan stock. Unlisted loans may be arranged with banks, insurance companies or pension funds. With only a single lender it may be possible to re-negotiate certain conditions of a loan if circumstances change. This is not feasible with listed loan stocks.

Companies with overseas interests may choose to borrow in foreign currencies, rather than in sterling. But where such loans are not fully covered by foreign currency earnings, changes in foreign exchange rates can have a serious effect. (This was one of the main factors leading to the collapse of Laker Airways in the early 1980s – see problem B5 in Chapter 19.)

Some issues of long-term loans are convertible into ordinary shares, at the holder's option, on prearranged terms. As long as the loan is not converted, it bears regular fixed-interest payments, and ranks as a creditor on liquidation. But upon conversion it ceases to bear interest and becomes ordinary share capital, ranking for dividends. The 'option' to take up ordinary shares at a low price if the company prospers will normally reduce the rate of interest payable on convertible loan stocks.

16.3.2 Other sources of debt

Several sources of debt finance may be of special interest to small and medium-sized businesses:

(a) Hire purchase

Acquiring an asset on **hire-purchase** terms involves an initial 'down-payment' of around 20 per cent of the total cost, followed by equal instalments (including interest at a fairly high rate) over between one and five years. The buyer does not become the legal owner until the last payment is made; but the balance sheet shows the total hire-purchase cost as a fixed asset (subject to depreciation), and all the unpaid instalments as a liability.

(b) Leasing

Leases give the lessee *use* of an asset in return for regular payments (of 'rent') to the lessor, who remains the legal owner. The lessor can claim tax allowances on the asset, and pass on (some of) the benefit in lower lease payments. The implied interest rate in leases may be high. It is useful to distinguish **operating leases**, which are short term and often for small amounts, from **financial leases**, which normally cover the whole of the asset's economic life, may be for large amounts, and are non-cancellable. In effect, financial leases put the lessee in almost the same position as if he had borrowed and purchased the asset outright. Hence accounts show financial leases as assets on the balance sheet.

(c) Factoring

Factors enable firms to reduce working capital tied up in debtors. The factoring company buys (some of) a firm's debts, at full value less a factoring charge, and then undertakes to collect them. Sometimes any bad debts remain to be borne by the firm itself, not by the factor (which affects the factor's charges). The service provided may also include sales ledger administration if desired.

(d) Finance houses

Finance houses finance the purchase by individuals of consumer durables, such as motor cars and television sets. They also finance industrial leasing, hire purchase, and instalment credit. Interest charges tend to be on the high side.

16.3.3 Preference capital

Preference share capital (see 4.4.3) may seem an unattractive alternative to debt (figure 16.3 A). It is usually more expensive than debt after tax, and often

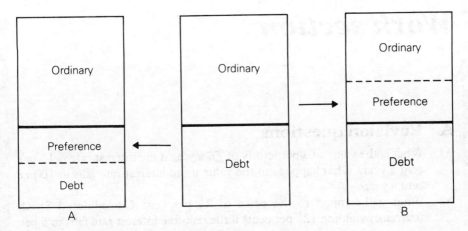

Figure 16.3 Alternative views of preference capital

seems nearly as risky. (There is, however, a big difference between a company being highly embarrassed if it has to omit preference dividends for a period and being *liquidated* if it cannot pay debt interest!)

But a company near its debt limit (see 18.3.2) may regard preference share capital as a useful alternative to *ordinary* share capital (figure 16.3 B) – as a way to increase its financial gearing. Preference capital may then be seen as cheaper than ordinary share capital, yet less risky than debt.

16.3.4 Financial institutions

The largest UK financial institutions are banks, building societies, insurance companies and pension funds. The banks are the main source of short-term and medium-term loans for business, while the insurance companies and pension funds provide long-term finance – both debt and equity – for larger firms.

The banks' main function is to provide an efficient mechanism for debt settlement, which they do through the transfer of deposits by cheque, standing order and direct debit. They are also important financial **intermediaries** receiving private savings in the form of deposits and then lending them out again to other persons and to businesses.

The building societies deal mainly with individuals. Their specialized function is to receive savings from people, and then to lend others the money to buy houses. The loan, together with interest, is repaid during the working life of the house-owner.

The life insurance companies and pension funds receive savings from individuals during their working lives, often through contracted arrangements. They pay these out again, together with accumulated interest, either during retirement (pensions) or on death (life assurance)

Work section

A Revision questions

A1 What is the value of a perpetuity of £6 a year if the interest rate is 12 per cent a year? What happens to the value if the interest rate falls to 10 per cent a year?

A2 What will happen to the price of $2\frac{1}{2}$ per cent Consolidated Stock (currently yielding $12\frac{1}{2}$ per cent) if the risk-free interest rate falls to 5 per cent a year?

A3 What is the difference between the 'flat yield' and the 'yield to redemption' on a government security?

A4 What is an 'index-linked' gilt? Why is the yield apparently so much lower than on ordinary gilts?

A5 How can one use current prices and yields in the gilts market to estimate the future rate of inflation?

A6 What has happened to the 'real' value of $2\frac{1}{2}$ per cent Consolidated Stock since the Second World War? Why?

A7 What is an 'upwards-sloping term structure' of interest rates? Outline two suggested explanations for its existence.

A8 Identify three specific questions which an applicant for a loan is likely to need to answer.

A9 Name three different ways in which a lender may try to reduce risk.

A10 What is the effect of a majority owner of a small limited company giving a personal guarantee to a bank granting his company credit?

A11 What are the main features which make an asset suitable collateral?

A12 What is a floating charge? How does it work?

A13 In what respect(s) does the position of a 'secured' creditor differ from that of an ordinary (unsecured) creditor in a winding-up?

A14 Give three examples of 'covenants' which might be attached to loans.

A15 What are the main characteristics of a bank overdraft? What is its main disadvantage to a borrower?

A16 How does a 'term loan' differ from a bank overdraft?

A17 What is a convertible loan stock? What are its advantages?

A18 What is the main advantage of financial leasing as a source of business finance?

A19 What is the difference between an operating lease and a financial lease?

A20 What is a factor?

B Exercises and case studies

B1 Refer to figure 16.1. Roughly what proportion of its 1979 'real' value had $2\frac{1}{2}$ per cent Consolidated Stock lost by 1989?

B2 Under what circumstances, if any, would you expect the market price of $2\frac{1}{2}$ per cent Consolidated Stock to rise from its present level of about £25 to a level of about £50 (per £100 nominal of stock)?

B3 The Arcadian government's irredeemable 4 per cent stock stands at 60.
   a. What is the rate of interest?
   b. What will the price of the stock be if the interest rate is:
      (i) 5 per cent?
      (ii) 3 per cent?

B4 If the rate of inflation falls from above 10 per cent a year to about 5 per cent a year, what would you expect to happen to the yield on an index-linked gilt which now stands at 3 per cent a year? Why?

B5 A company is declared bankrupt, having assets of £10 million on realization, and total liabilities of £13 million, as follows:

8 per cent mortgage debenture (secured on the company's £3 million office block)	£1 million
9 per cent unsecured loan stock	£1 million
Other liabilities	£11 million

There are 2 million ordinary shares in issue, of nominal value 25p each. You own £100 nominal value of *each* of debenture stock, loan stock, and ordinary shares.
   a. How much money do you receive in total?
   b. How much would you receive if the assets were worth £4 million more, and the company were still 'wound up'?

B6 Fidler Ltd has 200,000 Ordinary £1 shares in issue; 60,000 $3\frac{1}{2}$ per cent cumulative preference £1 shares; and £80,000 10 per cent debentures, repayable in 1989. Retained profits total £60,000. Calculate:
   a. the debt ratio;
   b. the amount per share the preference shareholders would receive if the company were liquidated and the total assets less the current liabilities realized £125,000 in cash;
   c. the amount per share the ordinary shareholders would receive if the total assets less current liabilities realized £190,000.

B7 A company going into liquidation has the following liabilities: trade creditors £172,000; bank overdrafts (secured by a floating charge) £65,000; bank overdrafts (unsecured, but with a personal guarantee from the managing director) £48,000; long-term 12 per cent loan (secured on land and buildings) £80,000.
   Ordinary shareholders' funds in the balance sheet are represented by:
   Ordinary shares issued (100,000 at 50p each nominal value): £50,000;

Retained profits and other reserves: £112,000;

Preference share capital amounts to £20,000 (in shares of £1 each).

How much will (i) unsecured creditors, (ii) ordinary shareholders, get:

a. if all the assets (book value £547,000) realize £750,000 in cash (of which land and buildings realize £220,000)?

b. if all the assets realize £500,000 (land and buildings £100,000)?

c. if all the assets realize £250,000 (land and buildings £50,000)?

B8 Refer to B7 above.

a. Draw up a list of the liabilities and shareholders' funds.

b. Draw up a revised list, on the assumption that the long-term loan is convertible into ordinary shares at 160p each, and that the holders decide to exercise their option to convert.

c. What difference(s) if any does conversion of such a loan into ordinary shares make:

   (i) to the company's profit and loss account in future (if it were to continue in business)?

   (ii) to the company's debt ratio taken from the balance sheet?

C Essay questions

C1 Why did the UK government start issuing index-linked securities in the early 1980s? Discuss the implications.

C2 'If the UK government continues to achieve budget surpluses, the National Debt might be completely repaid by the end of the century. Then there would be no gilt-edged securities outstanding.' Discuss the consequences.

C3 'It's absurd to call a government stock like $2\frac{1}{2}$ per cent Consolidated Stock 'risk-free' when it has lost more than 98 per cent of its real value since 1946'. Discuss.

C4 Is a banker 'someone who will lend you money only when you don't need it'?

C5 Discuss the relative advantages and disadvantages to a company of a bank overdraft and a term loan.

C6 Why have variable interest loans become more popular in recent years?

C7 What would be the pros and cons to a company of borrowing long-term on an index-linked basis?

C8 Would it be a good idea for a UK company to borrow Swiss francs at a much lower rate of interest than if it borrowed pounds sterling?

C9 Why might a medium-sized company choose to factor its debts?

C10 Is there a role for preference share capital in a company's capital structure? Why or why not?

17

Equity

Plan of the chapter:

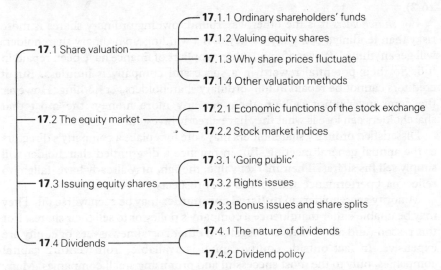

Fig.17.0

Objective *To outline a 'present value' model for valuing shares, and to describe other valuation methods; to identify the stock exchange's economic functions; to distinguish the various ways of issuing equity shares; and to discuss dividend policy.*

Synopsis: *Equity investors value company shares by discounting expected future dividends at their after-tax opportunity cost, the key factors being expectations as to future profits, risks, and interest rates.*

The stock exchange functions as a secondary market as well as helping companies (and governments) to raise new capital. It was not until 1987 that the level of the UK equity market again reached its 1972 peak, in real terms.

An unlisted company can raise new equity share capital by 'going public' (by one of three main methods); listed companies by making rights issues to existing shareholders.

In theory, in a perfect capital market dividends wouldn't matter. In practice they often signal management's views about prospects for future earnings.

17.1 Share valuation

17.1.1 Ordinary shareholders' funds

New issues of ordinary shares, like retained profits, are 'shareholders' funds' (equity). From the *company's* viewpoint, ordinary share capital is less risky than borrowing, for three main reasons. Unlike debt interest, there is no legal commitment to pay any dividend; the company need never repay equity until it is finally wound up (whereas most loans must be repaid on the agreed date); and equity capital is free from the restrictions often attached to borrowing (see 16.2).

For *shareholders* it is the other way round: owning ordinary shares is more risky than lending a company money. On a winding-up ordinary shareholders will get anything left over after all other suppliers of finance have been repaid in full. So their potential reward in a successful company is limitless. But if creditors cannot be repaid in full, ordinary shareholders get nothing. However the company cannot call on them for any more money: the most that shareholders can lose is what they have already invested.

Dissatisfied ordinary shareholders may vote to replace a company's directors at the annual general meeting. But in practice a disgruntled shareholder will simply sell his shares. Their market value, though, may already have fallen, to reflect past performance and poor future prospects.

Minority shareholders in **unlisted companies** may be even worse off. They may be unable either to influence a company's policy or to sell their shares. For this reason (and also because of legal and other costs) new issues of equity are expensive. In fact outside equity capital is available, from venture capital companies, only to the most successful and promising small companies. Many small businessmen anyway prefer to avoid new equity issues, since (unlike 'Aunt Agatha') few independent investors will provide equity money for small companies without wanting to influence policy.

17.1.2 Valuing equity shares

We can value equity shares in the same way as risk-free securities (see 16.1.1). Thus we discount the expected future cash receipts from owning the shares, at the opportunity cost of capital. Instead of a regular fixed money **annuity,** we now have to deal with dividends which can fluctuate. A common assumption is that, in money terms, the latest annual net dividend per share will grow at a *constant* rate in future.

A shareholder's 'return' from holding shares consists of two parts: dividends plus **capital gain.** Yet the stock market can value a company's equity shares *solely* on the basis of expected future cash dividends.

It is true that an individual mortal shareholder (A) (or his estate) will ultimately sell his shares. But he will sell to some other shareholder (B), who will value the shares on the basis of future dividends plus ultimate sales proceeds. Figure 17.1 shows how we can 'cancel out' the various intermediate purchases and sales on the secondary market, ending up with the value of the shares depending only on the stream of future dividends. For simplicity we assume that shareholders A, B, C, D, etc., hold the shares for exactly ten years each. Obviously we could pursue the logic right through the alphabet.

Share- holder	*Cost of purchase*				*Sales proceeds*
A	Value EOY 0	=	Dividends EOY 1–10	+	~~Value EOY 10~~
B	~~Value EOY 10~~	=	Dividends EOY 11–20	+	~~Value EOY 20~~
C	~~Value EOY 20~~	=	Dividends EOY 21–30	+	~~Value EOY 30~~
D	~~Value EOY 30~~	=	Dividends EOY 31–40	+	~~Value EOY 40~~
E	~~Value EOY 40~~	=	...		
...					

	Value EOY 0	=	Dividends EOY 1-40 ...

Figure 17.1 Valuing shares solely on future dividends

Applying the present value model to share valuation is straightforward enough in theory, though of course in practice guessing the actual numbers is not easy.

If the latest annual net dividend per share is d, the expected (assumed constant) rate of growth in future dividends per share is g, and the opportunity cost of equivalent-risk equity shares is k, then we find the present value per share (p) by discounting as follows:

$$p = \frac{d(1+g)}{(1+k)} + \frac{d(1+g)^2}{(1+k)^2} + \frac{d(1+g)^3}{(1+k)^3} + ... \frac{d(1+g)^\infty}{(1+k)^\infty}$$

This can be simplified* to: $p = \dfrac{d^1}{k-g}$ or $k = \dfrac{d^1}{p} + g$

*Multiply both sides of the equation shown by $\dfrac{(1+k)}{(1+g)}$

Then from the resulting product, subtract the equation shown above.

This gives: $\dfrac{p(1+k)}{(1+g)} - p = d^0 - \dfrac{d(1+g)^\infty}{(1+k)^\infty}$

Since k > g, the final term collapses to zero, which leaves:

$$\frac{p(1+k)}{(1+g)} - p = d^0$$

leading to $p(1+k) - p(1+g) = d^0(1+g)$

hence $p(k-g) = d^1$.

Example: Burnham Ltd is expected to pay a net dividend this year on ordinary shares of 11p, the expected future growth rate in dividends per share is 10 per cent a year, and the opportunity cost of equity capital is reckoned to be 15 per cent a year. Burnham Ltd's ordinary shares would be valued at 220p each:

$$Value = \frac{11}{0.15-0.10} = \frac{11}{0.05} = 220p$$

To determine the opportunity cost of equity capital, we simply add the assumed constant growth rate of 10 per cent a year to the net dividend yield of 5 per cent a year (based on d^1–the end-of-current-year dividend). This gives a cost of equity capital of 15 per cent a year.

Both k and g are only rough estimates, so the difference between them (k–g) must be subject to a very large margin of error.

17.1.3 Why share prices fluctuate

There can be three kinds of reason why a share's price may fluctuate:

1 There may be a change to the current year's net dividend. Clearly a change that the market has already anticipated will not affect the share price: only unanticipated changes will do so. This is one reason why the share price sometimes goes up when a company announces bad news: the market may have been expecting even worse.

2 The expected future growth rate in dividends per share may vary, perhaps more or less in line with expected future growth in *earnings* per share. There are many possible reasons for future *earnings* to vary: new management (perhaps resulting from a takeover), technological inventions, competitive activity, changes in customer tastes, new government policies, etc.

3 A change in the 'opportunity cost of capital' could also cause the share price to vary. There are many reasons why the market's view of the riskiness of a particular company might alter. An analysis of all the reasons might start by distinguishing between 'business risk' and 'financial risk' (see 1.4.4).

Thus any change in the future prospects of a business – especially its expected future returns or the risks involved – may affect a share's present market value. Since life is uncertain, with new information, new conditions, and new perceptions of the future continually developing, it is hardly surprising that share prices continually fluctuate. Only in an unchanging world where everything in the future had already been fully and correctly foreseen would this not be so.

17.1.4 Other valuation methods

(a) Price/earnings ratio

When we already know the market price per share, we can divide it by the latest earnings per share to determine the price/earnings ratio (see 9.3.3). But for an unquoted company we might know the earnings and want to estimate the value (either per share, or for the whole company).

We might take the current price/earnings ratio for a listed company in the same industry, and reduce it slightly to allow for the extra risks of an unquoted company. We could then multiply the unquoted company's earnings by the adjusted price/earnings ratio, to estimate the value.

Clearly a higher price/earnings ratio means a higher market value for any given level of earnings. A higher price/earnings ratio implies either a faster growth rate in future dividends (*g* in our formula), or else a lower cost of capital (*k*). But this is fair enough: if we value returns and dislike risk, then we would expect a higher value for a company with either higher returns or lower risks than another.

The price/earnings ratio does not represent literally the 'number of years' future earnings' included in the price. The discounting process means that future earnings are worth less than the same amount of earnings this year. Thus a price/earnings ratio of 9.0 does *not* mean that we are looking only nine years ahead: as we know, in principle our valuation formula includes expected future dividends *forever.*

(b) Book value

Another method simply assumes a company's equity to be 'worth' the book value shown in the latest balance sheet. This is not really adequate (see 2.3.1), since historical cost balance sheets do not pretend to show current values: they merely show the original cost of some assets, less amounts written off. (Even inflation-adjusted balance sheets may leave out many assets.)

Still, for unquoted companies, partnerships and sole traders, book values are at least *available;* and despite their serious disadvantages, they are quite often used in practice at least as a starting point for valuing firms.

(c) Liquidation value

Liquidation value (or break-up value) is the minimum value of assets of a business. If expected future cash earnings have a present value less than the assets could be sold for, then we should sell the assets now. We would value the company at the total net realizable value of its separate assets (less creditors).

But whoever buys the assets must be planning to earn future cash flows from them, which he presumably expects to produce a present value higher than the purchase price. For the seller it is the other way round. The buyer thinks he can use the assets more profitably or less riskily than the seller thinks he (the seller) can. Their different valuations of the assets are what makes a deal possible.

Indeed the same logic underlies the whole idea of competing buyers and sellers in markets, combined with private ownership of property. The aim of maximizing wealth, combined with the freedom of owners to buy and sell assets, leads in theory to the most profitable use of scarce resources.

17.2 The equity market

17.2.1 Economic functions of the stock exchange

The stock exchange is a market on which investors can buy and sell securities of leading British and international companies, and of governments. New issues of equity shares are far less important sources of funds for companies than retained profits.

In December 1989 there were just over 100 different British government securities outstanding with a total market value of some £150 billion. UK listed equity shares of about 2000 companies had a market value of about £88 billion.

The trend of the past 30 years shows a decline (mainly for tax reasons) in the proportion of quoted equities held by individuals, and an increase in that held by insurance companies, pension funds, unit trusts and investment trusts. It is not yet clear whether even the massive privatizations of the later 1980s (British Telecom, British Gas, the water companies,) will reverse this trend.

The main function of **unit trusts** and **investment trusts** is to invest in ordinary shares on behalf of individuals, who thus get the benefit of a diversified portfolio (see 18.2), expert management, and lower dealing costs. A unit trust is 'open-ended': it can expand if people want to buy more units, or contract if people want to sell back units. An investment trust is an ordinary limited company, whose purpose is to invest in securities.

Most stock exchange transactions involve the exchange of existing securities between investors. Only a small proportion of transactions consists of *new* issues, by companies or by governments.

Since investors value liquidity – the ability to sell quickly if they need the money – the existence of a **secondary market** makes it much easier to raise money on the **primary market** than it would otherwise be. Figure 17.2 illustrates the difference between (a) the primary and (b) secondary functions of the stock exchange. In (a) the company is issuing new shares to A, B, C

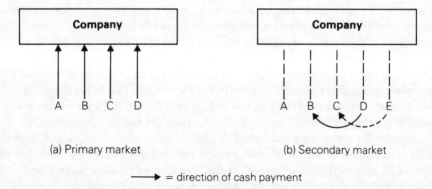

Figure 17.2 The stock exchange: primary and secondary markets

and D, and receives the cash. In (b) *the company* is not directly involved in the transactions, and doesn't receive any cash: shareholder A is not dealing; B is selling shares to D; and C is selling shares to E, at the market price at the time of each deal.

The capital invested by companies and by governments is often reflected in fixed physical assets, such as equipment, buildings, roads, etc. Thus businesses and their employees may tend to be 'anchored' to a particular location or type of business. But if a market exists where investors can buy and sell shares in the ownership of these assets, a shareholder possesses wealth which is 'mobile'. He can sell his shares to someone else if he needs the cash, or if he wants to invest in another kind of business or in another country.

The presence of short-term **speculators** helps the market. **'Bulls'** buy shares expecting them to rise, while **'bears'** look for prices to fall. They either sell shares they don't even own **('selling short')**, hoping to buy them later at lower prices; or at least refrain from buying yet, planning to do so more cheaply later. If on balance speculators make profits, that implies their views were 'more correct' than other people's. Their actions drive market prices *sooner* to levels they would otherwise take longer to reach. (This is also true of 'insiders'.)

17.2.2 Stock market indices

There is interest in the equity market as a whole, as well as in specific industries and companies. Three main indices show how the whole equity market is performing.

(a) The FT ordinary share index

The 30-share FT ordinary share index contains leading shares from most industry sectors. It began as long ago as 1935, though most of the shares comprising it have changed since then. The index is quoted hourly to show how leading shares have moved in the short term. It is computed as a geometric average (taking the 30th root of all the share prices multiplied together), and is not suited for long-term comparisons.

(b) The FT-Actuaries 500-share index

The 500-share index, started in 1962, gives a wide coverage of UK industrial shares. (There is also an All-Share Index, which includes another 200 financial shares.) The 500-share index, computed as an arithmetical average, is suitable for long-term comparisons: figure 17.2 overleaf shows it from 1963 to 1989, adjusted for inflation.

The very sharp (75 per cent) fall in 1973 and 1974 is striking; it contrasts with the 25 per cent fall in the 1987 'crash' (which, however, happened almost overnight). The five-year bull market of 1982–87 roughly tripled the real level of equities; but it was only in 1987 that the previous peak of 1972 was breached.

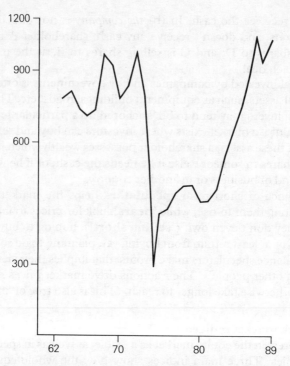

Figure. 17.3 FT-Actuaries 500-share index, 1963-89 (in constant January 1989 pounds)

(c) The FT-SE 100-share index

The FT-SE 100-share index ('Footsie') was started in 1984. The Footsie index is calculated minute-by-minute on the basis of the 100 largest quoted companies. Together they represent about two–thirds of the total value of the UK equity market. Prices are taken directly from the Stock Exchange Automated Quotations system (SEAQ).

17.3 Issuing equity shares

17.3.1 'Going public'

A company may wish its ordinary shares to be quoted on the stock exchange for two main reasons: to raise additional share capital from the public or to enable existing shareholders to sell some of their shares.

When a company 'goes public' it must issue a **prospectus** giving the names of the directors, the history of the company, its recent financial results, and certain other details. It must also agree to abide by the rules of the stock exchange. Normally at least 25 per cent of the ordinary share capital must be offered to the public in order to ensure a reasonably free market in the shares.

For shares in smaller companies there is the **unlisted securities market** (USM) with less stringent requirements. A company would normally need to have equity capital worth at least £2 million to be suitable for the USM; but need offer only 10 per cent of the shares to the public.

Pricing new shares may be difficult, especially if there are few directly comparable shares already listed. If the price of a new issue (fixed some days in advance) is too high, nobody will buy, and the shares will be left with the **underwriters;** but if the price is too low, the issuing company's existing shareholders will find their equity interest **diluted.**

The costs of issuing shares to the public can be high. In addition to a price discount (of between 10 to 20 per cent) needed to attract buyers of new shares in a relatively risky little-known company, administrative expenses would be at least $7\frac{1}{2}$ per cent for issues up to £2 million, and 5 per cent or so above that level. These include underwriting costs, fees to professional advisers, printing and advertising costs.

There are three main methods of going public:

1   An offer for sale (for larger issues) to the public at large, at a fixed price. The issuing house may take up all the shares prior to selling them on to the public.

2   A placing means that a new issue (below a certain size) is 'placed' privately by the issuing house with particular clients, including financial institutions, at a price fixed in advance. A proportion has to be made available to market makers to ensure a market. There may be lower expenses than for other methods of issue, but a higher market discount. There may also be a danger of ending up with large blocks of shareholding, which could threaten control.

3   The **tender method** is a third method for new issues. Here no fixed price is set in advance. Instead offers from the public are solicited, and the highest price which will raise all the required money becomes the asking price for all successful purchases. The market discount is likely to be small, which discourages **stags** (bulls of new issues).

17.3.2 Rights issues

The methods of issue just described in 17.3.1 applied to companies 'going public', whose shares were previously unlisted. Companies whose shares are already listed use a **rights issue** to raise more equity money, which the stock exchange regards as being fairest to existing shareholders.

A rights issue offers extra shares to existing shareholders, in proportion to their holdings, priced at some discount from the current market price per share. In contrast to the importance of pricing new issues, in theory it doesn't matter at what price a rights issue is offered. An existing shareholder who is unwilling to take up the new shares on offer can always sell his 'rights' in the market for their fair 'value', and thus avoid any loss.

Example: Thomas Lodge plc with 5 million ordinary shares already in issue, with a current market value of 140p each (= total value £7 million), plans to raise a further £2 million by means of a rights issue. Thus the new total value of the equity will be £9 million. Figure 17.4 shows two different ways of achieving this (ignoring transaction costs): either issuing 1 for 1 @ 40p, or else issuing 2 for 5 @ 100p.

	1 for 1 @ 40p	2 for 5 @ 100p
Number of new shares issued	5 million	2 million
New total number of shares (n)	10 million	7 million
New share price (£9 m./n)	90p	128.57p
Value of the 'rights'	50p	28.57p

Figure 17.4 Rights issue alternatives

17.3.3 Bonus issues and share splits

So far we have been discussing two kinds of share issues on the stock exchange: new listings, which usually raise new money for the company, but which may merely transfer shares from existing shareholders to new ones; and rights issues, by which listed companies raise new capital from their existing shareholders (or from those who buy the 'rights' to subscribe).

Two kinds of share issues which raise *no* new money for companies must also be understood, as they can affect the meaning of certain stock exchange ratios (see 9.3.3).

1 **Bonus issues** (scrip issues) capitalize some of a company's reserves, by transferring them on the balance sheet to called-up share capital. (This is purely a book-keeping entry.) The *total* amount of shareholders' funds remains unchanged, since no new money has been raised; but some of the company's retained profits, or other reserves, have now been turned into called-up ordinary share capital, and are no longer available to be paid out in dividends.

2 **Share splits** simply 'split' shares into smaller units, without even affecting balance sheet amounts.

Example: Giant plc has 600,000 ordinary £1 shares in issue, with a market price of £12 each. After the company makes a '4 for 1' share split, it will have 2.4 million ordinary shares of 25p each in issue, each with a market value of 300p.

Notice that a '4 for 1' share split means 4 new shares *instead* of each existing share held; whereas a '4 for 1' bonus issue means 4 new shares in *addition* to each existing share held, making 5 in all.

In making comparisons of earnings per share (or other 'per share' amounts) over time, it may be necessary to adjust earlier years' figures to allow for subsequent share splits or bonus issues.

17.4 Dividends

17.4.1 The nature of dividends

Ordinary dividends are cash payments by a company out of profits to its shareholders. Most listed UK companies pay an interim and a final dividend each year, with the final dividend usually being larger. (This contrasts with the American practice of equal quarterly dividends.)

At an annual general meeting, shareholders may vote to *reduce* the amount of a proposed final dividend, but they cannot increase it. (Thus they can increase, but not reduce, the amount of retained earnings for a year.) In fact open opposition to a company's dividend policy is rare.

In a 'perfect' capital market with no taxes, no **transaction costs**, and perfect information, dividend policy would not matter, since it would not affect shareholders' wealth. Dividends would transfer cash to shareholders, but any retained profits would be precisely reflected in the market value of the shares. Any shareholders who wanted larger 'dividends' than a company paid could simply sell some of his shares for cash (and vice versa). In effect, shareholders could 'declare their own dividends'.

Example: To begin with, John Smith owned 25 per cent of the shares in both Adam plc and Bede plc, two companies which were the same size and earned the same rate of return on assets (at the same level of business risk). But Adam paid out all its profits in dividends, whereas Bede retained all its profits for reinvestment. Smith maintained his 25 per cent shareholding in Adam which, with no retained profits, remained the same size. Bede, which retained all its profits, grew in size; but each year Smith sold enough shares in Bede to provide the same amount of cash as Adam's dividends. (In a perfect market there are no taxes and no transaction costs.)

Figure 17.5 shows the position after some years:

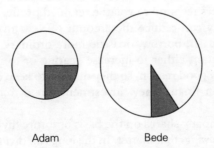

Adam   Bede

Figure 17.5 Smith's shareholdings in Adam and Bede after some years

Bede is now larger than Adam: but Smith's reducing share in Bede is worth exactly the same as his constant 25 per cent share in Adam. Since Smith has also received the same amount of cash from his shareholding in each company, the different dividend policies have (in theory) had exactly the same effect on Smith's wealth.

In reality, the tax position of shareholders can vary, from tax-exempt pension funds at one extreme to higher-rate tax-payers at the other. This can make it hard for companies to tell what dividend policy might be best for 'shareholders as a whole'. Basic rate income tax is 'deducted at source' from dividends, so companies pay only the 'net' amount in cash to shareholders.

Transaction costs, too, can be significant, especially for smaller shareholders. It would also be quite a nuisance for them to have to keep adjusting their holdings. A company which paid 'too, much' dividend one year would certainly find it very expensive to make a rights issue (which might be regarded as a 'negative dividend'!) the next year to remedy the position.

17.4.2 Dividend policy

Should a company decide on the dividend first, and regard any profits left over (retained profits for the period) as a residual? Or should it first choose how much to reinvest, and then treat *dividends* as the residual? Most companies take the former course: they base the current year's dividend on last year's amount. Dividends normally increase from year to year, partly to keep pace with inflation, and also to reflect increased real earnings on last year's retained profits.

Retained profits have been the most important source of funds for UK companies. (But historical cost accounts, which overstate profits (see Chapter 8), overstate *retained* profits too!) Where companies treat dividends almost as 'fixed' amounts, it is clear that the retained profits for a period can fluctuate even more sharply than earnings. Retained profits can even be *negative* if dividends exceed profits for a period, or if losses are incurred.

How can managers respond to volatile retained profits as a source of funds – say to a fall? They can reduce the amount of new investment, turn some existing assets into cash, borrow, or issue more ordinary share capital. Most companies are reluctant either to increase gearing or to issue more ordinary shares without a very good reason; so they may try to keep dividends down to a level where they can finance new investment out of retained profits (plus depreciation).

We can value company shares on the basis of future dividends (see 17.1.2), but ultimately it is *earnings* that matter. In the long run dividends cannot exceed earnings. In fact many companies try to keep their **dividend payout ratio** (DPR) fairly constant - in which case dividends per share will grow at much the same rate as earnings per share.

Inflation affects dividend policy. For example, a company's policy might be, on average, to pay out 50 per cent of inflation-adjusted profit. This might mean paying out only 30 per cent of historical cost profit. (A changing rate of inflation could affect the relationship.)

Companies with few profitable investment opportunities may tend to pay out a high proportion of their after-tax profits in dividends; while companies with many projects to invest in may prefer a lower payout ratio. But this would be a medium-term policy: it need not imply a constant payout ratio every year. For most companies the dividend payout tends to follow the 'step-like' pattern of figure 17.6 A, rather than closely following earnings from year to year, as in B.

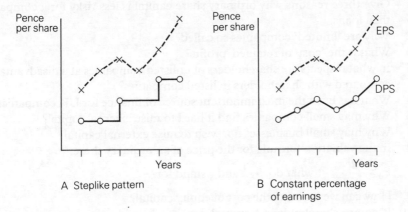

Figure 17.6 *Two patterns of dividend payout*

A loss-making company might not omit its dividend, or even reduce it from the previous year's level. The stock market would probably take maintenance of the dividend as a signal that earnings would soon recover. In contrast, cutting the dividend could signify that the decline in earnings would take longer to reverse. In the same way, a dividend increase higher than an increase in earnings might signal expected future earnings strength.

Probably the best dividend policy is to follow two general rules. First, tell shareholders clearly what a company's dividend policy *is*. Second, try not to change it without warning.

Work section

A   Revision questions

A1   Give three reasons why ordinary share capital is less risky for a company than loans.

A2   Why are 'limited' companies so called?

A3   What is the 'cost' of retained profits?

A4   In what respects are shareholders of unlisted companies at a disadvantage compared with shareholders in listed companies?

A5   What has been the most important source of finance for UK companies?

A6   Why may small companies find it hard to raise external capital?

A7   Why may small businesses not wish to raise external capital?

A8   In the valuation formula for the price of an ordinary share:

$$P_0 = \frac{d^1}{k-g}, \qquad \text{what do } d^1, k \text{ and } g \text{ stand for?}$$

A9   How can we estimate the cost of equity capital?

A10 If equity shareholders' 'returns' consist of dividends *plus* capital gains, how can it be correct to value shares *solely* on the basis of expected future dividends?

A11 Identify three reasons why equity shares might fluctuate.

A12 Explain why a company with poor prospects for profit growth may experience an above-average rise in its share price in the next year.

A13 Describe three alternative methods of valuing equity shares.

A14 Why is 'book value' likely to be an unsatisfactory estimate of the current value of an equity share?

A15 Distinguish between the stock exchange's primary and secondary functions.

A16 Since most ('normal') stock exchange transactions do not provide finance for companies, what use is the stock exchange to them?

A17 How can an individual investor remain 'mobile', while company (and government) assets are often 'fixed'?

A18 What is the difference between an investment trust and a unit trust?

A19 What are the main differences between the 30-share FT ordinary share index and the FT-Actuaries 500-share index?

A20 What are the two main reasons for a company wishing to have its equity shares quoted on the stock exchange?

A21 What is the Unlisted Securities Market? What are its two main advantages compared with the ordinary Listed Market?

A22 Name three methods of making a new issue of equity shares.

A23 Why is pricing a new issue of shares important when a company goes public? Why is it difficult?

A24 What are the two main types of expense of issuing new shares when a company goes public?

A25 What is a rights issue? Explain the mechanics.

A26 Why should an existing shareholder not lose whether he takes up his 'rights' or not?

A27 What is a bonus issue of shares (also called a scrip issue)? How does it affect the value of a shareholder's total holding?

A28 Why do dividends matter: (a) to companies; (b) to shareholders?

A29 How do taxes affect dividends?

A30 What two practical rules were suggested as a guide to dividend policy? What is the reason for them?

B Exercises and case studies

B1 A company has issued 250,000 8 per cent preference shares of £1 nominal value and 400,000 ordinary shares of 25p nominal value. The directors retain for future expansion one half of anything that remains once the preference dividend has been paid. Calculate the rate of preference dividend and the amount of ordinary dividend per share if profits are:

(a) £20,000;   (b) £60,000;   (c)£100,000.

B2 A company reports as follows in its 1990 profit and loss account:
Profit before tax £78,000; Preference dividends £3000; Interest payable £12,000; Depreciation £27,000; Taxation £34,000; Ordinary dividends £18,000.

a. Draw up a statement showing these items in the order you would expect to find them in a profit and loss account.

b. How much are retained profits for the year?

c. How much are net funds generated from operations ('cash flow')?

B3 From the latest annual reports of two different companies, study the funds statement, and draw up a brief summary of the sources of funds for each company for each of the two latest years, distinguishing between equity and debt; between retained profits and new ordinary shares; and between short-term and long-term debt.

B4 MD Enterprises Ltd expects to pay a net dividend this year of 6.0p; and the market expects the dividend to increase by 5 per cent a year.
The company's cost of equity capital is estimated at 15 per cent a year. Using the 'present value' formula discussed in the text, what would you expect the company's market price per ordinary share to be?

B5 Refer to B4. MD Enterprises has run into trouble. The company's policy is to pay out a constant proportion of its earnings in dividends each year; but earnings per share are now expected to grow by only 2 per cent a year for the foreseeable future. Instead of 6.0p a share, the company is now planning a dividend of only 4.0p this year. The prospects for the industry look gloomy, and the risk premium applicable to the company has increased, so that the cost of equity capital is now reckoned to be 20 per cent a year. What combined effect will all these changes have on the company's market price per ordinary share, as calculated in B4?

B6   Refer to figure 17.3, showing the FT-Actuaries 500-share index from 1963 to 1989, adjusted for inflation.

Roughly what percentage of its peak 1972 value had the index lost
a. at the end of 1974;
b. at the end of 1981;
c. at the end of 1988?

B7   If the rate of inflation is 12 per cent a year, the 30-share FT Ordinary share index is around 800, and the level of equity prices is 'keeping pace' with inflation, how much would you expect the 30-share index to increase *each day?* (Hint: assume 20 working days per month.)

B8   How would a market-maker react to each of the following events concerning one of his companies:
a.   a surprise announcement of a take-over bid for the company at 225p a share (compared with the present price of 170-172p)?
b.   press comment that such a take-over might occur?
c.   an announcement of unexpectedly poor results by the company?
d.   a government announcement of measures that might be expected to help the industry this company is in?

B9   Refer to the example in 17.3.2. For each of the two alternative rights issues, show the position:
a. of a shareholder who takes up his rights;
b. of a shareholder who sells his rights.

B10   Refer to figure 17.4. Suppose a 1 for 2 rights issue were made at 80p. Complete a third column as for figure 17.4

B11   Kay Ltd, Tar Ltd and Lupus Ltd each have an issued ordinary share capital of £120,000 in £1 shares, an accumulated balance of £70,000 on profit and loss account, and no other reserves. The authorized share capital in each case is £200,000.

The companies make the following ordinary share issues, and you are asked to show the details of share capital and reserves after the issue for each company:
a. Kay Ltd issues 20,000 new shares to employees at £1.50 each.
b. Tar Ltd makes a 1 for 3 bonus issue.
c. Lupus Ltd makes a 1 for 4 rights issue at £2.00.

B12   Refer to B11. If the market price per share for each company were 240p before the ordinary share issue concerned, what would you expect it to be in each case after the issue? Why?

B13   Whizzo Ltd, an unquoted company planning to go public, wants to raise £2.0 million additional capital net of all expenses. The two controlling families own 40 per cent of the 6 million ordinary 50p shares currently in issue: they plan to sell one third of their combined holdings. The shares can be sold on the market at 160p, and it is thought that 150p per share will be left after underwriting commissions and certain other costs. In addition, printing and advertising costs, together with professional fees, are expected to total £100,000.

a. How many shares will be offered to the public?

b. If the shares go to a 10 per cent premium over the issue price, what will the market value of the enlarged equity amount to?

c. If a net dividend of 4.0p per share is expected to be paid on the enlarged capital, with a dividend cover of 2.5 times, what is the envisaged price/earnings ratio based on the issue price?

B14 As part of his longer-term planning of the company's finances, James Park has been wondering whether the time has yet come for Park Products to 'go public' by issuing shares to members of the public. He is anxious to get some idea of the likely market price of each ordinary share. Park is too small for a full listing; so if it were to go public, it would be on the Unlisted Securities Market. No more than ten per cent of the equity would need to be made available to 'outsiders'.

Some of the relevant financial information is shown below:

Shareholders' funds:	200,000 issued 25p shares	£50,000
	Retained profits	£150,000
Annual pre-tax profits		£160,000
Annual growth rate in profits (approx.)		15%
Latest annual dividend (net of tax)		£20,000

Typical price/earnings ratios and dividend yields for the industry:

	P/E ratio	Net dividend yield (%)
A fast-growing company	15	3
A medium-growth company	10	6
A poor-growth company	7	9

Assuming a 35 per cent corporation tax rate, what would you expect might be the quoted stock exchange price of each ordinary share if Park Products were to go public:

a. based on price/earnings ratio;

b. based on dividend yield;

c. based on book value of assets;

d. based on the dividend growth formula?(Assume the cost of equity capital is estimated at 25 per cent a year.)

B15 Langley's finance director was thinking about ways for the company to raise money. One obvious possibility was a rights issue of ordinary shares to existing shareholders. Langley's 4 million 25p ordinary shares issued were currently quoted on the stock exchange at 40p each; and in order to raise £350,000 the finance director was considering a 1 for 4 rights issue at 35p. The net dividend currently cost £120,000. (See also the balance sheet in Chapter 18, problem B12.)

a. What is Langley's current:
   (i) earnings per share?
   (ii) price/ earnings ratio?
   (iii) net dividend yield?

b. What would Langley's 'shareholders' funds' on the balance sheet consist of after the proposed rights issue?

c. Does it matter that Langley's market value of equity is considerably less than the balance sheet book value? Why or why not?

d. Consider the position of two Langley shareholders, each holding 4,000 shares at present. Mr Smith would take up his rights, while Mr Jones would sell his on the market.
   (i) How much money would Mr Smith have to put up in subscribing for his rights under the proposed issue?
   (ii) How much money would Mr Jones receive for selling his rights under the proposed issue?
   (iii) What would Mr Smith's and Mr Jones's respective shareholdings in Langley be worth after the rights issue?

C Essay questions

C1   Why, if at all, might the directors of a public company be worried by a sharp fall in the share price of its ordinary shares?

C2   'It's impossible to privatize loss-making companies, and unfair to the taxpayers to sell off profit-making nationalized industries.' Discuss.

C3   If the valuation formula for ordinary shares includes expected future dividends *forever*, how can the City be accused of 'short-termism'?

C4   The stock exchange is sometimes called a 'casino'. Is this an accurate description?

C5   Financial institutions now own more than half of UK listed equity shares. Does it matter? What (if anything) might reverse the trend?

C6   The tender method is claimed to have significant advantages to a company issuing new shares. So why isn't it more widely used?

C7   'In a rights issue, companies should offer shares at a large ("deep") discount, and thus avoid any need to pay underwriting commission.' Comment.

C8   'In making money on the stock exchange, what matters is not whether the particular company in which you buy shares is 'good' or 'bad', but the *price* you have to pay.' Discuss.

C9   'I'm fed up with holding my shares in ICI; but unfortunately I bought when the price was much higher than it is now, and I can't afford to take a loss.' Discuss.

C10 How should a company choose its dividend policy?

18

Long-term finance

Plan of the chapter:

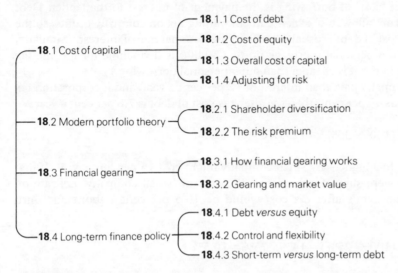

Fig.18.0
Objective: *To identify the costs of debt and equity capital, and show how to combine them to set the minimum required rate of return on average-risk investments; to describe how financial gearing works and how it affects firms' market value; and to discuss key aspects of long-term finance policy.*

Synopsis: *Debt costs less than equity both because debt interest is tax-deductible and because the investor's risk is less. The 'cost of equity' is the shareholders' opportunity cost. Combining debt and equity costs, weighted by market values, produces an overall 'weighted average cost of capital'. This is the rate at which to discount expected future cash flows in average-risk capital investment projects. (Or one can add a 'risk premium' to the risk-free rate of return, as modern portfolio theory (MPT) suggests.)*

    How a company invests funds determines its business risk; how it finances them, its financial risk. The traditional view of financial gearing suggests an optimal range: 'Not too little and not too much'. In choosing financial policy most company managements are likely to be concerned with control and flexibility as well as cost.

18.1 Cost of capital

A firm's **cost of capital** is 'that rate of return which its assets must produce in order to justify raising the funds to acquire them'. In this section we discuss the costs of the two main kinds of capital, debt and equity. They form the basis, when suitably combined, for a 'criterion rate' for capital investment projects, which we used in Chapter 15.

18.1.1 Cost of debt

The direct 'cost' of borrowing is the payment of interest to the lender. Debt interest is an 'allowable' expense in computing tax on company profits, so the after-tax cost of debt is usually less than the nominal rate of interest. (Similarly, interest on a personal mortgage up to £30,000 is deductible for income tax purposes; hence it is cheaper than other personal borrowing.)

If a company pays loan interest of 12 per cent a year, and if corporation tax on profits is 35 per cent, then the after-tax cost of debt is 7.8 per cent a year.

$$12\% \times (100\%-35\%) = 12\% \times 65\% = 7.8\%$$

A loan to a higher-risk small company might cost 14 per cent a year. If that company were subject only to the 25 per cent 'small company' tax rate on profits, the debt's after-tax cost would be 10.5 per cent - about one third higher:

$$14\% \times (100\%-25\%) = 14\% \times 75\% = 10.5\%$$

The tax laws do not recognize inflation accounting: they refer to monetary units and not to units of constant purchasing power (see Chapter 8). So the 'real' gain to the borrower in respect of inflation *is not taxable*.

Example: Suppose a 14 per cent annual interest rate comprises: (a) 3 per cent pure time preference: (b) 3 per cent risk premium; and (c) 8 per cent inflation premium (assumed correct). Then the purchasing power needed to repay the loan will be $\frac{8}{108}$ (= 7.4 per cent) a year less than that originally borrowed. The tax system allows a company borrower to deduct from taxable profits all the money interest paid; but it is not *taxed on the 'real' gain resulting from the actual inflation. Hence the after-tax cost can be very small. (Given high enough inflation it could even be negative.)*

Before-tax interest rate	*14.0%*
Less: corporation tax at 35%	*4.9*
= After-tax interest rate	*9.1*
Less: purchasing power gain	*7.4*
= 'Real' after-tax interest rate	*1.7%*

18.1.2 Cost of equity

Dividend payments do *not* represent the whole cost of equity capital. Equity capital still has an 'opportunity cost' even for a company which pays no dividends: it is what the shareholders could otherwise have done with the money. Hence it is the discounting rate that shareholders (presumably) apply to the expected future dividends.

We saw in 17.1.2 that $k = \frac{d}{p} + g$. In words: the cost of equity (k) is the expected current-year net dividend yield $(\frac{d}{p})$ plus the annual (assumed constant) rate of growth (g) in net dividends per share. A company paying *no* dividend will still have a positive share price, representing suitably discounted expected *future* dividends. (Because shareholders may have different tax positions, estimating the 'after-tax' amount of dividends can be difficult. One normally simply takes the net dividend, after deduction of basic rate income tax.)

> *Example: Phillipson Ltd's expected current-year net dividend is 9.0p per share. Dividends per share are expected to grow at 10 per cent a year, and the current market price is 150p per share. Then Phillipson's after-tax cost of equity capital is 16.0 per cent:*

$$k = \frac{9}{150} + 10.0\% = 6.0\% + 10.0\% = 16.0\%$$

Another way to estimate the cost of equity capital is set out in 18.2.2.

18.1.3 Overall cost of capital

We have discussed briefly how to calculate a company's after-tax cost of debt capital and its cost of equity capital. Combining them gives the company's overall **weighted average cost of capital** (WACC). This is the basis for a discount rate to use in evaluating capital investment projects.

> *Example: If a company has equity capital with a market value of £12 million, and debt capital with a market value of £4 million, weights of $\frac{3}{4}$ and $\frac{1}{4}$ respectively apply to the cost of equity and the cost of debt. Using the costs from the previous two sub-sections of 16.0 per cent for equity and 7.8 per cent for debt, the result is an overall cost of capital of 13.95 per cent. ($[\frac{3}{4} \times 16.0] + [\frac{1}{4} \times 7.8]$). In practice we would round this up, and use 14.0 per cent.*

We need to establish what it costs a company to raise more capital, in order to find out the minimum rate of return it must earn on any capital investment of funds. But remember that nearly all the numbers are only *estimates:* the future cash flows from a capital project (both the amounts and the timing), the cost of debt and the cost of equity.

As a rule businessmen think in terms of a 'pool' of funds. They *separate* two questions: (a) whether a project is worth investing in or not; and (b) if so, how to finance it. As a result, even if a company is going to finance a specific project by borrowing, it still bases the required rate of return on the *overall* cost of capital. Otherwise a 'worse' project to be financed by debt might (wrongly) be preferred to a 'better' project to be financed by equity.

18.1.4 Adjusting for risk
Rather than using WACC itself as the hurdle rate for *all* capital projects (the horizontal line in figure 18.1), we may choose to adjust the WACC upwards (= 'require a higher return') for 'high-risk' projects – and to adjust the WACC *downwards* for 'low-risk' projects.

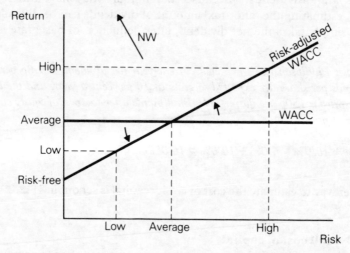

Figure 18.1 Risk-adjusted after-tax weighted average cost of capital

How much to adjust for risk in the context of WACC is a matter of guess-work (often called 'judgement'). In practice the cash flows for capital projects are usually based on such fallible estimates that a difference of one or two percentage points in the discount rate is unlikely to be critical.

We must also remember that managers are not merely trying to *measure* levels of risk and required return. They are also trying to *manage* the projects in order to 'move' their position to the 'north-west' – either to the 'west' (by reducing the risk), or to the 'north' (by increasing the return).

We saw in 16.2.2 how *lenders* may seek to reduce their risk (by personal guarantees, by taking security, or by loan covenants). Similarly, business managers might aim to reduce risk by various means, such as: extensive market research, arranging long-term sales contracts, or ensuring alternative sources of supply. Managers might also try to increase returns, for example by: expanding the volume of sales, increasing selling prices, or keeping careful control of costs. (It will be recognized that these are easier to say than to do!)

18.2 Modern portfolio theory

18.2.1 Shareholder diversification

Modern portfolio theory (MPT) suggests that investment involves two different kinds of risk: market risk and unique risk. **Market risk** stems from the uncertainties of the whole economy: equity investors cannot avoid it. **Unique risk**, in contrast, relates to a particular company or project: it can be **diversified** away by investing in a number of different kinds of projects (or shares).

An investor who splits his equity holdings equally among a dozen different shares can diversify away more than half the total risk he would bear by investing everything in a single equity share. In effect, a **portfolio** 'averages out' the unique risk of the different shares. About one third of the total risk of a single security *cannot* be diversified away however many shares are held. It represents the residual non-diversifiable market risk to which all shares (and projects) are subject. Increasing the number of holdings beyond about a dozen equity investments makes little further difference in reducing unique risk.

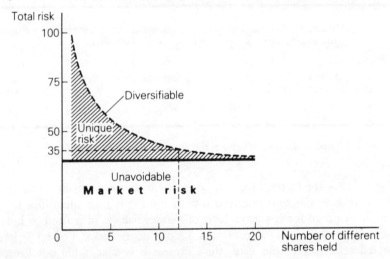

Figure 18.2 Unique risk and market risk

18.2.2 The risk premium

Modern portfolio theory says that no investor *needs* to take on unique risks: he can get rid of them by diversifying his portfolio, and holding shares in several *different* companies. Hence market returns will compensate only for 'market risk'. Based on actual past results over many decades, an investment in the equity market as a whole requires an after-tax risk premium of about 8 per cent a year on top of the 'risk-free' rate of return on government securities.

The theory says that the return on any particular share bears a definite relationship (known as **beta**) to the return on an investment in the 'market' as a whole. ('Return' means dividend plus capital gain.) Betas for listed shares are published, but determining the beta for a single capital project is not at all easy.

An investment with a beta of less than 1.0 is less 'risky' than the whole market; with a beta of more than 1.0, more risky. ('Risk' in this context means the volatility of a share's returns.) To find the *required* rate of return for a particular investment, simply add a risk premium to the risk-free rate of return. In MPT this risk premium is the whole market's required after-tax risk premium (estimated at 8 per cent a year, as noted above), *multiplied by the investment's beta.*

Example: Project E (which might be an ordinary share in Company E), with an estimated beta of 0.5, will have a required risk premium of 4.0 per cent, while Project F, with a beta of 2.0 will have a required risk premium of 16.0 per cent. Assuming the required risk-free after-tax money return is 6 per cent, the required project rates of return will be 10 per cent and 22 per cent respectively, as set out in figure 18.3:

Project	Required after-tax risk-free return	+	Estimated beta	×	Required market risk premium	=	Required project risk premium	=	Required project rate of return
E	6%	+	[0.5	×	8%]	=	4%	=	10%
F	6%	+	[2.0	×	8%]	=	16%	=	22%

Figure 18.3 Required rates of return for Project E and Project F

Figure 18.4 shows the capital market line with a straight-line relationship between market risk and required rate of return. It thus quantifies the risk premium required for any given level of market risk (as measured by beta). If project E has an expected return of 12 per cent, and if Project F has an expected return of 18 per cent, then Project E is acceptable but Project F (which is higher-return but also higher-risk) is not.

The capital market line in figure 18.4 starts from the 'risk-free rate of return' (assumed to be 6 per cent), and adds a 'risk premium' found by multiplying the estimated 'market' risk premium of 8 per cent by the project's own estimated beta. The beta refers *only* to 'market risk'. It ignores a project's 'unique risk', on the grounds that any investor can avoid it by holding a diversified portfolio.

This points to an important difference of outlook between managers of a company and its shareholders (see 19.4.3). Managers (like workers) are committed largely to a particular company, and may therefore be concerned with its *total* risk (that is, both 'market risk' and 'unique risk'). Shareholders, on the other hand, are 'mobile' (see 17.1.1), and presumably hold diversified portfolios: so the theory says they need care only about 'market risk'.

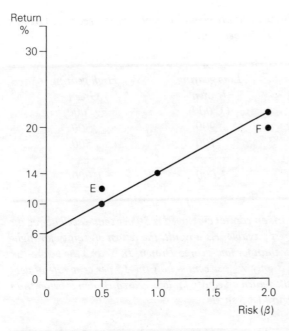

Figure 18.4 The capital market line

18.3 Financial gearing

18.3.1 How financial gearing works

How a company *invests* funds determines its business risk, how it *finances* them determines its financial risk. Top management can adjust a company's financial risk ('gearing') by changing the proportions of debt and equity in its capital structure:

Equity	{ (1) by retaining profits or paying out dividends
	{ (2) by issuing new shares or buying back shares in issue
Debt	(3) by borrowing more or repaying existing debt
Both	(4) by converting debt into equity

Financial gearing means borrowing to finance the business, rather than using only equity capital. If the rate of return on assets financed by debt exceeds the cost of borrowing, the 'profit' is added to equity earnings, and thus benefits the ordinary shareholders. Conversely, debt interest must be paid, even if the company's rate of return on assets is lower than the rate of interest on borrowing. When operating profit is high, then high gearing will benefit shareholders, and vice versa.

309

Example: Green Ltd and Brown Ltd are similar except for their gearing. Green's debt ratio is 10 per cent, Brown's 50 per cent.

	Low gearing Brown (£'000)	High gearing Green (£'000)
Equity	900	500
Debt (at 15% interest)	100	500
= Total capital employed	1,000	1,000

In Year 1 the before-tax return on capital employed is 30 per cent – well above the 15 per cent rate of debt interest payable. As a result, the return on equity for high-geared Green is much higher than for low-geared Brown. In Year 2 the before-tax return on capital employed is only $7\frac{1}{2}$ per cent – half the 15 per cent rate of debt interest payable. This time the return on equity for low-geared Brown is better than for high-geared Green, as figure 18.5 shows:

	Year 1		Year 2	
	Brown (£'000)	Green (£'000)	Brown (£'000)	Green (£'000)
Profit before interest and tax	300	300	75	75
Debt interest payable (@ 15%)	15	75	15	75
Profit before tax	285	225	60	0
Tax (@ 35%)	100	79	21	0
Profit after tax	185	146	39	0
Return on equity:	21%	29%	4%	0%
Interest cover:	20	4	5	1

Figure 18.5 Brown and Green, return on equity, Years 1 and 2 compared

We have looked at only two years' results; but (given our assumptions), figure 18.6 plots return on equity (on the vertical axis) against *any* rate of return on capital employed (on the horizontal axis).

The after-tax return on equity is the *same* for both companies at $9\frac{3}{4}$ per cent; which is what we would expect – the 15 per cent rate of debt interest less the tax rate of 35 per cent.

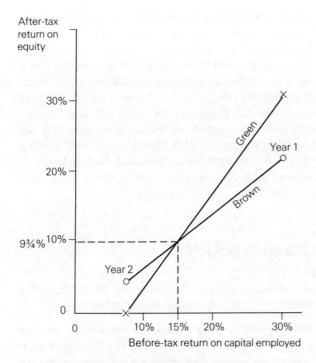

Figure 18.6   The effect of financial gearing

18.3.2   Gearing and market value

The 'traditional' view of gearing is that there is an 'optimal range' of capital structure, and that by moving towards it a company can increase its total market value. Over a wide range of moderate gearing, the overall cost of capital is almost flat and a firm's market value is *not* very sensitive to minor changes in gearing. Outside the range, however, a company may have too much debt or too little. It can then increase its overall market value (equity plus debt capital) by adjusting its financial gearing (figure 18.7).

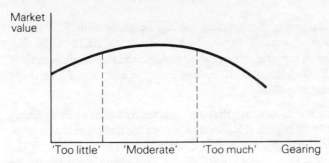

Figure 18.7   Gearing and market value

311

Debt is normally cheaper than equity, partly because it is lower-risk to the investor (see 17.1.1), and partly because interest is tax-deductible. So using debt instead of equity should reduce a company's overall cost of capital (WACC). This would reduce the discount rate applying to future cash flows, which means increasing the overall present market value. If there is 'too much' debt, however, then the extra risks will begin to increase the cost of both debt and equity. At some level of debt the firm's market value will begin to fall. There is not yet a convincing theory saying at what level of gearing there is 'too much' debt. We would expect that a company with high 'business risk' (such as exploring for oil) would not be able to bear much 'financial risk' (gearing) on top; whereas a 'safe' company with low business risk (such as some food companies) might be able to take on quite high levels of gearing.

18.4 Long-term finance policy

18.4.1 Debt versus equity

How can a company choose between debt and equity capital? Borrowing often appears *cheaper* after-tax than equity capital; but the *risk* is higher.

Example: Rutherfords Ltd's current level of earnings before interest and tax (EBIT) is £15 million a year; current debt interest payable is £3 million a year; and 40 million ordinary shares are outstanding. Earnings per share (EPS) are 15p.

The company requires £20 million of new capital to finance investment projects which it expects to increase profits by £4 million a year before interest and tax. There are two main alternatives: (a) to issue 10 million ordinary shares at 200p (a discount of one-sixth from the current market price of 240p per share), or (b) to borrow £20 million 10-year debentures at 12 per cent a year interest.

Should Rutherfords choose debt or equity? On what basis should the company decide between the two methods of finance? One approach would be to ask: which alternative would be better for the ordinary shareholders? (This amounts to asking: under which method of finance would the market value of each ordinary share be higher?)

As a start towards answering this question, we can calculate what EPS would amount to under each alternative. Figure 18.8 shows that if EBIT really does increase by £4 million as expected after raising the new capital, then the new EPS would be 20.8p if Rutherfords issue 10 million equity shares, and 22.1p if the company borrows the £20 million.

But we are *not* entitled to assume that the market value of each ordinary share would necessarily be higher if Rutherfords goes for debt merely because EPS would be higher. That would imply the same price/earnings ratio if the company borrows as if it issues new equity shares. But debt, being riskier for the company, might result in a *lower* price/earnings ratio than the equity issue.

	Now	*With increased capital*	
		Equity	*Debt*
	(£ m.)	*(£ m.)*	*(£ m.)*
EBIT	15.0	19.0	19.00
Interest payable	3.0	3.0	5.40
Profit before tax	12.0	16.0	13.60
Tax (at 35 per cent)	4.2	5.6	4.76
Profit after tax	7.8	10.4	8.84
Ordinary shares issued (m.)	40	50	40
Earnings per share (pence)	19.50	20.80	22.10

Figure 18.8 *Rutherfords Ltd: earnings per share calculations*

Just how risky is it for Rutherfords to borrow another £20 million? It would increase the debt ratio from about 24 per cent to about 36 per cent; and it would reduce interest cover from 5 to $3\frac{1}{2}$. In each respect that would seem to be getting towards the maximum comfortable level of debt. (You may wish to see if you can check where these numbers come from.)

Another calculation we can make is to see what is the 'break-even' EBIT level, at which EPS would be the *same* under the two alternative methods of finance. For Rutherfords, the break-even point comes at an EBIT level of £15 million; as we can show by simple algebra:

$$[Debt] \quad \frac{65\% \, (x - 5.4)}{40} = \frac{65\% \, (x - 3.0)}{50} \quad [Equity]$$

$$50(x - 5.4) = 40(x - 3.0)$$
$$50x - 270 = 40x - 120$$
$$10x = 150$$
$$x = 15$$

This means that above the 'break-even' level of £15 million EBIT, EPS will be higher with debt (due to the effect of gearing); whereas *below* it, EPS will be higher with the equity issue. In practice, uncertainty about the price at which equity shares can be sold may be important (see 17.3.1); more than one debt package may be available; and issuing preference shares may be another possibility. The main difficulty is not in calculating the numbers (on particular assumptions). It is exercising commercial judgement about balancing risks and returns.

For example: how likely is EBIT in future to fall below the break-even level? how much does it matter if that does sometimes happen? what might be the impact of future inflation? what effect, if any, might the increased risk of debt have on the price/earnings ratio?

18.4.2 Control and flexibility

Decisions about which method of long-term finance to employ are not solely a matter of calculation. Many of the estimates can only be approximate. Moreover two other aspects of long-term finance are hard to quantify, but may be of paramount importance: control and flexibility.

(a) Control

For small and medium-sized companies, the question of *control* of the company's equity capital is often over-riding. The current controlling shareholders (probably members of one or two families) may not be able to subscribe in full for their share of any rights issue of new shares. Hence they may not want an issue which would dilute their own equity interests.

'Control' need not refer only to the ownership of voting equity shares. Certain borrowing arrangements may involve covenants and other restrictions which managers think unacceptable. As a result, some companies might prefer to cut back on their investment plans and possible rate of expansion – even at the cost of shareholders forgoing large potential profits.

(b) Flexibility

Even in larger companies (where no small group owns a significant interest in the equity capital), management will usually value *flexibility*. Managers like if possible to keep open several alternative future courses of action. Thus they might not want to borrow all the way up to some supposed 'optimum' level of gearing, if that would rule out borrowing any more for a number of years.

Making a *loss* reduces a company's accumulated retained profits, and therefore the size of its balance sheet equity. (The same is true of paying dividends.) A seemingly adequate debt ratio, therefore, can soon become unacceptably high through one or two years' losses combined with further borrowing in order to finance current operations.

So it is not surprising if managements sometimes seem to the outsider to be rather cautious. In practice some company managements – both of large and of smaller firms – seem to prefer safety and flexibility for themselves to (higher-risk) profit for shareholders.

18.4.3 Short-term versus long-term debt

The choice between short-term and long-term borrowing depends mainly on comparing the relative costs and risks. To avoid uncertainties, a firm might try to 'match' the period of its borrowing to the period for which it needed the money. Thus it would finance long-term needs (says for a new plant expected to last 15 years) by long-term money, and short-term needs (say to finance temporarily high raw material stocks) by short-term sources. As a rule one might expect longer-term money to have a higher cost (see 16.1.4).

But a company may not be sure *how much* money it requires, nor for *how long*. Estimates of the amount and timing of capital projects can be subject to wide margins of error. It may often make sense to think of a company's needs as consisting of a long-term 'base load' which it can forecast with fair certainty, and a varying balance of short-term needs depending on the nature of the business (see 14.1.2).

Work section

A   Revision questions

A1   Why might borrowing be a sensible reaction to inflation?

A2   What is a 'negative real interest rate'?

A3   Name two reasons why the cost of borrowing might be higher for a small company than for a large one.

A4   In the formula: $k = \dfrac{d}{p} + g$, what does each letter stand for?

A5   Describe how to calculate a company's overall weighted average cost of capital.

A6   What is the difference between market risk and unique risk?

A7   Why does diversification reduce shareholders' risk?

A8   What is beta?

A9   How is beta used to determine a risk premium?

A10 Why may company managers and shareholders have different attitudes towards risk?

A11 What is the difference between financial risk and business risk?

A12 What is 'financial gearing'? Give a numerical example.

A13 Name three ways in which a company can adjust its level of gearing.

A14 Explain how financial gearing can 'work both ways'.

A15 What is the 'traditional' view of gearing?

A16 Why might a company *not* choose the debt/equity alternative producing the higher earnings per share at the expected level of EBIT?

A17 What is meant by the 'break-even level of EBIT'?

A18 Why might a strong desire to retain control lead owners to restrict the rate of their company's growth?

A19 How does making a loss affect financial gearing?

A20 How might a company choose between short-term and long-term borrowing?

B   Exercises and case studies

B1   The nominal rate of interest on a five-year loan is 15 per cent. What would the after-tax cost be for:
a. a large loss-making company;
b. a small profit-making company;
c. a sole trader subject to basic rate income tax?

B2   Refer to B1. What would the 'real' after-tax cost be in each case if inflation is running at 10 per cent a year?

B3 The risk premium on the whole equity market is estimated to be 8.0 per cent a year, after tax.
   a. What will the required after-tax market return be if risk-free government securities yield 6.0 per cent after tax?
   b. What will be the required after tax return for a company with a beta of 1.5?
   c. What will it be for a company with a beta of 0.8?

B4 F.G. Porter Ltd, with an issued share capital of £$7\frac{1}{2}$ million in 25p ordinary shares, is paying a final dividend of 14p per share.
   a. What is the cash cost to the company of the dividend?
   b. How much will Robert Jacks, who owns 2,000 ordinary shares in F.G. Porter Ltd, receive in respect of the dividend?
   c. How much income tax will be deemed to have been 'deducted at source' from the dividend paid to Mr Jacks?
   d. How much extra tax will Mr Jacks have to pay if his marginal tax rate is 40 per cent?

B5 Refer to the Rutherfords example (18.4.1). Confirm that EPS is the same under both debt and equity alternatives at an EBIT level of £15 million by calculating what EPS would be.

B6 Refer to the 'real interest rate' example at the end of 18.1.1.
   a. What would the real interest rate be if both the inflation premium, and the actual inflation rate, were not 8 per cent but 18 per cent a year?
   b. What if, in the original example, the tax rate were not 35 per cent but 50 per cent?

B7 Refer to the 'real interest rate' example at the end of 18.1.1.
   a. What would the real interest rate be if the inflation premium were 12 per cent and the *actual* inflation rate were 6 per cent?
   b. What would the real interest rate be if the inflation premium were 6 per cent and the *actual* inflation rate were 12 per cent?

B8 Davis Ltd and Hendry Ltd, two companies in the same industry, are similar in most respects, but have different financial gearing. In 1988 each company made an operating profit of £40,000, in 1989 each made £150,000. Each company has capital employed in each year of £1.0 million (including 2 million ordinary 25p shares in issue); but Davis has a debt ratio of 5 per cent, Hendry one of 40 per cent. The debt in each case carries an interest rate of 15 per cent a year.
   a. Prepare a table similar to that in 18.3.1, showing the after-tax return on equity for each company for each year. Assume a 40 per cent tax rate.
   b. What is each company's earnings per share for each year?
   c. Draw a chart similar to figure 18.6, showing the effect of gearing on return on equity for each company. What is the 'break-even point'?

B9 Refer to figure 18.6. Redraw the chart on the basis of an interest rate of 10 per cent a year and a tax rate of 40 per cent.

B10 Refer to the Rutherfords example (18.4.1). Draw an 'EBIT chart' showing the EPS in pence at various levels of EBIT in £ million for both the debt and the equity alternatives. Show EPS on the vertical axis and EBIT on the horizontal.

Hints: (i) We know that the 'cross-over' (or 'break-even') point comes at an EBIT level of £15 million.

(ii) We have already calculated what EPS will be under each alternative at an EBIT of £19 million.

(iii) At what level of EBIT in each case will EPS be *zero*?

B11 Park Products Ltd is a small but rapidly-growing engineering company owned by three brothers who are also its top management. Colin Park is the production director, Gordon is in charge of marketing, and James is the financial director. The company has borrowed substantially from the bank, but its problem has been to borrow fast enough to provide the machinery it needs to expand output in line with market opportunities. The company's shares are all owned by the three brothers (and their families): as yet they are not quoted on the stock exchange, nor, therefore, are they available to members of the public. Park Products has a high return on capital, and on the whole it is a company that takes risks to gain its objectives.

Langley Engineering Ltd is a medium-sized company, supplying various capital goods firms. It has a cautious but steady growth record, and its shares can be bought and sold through the stock exchange by members of the public. Most of the shares are still held by members of the Langley family, although the recently-appointed managing director is not one of them. Langley relies substantially on its own retained profits to finance its growth; when it does borrow, it tends to do so for specific projects rather than for general expansion. The company owns its offices and factory. Its return on capital is about average for the industry. Langley is in the same industry as Park, but has less export business and deals with less technically-advanced products.

Summarized balance sheets at the end of June for Park Products and Langley Engineering are set out in figure 18.9, together with figures for the most recent year's sales and profits.

a. Consider Park and Langley each raising £200,000 for investment in machinery. Discuss, with reasons, whether one company might be particularly influenced by cost, while the other's choice might be dominated by questions as to flexibility.

b. Might one company have wider access to sources of finance than the other? Why?

c. How do Park's and Langley's needs differ? How might these different needs be reflected in their approach to borrowing?

d. How do Park's objectives appear to differ from Langley's?

e. How financially 'well balanced' is each of the two companies?

Balance Sheets (end of June)	Park Products (£'000)	Langley Engineering (£'000)
Fixed assets		
Buildings	–	600
Machinery	300	1,000
	300	1,600
Current assets		
Stocks	200	1,500
Debtors	300	900
	500	2,400
Less: Current liabilities		
Bank overdraft	300	600
Creditors	100	400
	400	1,000
Working capital	100	1,400
= Net assets	400	3,000
Shareholders' funds	200	3,000
Long-term loan	200	–
= Capital employed	400	3,000
Latest year's sales	1,200	3,600
Latest year's profits (after tax)	80	240

Figure 18.9 Balance sheets for Park Products and Langley Engineering Ltd

B12 *Bexhill Manufacturing Limited*

In November 1991, Mr Watson, finance director of Bexhill Manufacturing Ltd, was considering how the company should finance its £3½ million expansion programme.

Bexhill made containers for industrial and commercial use. A significant volume of sales related to small tins for packing delicate instruments, used in aircraft. The level of sales and profits had fluctuated over the years, but the company had recently gained contracts to supply several pharmaceutical firms with tins for pills and small bandages, which had helped to add a needed element of stability to demand.

Late in 1991 the Bexhill management decided to modernize and enlarge a small plant near Walsall which had been acquired in 1975. New fixed assets would require £2.1 million, and extra working capital £1.4 million. The proposed investment was expected to net £1.0 million in extra profits before tax. Originally it had been hoped to provide the funds from retained profits, but a general inflationary increase in working capital requirements made this seem inadvisable. It was therefore planned to seek the necessary capital from external sources. Management policy had traditionally avoided long-term debt; and in 1991 the company's balance sheet contained no fixed indebtedness of any kind. The book value of shareholders' funds was £24.2 million.

For some years both Mr Sidney , the company chairman, and Mr Watson had been disappointed in the market price of Bexhill shares of which 12 million were outstanding. They believed the possibility of more stable earnings in future might justify a change to the company's established practice of avoiding long-term debt. The average annual rate of growth in dividends per share had been 8 per cent over the last 5 years.

Descendants of the company's founders still retained a large share-holding, but more than half the shares were publicly held, though there was only a thin market. Mr Watson thought that a rights issue of ordinary shares could probably be sold at 185p per share, to leave the company net proceeds of 175p per share after underwriting expenses and other fees. Thus raising £3 $\frac{1}{2}$ million would require issuing an extra 2.0 million equity shares.

Alternatively, the company could raise the £3 $\frac{1}{2}$ million from institutional investors through the sale of 15-year 18 per cent debentures. Repayment of £200,000 of the issue would be required every year, leaving £500,000 outstanding at maturity. Mr Sidney viewed the 18 per cent interest rate as equivalent to 11.7 per cent after 35 per cent corporation tax (which was the rate the company used in all its forward planning). In contrast, he reckoned that the share issue at 175p per share, and with a 7.5p net dividend, would cost the company 5.7 per cent a year gross. But he wondered whether the debenture issue might be desirable, after allowing for expected inflation. (The current level of inflation was between 5 and 10 per cent a year.)

The board had agreed to the proposal to enlarge the Walsall plant, if satisfactory financing could be arranged; and early in November 1991 Mr Sidney decided to sound out board sentiment on debt financing. To his surprise an acrimonious discussion developed.

Mr Hartley calculated the annual 'sinking fund' payment to be 10 per cent of the average size of the debenture issue over its 15-year life: to him, the cost of the share issue seemed much less than that of debt. He emphasized the cash outlay called for in the debenture programme, and the £500,000 maturity. He further argued that the extra risks from borrowing would make the ordinary shares more speculative, and cause greater variation in the market price in future.

On the other hand, Mr Harris claimed that ordinary shares were a giveaway at 175p. At today's prices Bexhill would be quite unable to replace fixed assets at anything like balance sheet net book value of 200p per share. The sale of ordinary shares at 175p would give new buyers a substantial part of the real value attributable to the company's present shareholders. (He dismissed as 'academic' Mr Bartholomew's suggestion that existing shareholders would be unaffected by any supposed rights issue 'discount' from the current market price.)

Two other directors, Messrs Gilbert and Lonsdale, compared debt and equity in terms of earnings per share. At the anticipated level of profits (£5.0 million a year, before interest and before 35 per cent tax – including the extra £1.0 million from the Walsall plant expansion), they calculated that earnings per existing share would become 23.21p with a rights issue netting 175p. In contrast, the sale of debentures would produce earnings per share of 23.67p. They didn't think it mattered that the annual repayment of debt would amount to 1.67p per share.

Mr Wilkinson argued for an equity issue because simple arithmetic showed the company could net £650,000 after tax a year from the new investment. Yet if 2.0 million ordinary shares were sold, the dividend requirement at the present rate of 7.5p per share net would amount to only £150,000 a year. He couldn't see how selling equity shares would hurt the interests of present shareholders.

Mr Joseph, a long-serving director, confessed he didn't fully understand all the calculations. But he was uneasy about changing the company's established policy towards borrowing, especially as the UK economic environment seemed likely to remain difficult for the next year or two at least. His motto was: 'Better safe than sorry.'

At the end of the discussion Mr Sidney had asked Mr Watson to evaluate the various arguments and make a definite recommendation to the board at its next meeting.

a. Calculate the 'break-even' level of EBIT.

b. Critically evaluate each of the arguments put forward by a director.

c. As Mr Watson, the finance director, what would you recommend to the board about financing the Walsall plant expansion? Why? How would you attempt to persuade the other directors?

B13 Kit Somerville Ltd's latest profit and loss account is summarized overleaf. The company has 120 million 10p ordinary shares in issue and 10 million £1.6 per cent preference shares. £25 million 16 per cent long-term debentures are outstanding. Retained profits amount to £37 million: there are no other reserves. The price/earnings ratio is 15.0.

		(£ m.)
Earnings before interest and tax		17.2
Interest payable		4.0
Profit before tax		13.2
Tax		5.7
Profit after tax		7.5
Preference dividends	0.3	
Ordinary dividends	4.8	
		5.1
Retained profit for the year		2.4

Calculate:

a. debt ratio.
c. dividends per share.

b. earnings per share.
d. dividend cover.

C Essay questions

C1 'Small companies grow by ploughing back profits; large ones employ other, more sophisticated financial methods'. What might these other methods be and why are they less often used by small firms?

C2 Why have many companies increasingly come to rely on short or medium term bank borrowing? Why might this be risky?

C3 How may inflation affect a company's financing policy?

C4 How would you expect inflation accounting to affect each of the two conventional measures of gearing? *(Hint:* Assume a substantial increase in the book value of depreciable fixed assets.)

C5 Given its tax advantages, why should a company limit the amount of debt in its capital structure?

C6 What do you understand by the term 'gearing', and how might it be measured? How might a finance house use gearing ratios when considering an application by a medium-sized manufacturing company for a loan of £5,000,000 for expansion purposes?

C7 How might the finance director of a group of companies view the riskiness of a particular capital investment project differently from a manager of a division of the group? How might a shareholder's view of a project's riskiness differ from both of them?

C8 In answer to the question: 'How much debt should a company have in its capital structure?', the traditional answer is quite definite: 'Not too little, and not too much!' Discuss.

C9 'Financial markets are relatively "efficient", so it makes little difference how a company finances its activities.' Discuss.

C10 Why should managers seek to maximize the wealth of their company's existing shareholders:

a. in their own interests;

b. in the interests of society as a whole?

19

Mergers and reorganizations

Plan of chapter:

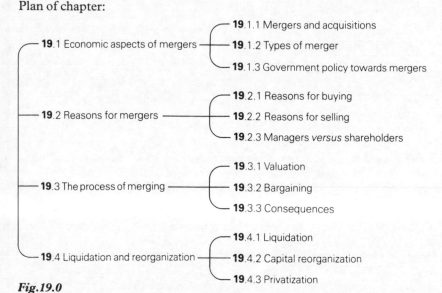

19.1 Economic aspects of mergers
- **19**.1.1 Mergers and acquisitions
- **19**.1.2 Types of merger
- **19**.1.3 Government policy towards mergers

19.2 Reasons for mergers
- **19**.2.1 Reasons for buying
- **19**.2.2 Reasons for selling
- **19**.2.3 Managers *versus* shareholders

19.3 The process of merging
- **19**.3.1 Valuation
- **19**.3.2 Bargaining
- **19**.3.3 Consequences

19.4 Liquidation and reorganization
- **19**.4.1 Liquidation
- **19**.4.2 Capital reorganization
- **19**.4.3 Privatization

Fig.19.0

Objective: *To discuss economic aspects of mergers and acquisitions; to list different reasons for them; to outline the process of valuation and bargaining; and to describe other forms of business reorganization.*

Synopsis: *Most business combinations are acquisitions of one entity by another, horizontal mergers (between companies in similar businesses) being the most common. Mergers may produce economies of scale and transfer resources to more capable management, but they may also lead to monopoly and reduced competition. There are many different reasons for acquiring businesses or for disposing of them. Shareholders in companies being acquired have on average received a 25 per cent premium, virtually all of the average economic gains arising. There are various forms of business reorganization, including liquidation, de-merging, and privatization.*

19.1 Economic aspects of mergers

19.1.1 Mergers and acquisitions

'Mergers' and 'acquisitions' both imply combining two or more separate businesses into one enterprise, with a single top management and common ownership. The term 'merger' is often used to cover both.

In a **merger** owners of the combining companies become the owners of a single company owning all the assets. For example, M and N pool their assets and liabilities, and each owner of shares in M or N receives *pro rata* in exchange shares in a new **holding company** MN.

An acquisition either eliminates the previous ownership interests in the acquired company (as when the price is all cash), or one of the combining companies is clearly dominant. The acquiring company A buys all (or most) of the equity shares or the net assets in the acquired company B.

19.1.2 Types of merger
From an economic viewpoint there are three main types of merger: (1) horizontal; (2) vertical; and (3) conglomerate.
1 **Horizontal mergers** combine firms in the same business: for example, a daily newspaper merging with a Sunday. Most mergers are of this kind. Horizontal mergers are most likely to yield economies of scale, but they may also lead towards monopoly.
2 **Vertical mergers** combine firms involved in the same 'industry', but at different stages of the overall production chain. Thus a producer of soft drinks might combine with a company making containers, or with a firm which distributes drinks. Vertical mergers might aim to control quality, to ensure sources of supply, or to move closer to the ultimate market for a firm's products.
3 **Conglomerate mergers** combine firms in different industries, often with no obvious connection: for example, a steel company and an oil company, or a mining company and a hotel chain. Such mergers are fairly rare. Economic benefits might stem from (a) management skills in the centre, (b) lower costs of borrowing, or (c) tax savings; but there should be no danger of monopoly. It can be difficult to interpret the group accounts of conglomerates, which add together numbers from quite different industries.

19.1.3 Government policy towards mergers
The government may refer mergers in the UK to the Monopolies and Mergers Commission (MMC) for scrutiny where:
1 the gross value of the assets involved exceeds £30 million; or
2 the merger would create or enhance a share of 25 per cent or more of the relevant market.

The MMC considers relevant *markets* (including imports), not just shares of domestic production. It is often not clear whether increased concentration will reduce or increase competition.

If the MMC finds a proposed merger would operate against the public interest, the government may forbid it, or allow the merger subject to certain conditions.

The government has referred an average of only about four mergers a year to MMC since 1965. Of these the MMC has found one-third to be against the public interest, one-third *not* to be, and roughly one-third have lapsed as a result of the reference.

19.2 Reasons for mergers

19.2.1 Reasons for buying
Figure 19.1 sets out many possible reasons for one business acquiring another.

Production
>   1 Expanding capacity
>   2 Economies of scale (reducing costs)
>   3 Acquiring technology
>   4 Vertical integration, for quality, control, or supply reasons

Marketing
>   5 Expanding market share
>   6 Extending product range (perhaps by patents or brand names)
>   7 Gaining entry to new markets (such as government agencies, or abroad)
>   8 Eliminating competition

Tactical
>   9 Target company's shares or assets 'under-priced'
>   10 Own shares 'over-valued'
>   11 Preventing a competitor from acquiring the target company
>   12 Making the acquiring company itself less attractive or less digestible

Miscellaneous
>   13 Acquiring management skills
>   14 Tax advantages
>   15 Diversifying business risk
>   16 Empire building

Figure 19.1 Reasons for acquisition

The acquiring company may want expansion more *quickly* than by internal growth. In some industries large size may be essential to compete globally. There may be a desire to avoid outside control: it is much harder for governments to interfere with intra-group transactions than with 'visible' market deals between autonomous companies.

Economies of scale vary between industries; and size can also bring disadvantages – remoteness of management control, extra layers of overhead cost, inflexibility, and undue caution.

19.2.2 Reasons for selling

Figure 19.2 sets out a number of reasons for selling companies.

Personal

1 Owner wants to diversify risk
2 Owner wants to avoid capital transfer tax problems on death
3 Manager(s) want to retire, no internal successor
4 Management inadequate, possibly following expansion or change of direction

Business

5 Needs additional source of finance
6 No longer fits with core business or strategy of selling group
7 Prospects poor under present control
8 Needs to benefit from economies of scale; cannot compete at present size

---

Figure 19.2 Reasons for disposal

Many commercial assets are for sale if the 'price is right'. People who have founded a business, or inherited it, may want either to retire or to diversify their risk by accepting cash or shares in a larger concern. (Shares in the latter can be disposed of gradually in an orderly way.)

Another reason for selling a business may be management problems, either succession or the ability to manage a larger business following a period of growth. The death or retirement of one or two key men can often reveal a need for new management. Or selling an ailing business may simply be 'a civilized alternative to **bankruptcy**'.

Another reason for disposing of a business may have to do with strategic focus. If a business, whatever its origins, no longer seems to be related to the core business, then managers may prefer to get rid of it. Sale as a going concern will normally produce a much better price than liquidating the business, as well as avoiding many human and legal problems.

19.2.3 Managers versus shareholders

One reason for managers wanting to merge may be to reduce a company's total risk. In theory this makes no sense for a company's *owners*, who can easily arrange to hold portfolios of shares and thus diversify away most of any company's 'unique risk' (see 18.2.1). Managers, however, have nearly all their eggs in one basket. So they may want to reduce the riskiness of the basket, even if it won't pay off for shareholders.

Managers who fail to maximize shareholder wealth ought to be vulnerable to a take-over bid for control of their company. That could yield large profits for anyone who organized such a bid (and then ran the company well). Some companies, however, may be largely exempt from this ultimate market discipline. Unquoted companies, for example, are not easy to buy control of; very large companies may be too big to be taken over; and there may be little incentive to take over very well-run companies.

In practice the short-term pressures on incompetent (or unlucky) managers may be less than theory suggests. But no doubt the pressures can be very powerful in the longer run.

The evidence suggests that not many mergers benefit shareholders in the acquiring firm. The 25 per cent premium (on the pre-bid price) which on average has to be paid to shareholders in the acquired company may absorb virtually all the economic gains from the merger.

19.3 The process of merging

19.3.1 Valuation

An acquiring company, A, may regard buying another company, B, as a capital investment 'project' (see Chapter 15). The amount of the investment is the purchase price, plus any extra amount to be invested in the business, less the disposal proceeds of any surplus assets. Estimates of the project's future cash flows must allow for **synergy,** or other expected changes, as well as for any further investment required. A may also allow for some terminal value for B at the horizon date.

To find the maximum purchase price payable, the acquiring company can discount the expected future cash flows to present value. The discount rate will be the required rate of return suitable for the riskiness of the *acquiree company*, B. Or A can calculate the project's internal rate of return in the usual way: by finding the discount rate which equates the various expected future cash flows to the initial net investment.

Other bases of valuation are also possible; such as price/earnings ratios applied to current levels of profit after tax: or even book values of assets (see 17.1.4).

19.3.2 Bargaining

An acquirer (A) will try to find out why the seller (S) wants to sell. Is S aware of adverse future factors unknown to A? Or are there personal reasons for selling? And S will seek to discover A's motives. Does A value some aspect of the business more highly than S? If so why? Both A and S should keep an eye on possible alternatives: A on other purchasers, or on internal growth; S on other buyers, or on continued ownership.

Both buyer and seller may have in mind a range of suitable prices. If they overlap, a deal should be possible. Of course the range may alter during the bargaining. In the excitement of an auction a 'successful' buyer can end up paying far more than he expected. Basing the purchase price partly on future profits defers some of the cost and insures the buyer against promised profits failing to occur. It may also motivate former owner-managers to continue working well.

In unwanted take-over bids, the interests of the victim's (V) top management may not coincide with those of V's shareholders. The City Code which governs take-over practice requires V's directors to provide full details to enable the shareholders to make an informed decision.

19.3.3 Consequences

(a) Organization
Over time most companies develop a style of their own; and it can be hard to combine two firms with different cultures. Making a merger work also takes management time and effort. The new group's top management will probably want to look in detail at every major aspect of the business: each major product line, every plant, the main markets, all senior personnel. And other results of a merger can be troublesome, such as integrating two different information systems.

(b) Workers
Human problems often arise among workers as a result of a merger. 'Economies of scale' may be an abstract way of saying that one person can do two people's jobs. So the other person may lose his job. Other employees may be demoted, or have to move to a new office or factory, perhaps far away from their present home and friends. Such 'redeployment' may often make economic sense; but requires great skill, understanding and tact on management's part. Telling the workers as much as possible as soon as possible about future plans is usually important.

(c) Financial structure
A merger may affect financial structure. For instance, a company with a 35 per cent debt ratio which acquires another company half its own size could end up with a debt ratio varying from 23 per cent to 57 per cent, depending whether none or all of the purchase price consisted of loan stock.

19.4 Liquidation and reorganization

19.4.1 Liquidation
Liquidation (or **winding-up**) is a legal process, triggered by **insolvency** (failure to pay debts due). It involves:
1 the appointment of a liquidator;
2 disposing of all the assets for cash; and
3 sharing out the cash proceeds among creditors and (perhaps) shareholders.

Except when members of a company *choose* to wind up their company, the effect of winding-up is to remove resources from the control of managements which have made losses or mismanaged their finances. (Lack of *profit* is not the same thing as lack of *cash.*) Of course, not all firms which lose money go into liquidation: the higher the proportion of equity in the capital structure, the lower the risk of that.

Figure 19.3 shows that 'compulsory' windings-up in the UK have risen sharply, from about 3,000 a year in the early 1970s to about 15,000 a year in the mid-1980s.

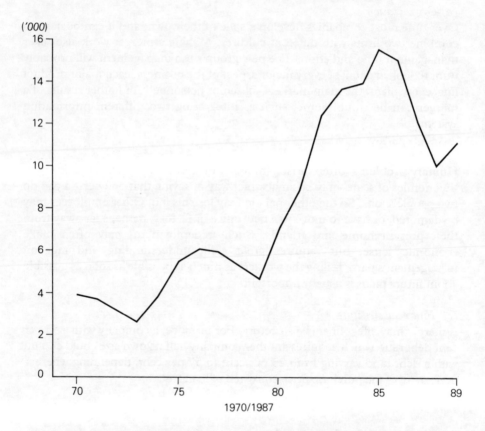

Figure 19.3 Compulsory liquidations in the UK, 1970 to 1989

When a firm goes into liquidation, its assets do not all disappear in a puff of smoke. They are sold, often for much less cash than their balance sheet book values. Then the proceeds are distributed in the order listed in figure 19.4.

1   The costs of liquidation
2   Creditors secured by a fixed charge on property
3   'Preferential' creditors:
    a)   one year's taxes due to government
    b)   wages of employees
4   Creditors secured by a floating charge
5   Unsecured creditors
6   Preference shareholders
7   Ordinary shareholders

Figure 19.4   *Priority of distribution in a liquidation*

19.4.2   Capital reorganization

There are three kinds of capital reorganization for a company which is to continue in business: (1) merging; (2) de-merging; or (3) formal reduction of equity capital.

1   *Merging.* We have already discussed most of the details of merging. Combining two formerly separate companies is likely to increase the total equity 'cushion', and thus to reduce the risk for existing creditors. Indeed, by reducing an enterprise's *total* risk (though perhaps not its 'market risk'– see 18.2.2), merging may encourage management to increase financial gearing.

2   *De-merging.* Recent changes in company and tax law have encouraged 'de-merging' (the opposite of merging). There are two versions:

(a)   Management buy-outs (called 'leveraged buy-outs' – LBOs – in the United States), where the managers of a subsidiary arrange to acquire all or most of the equity, often heavily assisted by institutional venture capital (both debt and equity). If this prevents a winding-up, it suits the management, who get continued employment with increased autonomy, as well as the chance of a large capital gain. The former parent company, which may cut out the subsidiary's losses, avoids possibly heavy costs of redundancies and winding-up.

(b)   Split-offs, where the holding company simply distributes the shares in a subsidiary *pro rata* to shareholders. If the two businesses are not closely enough related, it may not make sense to continue to manage them as a single enterprise.

3   *Formal reduction of equity capital.* The courts have to agree this, as a rule, because of the obvious threat to the interests of creditors. There are two main types:

a)   For tax reasons it was until recently difficult to repay to ordinary shareholders any liquid resources surplus to a company's needs. Yet it seems a good idea to let scarce resources flow to where they can best be used. An extra pressure to this end could result from changing company law to allow ordinary shareholders to vote to *increase* the dividends proposed by their company's directors (that is to *reduce* the amount of retained earnings).

b)   It can be awkward to recognize formally that a firm has permanently lost part of its capital, because the interested parties are sharing out losses not gains. But it may sometimes be necessary before introducing new capital. Explicit writing-off of losses has often occurred in the nationalized industries; but since the government is usually the major loan creditor, as well as the equity owner, no conflict of interest need arise between different classes of investor.

19.4.3 Privatization

During the decade of the 1980s many of the largest nationalized industries were privatized, including British Gas, British Telecom, and the regional water companies. The aims of privatization were: to make the industries more competitive and responsive to their customers; to change the climate for wage-bargaining; to reduce political interference; to relieve taxpayers from bearing any future losses; and to increase the number of individual shareholders.

The process of privatization has involved restructuring the business, strengthening top management, establishing a new regulatory system, and marketing the shares. The capital markets have shown an impressive capacity to cope with an enormous transfer of resources out of the public sector and into the private sector. Because of the huge size of some of the utilities, the shares have been paid for in two or three instalments. Proceeds from sales of government-owned businesses have averaged about £5,000 million a year since 1985.

Work section

A   Revision questions

A1   What is the difference between a 'merger' and an 'acquisition'?

A2   Which of a company's issued securities *must* be acquired for it to be 'taken over'?

A3   What is the difference between a 'horizontal' and a 'vertical' merger? Give one example of each.

A4   What is a 'conglomerate' merger?

A5   What kind of merger is most likely to yield economies of scale?

A6   What has been the overall result of the 100 odd references since 1965 to the Monopolies and Mergers Commission?

A7   Why may the government have mixed feelings about mergers?

A8   Name two production reasons for a company to make an acquisition.

A9   Name two marketing reasons for a company to make an acquisition.

A10 Name two reasons for wanting to sell a company.

A11 Why might managers and shareholders take a different view towards a company policy of diversification?

A12 What incentives are there to take over poorly-managed companies?

A13 Why will an acquiring company probably need to find ways of substantially increasing profits in order to make a take-over pay?

A14 What alternatives are likely to be open to a buyer? to a seller?

A15 Who seems to gain from mergers in financial terms?

A16 How does the existence of known priorities in the event of liquidation help companies to borrow?

A17 Why is a company with plenty of equity capital less likely to go into liquidation than one with little equity capital?

A18 What happens to assets disposed of on a liquidation?

A19 Name two possible reasons for 'de-merging'.

A20 Why might a company wish to *reduce* its equity capital?

B   Exercises and case studies

B1   Goliath Ltd acquired 100 per cent of David Ltd for 3 million £1 ordinary shares valued at £4.00 each on 31 March 1990, when their respective balance sheets were as summarized overleaf.

The acquisition method of accounting is to be used. Show the consolidated balance sheet after the acquisition:

a. if any resulting goodwill is left on the balance sheet.

b. if any resulting goodwill is written off against reserves.

	Goliath (£ m.)	David (£ m.)
Fixed assets, net	35	5
Working capital	25	5
	60	10
Issued £1 ordinary shares	15	2
Retained profits	35	5
	50	7
Long-term debt	10	3
	60	10

B2 Hollyhock Ltd is proposing to acquire all the equity capital of Snapdragon Ltd. Future cash inflows for Snapdragon as a separate company are estimated at £400,000 a year after tax; but Hollyhock's management reckons that economies of scale can add a further £200,000 a year after tax, to achieve which an immediate capital investment of £500,000 (which is stated net of tax allowances) will be required.

Regular fixed capital investments needed to maintain Snapdragon's profits are to be taken as equal to the company's present current cost depreciation of £250,000 a year. Surplus Snapdragon assets to be sold immediately after acquisition (without significantly affecting profits) are expected to realize £100,000 net.

If the appropriate after-tax discount rate is 12 per cent a year, what is the maximum purchase price for Snapdragon that Hollyhock should be prepared to pay:

a. using a horizon period of 10 years;
b. using a horizon period of 15 years?

B3 Runge Ltd is planning a major acquisition costing £5.0 million. The company's present capital consists of 10 million 50p issued ordinary shares, £4.0 million retained profits and £3.0 million 10 per cent Secured Debentures.

Runge can pay for its acquisition either by (a) issuing 4 million ordinary shares at £1.25 each, or (b) issuing £5.0 million 12 per cent loan stock. Present EBIT of £2.5 million a year is expected to rise to £3.5 million as a result of the acquisition.

For each of the two alternatives, compare (i) debt ratio, (ii) interest cover, (iii) earnings per share after the acquisition with Runge's present position. Assume a tax rate of 35 per cent.

B4 Bridge Steel Ltd has been trading unprofitably for several years. A potential investor, George Simpson, is prepared to put up another £2 million of new equity capital to try to restore its fortunes, on condition that there is a capital reconstruction. It is reckoned that the net assets would realize just under £1.0 million now if the company were put into liquidation.

The present capital employed appears on the balance sheet as shown:

	(£ m.)
Ordinary shareholders' funds	
5.0 million ordinary £1 shares in issue	5.0
Less: accumulated losses	(4.0)
	1.0
8 per cent £1 cumulative preference shares	0.5
Add: five years' dividends in arrears	0.2
12 per cent loan stock	1.2
	2.9

Losses have been running at £500,000 a year, but Mr Simpson believes he can turn the company round and earn at least £300,000 a year before tax and interest from now on. (Tax losses brought forward exceed £3.0 million.) He proposes the following scheme of reconstruction:

1 The present ordinary shares to be written down to 20p each.
2 The preference shareholders to waive the dividends in arrear.
3 The loan stock to be reduced to £1.0 million, still at 12 per cent a year.
4 The new equity capital of £2.0 million to be subscribed in return for 2.5 million new 20p ordinary shares.

a. Draw up a summary of capital employed for Bridge Steel Ltd after the proposed capital reconstruction.
b. Does the scheme seem reasonably acceptable, from the viewpoint:
   (i) of the loan stockholders;
   (ii) of the preference shareholders;
   (iii) of the existing ordinary shareholders;
   (iv) of Mr Simpson?

B5   *Laker Airways*
On 5 February 1982, at the request of the company, the Clydesdale Bank appointed Messrs Mackey and Hamilton (of Ernst & Whinney) as joint receivers of the Laker companies. The appointment followed more than six months of negotiations between Laker Airways, its bankers and aircraft manufacturers to resolve continuing and mounting cash flow difficulties. Within a week two of the Laker subsidiaries, Arrowsmith Holidays and Laker Air Travel, had been disposed of, to Greenall Whitley (a brewery company) and Saga Tours respectively.

It was thought that Sir Freddie Laker himself (who together with his wife owned all the equity shares in Laker Airways) would probably lose a relatively modest amount compared with the losses of his financial backers. Lacker's three Airbuses were mortgaged to a banking consortium headed by Midland Bank, and its 11 DC-10s were similarly mortgaged to a consortium of largely US banks.

One important reason for the crash had been changes in the dollar/sterling foreign exchange rate:

At 31.3.80 £1.00 = \$2.16; at 31.1.82 £1.00 = \$1.88. The average rate for the year ended 31.3.81 had been £1.00 = \$2.35.

At the time of the crash, the most recent Laker accounts available were for the year ended 31 March 1980. They are summarized below:

Laker Airways (International) Limited
Balanced Sheet at 31 March 1980

	1980 (£ m.)	1979 (£ m.)
Shareholders' Funds		
Issued ordinary £1 shares	5[1]	5[1]
Foreign exchange fluctuation reserve	5	3
Profit and loss account	13[2]	5
	23	13
Secured US dollar loans (\$235 m.)	109[3]	61
Sterling loans	3	–
Current liabilities	31	22
	166	96
Fixed Assets		
Aircraft and spares (net of acc. depn. 20)	136[4]	74
Other	10	8
Current assets	20	14
	166	96

Notes

[1] Adjusted (retrospectively) for a 9 for 1 bonus issue in September 1980, which increased issued share capital from £$\frac{1}{2}$ m. to £5 m.

[2] Including prior year adjustments of + £8 m.

[3] (a) \$235 m. loans translated at 'closing rate' of \$2.16 = £1.00.
   (b) \$41 m. loans repayable within next 12 months.

[4] Capital commitments (relating mainly to new aircraft): £275 m.

Laker Airways (International) Limited
Profit and Loss Account, year ended 31 March 1980

	1980 ($£$ m.)	1979 ($£$ m.)
Sales turnover	111	92
Profit before depreciation	13	10
Depreciation (aircraft and spares: $5\frac{1}{2}$)	7	5
Earnings before interest and tax	6	5
Interest payable	6	$2\frac{1}{2}$
Profit before tax[1]	–	$2\frac{1}{2}$

Note
[1] In both years, no tax charge or ordinary dividends.

Figure 19.5 Laker Airways Ltd: balance sheet and profit and loss account

a. As at 31 March 1980:
   (i) what is the current ratio?
   (ii) what is the debt ratio?
b. Assume:
   (1) A loss of £11 million was incurred in the 22 months ended 31 January 1982, exactly equalling depreciation charged on aircraft and spares in that period;
   (2) New American loans of $611 million net were incurred during the year ended 31 March 1981, to buy new aircraft.
   Note: The above assumptions are deliberately over-simplified. They do *not* purport to represent actual financial events.
   (i) Prepare an estimated balance sheet for Laker Airways as at 31 January 1982. (Use the 'closing rate' method of translating $s.)
   (ii) What is the debt ratio?
   (iii) What were estimated foreign exchange losses over the 22 months?
c. What alternative financial arrangements might have been desirable for Laker Airways after March 1980?
d. What went wrong? Could it have been prevented?

B6 Purton Plastics Ltd is considering making a bid for control of Marsham Mouldings. The company's directors have taken a five year view. Marsham's predicted cash flow for the first year is a surplus of £800,000, and it is expected that this will rise by £100,000 per annum for each of the next four years. If Purton's bid is successful, it is believed that the

annual surplus can be increased by a further £400,000 per annum, but only if £1 million is invested at once and a further £300,000 is invested at the end of each year thereafter, to maintain the plant.
a.   Construct a table of cash flows for each of the coming five years.
b.   What is the maximum price that Purton should pay for Marsham? Assume a discount rate of 10% and a five year time horizon for the acquisition.
c.   What factors might the company consider when deciding on a discount rate of 10%?
d.   How else might Purton Plastics Ltd value Marsham?
(UCLES International Examinations, 1988, GCE A level Business Studies)

C   Essay questions

C1   What is the purpose of conglomerate mergers?

C2   'Mergers and acquisitions are, among other things, a civilized alternative to bankruptcy.' Discuss.

C3   Is there any need for a Monopolies and Mergers Commission? Why or why not?

C4   Your firm has decided to make a take-over bid for a firm supplying you with raw materials. What factors should be taken into account when making the decision whether to offer equity capital or cash? What might be the financial consequences for shareholders of the company being taken over?

C5   Most cigarette companies have been diversifying into other industries. How does this affect their shareholders?

C6   Discuss possible conflicts between managers and shareholders with respect to: (a) financial gearing; (b) dividend policy; (c) mergers.

C7   In what ways can a merger fundamentally alter the bidding company's financial position?

C8   Why may it be difficult to value the net benefits to be expected from a merger?

C9   Why might 'de-mergers' be desirable?

C10   Is it desirable for companies to be allowed to buy back some of their own issued equity shares? What 'safeguards' (if any) might be necessary? Why?

Appendix 1

Retail Prices Index (RPI)

(January 1987 = 100)

	Average for year ending December	RPI for December	Annual inflation year to December
1950	8.4	8.5	2%
1960	12.5	12.6	2
1970	18.5	19.2	8
----	----	----	----
1971	20.3	20.9	9
1972	21.7	22.5	8
1973	23.7	24.9	11
1974	27.5	29.6	19
1975	34.2	37.0	25
1976	39.8	42.6	15
1977	46.2	47.8	12
1978	49.9	51.8	8
1979	56.7	60.7	17
1980	66.9	69.9	15
1981	74.8	78.3	12
1982	81.2	82.5	5
1983	85.0	86.9	5
1984	89.2	90.9	5
1985	94.6	96.0	6
1986	97.8	99.6	4
1987	101.9	103.3	4
1988	106.9	110.3	7
1989	115.2	118.8	8

Appendix 2

Accounting abbreviations and acronyms

ACT   Advance Corporation Tax
AGM   Annual General Meeting
BS   Balance Sheet
BV   Book Value
CA   Current Asset
CCA   Current Cost Accounting
CL   Current Liabilities
COGS   Cost Of Goods Sold
CPP   Constant Purchasing Power
DCF   Discounted Cash Flow
DPR   Dividend Payout Ratio
DPS   Dividend Per Share
EBIT   Earnings Before Interest and Tax
ED   Exposure Draft
EOY   End Of Year
EPS   Earnings Per Share
FA   Fixed Assets
FG   Finished Goods
FIFO   First In First Out
FT   Financial Times
HC   Historical Cost
HP   Hire Purchase
IRR   Internal Rate of Return
LIFO   Last In First Out
Ltd   Limited
MI   Minority Interests
MMC   Monopolies and Mergers Commission
MPT   Modern Portfolio Theory
MV   Market Value
NBV   Net Book Value
NPV   Net Present Value
NRV   Net Realizable Value
P&L   Profit and Loss
PAT   Profit After Tax
PBT   Profit Before Tax
P/E   Price/Earnings (ratio)

plc	public limited company
RC	Replacement Cost
RE	Retained Earnings
RM	Raw Materials
ROI	Return On Investment
RPI	Retail Prices Index
SL	Straight Line (depreciation)
SSAP	Statement of Standard Accounting Practice
SYD	Sum-of-the-Years'-Digits (depreciation)
USM	Unlisted Securities Market
VAT	Value Added Tax
WACC	Weighted Average Cost of Capital
WC	Working Capital
WIP	Work In Progress

Appendix 3

Discounting factors

The mechanics of discounting are not difficult; and two sets of Tables (A and B), set out on the following pages, contain discounting factors.

Table A shows the present value of £1 receivable at the end of *n* periods. Thus, given an interest rate of 8 per cent a year, £1,000 receivable at the end of four years (EOY 4) has a present value of £735.

Compounding factors (the reciprocals of discounting factors) are not shown here. At an interest rate of 8 per cent a year, £1,000 will compound to £1,361 by the end of year four. We could calculate this by *dividing* £1,000 by 0.735 (the discounting factor we found above).

Normal practice (used in the tables) is to assume that amounts invested will compound once a year at the end of each year (rather than continuously).

Table B shows the present value of £1 *per period* receivable at the end of *each* of the next *n* periods. Thus given an interest rate of 8 per cent a year, an annuity of £1,000 for the next four years has a total present value of £3,312. (This is the *sum* of the present values of £1,000 receivable EOY 1 plus £1,000 receivable EOY 2 *plus* ... Thus: £926 + £857 + £794 + £735 = £3,312.)

Where expected cash inflows are the *same* each year (annuities), instead of 'capitalizing' them and comparing their present value with the initial investment (as in the net present value method), it can sometimes be more convenient to 'annualize' the initial investment, and then compare that '**annualized cost**' with the (equal) annual cash inflows.

Example: A project costing £3,000 is expected to produce equal annual cash inflows of £1,000 for each of the next four years. With an interest rate of 8 per cent a year, we know already that their present value is £3,312. Therefore the project is 'acceptable', with a net present value of + £312. Alternatively the 'annualized cost' is: £3,000/3.312 = £906.
Thus the project is seen to be acceptable, since the (annualized) cost of £906 is less than the annual cash inflow of £1,000.

Where we are not starting from EOY 0, the procedure may require more than a single stage.

Example: To find the present value (at an 8% a year rate of interest) of an annuity receivable at the end of each year from EOY 4 to EOY 7, two simple steps are needed, using Table B:

First:	find the factor for amounts receivable at the end of *each* of years 1 to 7	5.206
Then:	deduct the factor for amounts receivable at the end of *each* of years 1 to 4	3.312
To show:	the factor for amounts receivable at the end of *each* of years 5 to 7	= 1.894

Where the amounts are *different* each year, then separate discount factors, as given in Table A, must be used for each future year.

Table A: Present value of £1

Years Hence	1%	2%	4%	6%	8%	10%	12%	14%	15%	16%	18%	20%	22%	24%	25%	26%	28%	30%	35%	40%	45%	50%
1	0.990	0.980	0.962	0.943	0.926	0.909	0.893	0.877	0.870	0.862	0.847	0.833	0.820	0.806	0.800	0.794	0.781	0.769	0.741	0.714	0.690	0.667
2	0.980	0.961	0.925	0.890	0.857	0.826	0.797	0.769	0.756	0.743	0.718	0.694	0.672	0.650	0.640	0.630	0.610	0.592	0.549	0.510	0.476	0.444
3	0.971	0.942	0.889	0.840	0.794	0.751	0.712	0.675	0.658	0.641	0.609	0.579	0.551	0.524	0.512	0.500	0.477	0.455	0.406	0.364	0.328	0.296
4	0.961	0.924	0.855	0.792	0.735	0.683	0.636	0.592	0.572	0.552	0.516	0.482	0.451	0.423	0.410	0.397	0.373	0.350	0.301	0.260	0.226	0.198
5	0.951	0.906	0.822	0.747	0.681	0.621	0.567	0.519	0.497	0.476	0.437	0.402	0.370	0.341	0.328	0.315	0.291	0.269	0.223	0.186	0.156	0.132
6	0.942	0.888	0.790	0.705	0.630	0.564	0.507	0.456	0.432	0.410	0.370	0.335	0.303	0.275	0.262	0.250	0.227	0.207	0.165	0.133	0.108	0.088
7	0.933	0.871	0.760	0.665	0.583	0.513	0.452	0.400	0.376	0.354	0.314	0.279	0.249	0.222	0.210	0.198	0.178	0.159	0.122	0.095	0.074	0.059
8	0.923	0.853	0.731	0.627	0.540	0.467	0.404	0.351	0.327	0.305	0.266	0.233	0.204	0.179	0.168	0.157	0.139	0.123	0.091	0.068	0.051	0.039
9	0.914	0.837	0.703	0.592	0.500	0.424	0.361	0.308	0.284	0.263	0.225	0.194	0.167	0.144	0.134	0.125	0.108	0.094	0.067	0.048	0.035	0.026
10	0.905	0.820	0.676	0.558	0.463	0.386	0.322	0.270	0.247	0.227	0.191	0.162	0.137	0.116	0.107	0.099	0.085	0.073	0.050	0.035	0.024	0.017
11	0.896	0.804	0.650	0.527	0.429	0.350	0.287	0.237	0.215	0.195	0.162	0.135	0.112	0.094	0.086	0.079	0.066	0.056	0.037	0.025	0.017	0.012
12	0.887	0.788	0.625	0.497	0.397	0.319	0.257	0.208	0.187	0.168	0.137	0.112	0.092	0.076	0.069	0.062	0.052	0.043	0.027	0.018	0.012	0.008
13	0.879	0.773	0.601	0.469	0.368	0.290	0.229	0.182	0.163	0.145	0.116	0.093	0.075	0.061	0.055	0.050	0.040	0.033	0.020	0.013	0.008	0.005
14	0.870	0.758	0.577	0.442	0.340	0.263	0.205	0.160	0.141	0.125	0.099	0.078	0.062	0.049	0.044	0.039	0.032	0.025	0.015	0.009	0.006	0.003
15	0.861	0.743	0.555	0.417	0.315	0.239	0.183	0.140	0.123	0.108	0.084	0.065	0.051	0.040	0.035	0.031	0.025	0.020	0.011	0.006	0.004	0.002
16	0.853	0.728	0.534	0.394	0.292	0.218	0.163	0.123	0.107	0.093	0.071	0.054	0.042	0.032	0.028	0.025	0.019	0.015	0.008	0.005	0.003	0.002
17	0.844	0.714	0.513	0.371	0.270	0.198	0.146	0.108	0.093	0.080	0.060	0.045	0.034	0.026	0.023	0.020	0.015	0.012	0.006	0.003	0.002	0.001
18	0.836	0.700	0.494	0.350	0.250	0.180	0.130	0.095	0.081	0.069	0.051	0.038	0.028	0.021	0.018	0.016	0.012	0.009	0.005	0.002	0.001	0.001
19	0.828	0.686	0.475	0.331	0.232	0.164	0.116	0.083	0.070	0.060	0.043	0.031	0.023	0.017	0.014	0.012	0.009	0.007	0.003	0.002	0.001	
20	0.820	0.673	0.456	0.312	0.215	0.149	0.104	0.073	0.061	0.051	0.037	0.026	0.019	0.014	0.012	0.010	0.007	0.005	0.002	0.001	0.001	
21	0.811	0.660	0.439	0.294	0.199	0.135	0.093	0.064	0.053	0.044	0.031	0.022	0.015	0.011	0.009	0.008	0.006	0.004	0.002	0.001		
22	0.803	0.647	0.422	0.278	0.184	0.123	0.083	0.056	0.046	0.038	0.026	0.018	0.013	0.009	0.007	0.006	0.004	0.003	0.001	0.001		
23	0.795	0.634	0.406	0.262	0.170	0.112	0.074	0.049	0.040	0.033	0.022	0.015	0.010	0.007	0.006	0.005	0.003	0.002	0.001			
24	0.788	0.622	0.390	0.247	0.158	0.102	0.066	0.043	0.035	0.028	0.019	0.013	0.008	0.006	0.005	0.004	0.003	0.002	0.001			
25	0.780	0.610	0.375	0.233	0.146	0.092	0.059	0.038	0.030	0.024	0.016	0.010	0.007	0.005	0.004	0.003	0.002	0.001	0.001			
26	0.772	0.598	0.361	0.220	0.135	0.084	0.053	0.033	0.026	0.021	0.014	0.009	0.006	0.004	0.003	0.002	0.002	0.001				
27	0.764	0.586	0.347	0.207	0.125	0.076	0.047	0.029	0.023	0.018	0.011	0.007	0.005	0.003	0.002	0.002	0.001	0.001				
28	0.757	0.574	0.333	0.196	0.116	0.069	0.042	0.026	0.020	0.016	0.010	0.006	0.004	0.002	0.002	0.002	0.001	0.001				
29	0.749	0.563	0.321	0.185	0.107	0.063	0.037	0.022	0.017	0.014	0.008	0.005	0.003	0.002	0.002	0.001	0.001					
30	0.742	0.552	0.308	0.174	0.099	0.057	0.033	0.020	0.015	0.012	0.007	0.004	0.003	0.002	0.001	0.001	0.001					
40	0.672	0.453	0.208	0.097	0.046	0.022	0.011	0.005	0.004	0.003	0.001	0.001										
50	0.608	0.372	0.141	0.054	0.021	0.009	0.003	0.001	0.001	0.001												

Years (N)	1%	2%	4%	6%	8%	10%	12%	14%	15%	16%	18%	20%	22%	24%	25%	26%	28%	30%	35%	40%	45%	50%
1	0.990	0.980	0.962	0.943	0.926	0.909	0.893	0.877	0.870	0.862	0.847	0.833	0.820	0.806	0.800	0.794	0.781	0.769	0.741	0.714	0.690	0.667
2	1.970	1.942	1.886	1.833	1.783	1.736	1.690	1.647	1.626	1.605	1.566	1.528	1.492	1.457	1.440	1.424	1.392	1.361	1.289	1.224	1.165	1.111
3	2.941	2.884	2.775	2.673	2.577	2.487	2.402	2.322	2.283	2.246	2.174	2.106	2.042	1.981	1.952	1.923	1.868	1.816	1.696	1.589	1.493	1.407
4	3.902	3.808	3.630	3.465	3.312	3.170	3.037	2.914	2.855	2.798	2.690	2.589	2.494	2.404	2.362	2.320	2.241	2.166	1.997	1.849	1.720	1.605
5	4.853	4.713	4.452	4.212	3.993	3.791	3.605	3.433	3.352	3.274	3.127	2.991	2.864	2.745	2.689	2.635	2.532	2.436	2.220	2.035	1.876	1.737
6	5.795	5.601	5.242	4.917	4.623	4.355	4.111	3.889	3.784	3.685	3.498	3.326	3.167	3.020	2.951	2.885	2.759	2.643	2.385	2.168	1.983	1.824
7	6.728	6.472	6.002	5.582	5.206	4.868	4.564	4.288	4.160	4.039	3.812	3.605	3.416	3.242	3.161	3.083	2.937	2.802	2.508	2.263	2.057	1.883
8	7.652	7.325	6.733	6.210	5.747	5.335	4.968	4.639	4.487	4.344	4.078	3.837	3.619	3.421	3.329	3.241	3.076	2.925	2.598	2.331	2.108	1.922
9	8.566	8.162	7.435	6.802	6.247	5.759	5.328	4.946	4.772	4.607	4.303	4.031	3.786	3.566	3.463	3.366	3.184	3.019	2.665	2.379	2.144	1.948
10	9.471	8.983	8.111	7.360	6.710	6.145	5.650	5.216	5.019	4.833	4.494	4.192	3.923	3.682	3.571	3.465	3.269	3.092	2.715	2.414	2.168	1.965
11	10.368	9.787	8.760	7.887	7.139	6.495	5.937	5.453	5.234	5.029	4.656	4.327	4.035	3.776	3.656	3.544	3.335	3.147	2.752	2.438	2.185	1.977
12	11.255	10.575	9.385	8.384	7.536	6.814	6.194	5.660	5.421	5.197	4.793	4.439	4.127	3.851	3.725	3.606	3.387	3.190	2.779	2.456	2.196	1.985
13	12.134	11.343	9.986	8.853	7.904	7.103	6.424	5.842	5.583	5.342	4.910	4.533	4.203	3.912	3.780	3.656	3.427	3.223	2.799	2.468	2.204	1.990
14	13.004	12.106	10.563	9.295	8.244	7.367	6.628	6.002	5.724	5.468	5.008	4.611	4.265	3.962	3.824	3.695	3.459	3.249	2.814	2.477	2.210	1.993
15	13.865	12.849	11.118	9.712	8.559	7.606	6.811	6.142	5.847	5.575	5.092	4.675	4.315	4.001	3.859	3.726	3.483	3.268	2.825	2.484	2.214	1.995
16	14.718	13.578	11.652	10.106	8.851	7.824	6.974	6.265	5.954	5.669	5.162	4.730	4.357	4.033	3.887	3.751	3.503	3.283	2.834	2.489	2.216	1.997
17	15.562	14.292	12.166	10.477	9.122	8.022	7.120	6.373	6.047	5.749	5.222	4.775	4.391	4.059	3.910	3.771	3.518	3.295	2.840	2.492	2.218	1.998
18	16.398	14.992	12.659	10.828	9.372	8.201	7.250	6.467	6.128	5.818	5.273	4.812	4.419	4.080	3.928	3.786	3.529	3.304	2.844	2.494	2.219	1.999
19	17.226	15.678	13.134	11.158	9.604	8.365	7.366	6.550	6.198	5.877	5.316	4.844	4.442	4.097	3.942	3.799	3.539	3.311	2.848	2.496	2.220	1.999
20	18.046	16.351	13.590	11.470	9.818	8.514	7.469	6.623	6.259	5.929	5.353	4.870	4.460	4.110	3.954	3.808	3.546	3.316	2.850	2.497	2.221	1.999
21	18.857	17.011	14.029	11.764	10.017	8.649	7.562	6.687	6.312	5.973	5.384	4.891	4.476	4.121	3.963	3.816	3.551	3.320	2.852	2.498	2.221	2.000
22	19.660	17.658	14.451	12.042	10.201	8.772	7.645	6.743	6.359	6.011	5.410	4.909	4.488	4.130	3.970	3.822	3.556	3.323	2.853	2.498	2.222	2.000
23	20.456	18.292	14.857	12.303	10.371	8.883	7.718	6.792	6.399	6.044	5.432	4.925	4.499	4.137	3.976	3.827	3.559	3.325	2.854	2.499	2.222	2.000
24	21.243	18.914	15.247	12.550	10.529	8.985	7.784	6.835	6.434	6.073	5.451	4.937	4.507	4.143	3.981	3.831	3.562	3.327	2.855	2.499	2.222	2.000
25	22.023	19.523	15.622	12.783	10.675	9.077	7.843	6.873	6.464	6.097	5.467	4.948	4.514	4.147	3.985	3.834	3.564	3.329	2.856	2.499	2.222	2.000
26	22.795	20.121	15.983	13.003	10.810	9.161	7.896	6.906	6.491	6.118	5.480	4.956	4.520	4.151	3.988	3.837	3.566	3.330	2.856	2.500	2.222	2.000
27	23.560	20.707	16.330	13.211	10.935	9.237	7.943	6.935	6.514	6.136	5.492	4.964	4.524	4.154	3.990	3.839	3.567	3.331	2.856	2.500	2.222	2.000
28	24.316	21.281	16.663	13.406	11.051	9.307	7.984	6.961	6.534	6.152	5.502	4.970	4.528	4.157	3.992	3.840	3.568	3.331	2.857	2.500	2.222	2.000
29	25.066	21.844	16.984	13.591	11.158	9.370	8.022	6.983	6.551	6.166	5.510	4.975	4.531	4.159	3.994	3.841	3.569	3.332	2.857	2.500	2.222	2.000
30	25.808	22.396	17.292	13.765	11.258	9.427	8.055	7.003	6.566	6.177	5.517	4.979	4.534	4.160	3.995	3.842	3.569	3.332	2.857	2.500	2.222	2.000
40	32.835	27.355	19.793	15.046	11.925	9.779	8.244	7.105	6.642	6.234	5.548	4.997	4.544	4.166	3.999	3.846	3.571	3.333	2.857	2.500	2.222	2.000
50	39.196	31.424	21.482	15.762	12.234	9.915	8.304	7.133	6.661	6.246	5.554	4.999	4.545	4.167	4.000	3.846	3.571	3.333	2.857	2.500	2.222	2.000

Table B: Present value of £1 received annually for n years

Glossary

Absorption costing: = full costing. System of costing which allocates all costs, including overheads, to cost centres, thence to products.

Accounts: Profit and loss account for a period, balance sheet as at the end of that period, and notes to the accounts, together with the auditors' report (and, for larger companies, a funds flow statement).

Accounts payable: = creditors. Amounts due to suppliers for goods or services purchased on credit.

Accounts receivable: = debtors. Amounts due from customers for goods or services sold on credit.

Accruals concept: The accounting principle of recognizing transactions in the period to which they relate, rather than when cash is paid.

Accrued charge: Liability not yet invoiced, often relating to period costs.

Accumulated depreciation: The total part of fixed asset cost (or valuation) charged as depreciation expense since purchase.

Acid test ratio: Yardstick of a firm's ability to pay its debts in the near future. Ratio of liquid assets (cash + debtors) divided by current liabilities. Usually close to 1.0.

Advance corporation tax: (ACT): Part of corporation tax liability, payable (at basic rate of income tax on gross dividends) at the same time as dividends, set off later against 'mainstream' corporation tax.

Amortization: Depreciation, usually of intangible fixed assets such as patent rights, leases or goodwill, or of a wasting asset such as a mine.

Annuity: Regular annual amount for a given number of years (in personal affairs, until death). For present values, see Appendix 3.

Appropriation account: Final part of the profit and loss account, disclosing how the profit has been 'appropriated' between dividends, transfers to special reserves, and retained profits.

Arbitrage: Buying in one market and selling in another to gain from price differences (which this process will reduce but, due to transaction costs, not eliminate).

Asset: Valuable resource which a business owns or controls.

Asset turnover: Annual sales revenue divided by net assets.

Associated company: = related company. Company in which another company (i) owns between 20 per cent and 50 per cent of the ordinary shares and (ii) influences management.

Audit: External examination of financial accounts (and records and systems) by independent professional accountants, to report whether accounts give a true and fair view.

Auditor: Independent professional accountant appointed by shareholders to check and report on company's financial accounts.

Authorized share capital: Amount of share capital which shareholders have authorized a company to issue.

Average cost: (a) Total cost of a product divided by the number of units produced. (b) Method of stock valuation (see 7.2.2).

Bad debt: Debt reckoned to be uncollectable.

Balance sheet: Classified statement of financial position of a business, showing assets, liabilities, and shareholders' funds at a particular date.

Bank of England: UK central bank responsible for integrity of the currency. Official 'authority' overseeing City institutions and markets.

Bank overdraft: Amount owing to bank repayable on demand. Amount borrowed, and rate of interest, may vary.

Bankruptcy: Legal process occurring when a person is unable to pay due debts. Equivalent for companies is liquidation or winding-up.

Bear: Speculator expecting prices to fall, who may sell assets he does not own, hoping to buy back later at a profit.

Below the line: The part of the profit and loss account below the line showing 'profit after tax on ordinary activities for a period'; containing extraordinary items as well as the appropriation account.

Beta: Coefficient relating the sensitivity of an investment's return to that of the whole market.

Bonus issue: = scrip issue. Issue of additional shares *pro rata* to existing shareholders 'free' (= in exchange for no cash or other assets).

Book-keeping: That part of accounting which records transactions in financial terms, in books or maybe on cards, tape or disk.

Book value: Balance sheet amount shown for asset. Under historical cost accounting usually means not 'value', but 'cost less any amounts written off'.

Budget: Financial or quantitative statement, prepared and agreed prior to the budget period, by those responsible, reflecting the policies to be pursued during that period to attain agreed objectives.

Bull: Speculator expecting prices to rise, who may buy assets (or options to acquire them) hoping to sell them later at a profit.

Business risk: The volatility of a business's operating profits, due to the specific assets in which funds are invested, regardless of how those assets are financed.

Capital: (a) Issued ordinary share capital. (b) = capital employed. (c) Contrasted with 'revenue'.

Capital allowance: = writing-down allowance. Tax equivalent of depreciation of fixed assets, calculated according to Inland Revenue rules. For most plant, 25 per cent on declining balance.

Capital budgeting: Planning use of investment funds, usually including methods of evaluating capital investment projects.

Capital employed: Shareholders' funds plus long-term liabilities. = total assets less current liabilities (net assets).

Capital expenditure: Expenditure treated as an asset on balance sheet, in contrast to revenue expenditure.

Capital gain: Part of 'return' on investment in securities, stemming from increase in market value, not from dividends or interest.

Capitalize: Record expenditure as an asset, not write it off as an expense.

Cash discount: Reduction in selling price of goods, offered in exchange for prompt settlement by debtor.

Cash flow: Usually defined as 'retained profits plus depreciation'.

Collateral: Asset serving as security for loan.

Conglomerate: Diversified group of companies whose subsidiaries operate in unrelated areas.

Consistency: Principle in accounting, and other statistics, of treating similar items in the same way, to produce meaningful results and to allow comparisons over time.

Consolidated accounts: = group accounts. Accounts for a group of companies, 'consolidated' by combining the separate assets and liabilities of all subsidiaries with those of the holding (parent) company.

Constant purchasing power (CPP) accounting: Method of inflation accounting which adjusts money of different dates by using the Retail Prices Index.

Contribution: = 'variable profit'. Sales revenue less variable costs.

Control: In management accounting means: planning, comparing actual performance with budget; finding reasons for significant variances; and taking action to improve matters.

Conventions: Accounting practices found useful by experience.

Convertible loan: Loan convertible at holder's option into ordinary shares on pre-arranged terms.

Corporation tax: Tax payable by companies on profits. 1990/91 rates: 35 per cent, or 25 per cent for smaller companies.

Cost: Amount given up in exchange for goods or services received. In accounts may appear either as an asset or as an expense.

Cost /benefit analysis: Process of trying to assess 'profitability' where either the costs or the benefits are hard to measure in financial terms. Often applied to social costs or benefits.

Cost centre: Unit or operation in respect of which costs are determined.

Cost of capital: Risk-adjusted weighted average of the (marginal) after-tax costs of ordinary share capital and debt. The criterion rate of return for capital investment projects.

Cost of goods sold (COGS): Costs identifiable with stocks, for example, raw materials and components, direct labour, and production overheads; but excluding distribution and administrative expenses.

Cost of sales adjustment (COSA): In current cost accounting, difference between the current cost of goods sold in period and their historical cost. Usually represents an extra deduction from profit in current cost accounting; but if specific values are falling it might *increase* HC profit.

Coupon rate: Nominal rate of interest payable on fixed-interest securities.

Covenants: Conditions attached to loan agreement restricting borrower's freedom of action (for example, *re* dividends, working capital, etc).

Credit note: A document crediting customer, often to correct or reduce an amount invoiced earlier.

Creditors: = accounts payable. Amounts due to suppliers for goods or services purchased on credit.

Criterion rate: Required rate of return on capital investment project.

Critical resource: Sometimes called 'limiting factor'.

Currency debasement: Process of reducing purchasing power of currency, originally by fraudulently adding base metal to precious metal, now by more sophisticated methods.

Current asset: Cash or any asset (such as stocks or debtors) expected to be converted into cash (or consumed in the normal course of business), within twelve months from the balance sheet date.

Current cost accounting (CCA): System of current value accounting which continues to use money as the unit of account, but shows assets and expenses at current replacement cost instead of historical cost.

Current liabilities: = 'creditors: amounts falling due within one year'. Amounts owing to others (such as trade creditors or tax) payable within twelve months from balance sheet date.

Current ratio: Measure of liquidity, current assets divided by current liabilities. Rule of thumb: should normally be between $1\frac{1}{2}$ and 2.

Current value: Usually means current replacement cost of asset, but may refer to net realizable value. Unlike historical cost, which is usually a definite known fact, current value is usually only a hypothetical estimate.

Days sales in debtors: Debtors divided by daily sales (that is, by annual sales revenue divided by 365). Ratio indicating how much trade credit customers are taking.

Debenture: Long-term liability. (Latin: 'They are owed.')

Debt (as opposed to equity): Negotiated borrowing.

Debtors: = Accounts receivable. Amounts due from customers for goods or services sold on credit. In balance sheet may include prepayments.

Debt ratio: Balance sheet measure of gearing. Long-term liabilities divided by total long-term capital employed (= debt plus equity).

Declining balance depreciation: Depreciation method which charges constant percentage of (declining) net book value each year.

Depreciation: Process of writing off as expense the cost of fixed asset, to spread total net cost over its economic life.

Dilution: Process which reduces a shareholder's equity interest when a company issues additional shares to other shareholders.

Direct cost: Cost that is directly identifiable with a specific product.

Directors' report: Report required with annual accounts, containing certain information if not published elsewhere.

Discount factor: Multiplier needed to reduce future cash amounts to present value.

Discount rate: Interest rate used in making present value calculations.

Discounted cash flow (DCF): Technique (for example, NPV, IRR) for evaluating capital projects, using interest rate as 'exchange rate over time'.

Disinvestment: Reducing investment by selling or abandoning asset(s).

Diversification: Adding or substituting investments with low or negative co-variance with existing holdings, to reduce total risk of portfolio.

Dividend: Cash payable to ordinary (or preference) shareholders, out of profits, if declared by a company's directors. May be 'interim' or 'final'.

Dividend cover: Profits divided by dividends for a year.

Dividend payout ratio (DPR): Reciprocal of dividend cover. Dividends payable as a percentage of profits available for a period.

Dividend yield: Dividends per share for a year (gross of basic rate income rate), divided by the market price.

Double-entry accounting: System of recording business transactions based on their two aspects: a 'source' of funds, and a 'use' of funds.

Earnings before interest and tax (EBIT): Operating profit for a year, used to calculate return on net assets, profit margin, and interest cover.

Earnings per share (EPS): Profit after tax divided by the number of ordinary shares in issue.

Earnings yield: EPS divided by market price per share.

Equity: Owners' equity, shareholders' funds.

Exceptional items: Items disclosed separately in profit and loss account, unusual on account of their size, included in calculating operating profit.

Expected value: Weighted average of subjective probabilities applied to all possible anticipated outcomes.

Expenditure: Amount spent = cost. May be either revenue (expense), or capital (asset).

Expense: Amount written off against profit in respect of goods or services consumed.

Exposure draft (ED): Proposed SSAP published for criticism and comment before (possibly amended) final version appears.

External finance: Funds raised from 'outside' the company; such as issuing new equity shares for cash, borrowing.

Extraordinary items: Profit and loss account items which appear 'below the line', being (a) material, (b) not expected to recur frequently, and (c) derived from events or transactions outside the ordinary activities of the business.

Factor: Company which buys trade debts at a discount for cash.

Final Dividend: Second dividend for a year, after interim dividend.

Financial accounting: External accounting, leading to published accounts for shareholders and other outsiders.

Financial lease: Lease giving lessee use of asset over most of its life, providing in effect another way to finance its 'acquisition'. Hence accounts now capitalize financial leases.

Financial objective: (of a company). 'To maximize the wealth of the present ordinary shareholders.'

Financial risk: Extra volatility of stream of equity earnings due to financial gearing; added to business risk (operational gearing).

Financial year: The 12-month period for which a firm chooses to prepare its financial accounts.

Finished goods: Stocks of completed manufactured products, held for sale.

First In First Out (FIFO): Method of valuing stock, assuming most recent purchases remain in stock at the end of an accounting period.

Fixed asset: Resource, either tangible or intangible, with long life, intended to be held for use in producing goods or services, not for sale in the ordinary course of business.

Fixed cost: = period cost. Cost which, within the 'relevant range' of output, is fixed for a given period whatever the level of output.

Flat yield: Interest yield ignoring capital gain (or loss) on maturity; annual interest divided by current market price.

Flexible budget: System of 'flexing' budget so that variable costs represent planned amount at actual rather than at budgeted sales volume.

Floating charge: Charge which is not secured against specific assets, but which 'floats' over all (otherwise unsecured) assets, 'crystallizing' only on occurrence of specified events.

Full costing: = absorption costing.

Funds flow statement: Accounting statement, required for companies with sales turnover exceeding £25,000 a year, showing sources and uses ('applications') of funds for a period.

Gearing: Proportion of negotiated borrowing in capital structure represents financial gearing. Proportion of fixed costs to total operating expenses represents operating (or 'business') gearing.

Gearing ratio: Long-term liabilities (perhaps plus bank overdrafts) divided by capital employed (long-term liabilities plus shareholders' funds).

Going concern: Assumption that a business entity will continue in operation for the foreseeable future.

Goodwill: Excess of purchase price paid on acquisition of another company over fair value of net separable assets acquired.

Group accounts: = consolidated accounts.

Guarantee: Undertaking to be responsible for the debts of another (person or company) if the nominal debtor fails to pay in full.

Hire purchase: System of paying for an asset by instalments.

Historical cost (HC): Traditional accounting convention of showing assets and expenses at actual past money cost, rather than at hypothetical current value (CCA), or at inflation-indexed past cost (CPP).

Holding company: = parent company. Company owning more than 50 per cent of equity shares in subsidiaries, directly or indirectly, or controlling composition of board of directors.

Horizon: Point in future beyond which financial calculations are not made explicitly (though including a 'terminal value' in capital project evaluation makes them implicitly).

Horizontal merger: Combination of firms making the same kind of product.

Income tax: Tax payable on personal incomes (such as dividends or trading profits of partnerships or sole traders). Basic rate 25 per cent (for 1990/91); higher rate 40 per cent on incomes above £20,000.

Incremental cash flows: Cash flows which occur as a result of action (for example, investing in capital project), but not otherwise.

Index-linking: indexation. Linking amount to the rate of inflation as measured by RPI. Examples: government securities, pensions, tax thresholds, capital gains.

Indirect cost: Cost not directly identifiable with product; allocated in full costing on some reasonable basis, in marginal costing not at all.

Inflation: Rise in 'general' level of money prices, usually measured by annual rate of increase in the Retail Prices Index. See Appendix 1.

Inflation accounting: Constant purchasing power (CPP) accounting. (Current cost accounting (CCA) is *not* a method of adjusting accounts for general inflation.)

Inflation premium: Part of the nominal rate of interest, depending on the expected future rate of inflation.

Insolvency: Inability to meet financial obligations.

Interest rate: Annual rate of compensation for borrowing or lending (money) for a period of time, comprising: (a) pure time-preference, (b) inflation premium, and (c) risk premium.

Interim accounts: Financial accounts for shareholders, covering a period of less than one year, not subject to audit.

Interim dividend: First (of two) dividends payable in respect of a year's profits, the second being the final dividend.

Intermediaries: Financial organizations which separate borrowing from lending and may alter the time-maturity of loans. They profit from economies of scale and specialization, and reduce risk by diversification.

Internal auditor: Employee responsible for reviewing the internal accounting system. Not to be confused with the external auditor.

Internal finance: Raising funds from 'within' a company, usually referring to retained profits plus depreciation (or perhaps selling off assets owned).

Internal rate of return (IRR): Rate of discount which, when applied to a capital project, produces a zero net present value.

Inventory: = stock.

Investment (real): Fixed capital formation; investment in fixed assets.

Investment (financial): Acquisition of a security, often from existing holder on the secondary market. Hence 'financial' investment need not imply any 'real' investment.

Investment trust: Company which holds a portfolio of company securities.

Invoice: Document showing details of goods sold, used as the basis for accounting records both by buyer and (a copy) by seller.

Irredeemable: Loan stock with no maturity date, whose annual interest is a 'perpetuity'. May be redeemable at issuer's option.

Last In First Out (LIFO): Method of valuing stock, very rare in UK, which assumes that most recent purchases have been used up in the current period, leaving earlier purchases in stock at the end of the period.

Lease: Commitment (by the 'lessee') to pay rent to the owner ('lessor') in return for the use of an asset.

Liability: Amount owing to a creditor.

Limited company: Form of business organization in which liability of owners (shareholders) for the company's debts is limited to the nominal (fully paid) amount of their shares. Abbreviated to 'Ltd', or to 'plc' (= public limited company) for larger companies.

Liquidation: = winding-up. Legal process of ending a company's life, by selling all its assets for cash, paying off the creditors (if possible), and distributing any residual amount to the shareholders.

Liquid resources: Cash in hand and at bank, plus short-term marketable securities.

Loan stock: Long-term loan to a company or government agency, often saleable on the Stock Exchange in the secondary market.

Long run: Period of time in which all fixed costs are reckoned to be variable.

Long-term liability: Liability not due for settlement until more than twelve months after the date of the balance sheet.

Loss: Negative profit, where expenses exceed sales revenue. Though not the aim, often the result of business.

Mainstream corporation tax: Main company liability to corporation tax on profits, payable nine months after end of accounting year; reduced to the extent of ACT paid at the same time as dividends.

Marginal costing: Costing method which allocates only variable costs, not fixed costs, to products.

Market risk: The non-diversifiable part of the total risk attaching to an investment, measured by 'beta'.

Master budget: Overall aggregation of various budgets for parts of a business, perhaps for part of a year, into a single profit and loss account budget, balance sheet budget, and cash budget for the whole company.

Matching principle: The accounting principle according to which balance sheets carry forward expenditures as assets only if there are expected to be sufficient sales revenues in future periods against which to match them.

Matching the maturity: Process of 'matching' the time-period of assets and liabilities, to reduce risk.

Maturity: Time at which a loan falls due for repayment.

Merger: A combination of two or more formerly independent businesses into a single enterprise.

Minority interests: Equity interests of minority shareholders in subsidiary companies which are less than wholly-owned. They appear in group accounts (a) as a long-term 'liability' on the balance sheet, and (b) as a deduction from profit after tax in the profit and loss account.

Modern portfolio theory (MPT): Distinguishes non-diversifiable 'market risk' from 'unique risk' which a properly diversified portfolio can eliminate.

Monetary asset/liability: Asset receivable or liability payable in terms of money, as opposed to 'real' assets, such as stocks or tangible fixed assets.

Monetary gain/ loss: In CPP accounting the gain arising in terms of constant purchasing power from owing money amounts in time of inflation (or the loss arising from being owed money amounts, or holding cash).

Negative interest rate: Real' interest rate, after-tax and net of inflation, which may be negative: (a) because while the inflation premium is tax-deductible, the 'real' gain from inflation is not taxable; or (b) because the actual rate of inflation is higher than was anticipated in the inflation premium.

Net assets: = capital employed. Total assets less current liabilities, that is fixed assets plus working capital.

Net book value (NBV): Cost (or valuation) of assets, less amounts written off.

Net current assets: = working capital. Current assets less current liabilities.

Net dividend: Amount of cash dividend paid to shareholders, net of basic rate income tax (at 25 per cent of gross dividend) deducted as ACT.

Net present value (NPV): Discounted estimated future cash inflows minus (discounted) cash outflow(s). If positive, indicates *prima facie* acceptability on financial grounds of capital investment project.

Net realizable value (NRV): Net amount for which asset could currently be sold. If less than cost, used for valuing stocks.

Net terminal value: As for NPV, but with the cash flows compounded to future horizon date instead of discounted back to present (value).

Nominal value: = 'par value'. Face value of security, unrelated to current market value. Usually refers to ordinary shares, with nominal value often of 25p each or £1 each, or to government securities with nominal value of £100.

Non-variable cost: = 'discretionary cost'. Cost which is neither fixed nor variable: it may change (not stay the same), but not necessarily in proportion to output, for example, advertising, research.

Notes to the accounts: Detailed notes forming part of the financial statements, explaining many items in more detail than on the face of the accounts.

Operating lease: Lease other than financial lease, usually for short period of time, and cancellable.

Opportunity cost: The hypothetical revenue or other benefit that might have been obtained by the 'next best' alternative course of action, which was forgone in favour of the course actually taken.

Ordinary share capital: Capital of a company, consisting of the amount called up on issued ordinary shares.

Overhead cost: = indirect cost.

Owner's equity: = shareholders' funds.

Partnership: Form of enterprise with two or more partners (owners), each with unlimited personal liability to meet the firm's debts in full.

Payback: Method of evaluating capital projects which calculates how long before initial investment is 'paid back' by later cash inflows. Ignores cash inflows after payback, so does not measure 'profitability'.

Period cost: = fixed cost, incurred in a period regardless of volume of output.

Perpetuity: Annuity payable forever.

Petty cash: Notes and coins. 'Cash' in accounts also includes amounts due from banks on current and deposit accounts. See also liquid resources.

Portfolio: Group of different investments held by a single owner, which diversifies away some of their 'unique' risk.

Preference share capital: Form of share capital entitled to fixed rate of dividend (usually cumulative) if declared, and to repayment of a stated amount of money on liquidation, with priority over ordinary shares.

Prepayment: Expense paid in advance of the period to which it relates, shown as a current asset on the balance sheet, often combined with debtors.

Present value: Discounted amount of expected future cash receipts, equivalent to the 'value' of an asset or security.

Price /earnings (P/E) ratio: Market price per ordinary share divided by the most recent annual earnings per share.

Price variance: Variance due to difference between budget price and actual price, calculated using actual volume.

Primary market: Market for securities which raises new money from public.

Product cost: Cost attributed to product, maybe equivalent to direct cost.

Profit: Surplus of sales turnover over expenses for a period.

Profit and loss (P&L) account: Accounting statement showing result (profit or loss) of business operations for a period (usually one year).

Profit centre: Business unit with manager responsible for sales revenue as well as for costs.

Profit margin: Operating profit (before interest and tax) as a percentage of sales revenue. Profit margin x net asset turnover = return on net assets.

Project finance: Method of finance whose repayments (and perhaps interest) are tied to a project's operating results.

Prospectus: Advertisement to members of public in respect of an issue of securities, subject to the rules of the stock exchange.

Prudence: = conservatism. Tendency of accountants to provide for all known losses, but to recognize sales revenue (and therefore profit) only when 'reasonable certainty' exists. Sometimes clashes with the matching principle.

Public limited company (plc): Name given to public limited company, in place of former 'Limited company' (abbreviated to 'Ltd').

Purchasing power: = value of money. What money will buy in real terms, usually measured by the 'basket of goods and services' comprising the constituent items in the Retail Prices Index.

Pyramid of ratios: Related network of financial and accounting ratios, stemming from the analysis of the 'return on net assets' ratio.

Qualified audit report: Audit report including a 'qualification', that is, an explanation of, or expression of disagreement with, some aspect of the financial accounts (for which the company's directors are responsible).

Quick assets: Assets which can quickly be turned into cash, for example, cash itself, marketable securities, and debtors.

Ratio analysis: Expressing one amount (often financial) in terms of another.

Raw materials: Input to manufacturing process, held for a time as stocks.

Realization: The concept in accounting that sales revenue (and therefore profit) is recognized only when it is 'realized' in cash or in other assets, the ultimate cash realization of which can be assessed with reasonable certainty.

'Real' terms: Amounts expressed after adjustments to allow for inflation (either CCA or CPP), as opposed to HC money amounts. 'Real' assets are those not comprising money amounts (for example, fixed assets and stocks).

Receiver: Official managing company's affairs on behalf of debenture-holders or others, often as a preliminary to winding-up.

Redemption: Repayment of loan or preference share capital.

Re-investment rate: Assumption (explicit or implicit) about the rate of return a business can earn on cash inflows 're-invested' during a capital project's life.

Replacement cost: Amount for which it is estimated that an asset held could currently be replaced. Basis for CCA. Not the expected ultimate cost if the asset actually is replaced in the future.

Required rate of return: The rate of return needed for a capital project to be profitable. Used as the discount rate for NPV, or as the criterion rate for IRR.

Reserves: Shareholders' funds other than issued share capital, including: share premium, revaluation reserves, cumulative retained profits. Need not be represented by cash (see 4.4.2).

Residual value: Net realizable value of fixed asset at the end of its economic life.

Retail Prices Index (RPI): Monthly government statistic measuring the weighted average of money prices of representative 'basket of goods'. Based on January 1987 = 100. See Appendix 1.

Retained profits: = retained earnings. Amount of profits earned by company (either for current period or cumulatively) and not yet paid out in dividends to shareholders.

Return on equity: Profit after tax divided by shareholders' funds.

Return on net assets: Operating profit before interest and tax, divided by net assets (= by capital employed). Apex of pyramid of ratios. = profit margin x net asset turnover.

Revaluation: Process of including asset in accounts at estimated current value when higher than historical cost.

Revaluation reserve: Increase in shareholders' funds needed to 'balance' increase in net book value of assets due to revaluation.

Revenue: (a) = sales revenue, turnover. (b) = as contrasted with capital, relating to the profit and loss account rather than to the balance sheet.

Revenue centre: Business unit whose manager is responsible for sales revenue.

Revenue expenditure: Expense, charged in profit and loss account, as opposed to capital expenditure, which relates to fixed assets.

Rights issue: Issue usually of ordinary shares, to existing shareholders, to raise cash.

Risk: Volatility about a mean (average) 'expected value'. More loosely, possibility of loss (either likelihood or extent). Sometimes treated as synonymous with 'uncertainty'.

Risk premium: Part of interest rate relating to perceived risk of investment.

Risk-free rate of return: Rate of return available in market on securities regarded as having no risk (usually only if government-guaranteed). An inflation premium is added separately.

Rolling budget: Budget which is continually updated by adding a new period at the end as the most recent past period is dropped.

Sales revenue: = turnover. A firm's gross trading income for a period.

Secondary market: Market for securities in which existing holders can buy and sell without directly involving the original issuer.

Secured loan: Liability 'secured' on asset, with lender having legal right to proceeds from sale of that asset on liquidation, up to the amount of the liability. Any balance of liability is 'unsecured'; while any balance of proceeds swells pool of funds available for unsecured creditors.

Security: (collateral): Legal charge on asset(s) by lender. In the event of default, secured creditor is entitled to priority of repayment out of proceeds of disposal of the charged asset(s).

Security: (share): Any stocks or shares, usually 'quoted'.

Selling short: Selling assets not owned, in the hope of buying back later, after the market price has fallen.

Share: Partial ownership of ordinary capital of company.

Shareholders: Usually refers to ordinary shareholders, who own company in proportion to number of shares held; but legally may also refer to preference shareholders.

Shareholders' funds: Amount shown in company balance sheets as attributable to ordinary (and sometimes preference) shareholders.

Share premium: Excess of issue price over nominal value of shares.

Share split: Process of dividing share capital into more shares of smaller nominal amount each. Reduces market price per share *pro rata*, without affecting the total market value.

Short run: Period within which not all factors of production are variable.

Solvency: Ability to pay liabilities in money.

Specific risk: Unique risk of security, which can be diversified away by holding a suitable portfolio.

Speculator: Anyone who acts on a view about the uncertain future.

Stag: Bull of new issues, hoping for an immediate rise in market price when dealings start, giving a quick profit on any shares allotted.

Statements of Standard Accounting Practice (SSAPs): Mandatory requirements issued by accountancy bodies regarding accounting treatment of certain items, for example, SSAP 9 on stock valuation, SSAP 12 on depreciation.

Stewardship: Original basis for financial accounting, to account regularly to dispersed shareholders. Partly intended for protection of steward.

Stock appreciation: Part of apparent HC accounting profit on stocks due solely to an increase in their price.

Stockbroker: Agent for investor, on whose behalf he buys or sells shares on the stock exchange.

Stocks: = inventories. Holdings of goods, either as raw materials and components, work-in-progress, or finished goods, with a view to sale (perhaps after further processing) in the ordinary course of business; also includes consumable stores (for example, cleaning and stationery).

Stock turnover: Annual sales revenue divided by the value of stocks held; ideally calculated using cost of goods sold (rather than sales revenue).

Straight line depreciation: Method of writing off cost of fixed asset in equal instalments over its estimated economic life.

Subsidiary: Company most or all of whose equity shares are owned by another (its 'holding' or 'parent' company).

Sum-of-the-years' digits (SYD): Method of accelerated depreciation of fixed assets. If life is 4 years, sum-of-years' digits is $10 (= 1 + 2 + 3 + 4)$; so first-year depreciation is $\frac{4}{10}$ of cost, second-year depreciation is $\frac{3}{10}$ of cost, and so on.

Synergy: What is hoped on merger to make $2 + 2 = 5$. Often elusive.

Taxable profit: Differs from 'profit before tax' in accounts (a) by deducting tax capital allowances instead of (book) depreciation; (b) by any accounting expenses disallowed by tax authorities; and (c) by any timing differences.

Taxation: In company accounts, means UK corporation tax plus any foreign tax on profits earned abroad. Excludes other taxes.

Tender method: Method of issuing shares to public, leaving price to be settled by demand for shares, thus discouraging stags, who can hardly expect much further appreciation when dealings start.

Term loan: Loan (probably from a bank) for a fixed period of time (often between one and seven years).

Term structure of interest rates: The pattern of interest rates over different periods of time, for example, from three months to 25 years.

Time preference: Ratio between someone's valuation of a good now and his valuation of an otherwise identical good at some future date.

Trade credit: Normal business arrangement to buy and sell goods 'on credit', that is, not settling in cash until some time later.

Trade investment: Investment (usually long-term) in another company connected with the business, but not more than 20 per cent.

Trading account: Name sometimes given to part of the profit and loss account ending with gross profit (or loss) before interest and tax.

Transaction cost: The cost of undertaking a transaction, for example, taxes, commissions, administrative costs, etc.

True and fair view: Aim of financial accounting, implying that generally accepted accounting concepts and conventions have been used.

Turnover: = sales revenue. The 'turnover' of the products being sold.

Uncertainty: Lack of knowledge about the future. Differs from 'risk', which usually assumes known probabilities of possible outcomes.

Underwriter: Person or firm agreeing, for a fee, to meet the financial consequences of a risk, for example, on new share issues.

Unique risk: Specific risk of company or project, which can be diversified away by holding a suitable portfolio (unlike market risk).

Unit of account: Numeraire in accounting. Traditionally the monetary unit, as in HC (and in CCA); but in times of inflation CPP accounting suggests an alternative - the constant purchasing power unit.

Unit trust: Financial enterprise holding range of securities; suitable vehicle for small unit-holder to spread his risk.

Unlisted company: Company whose shares are not quoted (listed) on the stock exchange. Hence shareholders may find it hard to sell their shares.

Unlisted Securities Market (USM): Market for securities of companies too small for full listing; subject to less stringent rules.

Unrecovered ACT: ACT unable to be set off fully against mainstream corporation tax, for example, due to losses or profits earned abroad, which has to be written off as an extra expense.

Usage method: Method of depreciating fixed asset based on usage in a period related to expected total usage over whole life. On this basis, depreciation becomes a variable expense (rather than fixed).

Value added: Difference between sales revenue and cost of bought-in materials and services. Roughly, profit plus wages.

Variable cost: Cost which varies directly in proportion to output.

Variance: Difference between budget and actual amount. (Not to be confused with statistical variance, which is a dispersion around the mean (average) value of a group of data.)

Variance analysis: Quantitative comparison between budgeted and actual results for a period. Basic components usually refer to quantity (or volume or usage) and to price (or rate or cost).

Vertical format: Modern form of balance sheet, showing net assets and capital employed underneath each other rather than side by side (as in horizontal format).

Vertical merger: Combination of two (or more) businesses engaged in different stages of production process in the same industry; for example, a brewery buying pubs, or a tyre manufacturer buying a rubber plantation.

Volume variance: Variance between budget and actual attributable to difference between budget and actual volume (both priced at budget price).

Wealth: Well-offness, expressed in terms of money, normally related to (ultimately) marketable assets.

Weighted average cost of capital (WACC): Average of the after-tax marginal costs of various kinds of long-term capital (debt, equity, etc.), 'weighted' by their market value (or their book value).

Winding-up: = liquidation.

Working capital: = net current assets. Excess of current assets over current liabilities.

Work-in-progress (WIP): Partly-completed stocks in manufacturing process; valued at lower of cost or net realizable value.

Write off: To charge an expenditure as an expense in the profit and loss account, as opposed to capitalizing it and recording it as an asset at cost on the balance sheet.

Yield: Rate of return on investment (usually security). Interest or dividend for a year, divided by current market price.

Yield to redemption: Yield on loan stock including element of capital gain (or loss) anticipated when principal (nominal amount) is repaid (at 'par') on maturity, in addition to the 'flat' yield of annual interest.

Index